CW00501484

Brilliance and Bravado, 1697–1766

KABUKI PLAYS ON STAGE

Volume 1, Brilliance and Bravado, 1697–1766

Volume 2, Villainy and Vengeance, 1773–1799

Volume 3, Darkness and Desire, 1804–1864

Volume 4, Restoration and Reform, 1872–1905

See page 390 for a complete list of plays in these volumes.

VOLUME 1

Kabuki Plays On Stage

Brilliance and Bravado, 1697–1766

EDITED BY JAMES R. BRANDON AND SAMUEL L. LEITER

UNIVERSITY OF HAWAI'I PRESS
HONOLULU

Publication of this book has been assisted by grants from the Nippon Foundation

and

Shiseido Co, Ltd., and the International Communications Foundation through the Association for 100 Japanese books.

Printed in Canada
07 06 05 04 03 02 6 5 4 3 2 1

University of Hawai'i Press books are printed on acid-free paper and meet the guidelines for permanence and durability of the Council on Library Resources.

Design by Stuart McKee Design, San Francisco

Printed by Friesens

Library of Congress Cataloging-in-Publication Data

Kabuki plays on stage / edited by James R. Brandon and Samuel L. Leiter.
p. cm.
Includes bibliographical references and indexes.

Contents:
v. 1 Brilliance and bravado, 1697–1766
v. 2 Villainy and vengeance, 1773–1799
v. 3 Darkness and desire, 1804–1864
v. 4 Restoration and reform, 1872–1905
1. Kabuki plays—Translations into English.
I. Brandon, James R. II. Leiter, Samuel L.

PL782.E5 K36 2002
895.6'2008—dc21 2001027912

ISBN 0–8248–2403–2 (v. 1. : alk. paper)
ISBN 0–8248–2413–x (v. 2. : alk. paper)
ISBN 0–8248–2455–5 (v. 3. : alk. paper)
ISBN 0–8248–2574–8 (v. 4. : alk. paper)

This series is dedicated to Professor Torigoe Bunzò
and his strong vision of kabuki
as an international theatre.

CONTENTS

PREFACE

The kabuki theatre of Japan, one of the world's greatest dramatic traditions, presently has an active repertory of 250 to 300 plays and dances, of which less than 20 have been translated into English. In addition, somewhat more than a dozen texts of the puppet theatre (widely known as *bunraku*), later adapted by kabuki, have been translated. Even taken together, this small number does not compare with the hundreds of translations of *nō* and *kyōgen* plays. Our intention in these four volumes is to begin to redress this gap by bringing to the reader translations of 51 previously untranslated kabuki plays. It is the first time in over twenty years that a collection of new kabuki translations is being published.

There are many reasons for this lack of translations, including the linguistic difficulty of understanding kabuki's ever-changing colloquial vocabulary, the complexities of transposing kabuki's elaborate verbal gymnastics and declamatory meter into another language, and the problem of establishing authentic texts in a domain where, in principle, the script of each production was newly written. Even today, as our experience working on this project often demonstrated, there are likely to be significant variations among certain scripts used by different actors. Moreover, as a practical matter, many of the plays are long. Finally, translation of the composite art of kabuki must take into account music, dance, acting, and staging as well as language.

The plays translated in these four volumes were selected with several criteria in mind. Most of all, the plays chosen by the editors and translators have exciting stories and charismatic characters; they are powerfully written and are brilliantly theatrical on stage. It often was difficult to limit our selection because many other plays also deserve translation.

The plays chosen for inclusion are also representative of major playwrights, chronological periods of playwriting, play types (history, domestic, and dance dramas), and performance styles. Plays from both Edo (Tokyo) and Kamigata (Osaka and Kyoto) kabuki are included.

All the chosen plays are in the current repertory, are regularly staged, and have not been previously translated. If only certain scenes or acts from a long play are presented today, then those scenes or acts have been translated. In a few cases, long plays, with their important scenes intact, have been slightly reduced in length, and where possible, a brief summation of the deleted passages has been provided by the translator.

We had not initially planned a four-volume effort, but as we combed kabuki's wonderfully rich repertory and as we consulted with our translators, the number of "must translate" plays grew beyond one, or two, or even three volumes. In the end, we selected fifty-one plays that we felt deserved translation, would be interesting to read, and might even be performed in English. The translations have been written by the editors and twenty contributors from Japan, England, Canada, Australia, and the United States, each person doing one or more plays. In addition to their love for kabuki and deep knowledge of its performing traditions, the translators share one vital quality: a passionate desire to transform these plays of two and three centuries past into living theatrical English. The translators bring different viewpoints to their work: some are scholars of literature and drama, some are practitioners of kabuki music and dance, some are kabuki theatre experts. As editors, we value each translator's unique voice and style of writing, and we hope the reader will enjoy the variety of tone and style within the series. We have, of course, made suggestions to the translators, but our major efforts have been to regularize the format and work for consistency of form.

As the series title implies, the plays are translated as if "on stage," with stage directions indicating major scenic effects, stage action, costuming, makeup, music, and sound effects. In some cases, complex stage action—such as stage fights—require several pages of careful description. We hope that such passages will read as clearly and interestingly as the dialogue. One translator may emphasize music and another action or scenic effects, according to the nature of the play and his or her interests. Each translation is based on the translator's choice of a text that approximates a performance on stage today (often this is an unpublished performance script), supplemented by attending public performances and by viewing performance videotapes. Because each performance is different, a translation reflects one performance example; it cannot reflect them all.

Each play is illustrated with a woodblock print *(ukiyo-e),* sometimes a series of them, and several stage photographs. The *ukiyo-e* artist commonly included on the print the name of the actor or character and, occasionally, a poem, commentary, or section of dialogue. These inscriptions, translated in the captions, are indicated by quotation marks.

Voice in kabuki is often sculpted into definite rhythmic measures. Narrative portions are sung or chanted by musicians on- or offstage (*takemoto* and *ōzatsuma* are two such styles). In the translations, the end of a phrase of sung or chanted lyric is indicated by a slash (/) between phrases, which we hope will suggest the original's general structure. Some translators directly reproduce the Japanese seven-five meter *(shichigochō)* in English, while others seek only to suggest the rhythmic structure of such lines.

The theatre, city, and date of the first production are mentioned before each translation. Stage directions are given in the standard way, from the actor's point of view: when facing the audience, right is the actor's right and left is the actor's left. Personal names are given in the Japanese fashion, with family name first, followed by the given name. A dozen or so Japanese terms that are generally known —kimono, obi, sake, samurai, daimyo, shamisen, and others—are not translated into English nor included in the glossary. In all other cases, translations of Japanese terms are given in the text. To facilitate reading, we have eschewed footnotes within the translations wherever possible in favor of including the pertinent information in the body of the translation, the stage directions, or the introduction. In years prior to 1873, months are given according to the lunar calendar; thus "first month 1865" means the first lunar month of 1865 (early to mid-February on the Western calendar). Dates after 1873, when the Japanese government adopted the Western calendar, are given in Western style (e.g., January 1899).

Translations are arranged in chronological order, and each translation is introduced by its translator. For each volume, the editors have written a general introduction, focusing on the historical development of kabuki drama, and have compiled a bibliography of sources and a glossary of terms. (For more detailed definitions of terms, see Samuel L. Leiter, *New Kabuki Encyclopedia: A Revised Adaptation of* Kabuki Jiten [1997].)

The editors wish to thank the many institutions, scholars, artists, and friends who have supported this undertaking. Publication of the four volumes is supported in part through a major grant to the University of Hawai'i Press from The Nippon

Foundation, for which we are enormously grateful. The Japan Foundation provided a six-month research fellowship to James R. Brandon for study in Tokyo, from January through June 1999, to get the project underway. A grant from the University of Hawai'i Research Council provided support for computer assistance and photo digitizing. Samuel L. Leiter received two PSC-CUNY Research Foundation grants that allowed him to work on the project in Tokyo in January 1999 and May 2000. A grant from the Asian Cultural Council assisted his research in January 1999. He also was awarded an Ethyle Wolfe Institute for the Humanities Fellowship that allowed him to spend a year working on the project free from teaching and administrative duties. Professors Torigoe Bunzō, former director, and Ito Hiroshi, current director of the Tsubouchi Memorial Theatre Museum of Waseda University (Waseda Daigaku Tsubouchi Hakase Kinen Engeki Hakubutsukan) and their staff generously opened the museum's vast kabuki collection to us. In particular, Suzuki Yoshio, Kozuka Kumi, Terada Shima, and Ikawa Mayuko searched out and provided 229 *ukiyo-e* prints and stage photographs as illustrations. Asahara Tsuneo, secretary-general of the Japan Actors' Association (Nihon Haiyū Kyōkai), kindly extended permission to use photographs under the association's jurisdiction. Hayashi Yukio, managing director of Engeki Shuppansha, and Umemura Yutaka, chief photographer of that theatrical publishing house, kindly provided many needed photographs that we were unable to obtain elsewhere. Karashima Atsumi and Orita Kōji of the National Theatre of Japan, Miyazaki Kyoichi of the Kabuki-za, Abiko Tadashi and Nakazato Takeshi of the Shōchiku Company, and chief librarian of the Shōchiku Otani Library, Ogawa Akiko, generously helped locate and obtain research materials. Among our colleagues, we are especially indebted to professors Kei Hibino of Seikei University for being an indefatigable negotiator on our behalf and, at the University of Hawai'i, Julie Iezzi for sharing her wide knowledge of kabuki music, Kakuko Shōji for writing English translations of many woodblock inscriptions, and Alexander Vovin for transcription assistance. Professors Kawatake Toshio, Mori Mitsuya, and Furuido Hideo; Kono Takashi of the *Nihon Keizai* newspaper; Konaka Yotarō, managing director of the Japan P.E.N. Club; and Fujita Hiroshi, general-secretary of the Japan Theatre Association (Nihon Engeki Kyōkai), have been staunch supporters of the project, opening many doors for us. And we are, as ever, indebted to our wives, Reiko Mochinaga Brandon and Marcia Leiter, for their limitless patience and support.

James R. Brandon
Samuel L. Leiter

INTRODUCTION

Samuel L. Leiter and James R. Brandon

Kabuki's birth coincided with the founding, in 1603, of the Tokugawa shogunate in the new city of Edo (Tokyo). By 1770, the end date of this volume, kabuki had developed into the single most important expression of popular, urban, mercantile culture of Tokugawa Japan. On the kabuki stage, as in real life, successful merchants visited courtesans in ostentatious and—because they were forbidden—daring displays of wealth and prestige. At the same time, kabuki plays aped the preoccupations of the ruling samurai class: the wielding and display of their power and the enjoyment of a sophisticated court culture. Then as today, popular audiences showed an insatiable relish for stories about the doings of the social elite. The characters that appear in these translations, whether aristocrats, warriors, or commoners, are depicted larger than life, for they inhabit the stages of kabuki's youth and adolescence, when brilliance and bravado were natural characteristics.

The first performances of kabuki, by the woman Okuni, around 1600 to 1610, and by troupes of female prostitutes or boy catamites *(wakashu)* from around 1610 until 1652, contained a strongly erotic component. Programs consisted of a melange of brief sketches (some suggested by *nō* and *kyōgen* theatre), popular songs, and sensuous dances designed to show off the physical appeal of the performers, who used the stage as an advertisement for their sexual availability. Okuni and her immediate followers performed on simple, roofed, raised platforms modeled on *nō-kyōgen* stages that were set up in open areas, such as dry riverbeds. Spectators, who had gathered in front of the stage, perhaps sitting on mats spread on the ground, were cheek-to-jowl with the performers. The actors' vivid self-presentation and the intense preoccupation with visual and aural beauty that began in these early performances have continued as touchstones of excellence throughout kabuki's history. It is commonly said that the chief aim of kabuki is "to be beautiful."

In 1629, because of the disruptions their presence caused among spectators, the shogunate banned female kabuki performers, although it took until the 1640s for such proscriptions to fully eliminate them. Their place was taken by the handsome *wakashu*, adolescent actors, who had begun appearing in the very earliest kabuki and who came to dominance in the 1630s. Their performances led to audience problems similar to those caused by the women, so, in 1652, the government

—fearful of any breach in its strictly demarcated social system—decided simply to ban kabuki altogether. A compromise was worked out, though, and the actors were allowed to return so long as they were adults *(yarō),* a status signified by shaving the youthful—and erotically appealing—forelock worn by boys. The period of *yarō* kabuki (1653–ca. 1688) marked the beginning of kabuki as an art form in which the overt sensuality of earlier performance was gradually replaced by a deepening of dramatic and aesthetic values. With women banned from the stage, it became necessary for female-role specialists *(onnagata)* to play women's roles and to do so by emphasizing more than their sensual attractiveness. Their artistry rose to such heights—especially following the career of Yoshizawa Ayame I (1673–1729)—that men playing women's roles became one of the most deep-rooted of kabuki conventions.

Still, kabuki remained associated with the world of prostitution, as evidenced by the word *kabuki.* Originally indicating behavior that was scandalous (from the verb *kabuku,* to incline, related to *katamuku,* which means the same thing but can also suggest "offbeat"), it came to be written with formal Chinese characters for "song" *(ka),* "dance" *(bu),* and "prostitute" *(ki),* the latter changing only in the Meiji period (1868–1912) to the character for "skill."

The conflicts in early *yarō* kabuki plays were ad-libbed *(kuchidate)* by the actors in what were, at first, programs of short, unrelated pieces *(hanare kyōgen),* each introduced to the audience by an announcement *(kōjō).* These were usually made by an assistant troupe manager *(tōdori)* seated at the side of the stage. The first multiact plays *(tsuzuki kyōgen)* date from 1664. In the same year, the draw curtain *(hikimaku)* was introduced, thereby facilitating transitions from scene to scene within these longer and more complex plays. In 1680, the actor Tominaga Heibei (dates unknown) was identified as a playwright *(sakusha)* on a printed playbill *(banzuke);* thereafter, playwriting became a specialized function within each theatre. In the Genroku period (1688–1704), which followed, kabuki developed rapidly in conjunction with growth in the visual and literary arts. Actors—using improvisation—and playwrights worked together to create a polished play during rehearsals, and the result, when written down, became the play text *(gikyoku* or *daihon).* Kabuki playwriting is best understood as "playmaking" because of the collaborative process in which actors shared much of the responsibility for script development with the writing staff.

The Edo actors Ichikawa Danjūrō I (1660–1704) and II (1688–1758) crafted lively theatre pieces filled with verbal gymnastics. Chikamatsu Monzaemon (1653–1725) of the Kamigata region, who had never been an actor, created increasingly profound psychological dramas. Revered as Japan's greatest playwright, he wrote plays in a variety of styles, including love plays—often with a double-suicide plot—that the Kyoto star Sakata Tōjūrō I (1647–1709) enhanced and polished through improvisation, to Chikamatsu's delight. He also composed exciting history plays for the puppet theatre *(ningyō jōruri,* now known as *bunraku)* in Osaka.

Before 1714, plays staged in Edo were housed at one of four large licensed theatres; in that year a scandal concerning an illicit affair between an actor and a lady of the shogun's court led to the liquidation of one theatre. Thereafter, audiences in Edo would have seen the plays translated here in one of the city's famed "three theatres" (Edo *sanza*), the Nakamura-za, Ichimura-za, and Morita-za. A theatre's license was signified by the presence of a drum tower *(yagura)* situated above its main entrance. Small theatres *(koshibai* and *miya shibai)* were also allowed to operate on a limited basis, but these minor theatres were not a source of new plays. Osaka and Kyoto also had a full complement of theatres, although managerial practices there were somewhat different from those in Edo. (See Volume 2 introduction.)

As plays grew in complexity during the eighteenth century, so did the architectural arrangements of kabuki theatres, which by the 1720s were roofed structures seating up to 1,000 spectators. Access to expensive seats in two tiers of box seats *(sajiki)* that lined the sides of the playhouse was through adjoining theatre teahouses *(shibai jaya),* which provided not only theatre tickets but food and drink and a place to rest during an all-day performance. Less expensive seats were in the gallery *(ōmukō)* facing the stage at the rear of the house. For a few coins, a poor laborer could buy a ticket from a barker in front of the theatre and sit on the ground with a throng of his fellow laborers in the large pit *(doma)* in the center of the house or even on stage in a section often called *yoshino.* The term *"yoshino"* derived from these spectators' ability to see the hanging artificial cherry blossoms that adorned many settings and that were reminiscent of the cherry blossoms on Mount Yoshino. Many important alterations made in theatres were the result of the frequent fires to which these all-wood structures were prone.

Actors performed on a relatively broad but shallow stage set up at one end of the theatre building. A side stage on the right, which had evolved from the *nō* runway *(hashigakari),* seamlessly abutted the main stage. Slightly off center, two front pillars supported a gabled roof, a reminder of the original outdoor stages of Okuni's time. This roof no longer served a practical function within the enclosed theatre building, but the pillars provided a frame for small scenic units, served as architectural elements in certain environments, and proved to be convenient places to hang signs giving play and act titles.

Kabuki's famous runway, the *hanamichi,* used in every play for major entrances and exits, appeared only intermittently in early kabuki but became a regular part of the playhouse in the 1730s. In its standard eighteenth-century configuration, it ran from stage right, through the auditorium on an oblique angle, ending at a curtained exit at the audience left side near the auditorium's rear. In *Just a Minute!* the heroic entrance of the superhuman Kagemasa onto the *hanamichi* after he has called out "Just a minute!!" from behind the exit curtain is enormously enhanced because of this unique physical structure. After entering, Kagemasa stops at a conventional *hanamichi* position *(shichisan)* to deliver one of kabuki's most famous speeches. Another magnificent use of the *hanamichi* is Danshichi's terrified flight through the auditorium after he has killed his father-in-law in *Summer Festival: Mirror of Osaka* (hereafter *Summer Festival*). Sanemori's exit on horseback in *The Sanemori Story* (hereafter *Sanemori*) is yet another memorable *hanamichi* moment.

By law, kabuki had to be performed during daylight hours, so audiences viewed actors primarily via natural light. Along each side of the theatre just below the ceiling a strip of windows was mounted with shutters that stagehands opened or closed on cue to brighten or darken a scene. Closer illumination of a scene could be provided by lighting candles set in stands across the front of the acting area, or a dramatic pose *(mie)* could be highlighted by moving a lighted candle attached to the end of a long bamboo pole *(sashidashi)* close to an actor's face. The nighttime murder scene in *Summer Festival* would be especially effective with the shutters closed to plunge the scene into darkness and candlelight reflecting off the wet and bloody bodies of Danshichi and Giheiji to create a sense of fear and horror. And in *Japan's Twenty-Four Paragons of Filial Piety* (hereafter, *Twenty-Four Paragons*), the flitting about in the dark of phosphorescent "fox fires" *(kitsune no bi)* on such poles would have been a truly eerie sight. There is also a good opportunity for playing with the contrast between light and dark in *Skylight*, when that eponymous set feature is opened as a major part of the plot's development. At any rate, fear of fire and government restrictions kept kabuki's use of candles to a minimum.

The years leading to 1770 were also remarkable for the genius of the many great actors who introduced the major roles in the plays translated here. The age saw the establishment of a system of actor families with actors inheriting the traditions of their forebears. For example, through 1770, five generations in the Ichikawa family assumed the name of Danjūrō: Danjūrō I (1660–1704), Danjūrō II (1688–1758), Danjūrō III (1721–1742), Danjūrō IV (1711–1778), and Danjūrō V (1741–1806).

The assumption of new and more prestigious names was publicly recognized in a formal name-taking ceremony *(shūmei)* held either within a scene of a play or as a separate, formal ceremony. Actors carried more than 800 family names during the Tokugawa period (1603–1868), of which some twenty important names continue today. Significant eighteenth-century acting families included several branches of the Ichikawa and Nakamura families as well as the Onoe, Bandō, Morita, Sawamura, Kataoka, Kawarasaki (also Kawarazaki), and Ichimura families. Each generation of actors strove to continue a family's unique style of performance, *ie no gei* (literally "family art").

The continuation of a strong current of tradition in acting is seen in stylized poses *(mie* and *kimari)*, codified fight sequences *(tate)*, specific vocal techniques, and in the use of music and percussive rhythms, which punctuate the action. These conventions, or *kata*, are performance "patterns" that form the building blocks of kabuki performance. *Kata* extend to every aspect of a presentation, including sets and costumes. An equally strong and continuing impulse in kabuki is toward innovation. *Kata* changed and evolved. Playwrights always sought to write new kinds of plays, with fresh characters and unexpected plot twists. The history of kabuki can be seen as a constant search for the right balance between tradition and change, between the excitement of the new and reverence for the past. Actors sought to stand out from each other in order to draw audience adulation, while at the same time they cherished and preserved the *kata* of their forebears. Kabuki is an art in everchanging flux, and numerous new conventions were constantly being created and old ones discarded. A simple example that sums up this maelstrom of stasis and change is the play *Just a Minute!* This old work, which came to be performed at each company's annual opening production in the eleventh lunar month, was revised on each occasion, and was only standardized in the late nineteenth century. Nevertheless, its famous *hanamichi* monologue, known as *tsurane*, is frequently altered to suit the actor performing it and the nature of the occasion.

One of the most interesting production practices, apparently beginning in the late seventeenth century, was the custom of employing a group of four to six house playwrights to compose plays jointly *(gassaku)*. Chikamatsu wrote his kabuki plays in collaboration with the actor Kaneko Kichizaemon (?–1728) and apparently introduced *gassaku* into the puppet theatre in the 1720s. By the eighteenth century, it was standard practice in all kabuki and the puppet theatre companies. Most plays in this volume were written by multiple authors. Even a play nominally attributed to a single author, as *Matahei the Stutterer* is attributed to Chikamatsu, had multiple, if uncredited, authors. And, while very early plays like *Just a Minute!* and *The Felicitous Soga Encounter* (hereafter, *Soga Encounter*) are attributed to Danjūrō I, their first star, the process of improvisational collaboration that first created them hints at the ease with which kabuki was able to adopt the *gassaku* system, whose roots were already in place in the process of kabuki playmaking. Star actors were the central attraction for audiences, and perhaps it is natural that, even after playwriting became a separate profession, they retained control of a "playmaking" process that was designed to demonstrate their charms and skills.

The task of the playwriting team was to fashion plays that highlighted the talents of their theatre company. The chief playwright *(tate sakusha)* was responsible for the overall structure of the play and assigned acts or scenes to second-level playwrights *(nimaime sakusha)* and third-level playwrights *(sanmaime sakusha)*.

Apprentice-level writing staff *(minarai* and *kyōgen kata)* wrote out parts, conducted rehearsals, and, when necessary, prompted actors in performance.

The most successful *gassaku* writing team of the time, headed by Takeda Izumo II (also known as Takeda Koizumo, 1691–1756) and including Miyoshi Shōraku (1697–1772) and Namiki Sōsuke (also known as Namiki Senryū, 1695–1751), wrote puppet plays for Osaka's Takemoto-za. Five plays in this volume—*The Sanemori Story* (hereafter *Sanemori*), *Skylight, Twenty-Four Paragons, Summer Festival,* and *The Secret Art of Rowing* (hereafter *Secret Art*)—are kabuki versions of puppet plays credited in part to one or more of these illustrious authors. This same writing team created the "three masterpieces" of *bunraku: Sugawara and the Secrets of Calligraphy* (Sugawara Denju Tenarai Kagami, 1746; trans. Ernst 1959, Leiter 1979, and Jones 1985), *Yoshitsune and the Thousand Cherry Trees* (Yoshitsune Senbon Zakura, 1747; trans. Jones 1993), and *The Treasury of Loyal Retainers* (Kanadehon Chūshingura, 1748; trans. Keene 1971 and Brandon 1982).

Kabuki playwrights were under enormous pressure to compose a new play every two months. Handwriting these lengthy scripts was tedious business, so generally just one or two copies of the full play text were written, intended for rehearsals and not for publication. Actors—as in the West—worked from "sides" *(kakinuki),* containing only their own dialogue. As a result, extant copies of early kabuki scripts are extremely rare. Despite the immense interest that popular audiences showed in going to the theatre and in purchasing *ukiyo-e* prints of their favorite actors, and the generally high level of literacy enjoyed by the merchant class, readers encountered kabuki plays primarily in the form of brief, abundantly illustrated synopses *(eiri kyōgen bon)* and a small number of handwritten copies produced outside the theatre for lending libraries. Puppet scripts, on the other hand, were regularly published and could be bought easily and read by the public. Therefore, an interested audience member could read the puppet versions of the kabuki plays that the actors had adapted for their own purposes.

Kabuki was contemporary drama, and new plays were written constantly to meet audience desires of the moment. Even when a play became well established in the repertory, performers and audiences alike valued some new twist in its revival. As a result, most of the plays in these volumes exist today in several versions. This is true of published texts as well as performance. A canonical text for a kabuki play is simply not desired. The compelling task for the playwright, producer, and actor was to stage, in interesting versions, core scenes while dropping those sequences or scenes that held little audience appeal. The *gassaku* system contributed to this process by its practice of assigning individual scenes to different authors, thus creating an imbalance leading to the eventual abandonment of weaker scenes. Only a few plays remain in which most of the original scenes still see regular performance.

The plays in this volume exemplify two stages of early kabuki drama, 1697 to 1720 and 1720 to 1770. The techniques that were established by 1770 continued to exemplify much kabuki playmaking through the nineteenth century. The first stage of development encompasses the vital Genroku period and the following decade and a half, during which the majority of plays were created directly for kabuki, often by actors. These "pure" *(junsui)* kabuki dramas include *Soga Encounter*, *Just a Minute!*, and *Medicine Peddler*. They meld rhythmic music, brilliant costuming, and makeup into sensuously ravishing spectacle.

Ceremonial qualities imbue each of these three plays, which are remarkable theatre pieces that reveal, and revel in, a fantastical world of superhuman heroes boldly confronting ultrapowerful villains. The Ichikawa Danjūrō family acting line in the city of Edo developed the forceful, bravura acting style called *aragoto* to portray Soga Gorō in *Soga Encounter* and Gongorō no Kagemasa in *Just a Minute! Aragoto* acting, which gloried in bombast, energy, confrontation, and lively humor, is typical of kabuki in its rambunctious early period. Edo, city of the shogun's residence, was bursting with country samurai, and Danjūrō's new *aragoto* plays reflected the masculine spirit of the rapidly growing metropolis. *Aragoto* actors, wearing oversized costumes and made up with striking masklike facial designs (*kumadori*), were believed to possess godly powers, so that being in the audience was tantamount to making a shrine visit.

Also part of the theatregoing experience was the time of year in which it occurred. Japanese have always felt an intimate relationship to the changing seasons, whose ceremonial ramifications are expressed in multifarious art forms. Playwrights were deeply committed to investing their work with qualities appropriate to the season, and a system of producing plays during specific seasons developed by the early eighteenth century. Some of these plays continue to be performed at traditional times of the year. Thus, for example, *Soga Encounter* is usually produced at the New Year, while *Summer Festival* is appropriate for the summer. Through most of the Tokugawa period, *Just a Minute!* was staged as part of the celebratory season-opening production in the eleventh month of each year.

The second stage of kabuki drama, lasting the next fifty years, until around 1770, saw the wholesale importation of plays originally written for Osaka's commercial puppet theatre. Chikamatsu's *Matahei the Stutterer* is typical of the nine plays in this volume that kabuki stole from the puppet theatre. From shortly after the start of the century through the Meiwa period (1764–1772), kabuki and the puppets competed for the same audiences, with puppets the victors for many years. Kabuki actors and audiences were enthralled by scenes of horrific conflict between duty *(giri)* and human feelings *(ninjō)* that were the staple of puppet drama. The puppets became so important as a source for kabuki drama that as much as fifty percent of today's nondance repertory is based on puppet plays. Some kabuki adaptations deliberately retained the puppet nature of their originals. The kabuki version of *Twenty-Four Paragons* strongly reflects its puppet theatre origin in its dramatic structure, characterization, and theme. Music and staging elements were borrowed from the puppets. In this play and in *Golden Pavilion* actors perform scenes imitating puppet movements using a technique called *ningyō buri*. Yet other plays were drastically reworked to capitalize on the human actor's abilities. In *Secret Art,* the climax in kabuki is a stylized battle *(tachimawari)* in which numerous skilled dancer-actors move in beautifully choreographed patterns, a conception that puppets are ill-equipped to imitate. The elaborate fight scene is typical of kabuki's brilliance and bravura. Puppet producers and manipulators originally conceived the murder scene in *Summer Festival,* in which Danshichi wallows in mud and washes himself with buckets of real water. The kabuki actor stripped to reveal an erotic body covered with tattoos, thereby recasting a grisly murder into an image of beauty, an example of kabuki's aesthetic of cruelty *(zankoku no bi)*. The use of real water and mud amidst stylized acting and impelling musical rhythms is a striking example of kabuki's ability to mingle earthy realism with exquisite theatricality.

The home of the puppet theatre was Osaka, so puppet dramas taken into kabuki invariably convey the atmosphere and tastes of the Kamigata region. During the eighteenth century, more dramas dealing with merchant life came from Kamigata, which was a commercial center, than from Edo, the military capital. And the plays of Kamigata were long respected for favoring "logical" character development and dramatic structure, while Edo's were tinged with fantasy and exaggeration. Kabuki was indelibly altered by its borrowing of puppet performance techniques and drama. By 1765, it was clear that the actors had come from behind to win the battle. That year, one of Osaka's two great puppet theatres, the Toyotake-za, closed its doors, with the Takemoto-za following two years later. Afterward, these theatres reopened sporadically, sometimes for kabuki performances, but the die was cast. The public had chosen kabuki, and the puppet theatre never again regained its previous popularity.

The plays in this volume represent the three major categories of kabuki drama: history or period plays *(jidaimono)*, domestic plays *(sewamono)*, and dance pieces *(shosagoto* or *buyō geki)*. Most of the scenes translated here are from history plays, concerning samurai from the centuries preceding the Tokugawa period, sometimes used as a blind for contemporary persons, since government magistrates forbade dramatizing events that concerned samurai of the current regime.

Many scenes that became popular in kabuki, such as the scenes produced as *Soga Encounter, Just a Minute!, The Stone-Cutting Feat of Kajiwara* (hereafter, *Stone-Cutting*), *Golden Pavilion*, and *Twenty-Four Paragons*, present gorgeous scenic backgrounds and stately actions representing the wealth and power of earlier samurai rulers. These are typical history or *jidai* scenes. But samurai are also portrayed in humble, even rustic, circumstances in *Matahei the Stutterer, Lady Kuzunoha, Secret Art*, and *Sanemori*, linking these Kamigata plays to that city's tradition of domestic drama. Such scenes, set in the pre-Tokugawa world, with samurai as leading figures involved in husband-and-wife, mother-and-child "family" situations, are usefully identified as *sewaba*, "domestic scenes" within history plays.

The second major type of play, the domestic drama, concerns merchants, servants, and townspeople of Tokugawa-period Edo, Osaka, Kyoto, and elsewhere and the alluring courtesans, prostitutes, and geisha who inhabited the licensed quarters of those cities. Two plays in this volume are full-fledged domestic dramas, *Summer Festival* and *Skylight.* While samurai appear in both plays, they are minor roles shown within the commoners' world. In fact, like the disinherited young samurai Isonojō in *Summer Festival,* samurai are often shown to be dysfunctional in the merchant's environment. The heroes of these plays are a sumo wrestler, a fisherman, a peddler, and a ne'er-do-well, while the heroines are their wives and a former prostitute. These are the kinds of people with whom the audience was instantly familiar: their dialogue reflected daily speech, their costumes, though heightened for stage use, closely resembled what the audience wore, their concerns were much the same as those of the average spectator, and the crises they faced—as in all good drama—were extreme examples of the kinds of experiences that might happen to anyone in the audience.

A third type of work is the dance play, either a short, independently created piece or a scene from a longer drama. Dance *(buyō)* has been integral to kabuki since Okuni performed her "kabuki dance" *(kabuki odori)* at Kitano Shrine in Kyoto in 1603, thereby identifying kabuki as a new genre of performance. Of the many hundreds of dances staged in kabuki during the period covered by this volume, most have disappeared. *Heron Maiden,* created for an *onnagata*—such specialists dominated kabuki dance throughout the period covered by this volume—is one of the few remaining.

Occasionally, dance sequences are motivated by events occurring within the drama. For example, in *Matahei the Stutterer,* Matahei dances to celebrate his success, and *Summer Festival* employs two dramatic dance insertions. In one, a pair of lion dancers dances into a house, their true purpose being to find a missing woman, while during the play's murder scene, a group of festival dancers encircle Danshichi after he has killed his father-in-law, Giheiji, providing a striking atmospheric contrast to the horror just enacted. The stylized and often acrobatic fighting sequences featured in *Secret Art, Summer Festival,* and *Just a Minute!* are related to, but distinct from, dance. The thrust and parry of weapons, blows to an opponent with fist or sandal, and the multitude of hand-to-hand combat techniques are features of kabuki *tachimawari,* which audiences find enthralling.

Whatever the type of play, writers began by choosing an appropriate "world" *(sekai)* of familiar dramatic materials from among the hundreds of worlds that existed. They then wrung every sort of variation from them and mixed chronologically different worlds with abandon so that characters living in different centuries could interact in the dramatic action. Perhaps the most often used world in kabuki drama is that of the semilegendary twelfth-century Soga brothers, who carried out a vendetta against the man responsible for their father's death. Using the basic characters and circumstances of the brothers' world, actors and writers have created more than five hundred Soga plays boasting many different plots *(shukō).* The "world of the Soga brothers" forms the basis for *Soga Encounter* and *Medicine Peddler* translated here. Many of the characters in the two plays are the same. *Stone-Cutting, Secret Art,* and *Sanemori* are all based on the eleventh-century historical world surrounding the civil war of the Heike-Genji clans. Another kind of world is that of the fox of Shinoda, dramatized, for example, in *Lady Kuzunoha. Summer Festival* is based on a domestic "world" in which commoners, Danshichi Kurōbei and Issun Tokubei, are the major figures. It is just one of a dozen domestic plays using the world of these popular Osaka "street knights" *(otokodate).*

Comedy is interspersed within all of the basic genres of kabuki drama. Humor of character is found again and again: in *Summer Festival,* old Sabu gives away his loincloth out of forgetfulness; Otoku is volubility itself on behalf of her stuttering husband in *Matahei the Stutterer;* and Yaegaki flirts outrageously with Katsuyori in *Twenty-Four Paragons.* These scenes are particularly effective because they provide comic relief in otherwise somber situations. Humor grows from physical action, as when Matahei moves back and forth around the water basin trying to make up his mind, when Danshichi twists and twirls the samurai Sagaemon like a human top, and when Gongorō lops off half a dozen heads with a single swipe of his immense sword.

One of kabuki's distinctive traits, and one often responsible for evoking laughter, is its self-referentiality or, one might say, metatheatricality. Audiences laugh delightedly when a character identifies an actor by "shop name" *(yagō),* as when Otsugi in *Summer Festival* calls out after her husband, "Three cheers for Matsushimaya," or whatever is the shop name of the actor playing that role. Name-saying takes on ritual dimensions in the specialized monologue *(tsurane)* in *Just a*

Minute! when the star actor refers to his own family's art. Other self-referential devices include the use of an actor's personal crest on clothing. In *Summer Festival,* the crest of the actor playing Danshichi is worked into the set design. And in the version of *Medicine Peddler* translated here, the actor announces his assumption of a new and more prestigious acting name, acknowledging his pride and asking for the audience's continued support.

History plays derived from the puppet theatre show us heroes and heroines who are locked into impossibly demanding moral choices that threaten to tear apart not only their own souls but those of the loved ones around them. In *Sanemori* and *Twenty-Four Paragons,* the struggle to lead a moral life is an intensely serious endeavor, fraught with cruel choices. Enormous discipline and fortitude are required to maintain one's dignity or self-respect. In scenes of lamentation and regret *(kudoki),* Lady Kuzunoha, Princess Yaegaki, and Otoko endure suffering that approaches operatic dimensions. Human actors on the kabuki stage perform the same fulsome displays of weeping that were developed for the inanimate puppets. The remarkable art of the chanter reaches its high points in scenes of tearful misery endured by agonized female characters. The emotionally powerful scenes that highlight the anguish of a male character—such as Kajiwara in *Stone-Cutting,* Matsuemon in *Secret Art,* and Sanemori in *Sanemori*—are descriptive narratives *(monogatari)* in which an unbearable event from the past, such as a killing or the death of one's child, is remembered. The actor recounts the past action, artfully using a fan to express himself. Such speeches occasionally reveal the motives that have caused the hero to act in a cruel or unpleasant way. Actors who portray the passionate feelings common in puppet performance are greatly aided by that theatre's deeply emotional *takemoto* narrative music, provided by a chanter *(tayū)* and shamisen player. In kabuki, this pair of *takemoto* musicians *(chobo)* describes and comments on characters' thoughts and feelings in sonorous passages while the actors mime the chanted words.

In a number of the plays in this volume, both history and domestic, emotionally powerful scenes of lamentation and narrative recollection are contrasted with interludes of romantic love. The woman may be a courtesan or prostitute (Kotoura in *Summer Festival*), a princess (Yaegaki in *Twenty-Four Paragons*), or a wife (the fox in *Lady Kuzunoha*). Interestingly, the male partner in each case is not a strong, masculine hero but, rather, a gentle, even helpless, young man acted in soft *wagoto* style. Isonojō in *Summer Festival*, Katsuyori in *Twenty-Four Paragons*, and Yasuna in *Lady Kuzunoha* are all gentle heroes. Soga Jūrō is acted in *wagoto* style also, in contrast to his robust brother, Gorō, who is acted in *aragoto* style. While Jūrō is not an active lover in either *Soga Encounter* or *Medicine Peddler*, his mild nature is intended to be erotically appealing to women, and his courtesan mistress, Ōiso no Tora, is always present to support him.

The plays show strong women who display extraordinary strength of will, in particular, dedication to lovers, husbands, and children. This is true even though women were an oppressed class during the Tokugawa period and, one might argue, were viewed as inferior to men in both Confucian and Buddhist morality. Female empowerment in kabuki—even though the female roles were played by men—must have been a factor in making this theatre so popular with female fans. Yaegaki in *Twenty-Four Paragons* and Yuki in *Golden Pavilion* are "red princesses" *(akahime)*, supposedly frail girls brought up in ultrarefined palace environments. But both are strong women who display remarkable fortitude in overcoming adversity to aid their loved ones. Yaegaki also reveals a decidedly forthright sexuality. Other women in these plays do not meekly follow the men in their lives. Otoku, in *Matahei the Stutterer*, is an independent spirit who uses her loquacity as a shield for her stuttering husband's disability. In *Secret Art*, Ofude—underlying the request that she be allowed to leave Matsuemon's home—is determined to avenge herself on her father's murderer. To protect her personal honor, Otatsu, in *Summer Festival*, purposely defaces herself with a hot iron so as to destroy the erotic beauty that Sabu finds threatening.

The courtesan is one of kabuki's most ubiquitous and important characters, yet she does not play a very active dramatic role in the plays translated here. There are courtesans in *Soga Encounter* and *Medicine Seller* whose function is mostly decorative, while Kotoura in *Summer Festival* has a more dramatic function, although she herself is passive. But the idea that women were sold into prostitution for limited terms by parents or spouses to earn much-needed money is a common dramatic device. The artist Shōgen in *Matahei the Stutterer* sells his daughter to raise money for the upkeep of his professional name, while Kozue in *Stone-Cutting* volunteers to be sold so her father can raise military funds. *Skylight*'s Ohaya, an ordinary housewife, had earlier served a term as a courtesan named Miyako before she was redeemed.

The majority of the plays in this volume are history plays delineating characters, male and female, who are imbued with the samurai code of ethics that called for loyalty to one's superior and implacable revenge *(adauchi* or *katakiuchi)* for slights to the honor of one's family. The motive of revenge is basic to *Soga Encounter* and is touched on in *Medicine Peddler, Sanemori,* and *Secret Art.* Not all samurai behave appropriately, of course, which allows for the presence of wicked warriors seeking to gain power, even to topple the emperor. Takehira is a tyrannical villain in *Just a Minute!* Kudō Suketsune, the object of the Sogas' revenge in *Soga Encounter,* enjoys aristocratic status. Nagao Kenshin in *Twenty-Four Paragons* is of such overwhelming malevolence that even his daughter betrays him. These villains are fascinating in their depravity. However, Matsunaga Daizen, the *go*-playing fanatic of *Golden Pavilion,* must appear to us as simply despicable when he uses his immense power to torture Princess Yuki, of whom he says he is fond. One of the most interesting villains is the samurai Senō in *Sanemori,* who—according to the convention of "return" *(modori)*—repents his misdeeds and allows the child Tarōkichi to wound him so that the boy may demonstrate his worth as a warrior. In a striking scene of self-slaughter, Senō then decapitates himself. Of course, each villain has his worthy samurai opponent who displays superior mental and physical powers to accomplish a seemingly impossible task, from Gongorō, who boldly faces down the evil aristocrat Takehira in *Just a Minute!,* to the undaunted Konoshita Tōkichi, who cleverly bests Daizen in *Golden Pavilion.*

Kabuki plays often provide sizable roles for child actors, who gain valuable training for their adult careers playing these roles. *Lady Kuzunoha, Secret Art,* and *Sanemori* contain significant roles for child actors. The boy actor is meticulously trained by his father and elders to move precisely and speak in a strong, falsetto monotone voice. And for audiences, the child is, above all, cute.

The roles of old people in kabuki range from the relatively simple and stereotypical to the complex and idiosyncratic. Commonly the elderly are depicted as benign—if occasionally stern—parents. A caring old mother is Oko in *Skylight,* while Rokurōdayū in *Stone-Cutting* is a noble old father and Gonshirō is a loving grandpa in *Secret Art.* Old Sabu, the delightfully short-tempered fisherman in *Summer Festival,* is not anyone's blood parent, but he acts in a protective, fatherly manner to the young lovers, Isonojō and Kotoura. In contrast to Oko's and Sabu's benevolence, Giheiji the cruel father-in-law in *Summer Festival,* acts out of a mountain of spite and vindictiveness.

Animals, too, often figure in kabuki plays, sometimes having been transformed into humans. For example, Lady Kuzunoha, ostensibly human, is actually a fox, and the *onnagata*'s highlights in performing her come about when Kuzunoha is unable to repress her inner nature. Foxes appear in *Twenty-Four Paragons* as well, a white tiger shows up in *Matahei the Stutterer,* and a horse in *Sanemori* has some rather complicated maneuvers to perform. The central character of *Heron Maiden,* of course, is captured in its title.

The plays in this volume are performed within certain aural conventions. Besides *takemoto* music that is heard in puppet-derived plays, several other styles of music can be called on in different dramatic circumstances. The mise-en-scène of *Heron Maiden* includes the twenty or so musicians of a full *nagauta* ensemble (shamisen, flute, and three *nō*-style drums) who play throughout the dance. *Ōzatsuma* musicians—mainly associated with *aragoto* plays—are seen onstage during *Soga Encounter, Just a Minute!,* and *Medicine Peddler.* All plays are accompanied by offstage music that sets an appropriate dramatic atmosphere. Musicians sit in a small room *(geza)* offstage right, where they are able to watch the action through slits in the scenery. For example, the melody called *kagen,* played by the offstage *nō* flute, large drum, and shamisen in imitation of *gagaku* court music, suggests the impressive grandeur of Kenshin's mansion in *Twenty-Four Paragons.* In *Summer Festival,* a plaintive solo song *(tada uta)* supports transitional moments. A quiet shamisen melody playing in the background *(aikata)* sets up important speeches by Oko and Chōgorō in *Skylight.* Rhythmic patterns of the large offstage drum *(ōdaiko)* help establish scenic location or mood: a wave pattern *(nami no oto)* suggests the seaside in *Secret Art,* a flowing water pattern *(mizu no oto)* indicates the canal in the last act of *Summer Festival,* and a continuous, suspenseful pattern *(dorodoro)* signals the supernatural appearance of a fox spirit in *Twenty-Four Paragons* and *Lady Kuzunoha.* Often, a large, offstage temple bell *(hontsurigane)* not only tolls the time of evening but creates a feeling of loneliness and sometimes dread; wooden clappers *(tsuke)* beat strong patterns on a board to highlight the running of a character or to emphasize an actor's powerful pose *(mie);* and the curtain is run open and closed to ringing sounds of hardwood blocks *(ki)* struck together.

The translations in this volume illustrate the verbal complexity of kabuki texts: dialogue in phrases of seven and five syllables *(shichigochō),* stichomythia of brief, repeated phrases leading to a vocal climax *(kuriage),* dialogue passed back and forth between two characters *(warizerifu),* and a thought continued by several people in sequence *(watarizerifu).* Long speeches, underscored with plaintive shamisen music, are featured in every play. Actors often share their speeches with *takemoto* chanters, adapting the traditions of puppet plays in which all the words are sung or chanted by the chanters. Characters unburden their hearts, admonish a friend, challenge a rival, or recall a nostalgic past. A delightful example of kabuki's verbal complexity is the intricate, punning peroration of the gentle hero in *Medicine Peddler,* clear evidence that, as the saying goes, "voice is the first skill" of the kabuki actor, followed by facial attractiveness, and then physique *(ichi koe ni kao san sugata).*

A secular theatre, kabuki nonetheless richly expresses strongly held popular religious beliefs, composed of elements from Buddhism, Shintoism, and Confucianism. Every common home had its Buddhist altar, and every community conducted seasonal festivals according to Shinto practice. Characters in kabuki plays are constantly praying to the "gods and Buddhas." The opening scenes of *Just a Minute!, Medicine Peddler, Summer Festival,* and *Stone-Cutting* are set in outer precincts of Shinto shrines, while the *Golden Pavilion* setting is the great gate of Kyoto's Temple of the Golden Pavilion. An idea of how a writer could effectively dramatize the everyday nature of religion in ordinary people's lives is seen in *Summer Festival.* Old Sabu prays before the Buddhist altar in his home. Always quick to fight, he has mastered his temper by hanging a Buddhist rosary of prayer beads over one ear as a reminder to remain peaceful. But when Good-for-Nothin' Gon and Slimy Hachi anger him, he tosses them and proceeds to fight. Princess Yaegaki and Lady Nureginu pray in tandem before altars, set up in separate rooms, seeking Buddha's mercy for the spirits of their dead lovers in *Twenty-Four Paragons*. The opening scene in which villagers mourn the soul of Oyoshi's first husband sets the elegiac tone of *Secret Art*. When, in *Stone-Cutting*, a famous sword is inspected for its authenticity, a formal procedure replete with sacred overtones is meticulously followed. Writers often drew explicit parallels between their plays and popular religion: Danshichi accidentally kills his father-in-law, Giheiji, during a village Bon festival dance, and the fugitive Chōgorō is given his freedom on the day of the Buddhist Ritual of Release, when caged animals are freed from captivity.

Beyond formal religions, kabuki plays reflect audiences' belief in magic and the supernatural. The hero's righteous decapitation of an entire line of attackers with one sweep of his gigantic sword in *Just a Minute!* is, on one level, mere fun and comic-book fantasy. Yet Gongorō's feat is grounded in the popular belief that he, as an extraordinarily powerful human, is imbued with the might of gods and deities and has become a protective "powerful human-god" *(arahitogami)*. In *Matahei the Stutterer,* audiences accepted the miraculous painting by Matahei, in which his image penetrated to the opposite side of the stone water basin, as evidence of the artist's spiritual endowment. And in the same play, the tiger's appearance and disappearance at the flourish of the paintbrush could occur because of the otherworldly powers of the painter. The sword in *Stone-Cutting,* whose authenticity is in doubt, proves to possess magical properties when it slices through the huge stone basin with ease. In *Sanemori,* a severed human arm is reattached to the woman's corpse from which it was separated and the corpse briefly comes back to life. Princess Yaegaki, in *Twenty-Four Paragons,* is so intent on saving her lover's life that magical foxes help her cross a frozen lake. And in *Golden Pavilion,* Princess Yuki, bound by ropes, wills the fallen cherry blossoms at her feet to transform into rats, which then chew through her ropes to free her. It may be that these scenes are a continuation of conventions established by Buddhist miracle stories in "old puppet drama" (*ko jōruri*) before the time of Chikamatsu and chanter Takemoto Gidayū (1651–1714).

Specialized stage props were developed in order to show the concrete effects of magic. In the plays translated here, a heavy stone neatly splits in two, a sword is so long it can scarcely be drawn from its scabbard, rats scamper, a helmet swoops through the air, a body falls into two parts, and severed heads appear instantly on the ground. A fox puppet is used in *Lady Kuzunoha.* Kabuki's most spectacular acting effects *(keren)* create a sense of magic, as when the fox Kuzunoha flies in the air *(chūnori)* over the stage and audience.

Kabuki drama in this period shows a strong didactic intent, emphasizing "rewarding good and punishing evil" *(kanzen chōaku).* According to the neo-Confucian values that were formally supported by the Tokugawa shogunate, the tie between vassal and lord extended over three existences, between husband and wife two, and between parent and child one. In a proper society, duty to one's feudal lord took precedence over family obligations. But this posed terrible dilemmas, and in play after play the human cost of feudal values is exposed. Kabuki's popular audiences cheered the Soga brothers for their obsession with avenging themselves on their father's murder, to the exclusion of any thought of duty to their rulers. Audiences were certainly on Princess Yaegaki's side when she defied her evil father in *Twenty-Four Paragons.* When she rescued his enemy—her lover—Yaegaki was not only unfilial but followed the dictates of her heart *(ninjō).* Danshichi, in *Summer Festival,* shows an admirable sense of duty when he helps Isonojō, the son of Danshichi's benefactor, but he abandons proper duty to Giheiji, his own father-in-law. When that carping, villainous old man taunts him beyond endurance, Danshichi kills him, and the scene that shows Danshichi being punished for his heinous act is only rarely performed.

Furthermore, playwrights capitalized on the dramatic possibilities of portraying a major samurai hero caught between overt loyalty to one side in the conflict and secret loyalty to the other side. The Heike-Genji civil war provided an especially fertile ground for the exploration of ambivalent loyalties. Audiences must have deeply appreciated seeing both the seemingly villainous Sanemori and Senō in *Sanemori* betray their allegiance to the Heike side in order to aid the sympathetic Genji supporters, thus suggesting that human factors precede legalistic ones. They also must have delighted in seeing the typically evil Heike samurai Kajiwara reveal a humanistic side in his decision to aid the Genji in *Stone Cutting.* On a strictly rational basis, such actions could be construed as traitorous, but audiences warmed to the display of the power of human sentiment to overcome formalistic necessities.

The demands of the parent-child relationship allowed playwrights to develop dramatic problems in complex ways. Authors of puppet plays, in particular, exploited the heartbreaking forced separation of parent and child *(kowakare)*. The old mother, Oko, in *Skylight,* is caught between love for Chōgorō, her son, who has killed four people, and her stepson, Yohei, the local magistrate responsible for arresting the murderer. Sobbing, she chooses her duty to her late husband and binds Chōgorō to turn him over to Yohei. The separation of the fox spirit from her son in *Lady Kuzunoha* is especially poignant because the child is so young. Out of deep maternal love, she selflessly urges him to leave her forever in order that he may have a human mother. In *Sanemori,* the parent-child separation encompasses three generations, with the emphasis on the young child, Tarōkichi, whose mother, Koman, has been killed by Sanemori, and on Koman's old parents, Kurosuke and Koyoshi. Tarōkichi clings to the mutilated corpse of his mother, pathetically attempting to revive her. Kurosuke reveals that Koman is actually a stepdaughter that he and Koyoshi have protected over the years in place of her real parents. Though no tie of blood exists, he weeps for her. A complicated web of parent-child relationships is laid out in *Secret Art.* Tsuchimatsu—the young son of the boatman Matsuemon and his wife, Oyoshi—and Komawaka—the noble son of Ofude—who are the same age, are accidentally exchanged during a battle. When Ofude reveals that soldiers executed Tsuchimatsu in the belief he was Komawaka, Matsuemon and Oyoshi grieve for their loss. But Matsuemon, loyal to his feudal lord, refuses to return Komawaka to Ofude, so she faces the agony of being parted from her beloved offspring. The conflict between Confucian duty and human feelings is bitterly expressed by Gonshirō, Tsuchimatsu's grandfather. When Matsuemon orders the boy in their care killed, Gonshirō, still believing the child to be Tsuchimatsu, rebels against killing his supposed grandchild simply to fulfill his samurai duty.

Two plays translated here revolve around a master-disciple relationship in an artistic or martial tradition. Both plays turn on the desire to gain knowledge of a secret tradition conceived in terms of an "art." And in each case, the secret tradition, known only to initiates, is handed down to the next generation during the dramatic action. The feudal structure of Tokugawa Japan encouraged artists to band together for self-preservation and continuation of their art in familylike groups. So in one sense, the plays reflect the actual world of kabuki theatre in which actors themselves lived within strict master-disciple relationships. The entire dramatic action of *Secret Art* concerns the struggle of Heike and Genji warriors to monopolize a secret naval strategy, the art of rowing in battle. In the play named for him, Matahei is a professional painter whose goal throughout is to receive the secrets of his art from his painting master, Shōgen Mitsuoki.

Finally, the shifting identity of a character is dramatically explored in several of the plays translated here, returning to the theme of a character in disguise, which Chikamatsu and Sakata Tōjūrō exploited and which can be traced as far back as *nō* plays of the fifteenth century. A character's true identity may be hidden and then revealed at a dramatically necessary moment. In *Twenty-Four Paragons*, Katsuyori—thought dead—disguises himself as the gardener Minosaku in order to retrieve an heirloom helmet. In *Secret Art*, the Heike warrior Matsuemon has assumed the lowly guise of a fisherman and raised a family as part of his elaborate plot to seek vengeance on the Genji leader, Yoshitsune. He defiantly reveals his true identity to the enemy in the final scene, when surrounded by them. Prior to the beginning of the play, the fox spirit in *Lady Kuzunoha* has transformed herself into the form of a human, impersonating Lady Kuzunoha out of love for her husband, Yasuna. Her fox nature is gradually revealed when the beautiful woman unconsciously expresses herself in foxlike actions, such as fingers curled into paws and hopping movements.

It is perhaps natural that the image of life presented on kabuki stages in the first two-thirds of the eighteenth century did not completely match the ideal society that Tokugawa officials envisioned or that neo-Confucian ideology demanded. After all, kabuki actors were classified as nonhuman *(hinin)*, below the four accepted social classes of samurai, farmer, artisan, and merchant. Feudal control over Japanese life in this period demanded the absolute separation of the four classes. Yet kabuki was a public art in which samurai and commoner mingled together in the audience, although angered government officials tried unsuccessfully to prevent samurai attendance at the theatre. Worse, playwrights and actors mixed commoners and warriors in the plays that these audiences came to see. The rigid social system constructed by the Tokugawa shoguns did not support vertical social mobility, but on kabuki stages samurai fell to commoner status (Isonojō is dismissed from samurai service in *Summer Festival*) and commoners could become samurai (Yohei in *Skylight* and Matahei in the play of that name). And while the reality was that a samurai could legally kill a commoner at will, kabuki plays regularly showed commoners standing up to samurai. Danshichi and Sabu in *Summer Festival* cheerfully abuse, ridicule, and beat Sagaemon, a samurai, without a hint of retribution to follow. The samurai code required unquestioned obedience, but a kabuki play could depict even a samurai acting against feudal obligation. It was no wonder government officials in eighteenth-century Japan attempted again and again to suppress the plays of this popular theatre. As a result, kabuki plays mirror the conventional social ethic of the ruling class and rebel against it at the same time.

The plays translated here open a door into the world of eighteenth-century Japan in a way unrivaled by other forms of art or literature. They let us see in startling color their characters' grandiose dreams and feel their powerful emotions, intense almost beyond bearing. They introduce us to the proud words and posturing of figures who present themselves to us with daring and panache as larger than life. In short, these plays present the unparalleled world of kabuki's brilliance and bravado during its first major period of dramatic development.

Three-panel woodblock print by Utagawa Toyokuni I (1769–1825) of *The Felicitous Soga Encounter,* New Year's 1817, Kawarasaki-za, Edo. The play's main title, *Soga Success in Kobiki Ward* (Kobikichō Soga Tamamono), is a punning reference to the fact that the play was at the Kawarasaki-za in Edo's Kobiki Ward. The honorable villain "Kudō Suketsune" ("Ichikawa Danjūrō" VII), center, poses elegantly with eyes crossed *(nirami).* The inscription refers to the actor's great fame in the city: "Great Edo, seeing Danjūrō's art, will prosper fragrantly." He confronts the two Soga brothers, who boldly face him, holding hunting hawks on their arms. Soga Jūrō "Sukenari," standing, also named "Ichiman," is played by the Kawarasaki-za's leading *onnagata,* the fifteen-year-old "Segawa Kikunojō" V. Soga Gorō "Tokimune," kneeling, also named "Hakoō," is played by "Iwai Matsunosuke" I, then thirteen years old. Above them, a *tanka* poem (composed of phrases of 5–7–5–7–7 syllables) reads, "Crests of two brothers, flowery chrysanthemum, butterfly and fan, dancing in the New Year's play, joyful felicitation." Courtesan Tora, disguised as "Nagi no Ha" ("Iwai Hanshirō" V), right, holds her fan in a position that indicates that the brothers' planned encounter with Kudō will take place at Mount Fuji. The inscription reads, "Here is the way an *onnagata* acts; everyone comes to see Hanshirō's movements as Yagi no Ha." (Tsubouchi Memorial Theatre Museum of Waseda University)

The Felicitous Soga Encounter

Kotobuki Soga no Taimen

Original Version Attributed to Ichikawa Danjūrō I (Mimasuya Hyōgo)

TRANSLATED BY LAURENCE R. KOMINZ

1697 NAKAMURA-ZA, EDO

The Felicitous Soga Encounter

INTRODUCTION

The Felicitous Soga Encounter is a short but grand New Year's pageant play, demonstrating both the seasonal rhythms of Tokugawa-period kabuki and the high histrionics of the Edo stage. The two avenging heroes, Soga Jūrō and his younger brother, Gorō, are more intimately associated with Edo kabuki than any other characters. They epitomize the two dominant and contrasting acting styles used for male heroes: Jūrō's portrayal in the gentle style *(wagoto)* and Gorō's bold posturing and flamboyant vocalizations in the bravura style *(aragoto)*. The brothers are dressed similarly, but Gorō's forelock shows that he is still a callow youth while his makeup *(sujiguma)* of red lines on a white background betrays his impulsive nature. Gorō is ever eager to set upon his father's murderer, even when to attack would be suicidal. Jūrō—who knows they must wait for the right moment—repeatedly restrains his impetuous brother. Together, the brothers represent an ideal samurai whole—youthful impetuousness balanced by mature calculation—with pure emotions subjected to reason in the interests of achieving honor and glory.

The Sogas were actual historical figures who, in 1193, avenged their father's murder by staging a daring night raid on their enemy during a grand hunt. The villain, a powerful minister of state named Kudō Saemon Suketsune, had orchestrated the murder of their father seventeen years earlier. Jūrō was slain in the melee immediately following the vendetta, and Gorō was captured, interrogated by the shogun the next day, and sentenced to immediate execution.

An oral tale about the vendetta and the three generations of strife that led up to it, sung primarily by blind, female minstrels, was in circulation within a few decades. By the 1300s, *The Tale of the Soga Brothers* (Soga Monogatari) was known to every Japanese. In the medieval period, playwrights of the *nō* and *kōwakamai* theatres created a number of plays celebrating the brothers' valor and self-sacrifice. Also recounted were the vicissitudes of the relationship between Jūrō and his devoted prostitute lover, Tora. In the early Edo period, the puppet theatre produced a wide variety of Soga plays. Some showcased special effects and the brothers' exploits, while others parodied the tradition.

The brothers came to the kabuki stage early. The vendetta itself was staged soon after the 1652 ban of boys' kabuki, and one of the first three-act kabuki plays,

Soga, was performed in 1665, only a year after such multiact plays were introduced. In the 1690s in the Kamigata region, a tradition was established of staging Soga plays in summer to commemorate Obon, the festival of the dead. Often, the great *wagoto* star Sakata Tōjūrō I (1647–1709), enacted Jūrō. From 1709 until 1868, each Edo theatre staged a Soga play at the New Year. As a result, over one thousand kabuki plays were written featuring the brothers.

In Edo, plays about the Sogas were called "spring plays" *(haru kyōgen)* because, according to the lunar calendar, the New Year ushered in spring. The congruence between Gorō's *aragoto* and New Year's rituals to dispel evil spirits was one reason for the strong seasonal character assumed by Soga plays, and the very word "Soga" came to represent the New Year holiday in Edo.

Beginning with the earliest medieval versions of the Soga story, Gorō's first encounter *(taimen)* with Suketsune was crucial. At the time of the encounter, Gorō was a temple acolyte, but, thanks to the meeting, he finally began to take the decisive actions necessary to become an active partner with his brother in their vendetta. The oldest surviving Edo encounter text dates from 1697, when Ichikawa Danjūrō I (1660–1704) played Gorō in *aragoto* style in a play that was crucially important to his career: *The Origin of the Soga Warrior* (Tsuwamono Kongen Soga). Soga Gorō became one of Danjūrō's archetypal *aragoto* superheroes, and the encounter scene in this play showed that Gorō attained his superhuman strength by praying to the tantric deity Fudō.

By the late eighteenth century, an encounter scene was the climax of almost every Soga spring play. There were several reasons for its importance: it was an important New Year's activity for all Japanese to visit senior relatives, benefactors, and professional superiors; its formality allowed the actors to express New Year's greetings directly to the audience; the confrontation between brash young heroes and an old villain suited the New Year's symbolism of the new replacing the old; the dramatic meeting of opposites was crucial to New Year's fertility rituals; the traditional encounter at Hakone Shrine was said to have taken place on the last day of the New Year's holiday; the word *"taimen"* has many felicitous New Year's associations.

Playwrights and actors worked hard to come up with interesting plot changes *(shukō)* to provide variety within the obligatory confrontation situation. One solution was to have one or both brothers approach Suketsune disguised as entertainers, giving the actors the opportunity to show their skills in song and dance (see *The Medicine Peddler* in this volume). Or the villain Kudō Suketsune might be disguised as a woman, as the villain's wife, as an impostor, or even as a fox. The scene's action could be set anywhere in eastern Japan, sometimes taking place in a snowstorm or an earthquake.

Soga Encounter, translated here, is the most often performed Soga encounter play today. In earlier times, it was usually staged as the last act of a three-act play, but now it is presented as an independent, celebratory piece. Most current productions use the text that Danjūrō IX (1838–1903) and Onoe Kikugorō VI (1885–1949) adapted in 1903 from several texts written by Kawatake Mokuami (1816–1893) in the late nineteenth century.

Soga Encounter is a play fraught with tension. The brothers meet their blood enemy at his New Year's celebration in 1193 but must wait five more months before they strike. The play takes place during a celebration of Suketsune's promotion to marshal of the shogun's hunt. In this grand environment, the brothers do not hesitate to brand the man of honor a murderer, an action that might be compared to Greenpeace activists today breaking into a corporate boardroom and hurling the company's foul waste products at the CEO. This sort of denigration of powerful authority figures is characteristic of Soga plays in general and was very enjoyable for Edo-period audiences. The play also follows a precedent set in the late eighteenth century of having an illustrious actor of heroic roles—often the company leader *(zagashira)*—play Suketsune, thereby making him an honorable villain. The epitome of civility and restraint, he invites the brothers to try their hand at attacking him after he has performed his important duty to the shogun.

Asahina is a secret ally of the brothers who leads them into the presence of their blood enemy. Asahina is a figure of fascinating contrasts. His purpose is a delicate and sensitive one, yet he is costumed and speaks and moves as a bombastic buffoon. With his "monkey makeup" *(saru guma)* of silly-looking horizontal red forehead stripes and huge handlebar mustache and the winglike "power paper" *(chikaragami)* protruding from his headdress, Asahina's appearance is unforgettable. Despite his outré appearance, Asahina joins Jūrō in restraining Gorō to help ensure the brothers' eventual success.

One purpose of staging *Soga Encounter* is to put every actor in the troupe on display, in a manner similar to *kaomise* (face-showing) plays, those produced during the Tokugawa period at the start of a new theatrical season. There is a wide range of costumes and makeup styles, and every actor, even the lined-up lords *(narabi daimyō),* is given at least a short opportunity to take stage.

The script translated here was used for a production celebrating the reopening of the Meiji-za in Tokyo in March 1993. The text is virtually identical to one written by Kawatake Mokuami for a performance to open the newly built Chitose-za (located on the site of today's Meiji-za) in 1885. The play's only significant departure from the more frequently performed 1903 version is the opening *ōzatsuma* chorus, which replaces introductory words by the assembled feudal lords.

CHARACTERS

KUDŌ SAEMON SUKETSUNE, *powerful minister of state*
SOGA GORŌ TOKIMUNE, *nineteen years old*
SOGA JŪRŌ SUKENARI, *twenty-one years old*
ŌMI KOTŌTA NARIIE, *close retainer of* SUKETSUNE
YAWATA NO SABURŌ YUKIUJI, *close retainer of* SUKETSUNE
KAJIWARA HEIZŌ KAGETOKI, *villainous feudal lord allied to* SUKETSUNE
KAJIWARA HEIJI KAGETAKA, *son of* KAGETOKI
ŌISO NO TORA, JŪRŌ*'s lover, a courtesan at the Tōkaidō Road post-station at Ōiso*
KEWAIZAKA NO SHŌSHŌ, *courtesan and* GORŌ*'s lover*
ONIŌ SHINZAEMON, *family retainer of the* SOGA *brothers*
KOBAYASHI ASAHINA, *son of a leading feudal lord, a strong and blustery samurai friendly to the* SOGAS
EIGHT FEUDAL LORDS, *present at the invitation of* SUKETSUNE
STAGE ASSISTANTS, *formally dressed* kōken
ŌZATSUMA, *narrator and shamisen player who set the festive mood and situation of the play*

(The curtain opens to the sounds of the ki *and offstage music* [geza], *simple flute and shamisen melodies punctuated with strikes on the large drum. White screens decorated with gold clouds and blue "plum blossom in a hermitage" crests—associated with* SUKETSUNE*—conceal the setting upstage of them. The* ŌZATSUMA *singer and shamisen player enter and stand left. The singer stands, holding his text out before him. The shamisen player stands with his right leg up on a wooden stool so that he can rest the shamisen on his knee. After a brief instrumental prelude, the singer begins.)*

ŌZATSUMA *(In a strongly rhythmic style):*
Since it is a time-honored, auspicious occasion, / this bountiful spring / we dedicate this kabuki / To a thousand autumns, ten thousand years of happiness, / and the gates to the everlasting joy of eternal youth.
(Instrumental shamisen interlude.)

Now we behold the entwined conjugal pines at Matsushima, / and Mount Fuji, soon to be the site of a shogunal hunt. / The senior minister of state has been chosen marshal of the hunt.

(Instrumental shamisen interlude.)

On the ceremonial dais, he is the pride of a generation. / It is an occasion of great celebration.

(The ŌZATSUMA *musicians bow and exit left. To the accompaniment of an offstage flute and drum, the screens slide offstage to left and right, revealing* SUKETSUNE*'s splendid mansion. The walls are gold, decorated with blue "plum blossom in a hermitage" crests. A blue and white checkerboard lattice is raised, framing the mansion from above.* SUKETSUNE, *dressed in a black kimono covered in the same crests embroidered in gold, is seated stage left on a high dais. Behind him sit* KAJIWARA KAGETOKI *and* KAGETAKA, *wearing persimmon-colored robes. Their red-painted faces and catfish mustaches indicate that they are comic villains. The* EIGHT LORDS *sit in a line at their right, wearing formal hats* [eboshi] *and ceremonial robes in varying hues of gray, green, and blue.* SUKETSUNE*'s retainers,* ŌMI *and* YAWATA, *sit, respectively, to the immediate left and right of his dais. They wear persimmon-colored formal vests* [kataginu] *over black kimono, with persimmon-and-white-striped* hakama *tucked up in footman* [yakko] *fashion.* TORA *and* SHŌSHŌ, *dressed in sumptuous courtesan's attire of overrobe* [uchikake] *and large, stiff, front-tied obi* [manaita obi], *sit to* YAWATA*'s right.* ASAHINA *is to their right. Sprays of pink and white plum blossoms* [tsurieda] *hang down from the proscenium, indicating that it is the time of the New Year's celebration.)*

SUKETSUNE *(Deliberately)*: Today I have been promoted to senior minister of state and made marshal of the shogunal hunt. It is a most weighty responsibility. I now celebrate my good fortune and express in words my thanks for a land at peace and a bountiful spring in a blessed reign.

ASAHINA *(Grandly)*: The sacred red-crested crane that lives a thousand years in happiness spreads his wings and flies calmly, joyfully, upward into the sky. Here, today, I, Asahina, welcoming the sacred crane, offer words of congratulations as bounteous as heaven's light to overspread the high minister's seat.

KAGETOKI *(With haughty pride)*: We of the Kajiwara clan, along with everyone here, in the radiance of our lord's reign at the mountains of Kamakura, don large-crested festive robes and feel brave-of-heart this misty spring day.

KAGETAKA *(With exaggerated hauteur)*: We spread out the sleeves of our robes in expanding good fortune, like the green of the everlasting pine, which grows ever greater with time, like the green of new buds, which every day we long to see.

ŌMI *(Straightforwardly)*: Once again spring is renewed and the shrimp energetically leaps out of the water. He is not to be scolded for splashing.

YAWATA: Just as the fruits swell and turn orange amid luxuriant branches and foliage, so our family thrives from generation to generation with persimmon the color of felicitation.

(ŌMI and YAWATA are dressed in formal garments [kamishimo] *of persimmon color—the color associated with the Ichikawa acting family—hiked up to the thigh in footman fashion. ŌMI and YAWATA's yellow* tabi *indicate that they are comic retainers.)*

TORA *(Confidentially)*: Among the many requests made to me came Lord Suketsune's invitation. I came as if summoned by the first east wind of spring, buoyant and full of cheer, from Ōiso, where I deign to perform the duties of a courtesan.

SHŌSHŌ: Tora brought me along to keep her company, incompetent though I am. Though our feelings are complex, even now the white plum is . . .

(All EIGHT LORDS proceed to praise SUKETSUNE, speaking in formal, declamatory style.)

FIRST LORD: Wonderfully fragrant, like cedar planks on the happy day that construction is complete on this celebratory pavilion . . .

SECOND LORD: Samurai, great and humble, open their homes—gates festooned in pine branches . . .

THIRD LORD: It feels like spring throughout the city of Kamakura. At every home they celebrate lucky omens . . .

FOURTH LORD: The ones who really require the most tolerance are those who noisily celebrate their happiness tipsy with sweet New Year's sake . . .

(The following LORDs' lines allude to various New Year's customs.)

FIFTH LORD: Like the groaning of the kites' humming strings, staggering revelers mumble felicitations at the gate . . .

SIXTH LORD: Like our trousers with finely pressed pleats, letters for good fortune tied to a branch . . .

SEVENTH LORD: Looking at the fortune papers that tell our future, everyone in the land learns that it will be a lucky new year . . .

EIGHTH LORD: All is at peace, the waves are calm, in splendor we at this gathering sing praises to the world.

ASAHINA: In the joy of today's auspicious celebration . . .

KAGETOKI: We Kajiwaras will be the first of all assembled here . . .

KAGETAKA: To express our deepest . . .

ALL *(To SUKETSUNE)*: Congratulations!

SUKETSUNE *(Matter-of-factly)*: I am most thankful for everyone's congratulatory speeches. I trust you will all please forgive me for taking the seat of honor.

ASAHINA *(Politely, though his rustic dialect begins to surface)*: Now I have a heartfelt request to make of Suketsune. It's just as I've asked you before. Would you please be so kind as to meet the two men who've been so longin' to see you?

SUKETSUNE: Since it is none other than Asahina who makes the request . . .

ASAHINA: Then you'll be so kind as to meet them?

SUKETSUNE: By all means.

ASAHINA *(Joyfully)*: Why, that's mighty kind of you. I reckon I'd better call them. *(To the beats of a small drum* [kotsuzumi], ASAHINA *removes his overrobe, assumes several poses, and makes his way in grand style to the edge of the* hanamichi. *Then, in a loud, formal voice, but with no trace of dialect.)* You two men who have withdrawn to the next room have received permission from Lord Suketsune and have been granted your request for an audience. You may visit him on this felicitous occasion—this everlasting spring. You are to come forth at once. *(He returns to his former place.)*

GORŌ and JŪRŌ *(Faintly audible from beyond the* hanamichi *curtain)*: We most humbly obey!

(The brothers enter to the accompaniment of offstage shamisen music [taimen sanju], *carrying gifts of miniature trees on ceremonial trays. Both wear short swords and ceremonial overrobes and long, trailing* hakama. JŪRŌ's *costume is decorated with plovers and* GORŌ's *with butterflies.* JŪRŌ *walks quietly down the* hanamichi *in a stately manner;* GORŌ *struts noisily.* GORŌ *pushes in front of* JŪRŌ *and tries to lead the way, but his older brother immediately retakes his position in the lead and dramatically restrains his sibling's advance. They pose in a dramatic* mie. *Meanwhile, the lined-up* FEUDAL LORDS*—whose function here is simply to provide vocal embellishment—repeatedly shout* "Look at that!" *and end with* "Well done!" *to accentuate the brothers' impressiveness.)*

KAGETOKI *(Contemptuously)*: Wait, wait, wait! Do you all see that? There are two young men we've never seen before.

KAGETAKA *(Derisively)*: Since they are traditional New Year's clowns, the one in back has got to be the one called Saizō.

(The EIGHT LORDS *follow* KAJIWARA*'s lead and speak derisively.)*

FIRST LORD: They come sauntering in, not even wearing proper hats . . .

SECOND LORD: Showing no deference to any of us . . .

THIRD LORD: Boors! Ignorant of rules and decorum . . .

FOURTH LORD: Look at them! As shabby as poor Sogas . . .

FIFTH LORD: Their bodies shaking like a couple of paupers . . .

SIXTH LORD: They come here quaking, all aflutter . . .

SEVENTH LORD: To appear here like this, the two of them . . .

EIGHTH LORD: Don't they look pathetic?

KAGETAKA *(Loudly and derisively)*: Hey, Dad, since laughter suits felicitous occasions, shall we have a good laugh?

KAGETOKI *(Contemptuously)*: Yes, laugh everyone, laugh!

EIGHT LORDS, KAGETOKI, and KAGETAKA: Ha, ha, ha, ha, ha, ha, ha!

(Hearing this, GORŌ *glares at the assembled lords, but* JŪRŌ *prevents him from moving toward them.* ASAHINA *does a* mie *to two* tsuke *beats.)*

ASAHINA *(Interrupts the laughter)*: Cut out all of that noise! The two men over there are to appear before Lord Suketsune. For a long time, I, Asahina, have been petitioning on their behalf, and it is I who have escorted them here.

TORA *(Compassionately)*: The two have been granted an audience through the good offices of Asahina, but even though it is a felicitous occasion, you abuse them, you boors who know nothing of tender feelings.

SHŌSHŌ: You talk like this, but you will get what is coming to you later on.

TORA: Use a little more discretion . . .

TORA and SHŌSHŌ *(Pleadingly)*: If you please.

SUKETSUNE *(Inquiringly)*: So, it is you who have been pressing Asahina to arrange a meeting with me? *(Authoritatively.)* There is no need to stand on ceremony. Come here, come here.

ASAHINA *(Stepping forth and speaking enthusiastically)*: Did you hear that, you two? Lord Suketsune, who holds the post of senior minister of state, says he's gonna meet you. You'd best mosey on out here now. And boldly, fearlessly, and without any shame, state your case—without delay! *(Strikes a comic pose, holding his hands out like paws.)*

GORŌ *(Angrily)*: We're on our way!

*(*GORŌ *prepares to charge onstage, but* JŪRŌ*, kneeling, restrains him.)*

JŪRŌ *(Deliberately)*: Wait Gorō! You must not do anything foolish.

GORŌ *(Intensely)*: Right you are!

(Offstage flute and shamisen play formal music [iwato kagura]. *The brothers pick up their gifts.* JŪRŌ *moves to the main stage.* GORŌ *follows, doing a strong sideways sliding move, his knees bent deeply.* ASAHINA *returns to his usual place before the brothers reach the main stage. As the brothers proceed, the* LORDS *accompany them with shouts of* "Look at that!" *as before. On the main stage,* GORŌ *passes his brother and makes a threatening move toward* SUKETSUNE, *but* JŪRŌ *immediately stops him. The brothers, along with* SUKETSUNE, *who glares at them, perform a* mie *to the accompaniment of the* LORDS *shouting,* "Well done!"*)*

SUKETSUNE: So, you are the two young men who have been brought into my presence through the good offices of Asahina. Why, you two very much resemble someone I used to know.

JŪRŌ *(Intently)*: You say we look like someone. . . . Just who is it . . .

JŪRŌ and GORŌ *(Deliberately)*: We resemble?

SUKETSUNE: Kawazu no Saburō Sukeyasu, a family relative.

JŪRŌ and GORŌ *(Emotionally)*: What are you saying?

SUKETSUNE: When I think back on it . . . *(He ponders, nods, and speaks loudly.)* Oh, now I remember . . . *(Offstage large and small drums play a strong rhythm.*

Soga Gorō (Nakamura Tomijūrō V), standing center, is restrained from attacking Kudō Suketsune by his supporter, Kobayashi Asahina (Kataoka Gatō V), left, and his elder brother Soga Jūrō (Nakamura Senjaku II, later Nakamura Ganjirō III), kneeling. Yawata no Saburō (Kataoka Ainosuke VI), a retainer of Kudō Suketsune, poses defensively, right. (Umemura Yutaka, Engeki Shuppansha)

Upstage screens open, revealing a view of Mount Fuji. Formally dressed STAGE ASSISTANTS [kōken] *remove the offerings brought by the brothers.* SUKETSUNE *takes out his fan and holds it in narrative posture.)* In 1176, in the tenth month, a hunt about ten days long was held at Okuno to entertain Lord Sukechika. It was when the young samurai were returning from the hunt . . .

JŪRŌ: At Minami Ozaki on Mount Akazawa, halfway down the mountain from Oak Pass, Sukeyasu sat astride a lustrous white horse, perhaps waiting for someone to catch up with him.

SUKETSUNE: That day he wore a hunting robe decorated with views of autumn fields, and he carried a bow whose ends were wrapped in wisteria.

JŪRŌ: A cold autumn wind suddenly blew off his bamboo traveling hat . . .

GORŌ: Unafraid of mountain tracks or cliffs, he walked his horse ever onward.

ŌMI: We lay in wait for him, taking cover behind three oak trees. The first brave warrior was I, Kotōta Nariie.

YAWATA: And the second brave warrior was I, Saburō Yukiuji. When I let fly, I didn't miss.

SUKETSUNE: The arrow glanced off the saddlebow of the swift horse he was riding, pierced the edge of his chaps, and, with a "thwack," drove right through his body.

GORŌ *(Emotionally)*: Though Sukeyasu had no peer among ten thousand warriors, he could not survive this grievous wound . . .

JŪRŌ *(Emotionally)*: He fell crashing from his horse, and his life vanished like the dew that covers Mount Akazawa.

SUKETSUNE: Your faces resemble that Sukeyasu. *(Lost in thought.)* Could it be that the two of you . . .

JŪRŌ: Since our looks make it so plain, why should we conceal it any longer? We brothers are the two sons left behind by Kawazu no Saburō Sukeyasu.

SUKETSUNE: The older was then named Ichiman. You have grown up . . .

TORA: To become the adopted son of Soga Sukenobu.

JŪRŌ *(Deliberately)*: My name is now Soga Jūrō Sukenari. *(He bows.)*

SUKETSUNE: The younger son, Hakoō, is now a samurai . . .

SHŌSHŌ: And came of age at a ceremony presided over by Lord Hōjō.

GORŌ *(Shouting in anger)*: I am now Soga Gorō Tokimune. *(Does a powerful* mie.*)*

SUKETSUNE: Now then, for you brothers . . .

JŪRŌ: And for Lord Kudō Saemon . . .

GORŌ: Suketsune . . .

SUKETSUNE *(Deliberately)*: This is a truly remarkable . . .

ALL THREE *(Emotionally)*: Encounter, isn't it?

GORŌ *(Briskly and angrily)*: Murderer of my father, prepare to die!

*(*GORŌ *frees his right arm from his overrobe and rushes toward* SUKETSUNE, *but* JŪRŌ *stops him.)*

JŪRŌ *(Rapidly)*: Now, don't cause a ruckus, my rambunctious younger brother. Just leave everything to your older brother before we carry out our crucial task.

GORŌ *(Loudly, in frustration)*: But . . .

JŪRŌ *(Slowly and full of emotion)*: Restrain yourself and be patient.

GORŌ *(Rapidly, in anger)*: I won't, I can't! My stock of patience has run out!

*(*GORŌ *again makes a move toward* SUKETSUNE, *but* ASAHINA *seizes his waist.)*

ASAHINA *(Placatingly)*: Hey, wait, brother! Don't do anything rash. I wouldn't steer you two wrong, so please come on and settle down. *(He moves grandiosely toward the brothers.)* If you'll just hold back for me now *(loudly)*, you'll have your lucky New Year's dreams.

(He places his hand on GORŌ *'s waist, holding him from behind while* JŪRŌ *continues to restrain him from in front. The three pose, acknowledging each other, then return to their places.)*

SUKETSUNE *(Matter-of-factly)*: Tokimune, you are a fool to be stalking me, thinking that I'm your father's murderer. Even dog-beating children know that Matano no Gorō had your father killed for besting him at sumo wrestling. I had nothing to do with killing him.

GORŌ *(Rapidly)*: No, you're a coward, Suketsune, for denying your role. Admit that you had my father killed!

ŌMI *(Commandingly)*: Why, you stupid, impudent brat! Will you shut up and listen? How dare you accuse my master to his face of being your blood enemy?

YAWATA: You speak rude words to Lord Suketsune, who holds the place of honor on this occasion. And to think that you are a distant relative . . .

(The LORDS *speak with more contempt than did* ŌMI *and* YAWATA.*)*

FIRST LORD: You don't have to pretend to be more than what you are. If you call on him every three days . . .

SECOND LORD: And wait cowering in a corner of his kitchen . . .

THIRD LORD: He may give you the head of a salted sea bream to munch on.

FOURTH LORD: If you come near him, you'll feel just like you're standing under a huge tree.

FIFTH LORD: It is best to get out of the way of the great.

SIXTH LORD: But if you stay here and bluster . . .

ŌMI: By his side stands Ōmi no Kotōta.

YAWATA: And Yawata no Saburō serves him, too, so . . .

ŌMI *(Loudly)*: Begone!

YAWATA *(Loudly)*: Get lost!

ŌMI and YAWATA *(Emphatically)*: We won't let you get away with it!

(The two do a mie, *posing with outstretched arms, protecting their lord.)*

SUKETSUNE: Desist, both of you. *(The two resume their at-ease posture.)* After all, in the past we were members of a close-knit family, and Asahina escorted the two men here. You are by no means to say anything foolish to them.

ŌMI and YAWATA: Yes, sir.

ASAHINA *(Cheerfully)*: Lord Suketsune, in the spirit of your words, which are too kind and generous, may I suggest an exchange of New Year's gifts to celebrate the coming of spring?

TORA: To the two brothers waiting patiently here . . .

SHŌSHŌ: Please, sir, would you offer . . .

TORA and SHŌSHŌ: A cup of sake?

SUKETSUNE: Yes, by all means, I shall offer them a cup of sake. Ōmi, Yawata, bring the ladle and cup.

ŌMI and YAWATA: As you wish, sir.

(Offstage music called sanbō kagura *begins. Moving with great formality,* ŌMI *and* YAWATA *turn around and receive a sake cup on a stand and a ladle from* STAGE ASSISTANTS. *They take them to the front of* SUKETSUNE*'s dais, and serve him.* SUKETSUNE *drinks one cup of sake.)*

SUKETSUNE: Since he is the elder brother, serve Jūrō first.

JŪRŌ: I accept most humbly.

(To the same music, TORA *and* SHŌSHŌ *receive the sake ladle and cup from* ŌMI *and* YAWATA. *The two women solemnly and formally serve* JŪRŌ. *After* JŪRŌ *drinks,* TORA *removes the sake cup and stand and returns to her place. She looks at* SUKETSUNE *and cocks her head inquiringly. He looks at* GORŌ *and nods to her, indicating that she should place the stand between* JŪRŌ *and himself, not put it away.)*

SUKETSUNE *(Commandingly)*: Now then, Gorō!

GORŌ: What is it?

SUKETSUNE: I'm offering you sake. Come. Come right over here and drink it.

GORŌ *(Rapidly, in anger)*: I'll drink it, yes I'll drink it!

(He rushes toward SUKETSUNE, *but the kneeling* JŪRŌ *stops him and they pose.)*

JŪRŌ *(Deliberately)*: Gorō, be sure you don't try anything foolish.

GORŌ *(Loudly, but in resignation)*: Right.

*(*GORŌ, *getting ready for action, flips his outer garment off his shoulders, revealing his red underkimono, and assumes a powerful, low posture, with legs apart. Wiggling his feet sideways in a shuffling movement known as* jirijiri, *he slowly advances on* SUKETSUNE, *pausing challengingly at several points, while delivering the following lines.)*

GORŌ *(Emotionally)*: What an auspicious day this is. For a long time, over and over, I have begged the gods and Buddhas to give me the chance to meet you, and my prayers have been answered. To be able to meet you now is like waiting 3,000 years for the miraculous *udonge* flower to blossom and then actually seeing it bloom. Thanks to today's meeting, good fortune comes to the three estates, and the wind of heaven will blow away the demons who have been there these past eighteen years. I'll partake of your sake . . . *(almost shouting)* by all means!

*(*GORŌ *sits in front of the sake stand, and glaring at* SUKETSUNE, *his hand shaking in anger, grasps the sake cup. Never taking his eyes off* SUKETSUNE, *he thrusts the cup out to his right for* SHŌSHŌ *to pour.* GORŌ *brings the cup to his lips but can't bring himself to drink. He then smashes the cup to pieces on the floor, and growls at* SUKETSUNE.*)*

SUKETSUNE: My, how fierce you are. You act as though you are deeply chagrined that your father was killed.

GORŌ *(Quivering with emotion)*: I am indeed.

SUKETSUNE: Are you angry about it?

GORŌ: I am indeed.

(Chagrined, he tightly clutches the sides of the sake cup stand, and it begins to crumple.)

SUKETSUNE: I would expect nothing less of you. But you will find it most unfortunate that I stand high in the esteem of the shogun and am a very great feudal lord, ruler of the three estates. When I am accompanied by my whole retinue, they number one to two thousand horsemen. When I travel in lesser state, one to two hundred personal horse guardsmen accompany me. So, you see that you will never manage to cross swords with me. *(Emphatically.)* I'm afraid it is quite impossible.

GORŌ: Damn it!

(He angrily smashes what remains of the stand and, clutching a fragment in each hand, stands and makes an aggressive move toward SUKETSUNE. JŪRŌ *rushes between his brother and their enemy and the two do a* mie, JŪRŌ *kneeling and* GORŌ *standing just upstage of him.)*

SUKETSUNE *(Briskly and authoritatively)*: And that is not all. The sword Tomokirimaru was lost some time ago and, as long as its whereabouts remain unknown, your foster father, Lord Sukenobu, will continue to be a suspect. Therefore, all of you Sogas must consider yourselves virtually under arrest by the shogun himself.

JŪRŌ: Does that mean that as long as Tomokirimaru . . .

JŪRŌ and GORŌ: Remains unfound . . .

SUKETSUNE: Yes, you are not permitted to attempt revenge.

JŪRŌ and GORŌ: Why, you! . . .

(The brothers groan in frustration. A voice is heard on the hanamichi.*)*

ONIŌ: Wait! Wait! *(*ONIŌ SHINZAEMON *runs noisily down the* hanamichi. *He is formally dressed and carries the sword Tomokirimaru wrapped in a brocade bag. He addresses the stage briskly and respectfully from* shichisan.*)* I have recovered the lost sword, Tomokirimaru.

ASAHINA: What? You say that you . . .

ALL *(Surprised)*: Have possession of Tomokirimaru?

ONIŌ *(Briskly)*: Yes, I, the Soga retainer Oniō Shinzaemon, do humbly proclaim that, at this moment, I have come bearing it in my possession.

ASAHINA *(Rapidly)*: Oh, Shinzaemon, well done! Bring it here at once.

ONIŌ: Yes, sir. *(He enters the main stage and kneels to the right of all the others.)* Please excuse my status as a lowly retainer of a vassal and forgive me for my intrusion. Lord Suketsune, may I take the liberty to request that you inspect this sword?

Soga Jūrō (Onoe Baikō VII), kneeling, and Soga Gorō (Onoe Shōroku II), standing left, face Kudō Suketsune (Ichikawa Ennosuke II), right, as courtesan Tora (Ichimura Uzaemon XVI) and Kudō's retainer, Yawata no Saburō (Kataoka Ichizō V), center, pose strongly. (Tsubouchi Memorial Theatre Museum of Waseda University)

*(*YAWATA *receives the sword from* ONIŌ *and presents it to* SUKETSUNE. SUKETSUNE *holds a wad of paper in his teeth to prevent his breath from sullying the blade, pulls the blade part of the way out of the sheath, and carefully inspects the sword. He slides the sword back in the sheath and holds the sheath in his left hand.)*

SUKETSUNE *(Matter-of-factly)*: This is indeed Tomokirimaru.

JŪRŌ *(Rapidly)*: Since it is once again in our possession . . .

GORŌ *(Loudly and rapidly)*: Proclaim that you are our blood enemy!

SUKETSUNE *(Interrupting)*: Now is out of the question. We must wait until the time is right.

GORŌ *(Loudly and rapidly)*: Suketsune, you are a coward to delay.

SUKETSUNE *(Interrupting)*: No, I am no coward. Until I have finished my duty as marshal of the shogun's hunt at Mount Fuji, late in the fifth month *(authoritatively)*, I absolutely cannot allow you to attempt your revenge.

ASAHINA: When Lord Suketsune says wait until the time is right . . .

TORA: He speaks words of wisdom . . .

ASAHINA *(Reassuringly)*: You'll have another chance to pay him back.

JŪRŌ: Does that mean that until you have finished your duty . . .

ONIŌ: As marshal of the shogun's hunt at Mount Fuji . . .

GORŌ *(Rapidly)*: Even though we've come all the way to the mountain of treasure, you'll send us home empty-handed? Jūrō . . .

JŪRŌ: Gorō . . .

GORŌ *(Angrily)*: Damn you Suketsune, it's infuriating!

(He throws down the fragments and stands up straight, arms crossed before his chest in an aragoto mie.*)*

SUKETSUNE *(Briskly)*: No, by no means will I send you home empty-handed. As a memento of our meeting today, I have something for you instead of a New Year's present, trifling though it is. Yawata . . .

*(*SUKETSUNE *takes a packet wrapped in a purple handkerchief out of his kimono and gives it to* YAWATA, *who takes it and hands it to* JŪRŌ. JŪRŌ *opens the packet and gives one pass to* GORŌ.*)*

JŪRŌ *(Excitedly)*: Look, here are . . .

GORŌ *(Joyfully)*: Two tickets to the hunt.

SUKETSUNE *(Emotionally)*: Tickets to strike and dispel your hatred for me, brothers.

JŪRŌ and GORŌ *(Nodding to each other and speaking with emotion)*: You don't have to tell us that!

ASAHINA: So, until the time . . .

SUKETSUNE: When Jūrō and Gorō . . .

JŪRŌ and GORŌ: Meet Lord Kudō Saemon Suketsune . . .

SUKETSUNE *(Decisively)*: At the base of Mount Fuji . . .

ALL THREE *(Grandly)*: Farewell!

(To geza *music,* JŪRŌ *and* GORŌ *circle each other and do a* mie *in which* JŪRŌ *again restrains his brother from approaching* SUKETSUNE. *The* EIGHT LORDS *shout,* "Look at that! Look at that!" *to accompany them. The brothers then turn and face backward, joining the other principals who have already done so, with the exception of* SUKETSUNE, *who remains facing forward the whole time. When, as a signal,* SUKETSUNE *snaps his head in a* mie *and makes a gesture resembling a blow to his throat—indicating his eventual fate—*ONIŌ, SHŌSHŌ, ASAHINA, JŪRŌ, GORŌ, TORA, YAWATA, SUKETSUNE, *and* ŌMI, *lined up in this order from right to left, turn and face forward and assume their final tableau.* ASAHINA, JŪRŌ, GORŌ, *and* SUKETSUNE *do* mie *just before the curtain closes and the play comes to an end. The closing tableau is famous for its supposed resemblance to Mount Fuji with a crane flying past it, an image of great auspiciousness.)*

Two-panel woodblock print by Toyohara Kunichika (1835–1900) of Ichikawa Danjūrō IX as Kamakura no Gongorō Kagemasa in the "face-showing" *(kaomise)* production at the Shintomi-za, Tokyo, November and December 1878. The huge personal *mimasu* crest of Danjūrō on the sleeves, bold *kumadori* makeup, and oversized costume, wig, and sword are characteristic of the actor's bravura *(aragoto)* acting style. The *haiku* poem alludes to the custom of placing on display a felicitous papier-maché or clay figure of an animal or person, perhaps an actor: "An auspicious doll, resting in an alcove niche, a clear frosty day." (Tsubouchi Memorial Theatre Museum of Waseda University)

Just A Minute!

Shibaraku

Original Version Attributed to Ichikawa Danjūrō I (Mimasuya Hyōgo)

TRANSLATED BY KATHERINE SALTZMAN-LI

Tsurugaoka Shrine Precincts

Tsurugaoka Shato no Ba

1697 NAKAMURA-ZA, EDO

Just A Minute!

INTRODUCTION

The Tokugawa-period kabuki year began in the eleventh calendar month with the "face-showing" *(kaomise)* production. As the opening program for the year ahead, it aimed not only at immediate production success but also to announce and advertise the artistic and entertainment possibilities of a troupe with continuing and newly contracted stars. The Edo *kaomise,* in particular, were always grand and showy presentations. Troupe leaders *(zagashira)* carefully planned them to be spectacularly attractive and to show off the coming year's stars to their greatest advantage.

Just a Minute! became a regular feature of the season's opening production (as its first main act) from the time of actor Ichikawa Danjūrō II (1688–1758). Performed annually throughout most of the Tokugawa period, it provided one of the most popular and representative opportunities for the display of Edo-style kabuki. Its connection to the bravura-style *(aragoto)* traditions of the Danjūrō acting line and its placement in the opening production put it at the center of Edo kabuki practices. Successive generations in the Danjūrō line followed in the footsteps of their founder, whose religious beliefs were deeply enmeshed in his art. His roles included deities, particularly the Buddhist god Fudō, and his acting was considered to have a religious, protective effect. *Just a Minute!* is one of the finest examples of the Danjūrō family style *(ie no gei),* its hero powered by godlike qualities of magnificence, might, and the ability to save weak victims from oppression. As the most eagerly awaited act of the Edo *kaomise* production, *Just a Minute!* not only offered brilliance and theatricality but also contained roles of every type *(yakugara),* thus effectively presenting the members of the new troupe through the display of their varied talents.

There was no fixed text for *Just a Minute!* during the Tokugawa period. Pre-Meiji versions of the play can be summarized better by their general idea than by their plot: evil designs and their perpetrators are undone by the sudden appearance of a brash *aragoto* hero of about eighteen years of age. He exposes the villains and puts an end to both their plans and their power. Over time, this situation was worked into a large number of often very complex plots. Major acting features shared among versions include the overpowering, larger-than-life hero, his grand entrance, his characteristic elocutionary and gestural styles, and his speech of self-introduction *(tsurane)*. Common plot devices involved a ledger and the explanation of its meaning or etymology, and lost and recovered objects (typically, governance seals and a famous sword). Each year, the setting and characters making up the play's world *(sekai)* would be newly determined, incorporating both the elements just listed and new plot and production elements *(shukō)*.

The earliest play containing elements of *Just a Minute!* was *The Great Ledger Book and Asahina's Hundred Stories* (Daifukuchō Asahina Hyaku Monogatari), in which the meaning of a certain ledger is explained. Written by Danjūrō I (1660–1704)—using the penname Mimasuya Hyōgo—for Edo's Morita-za in 1692, the author also played the major role of Asahina. Five years later, in 1697, Danjūrō performed *Just a Minute!* in *Meeting with Nagoya* (Sankai Nagoya) at the Nakamura-za. Both this history play *(jidaimono)*, which is considered the first actual version of *Just a Minute!*, and the 1692 play were performed in New Year's productions. However, the play that became the basis for later performances was performed in the eleventh lunar month, thus initiating the *kaomise* connection. In Danjūrō II's 1714 Nakamura-za production of *The Nation's Great Ledger* (Banmin Daifukuchō), the hero was, for the first time, called Kamakura no Gongorō Kagemasa, his most usual name in subsequent versions.

In 1840, *Just a Minute!* became an independent play with its now familiar title when Danjūrō VII (1791–1859) included it in the "Eighteen Famous Kabuki Plays" *(Kabuki Jūhachiban)* collection, the most popular pieces of the Danjūrō line of actors, most of them in *aragoto* style. The one-word Japanese title is taken from the hero's offstage call to the onstage villains just before his entrance on the *hanamichi*. A famous anecdote from Danjūrō II's early acting days accounts for the title: rivalry with Yamanaka Heikurō I (1642–1724), the actor playing the role of the chief villain, Takehira, resulted in Danjūrō's delayed entrance and the repetition of his line, "Just a minute!" The effect of his entrance was inadvertently enhanced, and the line's repetition worked its way permanently into scripts. (Interestingly, the *hanamichi* was still just a provisional part of theatre architecture at the time, not becoming permanent until, perhaps, the 1730s. Thus the story, if true, demonstrates an early example of *kabuki*'s discovery of the runway's latent dramatic possibilities.) *Just a Minute!* also serves as an appropriate title because of the line's importance in the play. It is delivered at a pivotal moment: with his call of "Just a minute!" the hero effects both a halt to further villainy and a switch to the ascendancy of good over evil.

The hero's entrance in *Just a Minute!* remains one of the great moments in which we may share the pleasure experienced by Edo spectators. As he enters on the *hanamichi,* wearing one of kabuki's most memorable costumes and wigs (described in the translation), all eyes are riveted with excited anticipation on his awesome presence. Countless portraits of actors in this guise effectively captured and represented the excitement and pleasure of Edo kabuki.

Having entered on the *hanamichi,* Kagemasa takes a seat at *shichisan,* where he is aided by a stage assistant *(kōken)* dressed formally in the standard Danjūrō colors of persimmon and black. Kagemasa introduces himself in a formal, lengthy speech *(tsurane),* a moment of both literary importance and heightened theatricality. Usually written in poetic meter of alternating seven and five syllables *(shichigochō)* and often composed with the literary techniques of extensive wordplay and exhaustive lists, this rhetorical highlight calls on the actor's elocutionary skill and ability to hold an audience. Many Tokugawa-period *tsurane* for this play were written by the actors themselves, who, with topical references and current locutions, would update the traditional model. When Danjūrō XII (b. 1946) spoke the *tsurane* at the performance celebrating the assumption of his name, he added many topical references regarding the significance of the occasion, such as, "Today I present myself as the twelfth in succession." In fact, although the *tsurane* translated here is the standard one given in most contemporary published versions of the play, the one spoken by Danjūrō XII when he took that name in 1985 demonstrates that these speeches are still subject to considerable revision, although certain traditional phrases may be retained.

Tsurane were the only published parts of *Just a Minute!* and other scripts, and fans collected them as part of their adoration of specific actors. Thus, the *tsurane* is a chief point of attention for both the actor and audience. Because of the elocutionary style employed, it is far more impressive in performance than on the page, especially in English, where its rhetorical devices and auditory flamboyance can barely be suggested.

The play contains other distinctive characters in addition to Kagemasa. Chief among them are the arch-villain Takehira, with his blue-lined face *(ai guma)* and his coolly elegant evil nature; the comical Priest Shinsai, who wears the strange *namazu guma,* a makeup suggestive of a catfish; and the highly exaggerated "belly-thrusters" *(haradashi),* Takehira's red-faced henchmen, whose large, exposed red bellies have their musculature painted on them.

An alternate version of the play called *Female Just a Minute!* (Onna Shibaraku, 1745 or 1746), features a powerful heroine, and a version written as a domestic play *(sewamono), Domestic Just a Minute!* (Sewa Shibaraku), was created in 1818 by Tsuruya Nanboku IV (1755–1829) for Danjūrō VII.

The script most often used today is based on that prepared in 1895 by Fukuchi Ōchi (1841–1906) for Danjūrō IX (1838–1903) for a Kabuki-za production. I have used the version published in Hattori Yukio, ed., *Kabuki On-Sutēji,* Vol. 10, together with a video of a 1985 production starring Danjūrō XII.

CHARACTERS

KIYOHARA NO TAKEHIRA, *an evil lord*

KASHIMA PRIEST SHINSAI, *comic priest used by* TAKEHIRA

BELLY-THRUSTERS, *large-bellied samurai in service to* TAKEHIRA:

- TOGANE TARŌ YOSHINARI
- ASHIGARA ZAEMON TAKAMUNE
- EBARA HACHIRŌ KUNITSURA
- HANYŪ GORŌ SUKENARI
- MUSASHI KURŌ UJIKIYO
- NARITA GORŌ YOSHIHIDE

TOYOSHIMA HEIDA, *samurai on the side of* TAKEHIRA

TAGATA UNPACHI, *samurai on the side of* TAKEHIRA

UNAGAMI TONAI, *samurai on the side of* TAKEHIRA

OSUMI HYŌJI, *samurai on the side of* TAKEHIRA

KAMAKURA NO GONGORŌ KAGEMASA, *the powerful young hero*

KAMO NO JIRŌ YOSHITSUNA, *son of an important governor*

KAMO NO SABURŌ YOSHISATO, *brother of* YOSHITSUNA

TAKARAGI KURANDO SADATOSHI, *samurai on the side of* YOSHITSUNA

WATANABE KOGANEMARU YUKITSUNA, *samurai on the side of* YOSHITSUNA

TERUHA, *in disguise as an attendant of* TAKEHIRA, *in reality* KAGEMASA*'s cousin*

KATSURA NO MAE, YOSHITSUNA*'s fiancée*

KURETAKE, *lady-in-waiting to* KATSURA NO MAE

EIGHT FOOTMEN, *in service to* TAKEHIRA

FOUR FEMALE ATTENDANTS, *in service to* KATSURA NO MAE

TWELVE MALE SHRINE ATTENDANTS

STAGE ASSISTANTS, *formally dressed* kōken *and black-garbed* kurogo

ŌZATSUMA, *two chanters and two shamisen players used in* aragoto *plays*

Tsurugaoka Shrine Precincts

(The curtain opens to offer a view of the Hachiman Tsurugaoka Shrine precinct, which is set back and raised by several steps, leaving the front of the stage for arrivals, departures, parading, and seating. The action occurs on the forestage before a painted flat depicting the shrine's outer wall of stone and red lacquered wood. The stage and hanamichi *floor are covered with dance platforms* [shosabutai]. *A border of plum blossoms* [tsurieda] *runs overhead at the front of the stage. The curtain opens to* haya kagura *music, traditional for the opening of the* kaomise *program. Two* ŌZATSUMA *chanters and two* ŌZATSUMA *shamisen players sit in full view, stage left, on a side extension to the stage. They wear the traditional persimmon-colored formal garb associated with the Danjūrō line. Offstage, lively music* [watari byōshi] *accompanies the procession.* EIGHT FOOTMEN [yakko] *parade in along the* hanamichi *with high and noisy steps. The outer garments of their matching costumes are tucked up behind them and they wear fringed aprons. All carry feathered lances with black-and-white-striped handles. The feathers alternate in color, four red and four white. The* FOOTMEN *stop, spread out along the* hanamichi, *lean on their left knees, and face the main part of the audience. Right arms are outstretched; left arms hold the lances vertically. They speak rapidly and in order, starting with the* FOOTMAN *closest to the stage.)*

ALL FOOTMEN: At last!

(Music stops.)

FIRST FOOTMAN: It is here! The month of the "face-showing," the auspicious tradition of Edo kabuki when the year's lineup of actors first appears.

SECOND FOOTMAN: At the first beat of the announcing drum, the feathered adornments of secondary attendants rush in.

THIRD FOOTMAN: Flurrying, is it snow or a hail of sweet warming sake that falls in this year-end cold? With the wrap-up of the final month . . .

FOURTH FOOTMAN: We share the measured wine of drinking companions at the familiar site of the dismount.

FIFTH FOOTMAN: We toss off a full half-pint, and it penetrates like an extractor.

SIXTH FOOTMAN: We discard our sandals at the entrance, the entrance of groveling sycophants.

SEVENTH FOOTMAN: For the lucky gallant, fame and adornments are the glamorous props on the stage of the day.

EIGHTH FOOTMAN: To the accompaniment of rousing music, we must, as always at this time of celebration . . .

FIRST FOOTMAN *(Raising spears)*: Be stirred by valor . . .

ALL FOOTMEN *(Standing straight)*: Our spirits high!

(They run onstage, holding the lances ahead of them, cross the stage, and exit left.)

ŌZATSUMA:

Like the profusion of flowers surrounding the Ch'in emperor's palace of old, / there is nothing more glorious than the power of those on high. / With the progression of time, / his lordship's influence has surpassed that of all rivals. *(Three* ki *beats mark the opening of the painted wall flat. It opens out from the center, revealing a full panoply of characters. Lower stage characters move out to sit where the flat was. The setting now reveals the full shrine. The covered vestibule, which encircles the open space of the precincts, is painted red. Metal lanterns hang from the eaves. On either side of the stage are plum trees.* Haya sagariha *music plays.* KIYOHARA NO TAKEHIRA *sits upper stage center on a raised platform with an open umbrella over his head. His blue makeup* [aiguma] *indicates his evil nature. He is dressed in white and holds a closed fan upright in his right hand. He wears a large black wig parted in the middle with a gold crown. The musculature on his padded belly is outlined with black lines. The ledger is displayed to his right and the sword to his left.* TOYOSHIMA HEIDA, TAGATA UNPACHI, UNAGAMI TONAI, *and* OSUMI HYŌJI*—in that order, with* HEIDA *closest to center—sit lower left, each dressed in elegant formal attire* [kamishimo] *and bearing the two swords—one long, one short—of the samurai. Upper left are the* KASHIMA PRIEST SHINSAI*—the so-called Catfish Priest—and* TERUHA, *pretending to be the younger sister of* Nasu no Kurō *and thus attending on* TAKEHIRA. SHINSAI *has foot-length sideburns hanging from his ears; an oversized red lacquer sake cup rests on a small stand of plain wood in front of him.* TERUHA *is dressed in a bright red long-sleeved kimono* [furisode] *and holds a plum branch. Shrine attendants sit behind them. The five* BELLY-THRUSTERS *sit on stools upper right, with shrine attendants behind them. They wear black-and-white-sleeved jackets under stiff, sleeveless, red-lined black jackets with Danjūrō box crests* [mimasu] *on the shoulders. Large padded red bellies, on which the musculature is outlined with darker red, show through their open jackets. Their red legs are similarly outlined, and they wear white sandals and white kneepads. They have distinctive black wigs, with ax blade–like top knots and a white forehead and pate. They sit in the order in which they most often speak: closest to* TAKEHIRA *is* TOGANE, *followed by* ASHIGARA, EBARA, HANYŪ, *and* MUSASHI. YOSHITSUNA, KATSURA NO MAE, YOSHISATO, KURANDO, KURETAKE, *and the* FOUR FEMALE ATTENDANTS*—with* YOSHITSUNA *closest to center—sit lower right. Their faces are white and they are all beautifully attired. The* EIGHT FOOTMEN *file in to sit behind them soon after the wall flat opens.)*

HEIDA: Today, after many trials, our lord, Kiyohara no Takehira . . .

UNPACHI: Comes here to the Tsurugaoka Shrine to obtain imperial appointment as leader of the land.

TONAI: From today, we four will fulfill our wishes for success.

HYŌJI: This is truly . . .

ALL FOUR: A joyous occasion!

TAKEHIRA: My time has arrived. I, Counselor Kiyohara no Takehira, have subjugated the Eastern provinces, an excellent omen that I will soon grasp the power of the land in my hands. Here at this shrine, I come attired to take myself to the heights.

(The BELLY-THRUSTERS *aligned to* TAKEHIRA*'s right speak without moving.)*

TOGANE: Indeed, our lord graciously commands. He stands first among the blooms of court, his face the hue of the winter red-blossomed plum.

ASHIGARA: The aligned faces are all red. Not caused by wine, this red is our custom.

SHINSAI *(Stiffly)*: I don't know anything about customs. To my half-tutored mind, the color of white blossoms wouldn't be surprising.

TERUHA: There is no one who would defy your authority, my lord. We are all ready for your commands. Even I, incompetent though I am, await your pleasure.

TAKEHIRA: Investigate the misconduct of these men who cross me, and we will punish them. That done, we'll shout "Hurrah!"

EBARA: We honor you in every way!

HEIDA: We offer . . .

ALL BELLY-THRUSTERS: Our congratulations!

YOSHITSUNA: Although you have distinguished yourself slightly during these three years of strife, this display is overblown.

KATSURA: To have taken down the ledger offered by Yoshitsuna!

YOSHISATO: And it is by your own command that you have donned the attire and accoutrements of a high official.

KURANDO: Your seizing political power could not be more arrogant or offensive.

KURETAKE: Your actions . . .

YOSHITSUNA: Are just too much.

TAKEHIRA: All these insults you hurl at me, you, whose father, Yoriyoshi, already bore me, Takehira, great ill will! But Katsura no Mae fascinates me, and I want her to be my attendant. Stand in my way and I'll deal with you!

YOSHITSUNA: You defy the laws of nature, Takehira! Why would she go with you?

KATSURA: As I have a man of my own choosing, why should I be unfaithful to him?

KURETAKE: No matter what, you must both flee this place to ensure your safety.

FIRST FEMALE ATTENDANT: Oh, please leave them alone!

SECOND FEMALE ATTENDANT: And kindly leave the ledger as it was. There is more than enough room in the votive hall . . .

THIRD FEMALE ATTENDANT: To hang your plaque elsewhere.

FOURTH FEMALE ATTENDANT: With prayers for peace . . .

FIRST FEMALE ATTENDANT: Please grant our wish . . .

FOUR FEMALE ATTENDANTS: Our earnest wish.

KURANDO: No, they must go to the capital and report everything to the emperor.

YOSHITSUNA: Yes, indeed we must. Brother come, let's go.

(He tries to stand up to go.)

TOGANE: So, you not only go against the emperor's wishes, but you would also go to the capital to make your own report. You are completely contemptible!

ASHIGARA: What do you expect from men with no one to serve?

EBARA: I'll strike them down, don't worry!

HANYŪ: Yes, do, and I'll help!

MUSASHI: I will too!

TERUHA *(Quickly)*: Please wait. What you say has reason, but if blood should flow at the shrine, it will anger the gods. Please forgo this matter for now.

SHINSAI: Sister Teruha here speaks as an ally, not from faintheartedness.

TOGANE: No, let's arrange to bring them to justice now! *(Elongating his vowels.)* Call for Narita Gorō.

*(*ASHIGARA, *upstage right, stands, walks past the other* BELLY-THRUSTERS *and descends the stairs.)*

ASHIGARA: Yes! *(He now stands at the stage end of the* hanamichi, *looking down it.)* Your devoted retainer, Narita Gorō, has been waiting at the vehicle outbuilding. *(Vowels stretched.)* At your request, he is hurrying here.

NARITA *(Offstage and powerfully)*: At your service!

(Onstage villains call out "Yo!" ASHIGARA *goes back to his seat.* NARITA GORŌ, *dressed in* kamishimo, *approaches down the* hanamichi. *He is dressed in the same way as are the other* BELLY-THRUSTERS. *Flute and drums accompany his passage down the* hanamichi. *He stops at* shichisan *and faces out to the audience.)*

ASHIGARA: Narita Gorō!

ALL BELLY-THRUSTERS: He has come!

NARITA *(Spoken toward audience)*: As I heard the summoning voice, the winter-red plum blossoms burst open, displaying the red of my face. On this day of *kaomise* revival, I, Narita Gorō Yoshihide, once again make my entrance and am here to serve you.

(He strikes his belly with both hands and then ends with a pose, leaning toward the stage on bended knee, elongating his last words.)

TAKEHIRA: We're all here for the same reason. Now, let's punish these men, one and all!

NARITA: Men who defy you should lose their heads. It won't take long to sharpen my sword. I've been waiting a long time for this!

TAKEHIRA: All right then, get ready!

ALL BELLY-THRUSTERS: Here we go!

("Shrine music" [miokagura] *of drum and flute. The five onstage* BELLY-THRUSTERS *move down the steps and spread out along the stage. Once in place,*

formally dressed STAGE ASSISTANTS [kōken] *come out from stage left, one for each man.* NARITA *remains at* shichisan *and a* STAGE ASSISTANT *comes out behind him as well. The six men hold their right arms out from their sides and stamp their left feet forward; then they thrust their left arms out and stamp their right feet forward. Then the* STAGE ASSISTANTS *help them strip their outer costumes to the waist, one arm at a time. A unison* "Yo!" *is followed by the* BELLY-THRUSTERS *moving their left arms to their sides and having their sleeves pulled off and down by the* STAGE ASSISTANTS. *They do the same for their right arms. Red upper costumes are revealed underneath. After making adjustments, the* STAGE ASSISTANTS *exit in the direction from which they entered. All* BELLY-THRUSTERS *stamp with their left feet, shouting the rhythmic* aragoto *nonsense syllables,* "Yattoko tottchaa, untoko na," *pause, and then do the same with their right feet, striking a simultaneous* mie.*)*

TAKEHIRA *(Still sitting formally and stiffly)*: Turn them into side dishes and we'll have them with wine! Ha-ha-ha!

SHINSAI: In that case Madame Teruha, you'll have to serve.

TERUHA: Oh?!

(Flute and drums. SHINSAI *and* TERUHA *get up, and the five* BELLY-THRUSTERS *turn around to face* TAKEHIRA. TERUHA *turns around and hands her plum branch to a black-garbed* STAGE ASSISTANT [kurogo] *and receives a golden sake dipper.* SHINSAI *carries the oversized sake cup on its stand over to* TAKEHIRA. TAKEHIRA *picks up the cup in both hands.* SHINSAI *bows, turns, and walks down the stairs as* TERUHA *walks over and mimes pouring sake from the dipper into the cup. Then she, too, walks down the stairs and over to* SHINSAI, *both she and he now taking their places with the men at lower left. The original five* BELLY-THRUSTERS *return to stand at their earlier upstage left spots while the platform on which* TAKEHIRA *is seated moves from center to left.* NARITA *walks from the* hanamichi *up the stairs to join the other* BELLY-THRUSTERS *and stands closest to* TAKEHIRA.*)*

NARITA: Okay, let their heads roll!

TOGANE: Prepare to meet your ends!

ALL SIX: Resign yourselves.

*(*TAKEHIRA *begins to drink sake from the large cup. The six* BELLY-THRUSTERS, *each with a white-clothed attendant sitting behind, growl, stamp their right feet, half unsheathe their exaggeratedly large swords, and hold them overhead with both arms, like rainbows, as they complete this group* mie. *As they hold the pose, the voice of* KAMAKURA NO GONGORŌ KAGEMASA *is heard coming from behind the* hanamichi *entrance.)*

KAGEMASA *(Elongated)*: Just a minute!

(The BELLY-THRUSTERS *sheath their swords.)*

ASHIGARA *(Surprised)*: Huh?!

TAKEHIRA *(Still holding the cup)*: Hold it, hold it, hold it. Why this interruption, just as we're about to punish these transgressors for their crime, just as I turn this cup in my hands?

NARITA: Hearing the sound of that voice, the voice which called out "Just a minute!" gives me the chills. I hope it's just the flu coming on.

TOGANE: Me too, me too.

ASHIGARA: Yes, indeed, I feel thoroughly uneasy, down to the soles of my feet. I have a bad feeling about this.

EBARA: If only we had tried out for a winning role!

HANYŪ: My heart's throbbing!

MUSASHI: Me too, me too. We're all like that from hearing that "Just a minute!" voice.

TERUHA: Isn't that so? When I heard that voice, I shuddered. *(She puts her hands up to cover her ears as if to protect them.)* It was louder than thunder!

SHINSAI: It's frightening, yes, but I'm brave. No one can scare me.

TOGANE: Whoever just yelled out "Just a minute! . . ."

ALL BELLY-THRUSTERS: Who are you?

KAGEMASA *(Still offstage, with great force)*: Just a minute!

ALL BELLY-THRUSTERS: What do you mean?

KAGEMASA *(Increasingly powerful)*: Just a minute! Juust a miinuuttte! Juuust a miiinnuuutttte!

*(*TAKEHIRA *puts the cup to his side. The* hanamichi *lights come on as the curtain is pulled open for* KAGEMASA*'s entrance. He is costumed in the most famous of kabuki getups: a hugely oversized, persimmon-colored outer garment* [suō] *whose square, winglike sleeves are decorated with the Danjūrō crest of three squares of graduated size, three measuring boxes* [mimasu] *one inside the other; long, trailing* hakama [nagabakama], *which hide tall clogs* [takageta] *worn to give the actor intimidating height; a "five-spoked"* [gohon kuruma bin] *wig topped with a court hat* [eboshi] *and large pieces of stiff hair paper* [chikaragami] *containing ritualistic implications; a pair of huge swords, the longer of which is over seven feet long; and masklike makeup* [sujiguma] *of red lines on a white background, designed to create a fiercely heroic appearance. He moves down the* hanamichi, *at first concealing his face with his large sleeve wings. About midway down the* hanamichi, *he turns and opens his arms, bends down incrementally, and strikes a* mie. *From before his entrance and as he proceeds to* shichisan, *the following is chanted.)*

ŌZATSUMA:

The sleeves of his costume speak of prosperity. / Today we return to the past, / the flower of Edo performing for this month of the face-showing. / What a spectacular occasion!

(A beat of the tsuke *accentuates each step until his arrival at* shichisan. *He swings the sleeve wings, stops, turns to the audience, closes the wings in front of him, and then swings them out to the sides as he sits on a stool* [aibiki] *provided by a formally dressed* STAGE ASSISTANT. *His sleeve wings are carefully arranged at his sides. He strikes a* mie.*)*

NARITA: Today, we are under strict orders to deal with anyone who transgresses.

TOGANE: Imagine yelling out, "Just a minute," you unwieldy brat!

ASHIGARA: While it would be a direct insult even to listen to him, still, well, let's hear what he has to say.

EBARA: You wretch . . .

ALL BELLY-THRUSTERS *(Elongating their words as they lean challengingly in* KAGEMASA*'s direction)*: Who are you?

*(*KAGEMASA *turns his head to the left and then to the right.)*

NARITA *(Stepping forward on his right leg, challengingly)*: Well, who are you?

(He steps back to align himself with the others.)

ALL BELLY-THRUSTERS: *(Nastily, as if daring him)*: Well?

*(*KAGEMASA *speaks his* tsurane, *which takes about five minutes, with great physical and oral intensity. He sits stock still, facing the audience to the stage left side of the* hanamichi *and delivering his lines in a booming bass, his words soaring into a series of rhythmically prepared exclamation points, vowels extended, as he moves from one swooping, operatic phrase to the next. Most powerful is the final phrase, after which the audience applauds.)*

KAGEMASA: We learn from the Chinese Han scholar Enanji that heaven bestows its blessings impartially, no matter what the amount, no matter what the purpose. The Genji samurai of the East have always purified and emboldened themselves in the dewdrops of the Tama River, that same river where I, Mimasu of the ninth generation, hail from. Called Kamakura no Gongorō Kagemasa by most, I am here this year in the winter-peony makeup, which recalls the many *kaomise* of old. Ready to appear again in this play for which my forebears have been famous, my coat is the color of the persimmon, its puckery flavor the refinement of the technique that has been transmitted to me. I take my turn and clumsily display my skills as an *aragoto* specialist. *Aragoto* is the height of Edo acting and the fame of my family. Permit me to show you. I speak with all due respect.

(Just after the completion of the tsurane, *as the others continue to speak, the importance of the moment is accentuated when a* STAGE ASSISTANT, *formally dressed in the colors of the Danjūrō line, walks down the* hanamichi *with a cup of tea and holds it up for* KAGEMASA *to drink. He looks the actor's costume over to make sure everything is perfect, takes a slight bow, and exits back up the* hanamichi.*)*

EIGHT FOOTMEN: Wow!

NARITA: Well, well. So this is Mr. "Just-a-minute." Since the beginning of kabuki, he's been the main branch of the Edo "Just-a-minute" specialty shop, always ready with a guarded witticism.

ALL BELLY-THRUSTERS: Yes!

TAKEHIRA: I heard that voice and then carefully looked him over after he made his appearance. I recognize him as that lad of the *aragoto* family of unmatched skill. Gongorō no Kagemasa, why have you detained us with your "just a minute?"

KAGEMASA: Why did you remove the ledger? Or if it wasn't you, then who did it?

(The following exchange regarding the ledger is often omitted in performance.)

TAKEHIRA: Do you even know the meaning of the word "ledger"?

KAGEMASA: What an absurd question! It is written with three characters. The first is *dai,* meaning "big" or "great." *Dai* stands on top of all. It is read simply as *"dai"* and written by adding the character for "people" to the character for the number "one." It contains within it the universe and the earth.

TAKEHIRA: What about *fuku,* the second character used to write "ledger"?

KAGEMASA: *Fuku* means "good fortune." The various components with which it is written remind us that blessings from above are directed below. In old writings, the people were considered the jewel of the country. The influence of a lord such as you truly cannot be described: it reaches past Japan as far as China and India; in a word, it is all-encompassing in its power of bestowal.

TAKEHIRA: And then *cho,* how do you explain this third character of the word "ledger"?

KAGEMASA: Inquiring into what we do not know, we find that the character for *cho* contains the idea of endurance, in the sense of everyone—the emperor and his entire nation—serving their offices as long as they are able. It also contains the idea of width, or breadth, with the understanding that when all necessities are provided, the country is at peace and the people are able to live in abundance. When the country is at peace, we can care for the people through civil administration; when disorder reigns, we must crush the enemy through military power. Upon consideration, we understand that military troops are a powerful weapon that must inevitably be used in order to keep control, just as the ancient Chinese leaders—Ryomo, Choryo, Kobu, and Taiso—understood in their administration of the realm. An ancient poem goes: "As with the moats and walls of a castle, the more firmly we establish ourselves, the greater the possibility for security; compassion destroys distinctions between friend and foe." With single intention in our relations with heaven, earth, and man, households will flourish and the country will prosper when conditions for peace obtain in the realm; wisdom, benevolence, and courage guide us at home and the Three Treasures bestowed on mankind are revered at home. This is the full meaning of the three characters used to write "ledger". Now, on an auspicious day of this most marvelous sixtieth year of Shōwa *(the current year is named)*, isn't it wrong to have offered up your plaque secretly? Whisper your reason to me.

(The ledger explanation ends here.)

TAKEHIRA: Your overly presumptuous words grate on my ears. Someone get rid of him!

ASHIGARA: Yes! It must be someone special for this job. Master Priest, I think it should be you.

SHINSAI: Yes, sir. It doesn't seem right, but I guess I've been chosen for the role. I'm not sure of how to go about this, but let's give it a try.

(He unties his outer robe with the help of a black-garbed STAGE ASSISTANT.*)*

ALL BELLY-THRUSTERS: Let's see how well he can pull this off. Let's see!

*(*SHINSAI *turns his back to the audience and a* STAGE ASSISTANT *helps him off with his sandals. Stamps energetically to stage right and pauses midstage.)*

SHINSAI: Hey, hold on. It's fine with me to take on the task, but it's tough not knowing what to do. I shouldn't have entered into it for nothing, but there's no turning back now. *(Sings a couple of bars of comic-sounding music, holding one hand open before the right side of his face and the other open before his chest.)* Ahh, ahh. Ohh, Ohh. Oh, my voice is awful. *(Hits himself on the top of his head.)* My, my, my . . . *(Stamps one foot forward with each* "my." *He approaches the* hanamichi. *Sharply.)* Hey brat, stand there! *(He poses defiantly, staring at* KAGEMASA.*)*

KAGEMASA *(Watching* SHINSAI*)*: What's this? A catfish monster?

SHINSAI *(Holding his long, pigtaillike whiskers and gesturing with them)*: Could be worse! I hale from the province of Hitachi. I'm known as Shinsai the Kashima priest. Nothing scares me, not even uncontrollable acts of nature. *(Sharply.)* Now, stand there at once! *(His manner changes and he movers closer to* KAGEMASA.*)* That is to say, if you would please be so kind, young man, as to stand there as I have requested.

KAGEMASA: Where is it you'd like me to stand?

SHINSAI *(Gesturing to curtain at* hanamichi *entrance)*: Over near the curtain.

KAGEMASA *(With a fearsome expression and increasing speed and ferocity of delivery)*: I would, but it might be the end of me. I could be finished off quickly, or if they weren't quite fast enough for me, it would be like being salted and nibbled.

SHINSAI: Oh my, oh dear, oh gosh!

(In consternation and fear, one hand held up over his head protectively, he crosses center. Meanwhile, TERUHA *moves toward him and they meet.)*

TERUHA: What's the matter, Shinsai?

SHINSAI: Oh geez, what a moment to be caught by a woman. *(Pointing behind him to* KAGEMASA.*)* Please go over and escort him away.

TERUHA: Now, why would you want me to do a thing like that?

SHINSAI: Well, how about we go together? Well, anyhow, come on.

*(*SHINSAI *moves behind* TERUHA *and puts his hands on her shoulders. She spreads her arms out and shifts her weight from side to side as* SHINSAI *stamps the matching foot on each side, yelling out,* "Come on now, come on now." *He pushes her forward. She runs halfway to* KAGEMASA, *then, in fear, turns and runs back to* SHINSAI. *He gestures her back. She turns front and back, front and back, gestures her quandary with a thoughtful pose, and moves decisively toward* KAGEMASA, *speaking as she goes.)*

TERUHA: Excuse me Master Narita-ya! *(*TERUHA *uses the actor's* yagō, *a kind of nickname—Narita-ya in the case of Danjūrō—which gets a laugh from the audience).*Would you mind very much, in spite of the bitter cold, coming over here for just a minute? I have a little something I would like to ask you. *(Kneeling at the stage end of the* hanamichi.*)* Would you kindly listen?

KAGEMASA: Well, who could this be? Why if it isn't *(he mentions the actor's* yagō, *in this case that of Onoe Baikō.)* Sister Otowaya. It's so unladylike of you to deal with me like this. How about helping me restrain this joke of a priest? But what is it you want with me?

TERUHA: It's nothing really, but could you please move just a little over this way?

KAGEMASA *(Louder and louder)*: Okay, I'll let you make your precious request just to help you out, but this is really getting annoying. If you take too long about it, I'll glare you down. *(Strikes a* mie.*)*

TERUHA *(In fear)*: Oh! *(Runs back to* SHINSAI.*)*

SHINSAI: You! What happened?

TERUHA: I couldn't get him to move.

*(*SHINSAI *switches places with* TERUHA *and shouts as he punches out with clenched fists. He strikes a threatening* mie *with hands overhead.)*

KAGEMASA *(Fiercely)*: What's that?

(Frightened, SHINSAI *pretends he was just moving his hands as accompanying gestures to a children's song, such as "This Old Man," and sings* "This old man, he played one, . . ."*—or an equivalent—timing his movements to cover up his attempted aggression. Instrumentalists provide background accompaniment.* TERUHA *goes along with his cover-up and lightly "plays knick-knack" on* SHINSAI*'s head until he falls flat on his rear end, legs out before him.)*

ALL BELLY-THRUSTERS: Cut it out!

NARITA: Stop this nonsense! *(To* HEIDA, UNPACHI, TONAI, *and* HYŌJI.*)* You four samurai, take care of him!

(The samurai HEIDA, UNPACHI, TONAI, *and* HYŌJI *rise from their positions at left and walk to center, as* SHINSAI *and* TERUHA *cross left to their places.)*

HEIDA: Must he go? What a burdensome responsibility.

UNPACHI: Yes, but when we succeed in getting rid of him, we'll be rewarded.

TONAI: That may be so, but this is awful. How about we four leave instead?

HYŌJI: You know the deal, we toil and the master benefits.

HEIDA: Well then,

ALL FOUR SAMURAI: If we must. *(They progress to the* hanamichi *with bold "six directions"—style* [roppō] *stamping movements, yelling.)* Here we come! Here we come!

HEIDA: Hey creep, come here!

(The four stamp their right feet out and turn their heads sharply toward KAGEMASA. *Sharply.)*

ALL FOUR SAMURAI: Right here! *(They strike a group pose.)*

KAGEMASA: This is absurd! Get near me and you'll end up six feet under.

HEIDA *(As they straighten up)*: What a man, with his abusive insults. We're not animals, you know.

UNPACHI *(Proudly)*: We are Lord Takehira's Four Almighty.

TONAI: Oh, Lordie, who art in heaven, trouble be thy name.

HYŌJI: We Almighty like to stir up trouble.

HEIDA: So, we'll get right to it.

(The four comically swing their bodies from side to side and jump up and down between phrases.)

ALL FOUR SAMURAI: Loudly bantering, boisterously clamoring. Loudly bantering, boisterously clamoring.

KAGEMASA *(Sharply)*: Hey, it's too noisy around here.

ALL FOUR SAMURAI: Hey brat, stand there!

*(*KAGEMASA *looks to one side, then back. He seems thoroughly disgusted and angry.)*

ALL FOUR SAMURAI *(Threatened)*: Oh!

(Alarmed, they flee back to their old positions left, behind SHINSAI *and* TERUHA. *As they go, the* EIGHT FOOTMEN *move out from their places behind* YOSHITSUNA *et al. and align themselves from center toward* KAGEMASA.*)*

FIRST FOOTMAN: From now on, we need a footman's guard. *(Imitating the voice of a guard.)* Who offers to keep watch?

SECOND FOOTMAN: Let's take him away!

(They make the same movements and calls as did HEIDA *et al. when they tried to approach* KAGEMASA.*)*

ALL EIGHT FOOTMEN *(With each stamp and swing of their arms)*: Here we come! Here we come! *(Repeated until stamping is done.)*

FIRST FOOTMAN *(to* KAGEMASA*)*: Hey, thug . . .

(They all take another step forward.)

ALL EIGHT FOOTMEN *(Pointing)*: Stand there!

*(*KAGEMASA *disdainfully turns his fierce face one way and then the other. The* EIGHT FOOTMEN *stamp and clap hands twice, once to each side.)*

Kamakura no Gongorō Kagemasa (Ichikawa Danjūrō XII) stands protectively at center stage shielding the virtuous characters, Yoshitsuna, Katsura, and Kuretake, left, from their evil opponents, rear and right. (Umemura Yutaka, Engeki Shuppansha)

ALL EIGHT FOOTMEN: Are you ready?

*(*KAGEMASA *makes a ferocious growl in their direction.)*

ALL EIGHT FOOTMEN: Yikes!

(Terrified, they rush back to their seated positions, spinning and miming their fear humorously.)

NARITA *(Scolding)*: Oh, cut it out! *(Referring to the* BELLY-THRUSTERS.*)* We have all been treated well. Therefore, let us do as our lord commands.

TOGANE: That rude and hateful fellow!

NARITA *(Introducing themselves in quick succession)*: I am Narita Gorō Yoshihide.

TOGANE: Togane Tarō Yoshinari.

ASHIGARA: Ashigara Zaemon Takamune.

EBARA: Ebara Hachirō Kunitsura.

HANYŪ: Hanyū Gorō Sukenari.

MUSASHI: Musashi Kurō Ujikiyo.

(The six BELLY-THRUSTERS *stand.)*

NARITA *(Stamping with his right foot)*: Come over here . . .

ALL BELLY-THRUSTERS: Or we'll have to get you!

(They tilt their heads in unison and strike a pose. Their attendants remove stools behind them.)

KAGEMASA *(Strongly)*: Don't get near me.

ALL BELLY-THRUSTERS *(Worried, their expressions exaggerated)*: Oh, gosh!

KAGEMASA: Just send someone to the family temple . . .

ALL BELLY-THRUSTERS: Oh, gosh!

KAGEMASA: To prepare your coffins!

ALL BELLY-THRUSTERS: Oh, gosh!

KAGEMASA: Well *(stands with a jump)*, here I come!

*(*KAGEMASA *moves onto the stage. As he proceeds, a repeated* "Here he comes" *is heard in unison from the group, accompanied by drums and a flute. After he arrives center, three formally dressed* STAGE ASSISTANTS *help rearrange his costume, removing the wings and sleeves of his outer robes from his shoulders and revealing an immense, blue bow knotted at his back and made from the ropes holding back his sleeves for action. While this is happening, all others parade around the stage and reposition themselves. The* STAGE ASSISTANTS *finish and align themselves upstage, behind* KAGEMASA. *The music and unison calling stop as* KAGEMASA, *with half-opened fan in one hand, turns and moves forward. He strikes one of kabuki's most grandiose* mie, *the* genroku mie, *named for the Genroku period* [*1688–1704*]. *It concludes with his sleeves held out by* STAGE ASSISTANTS *to either side in giant squares, his weight on his right leg, his right hand in a raised fist, his great sword held against him in his left hand with its handle near the floor and its sheath tip forming an arc above him to the left, and his glaring gaze directed downward to the left. At its completion, the* BELLY-THRUSTERS *sit, the* STAGE ASSISTANTS *relax and fold up the sleeves, then exit.* YOSHITSUNA *and* KATSURA *come forward a bit.)*

YOSHITSUNA: Oh, Kagemasa, you're here!

KATSURA: We've been waiting for you!

KAGEMASA *(Spoken in their direction)*: Since I am here, please rest assured and relax now. *(Turning his head slightly toward* TAKEHIRA, *behind him to his left, he speaks with great ferocity.)* I'd like to know why you were going to slay them.

TAKEHIRA: Kagemasa, you overly meddlesome brat, you youthful nobody. You're too much! You're a huge pain!

KAGEMASA: Start from the beginning. Where did you receive permission to proceed with your plan?

(There follows a kuriage *section of rising intensity and pace, leading to a climactic outburst.)*

TAKEHIRA: Well, uh . . .

Formally dressed stage assistants stretch out the huge sleeves of the exaggerated costume worn by the superhuman hero Kamakura no Gongorō Kagemasa (Ichikawa Somegorō VI, later Matsumoto Kōshirō IX), center. He poses aggressively, protecting young lord Yoshitsuna (Ichikawa Komazō XI), left, and Yoshitsuna's fiancée, Katsura no Mae (Matsumoto Kōjaku I), right. Kiyohara no Takehira (Matsumoto Kōshirō VIII, later Matsumoto Hakuō), seated on the platform, is marked as an aristocratic villain by his bold grey and blue makeup. (Umemura Yutaka, Engeki Shuppansha)

KAGEMASA: Did you grant it to yourself?

TAKEHIRA: Well . . .

KAGEMASA: Well?

BOTH MEN: Well, well, well.

KAGEMASA *(Threateningly)*: One might wonder. *(He stamps and, with a conventional* aragoto *throat-clearing and snorting noise, moves his closed fan steadily and jerkily toward his chest, ending with a shout.)* Idiot! *(He straightens and speaks faster.)* This sword that you offer on behalf of the court, what a deception to call it Ikazuchimaru. Instead, it's a sword that could bring misfortune to His Imperial Majesty.

TAKEHIRA: What absurdities are you uttering? The famous Ikazuchimaru sword was given its name due to a gracious duel during which it protected the court, a duel with a thunderbolt that threatened the Imperial Palace.

KAGEMASA: Did it battle the thunder of stormy weather or the thunder of dry weather, which gives rise to fires? If it was storm thunder, the sword can cut down anything, formed or formless. If it was fire thunder, it would inflame the sword and weaken the blade, most likely rendering it useless. *(He gestures with his closed fan as he speaks to the others.)* Now, you big boys be good and hand over the governor's seals, which are probably hidden in one of your little kimono.

(He stamps as he screams the last elongated words.)

NARITA: What?!

ALL BELLY-THRUSTERS *(Punctuating words with head movements)*: What makes you think that?

KAGEMASA: Well, if none of you know anything, then your leader and master Takehira must have them. *(He throws his fan behind him, then stamps toward* TAKEHIRA. *He elongates vowels and yells.)* Produce them!

*(*KAGEMASA *strikes a powerful* mie. *At this point,* TERUHA *hurries over to him. Taking out of her kimono the governor's seals, which are wrapped in a purple cloth, she kneels in front of* KAGEMASA, *all the while explaining.)*

TERUHA: Excuse me, the lost seals, which caused Master Yoshitsuna's disinheritance, have found their way back into my possession. *(She hands them to* KAGEMASA. *As she gets up,* KAGEMASA *gives the seals to* YOSHITSUNA, *who kneels at his side.* TERUHA *hurries to the* hanamichi, *standing at its stage juncture.)* Furthermore, Koganemaru Yukitsuna, who attends here, will quickly bring the irreplaceable sword, the famous Ikazuchimaru.

KOGANEMARU *(Offstage)*: Right away! *(*WATANABE KOGANEMARU, *dressed as a boyish shrine attendant, and carrying the sword, runs noisily down the* hanamichi *to* batabata *beating of* tsuke *to offer* KAGEMASA *the sword, wrapped in brocade cloth. He rushes onstage and seats himself next to* TERUHA, *who has just sat down near the* YOSHITSUNA *group.)* As requested, here is the master's family treasure.

(He walks over and hands the sword to KAGEMASA. KOGANEMARU *goes back to his seat.* KAGEMASA *unwraps and partly unsheathes the sword, turning it over twice to examine it. He then resheathes and rewraps it, speaking as he wraps.)*

KAGEMASA: With this, Yoshitsuna may be reinstated in his family and properly carry through with his engagement to Katsura no Mae. *(He acknowledges the sword's authenticity by holding it up and striking a fierce* mie. *He turns toward* YOSHITSUNA.*)* And now I must turn this over to you.

*(*YOSHITSUNA *gives the seals to* KATSURA NO MAE *to examine, and* KAGEMASA *gives the sword to* YOSHITSUNA.*)*

YOSHITSUNA *(Facing* KATSURA*)*: I am so grateful to have the governor's seals back.

KAGEMASA: Let us give a congratulatory round of applause! *(As villains observe, all nonvillains—except for* YOSHITSUNA, KATSURA, *and* TERUHA, *who sit quietly—clap hands rhythmically with* KAGEMASA. KAGEMASA *energetically*

Kamakura no Gongorō Kagemasa (Onoe Shōroku II) strikes a defiant *mie* before two Belly-Thruster *(haradashi)* opponents. The strong *kumadori* lines on Kagemasa's face and on the Belly-Thrusters' bodies as well as the extremely long sword, halolike wig with protruding paper decorations, and oversized costume crests are typical exaggerations of *aragoto* style. (Tsubouchi Memorial Theatre Museum of Waseda University)

and verbally punctuates the clapping.) Yes, yes, yes! Con-grat-u-la-tions! *(Bows in* YOSHITSUNA*'s direction.)*

NARITA: We'll clap too.

ALL BELLY-THRUSTERS *(With feigned disinterest and mocking synchronized applause)*: Yeah, yeah, yeah. Yeah, yeah, yeah. Yeah, yeah, yeah, yeeaahhh.

SHINSAI *(Hand raised)*: Let's hear it for them!

ALL BELLY-THRUSTERS *(All put a hand on their heads as they mock a bow)*: Yo!

TAKEHIRA *(With an intense gaze, to* TERUHA*)*: You accompanied us pretending to be the younger sister of Nasu no Kurō, but you're a spy!

TERUHA: In order to be entrusted with such an important task, so unsuitable for a woman, I carried out my deception as Nasu no Kurō's younger sister.

NARITA *(Angry)*: How sneaky!

ALL BELLY-THRUSTERS *(Slowly, measured)*: Yes, yes, yes!

KOGANEMARU: And I am Koganemaru Yukitsuna, retainer to Lord Yoshiie and one of those who passes his evenings with Watanabe Kingo. You Takehira fools . . .

ALL BELLY-THRUSTERS: Eh?

KOGANEMARU *(Shouted and elongated)*: Are you shocked?

ALL BELLY-THRUSTERS: Yes!

KAGEMASA: Thanks to Teruha's reports, your treasonous plan was fully discovered. Wait until we deal with you! *(Turns slightly in seated* YOSHITSUNA*'s direction.)* But first, arrangements for Yoshitsuna's return must now be made.

YOSHITSUNA *(To* KAGEMASA*)*: My gratitude is beyond words.

KATSURA *(Anxious to leave, to* YOSHITSUNA*)*: We mustn't linger. Please, it is time to hurry.

YOSHITSUNA: Yes, let us go.

TAKEHIRA: This gets worse and worse.

KAGEMASA *(Turning slightly back toward* TAKEHIRA *and getting angry)*: Hey, if you've got any complaints, let's hear them.

ALL BELLY-THRUSTERS *(Showing fear)*: As for complaints . . .

KAGEMASA *(Angry and yelling)*: Yes?

ALL BELLY-THRUSTERS: We have . . . *(pause, then a quick bow of the head)* none!

KAGEMASA: Good, otherwise there might have been trouble. And now, let's leave.

ŌZATSUMA:

In parting, / the vigor and courageousness of a hero heading off alone, / here in the Land of the Rising Sun.

(During the chanting, YOSHITSUNA, YOSHISATO, KURANDO, KATSURA, KURETAKE, *the* FOUR FEMALE ATTENDANTS, *and* TERUHA *stand, facing upstage, and are prepared for exiting by black-garbed* STAGE ASSISTANTS [kurogo]. *As* YOSHITSUNA *begins to go,* KAGEMASA *bows to him, and* YOSHITSUNA *gives a slight bow back. After a brief pause at the beginning of the* hanamichi, *he leads the others off down the* hanamichi. KATSURA NO MAE *follows, also taking a slight pause before starting down the* hanamichi. *The others follow, including the* FEMALE ATTENDANTS *and, finally,* KOGANEMARU. TERUHA, *shouldering her plum branch again, has waited behind and takes her exit alone, moving with quick, fluid steps. The music and chanting stop. A* STAGE ASSISTANT *has been helping prepare* KAGEMASA *for the next encounter.)*

NARITA: Get him!

ALL BELLY-THRUSTERS: Yes!

*(*SHRINE ATTENDANTS *rush over to* KAGEMASA, *their hurried movements heightened by loud, fast* tsuke *beats.)*

SHRINE ATTENDANTS: Don't move!

(They surround KAGEMASA *in a line, bending upstage toward him with their backs to the audience.* KAGEMASA, *also facing upstage, unsheathes his gigantic sword. Turning, he lops off their heads with one sweeping slice. To represent this, each "headless" man pulls a red cloth over his head and runs offstage while red cotton head props are flung down by* STAGE ASSISTANTS. KAGEMASA *strikes another* mie, *with his sword held vertically to his right like a baseball bat, as* STAGE ASSISTANTS *clear away the heads.)*

TAKEHIRA: Kamakura no Gongorō . . .

ALL BELLY-THRUSTERS: Kagemasa!

KAGEMASA *(With great force as he grandly brandishes his sword)*: In-sects!

*(*KAGEMASA *holds the sword to his right side and glares out toward the audience.)*

ALL BELLY-THRUSTERS *(Elongated)*: And Now We Take Our Leave!

*(*KAGEMASA *glares several seconds longer. Drum and flute music accompany a group* mie. KAGEMASA *moves toward the* hanamichi*, sword overhead, as he makes his way around the* EIGHT FOOTMEN *coming at him one by one, or two by two. When he arrives at the* hanamichi *juncture, he and* TAKEHIRA, *who is now standing center at the front of the platform, glare at each other.* KAGEMASA *holds the sword vertically. All remaining characters—who have arranged themselves standing across the stage with the* BELLY-THRUSTERS *in front—strike* mie. *The curtain is drawn closed in preparation for an "outside-the-curtain exit"* [maku soto no hikkomi]. *The drum and flute music stops. With his huge sword over his shoulder,* KAGEMASA *snorts and, to the rapid beating of the* tsuke, *performs a final grand* mie *before the curtain, leaning in the direction of the* hanamichi *curtain. Drum and flute exit music, gradually increasing in intensity, together with the repeated* aragoto *verbal call,* "Yattoko tottchaa, untoko na," *accompany* KAGEMASA*'s grand and triumphant* roppō *departure down the* hanamichi. *Music continues for several moments after his exit.*

Two-panel woodblock print by Utagawa Kunisada I (later Utagawa Toyokuni III, 1786–1864). Nakamura-za, Edo, seventh month 1828. "Matahei the Stutterer" ("Nakamura Shikan" II, later Ichimura Uzaemon IV) prepares to paint on the water basin while his wife Otoku (identified as "wife Ofude," played by "Segawa Kikunojō" V), gestures encouragingly. (Tsubouchi Memorial Theatre Museum of Waseda University)

Matahei the Stutterer

Domo Mata

Chikamatsu Monzaemon

TRANSLATED BY HOLLY A. BLUMNER

Tosa no Shōgen's Residence

Tosa no Shōgen Kankyo no Ba

1708 TAKEMOTO-ZA, OSAKA

Matahei the Stutterer

INTRODUCTION

Matahei the Stutterer (Domo Mata) was originally part of the longer scene "The Bay of Kehi" (Kehi no Ura) in Chikamatsu Monzaemon's (1653–1725) *The Courtesan of the Hangon Incense* (Keisei Hangonkō), a puppet play first performed at Osaka's Takemoto-za in 1708. The first kabuki adaptation was staged at Osaka's Kadono Shibai by the Arashi Sangorō troupe in the third month of 1719 with the famous actor and troupe leader *(zamoto)* Arashi Sanemon III (1697–1754) playing the demanding role of Matahei. The story of Matahei the Stutterer proved popular with audiences, and variations on the theme were frequently performed thereafter in both kabuki and the puppet theatre.

Chikamatsu's three-act drama is a feudal house play *(oiemono)* concerning the affairs of the great court painter Tosa no Shōgen and his family. None of the grand history scenes *(jidaimono)* are performed today. What has continued to be popular with audiences, and the only scene to survive, is "Matahei the Stutterer," a domestic-style scene *(sewaba* or *sewamono)* that focuses on the lowly samurai and painter Matahei, whose speech impediment has prevented him from rising to a position of success. It seems likely that kabuki's plebeian audiences felt an affinity with the humble man who struggles and overcomes both poverty and physical imperfection to become a hero.

In this scene, Matahei moves from the depths of depression to exaltation. And he moves from a *sewamono* world of degradation to a *jidaimono* world of status and pride. Condemned to eking out a living by selling cheap pictures to tourists passing through the town of Ōtsu, and discouraged because his master, Tosa no Shōgen, has refused to award him the Tosa name, Matahei is about to commit ritual suicide to salvage his honor. In the highly dramatic sequence that provides the climax of the scene, Matahei's greatness of spirit is shown when the self-portrait that he paints on a solid granite water basin miraculously shows through to the opposite side. Because only a painter of superior talent could perform such a feat, Shōgen, deeply impressed, relents and awards Matahei the Tosa name. At this point, the scene returns to the *jidaimono* story line of the full-length play: Matahei is transformed into a self-confident samurai who no longer stutters and who happily sets off to fight the enemy.

Highlights of *Matahei the Stutterer* include the felicitous song and dance that

Matahei performs to celebrate his new elevated status. Ostensibly, it is a *nō* dance, its execution in time to the rhythmic accompaniment of *takemoto* shamisen music. Another highlight is when, in a brief appearance, the warrior-messenger Utanosuke gives a dramatic battle account using strong gestures and poses, typical of puppet history plays. His use of the musical-narrative convention called "riding the rhythm" *(nori)* marks the play as originating in the puppet theatre.

Humor and pathos are mixed in the assertive chattering of Matahei's wife, Otoku, who is obliged to speak on her husband's behalf. Her long monologues are unusual for a female character and mark Otoku as one of the three most challenging wife roles (a trio known as *san nyōbo*) in kabuki. A key element of success in a production lies in the skill with which the actors portraying Matahei and Otoku are able to convey the deep affection husband and wife, tied closely by his impediment, feel for each other. Performers must be skilled in improvising dialogue *(sutezerifu)* in long segments of the play, notably in the extended sequence in which Matahei executes the astonishing painting and at the end when Otoku helps Matahei depart for battle as a samurai. To show Matahei's stuttering, each actor is free to ad lib and develop his own style *(kata)* for the role.

Chikamatsu is reported to have written his play for the two hundred and fiftieth anniversary of the death of the court painter Kanō Shirōjirō Motonobu in 1559; Shōgen refers to one of his well-known paintings. Other noted Chinese and Japanese classical painters, as well as famous Japanese paintings, are alluded to in the scene. It was not uncommon for actual persons to be dramatized in fictional situations on the puppet or kabuki stage, although prohibitions against the depiction of members of the samurai class forced playwrights to place their stories in a pre-Tokugawa period. To Japanese audiences of the time, these names would have been as familiar as Monet or Picasso are to Western audiences. Typical of puppet-derived stories, two miraculous events occur in what is otherwise a purely ordinary, domestic situation: a painted tiger comes alive to ravage the fields of local farmers, and the portrait that Matahei paints uncannily penetrates solid granite. In these moments, we see links to the puppet theatre's origins in religious miracle plays of old-*jōruri (ko jōruri),* the early, pre-Chikamatsu puppet theatre.

The role of Matahei is considered difficult to carry off successfully. The actor must be able to express Matahei's earnestness and frustration, through bouts of stuttering and repeated words, and balance this with a hint of comic relief. Matahei's quick transition from disgraced disciple to acclaimed samurai and painter is another challenge to the actor. The agony of the character must be shown mainly through physical action and gesture, as he is denied the use of clear speech. On top of this, Matahei is considered a *wagoto*, or gentle-style character, who should be unassertive in behavior. Two main interpretations of the scene are those performed by the Ichikawa Danjūrō and the Kataoka Nizaemon acting families.

This translation is based on the text in Torigoe Bunzō, ed., *Kabuki On-Sutēji,* Vol. 12 and on the unpublished production script *(daihon)* of the Kokuritsu Gekijō (National Theatre of Japan) of July 1998.

CHARACTERS

UKIYO MATAHEI SHIGEOKI, *disciple of the samurai and great painter* SHŌGEN MITSUOKI

OTOKU, *wife of* MATAHEI

TOSA NO SHŌGEN MITSUOKI, *samurai and great artist, currently under house arrest by order of the emperor*

KITA NO KATA, *wife of* SHŌGEN MITSUOKI

SHŪRINOSUKE MASAZUMI, *young disciple of* SHŌGEN MITSUOKI

KANŌ UTANOSUKE, *young disciple of* KANŌ SHIRŌJIRŌ MOTONOBU, *ordered to protect Princess Itchiyō no Mae*

SHŌEMON, *a farmer*

KAMASAKU, *a farmer*

TOYŌZO, *a farmer*

BEISAKU, *a farmer*

FARMERS

STAGE ASSISTANTS, *black-garbed* kurogo

TAKEMOTO, *narrator-chanter and shamisen player who accompany the action*

Tosa no Shōgen's Residence

(Offstage [geza] *drum and flute music, shamisen, and singing set the mood as the curtain opens to an accelerating* ki *pattern. The scene is* SHŌGEN MITSUOKI*'s humble residence. A simple room, covered with a worn-looking roof, has sliding paper doors leading to another room, left, and a rustic gate leading to the entry, right. Center are two sliding wooden doors decorated with Chinese characters. Numerous painted panels and rolled scrolls lean against the right back wall. On a set of shelves is a shoulder drum* [tsuzumi] *covered by a purple cloth. At the front of the room,*

three steps lead down into a garden in which stands a granite water basin with a wooden ladle. It is dusk. A loud ki *signals the offstage* TAKEMOTO *chanter-singer, seated behind a screen up left, to begin.)*

TAKEMOTO:

The spirit of a tiger has been running through the fields, / devouring the crops the farmers have grown. / The neighborhood farmers are troubled . . .

(Offstage the big drum plays ominous dorodoro. *A group of some twenty* FARMERS, *led by* SHŌEMON, KAMASAKU, TOYŌZO, *and* BEISAKU *enter on the* hanamichi. *They are carrying hoes and long poles to hunt the tiger and lanterns to see in the dark of night. They stop at* shichisan.*)*

SHŌEMON *(Frustrated)*: We have traveled from Mii Temple to Fuji no Ō, searching and searching.

KAMASAKU: We've stalked him from Shina Mountain all the way here, and he is nowhere to be found.

TOYŌZO: Let's take him by the skin and kill him.

BEISAKU: Let's go . . .

FARMERS: Kill him!

(Offstage gongs and drums.)

TAKEMOTO *(Offstage left)*:

Hearing the clamor outside, Shūrinosuke emerges from the residence to see what the commotion is about.

*(*SHŪRINOSUKE, *a young samurai, comes through the sliding doors of the residence, carrying a long wooden staff as a weapon. Coming down the steps, he puts on clogs* [geta] *and makes his way to the gate to meet the farmers.* SHŪRINOSUKE*'s plaid kimono is tucked into striped* hakama. *He wears a samurai's two swords and his hair is still worn in youthful style with a forelock.)*

SHŪRINOSUKE *(Striking the pole on the ground once and speaking officiously)*: What is this talk of killing I am hearing on the grounds of this residence? State your business!

SHŌEMON: We are farmers from Yabase and Awazu. A tiger has come down from Shigaraki Mountain.

KAMASAKU: The tiger has destroyed a field and is eating our crops. We have gathered from five villages to hunt him down.

TOYŌZO: We've looked all over and we're sure he is in these thickets.

BEISAKU: Allow us to search around here . . .

FARMERS: Please do.

TAKEMOTO:

Shūrinosuke scoffs at them.

SHŪRINOSUKE: There is no evidence of any tigers living in Japan, I assure you. What a ridiculous notion!

SHŌEMON: Yes, but there's one here now . . .

FARMERS: In this thicket.

SHŪRINOSUKE *(Self-importantly)*: What? Are you still saying that? Are you in league with thieves? This is the residence of the painter Tosa no Shōgen Mitsuoki who was censured by the emperor last year. I am his disciple, Shūrinosuke Masazumi. Now, if I hear another word from any of you, I will cut you down so fast you won't see my hands move.

*(*SHŪRINOSUKE *strikes the pole on the ground and swings it in a figure eight. He poses threateningly.)*

TAKEMOTO:

They suddenly turn around.

(Cowed, the FARMERS *bow their heads and retreat two or three steps.)*

SHŌGEN *(From offstage)*: Wait a minute, wait a minute.

TAKEMOTO:

After a moment, Shōgen and his wife make their entrance.

(From the sliding doors left, the elderly SHŌGEN *and his wife,* KITA NO KATA, *enter. He wears an elegant kimono and* haori *in shades of gold. She wears a deep gray kimono and a dark gray* haori. *Her hair is an asymmetrical topknot, typical of an upper-class samurai wife. She carries a candle to light the way.)*

SHŌGEN: I heard everything. *(Tongue-in-cheek.)* If such a creature exists between the heavens and the earth, I am sure we have one here as well. Take a look around the grounds. Go ahead, look around.

FARMERS: Yes, sir!

(The FARMERS *explore the thicket behind the house, striking with poles and hoes while talking quietly among themselves.)*

TAKEMOTO:

Grabbing spears and rakes / and carrying torch lights, / the farmers begin the hunt. / Lifting their torches in the firelight, / they see the fierce-looking tiger, / who has destroyed so many fields, / resting quietly in the grass.

(Large offstage drum plays rapid dorodoro. *A tiger's head appears at the top of the thicket.)*

SHŌEMON: Just look at that!

FARMERS: There he is!

(With a fearful cry, the FARMERS *pull back from the thicket in panic.)*

SHŌGEN: Where?

TAKEMOTO:

Moving ever so quietly, / Shōgen approaches this miraculous sight.

*(*SHŌGEN *comes down the steps and slips into a pair of clogs.)*

He pulls his spectacles / from the recesses of his kimono.

(Before the thicket, he puts on a pair of glasses and looks carefully at the tiger, SHŪRINOSUKE *holding up a candle to light the scene.)*

Carefully, he scrutinizes the scene before him.

SHŌGEN *(Turning front)*: Well this is quite unbelievable! He looks like he has been painted by the great Chinese master, Ganhi, himself! It closely resembles his painting of the tiger in the bamboo forest. It is such a lifelike picture, it's as if the spirit of the tiger was lifted right from the painting! He looks like a fierce tiger! Look at his eyes! But, he looks freshly painted. This incredibly lifelike tiger could only be the work of the young painter, Shirōjirō Motonobu. He is absolutely beautiful! Beautiful!

TAKEMOTO:

It is a masterpiece!

SHŌGEN: Farmers, listen. This is not a real tiger. When the painter created this piece of art, he put his heart and soul into the painting and the spirit of the tiger walked right out of it. There is a way to prove whether he is real, once and for all. If he is not real, there will not be any paw prints. Let's take a look.

TAKEMOTO:

They divide and search the dense bamboo thicket, / but find no tiger prints.

(The FARMERS *nod their heads in assent and search for paw prints.)*

SHŌEMON: Well, after careful examination . . .

KAMASAKU: There isn't anything here . . .

FARMERS: That resembles a paw print.

(The FARMERS *sit cross-legged along the* hanamichi. *They bow their heads in awe after finding no paw prints.)*

SHŌGEN: That was nothing! Now I will show you something even more unbelievable. I will erase this tiger in front of your very eyes!

SHŪRINOSUKE *(Bowing humbly before* SHŌGEN*)*: Please, sir. I am only your humble student. But this beautiful tiger inspires me to acquire greater wisdom in the philosophy of painting. Do let me take a brush and erase the tiger myself, in order to increase my understanding. Please allow me the honor, master.

SHŌGEN: Well, if you would like to learn more about the way of painting and you say you would like to erase the tiger, very well, I will allow you to do so. And I will lend you a special brush. If you are going to be successful, you must clear your mind of everything else. You must erase the tiger by drawing with a pure and tranquil heart.

SHŪRINOSUKE: Thank you, sir.

TAKEMOTO:

Shūrinosuke humbly receives the special brush.

*(*SHŪRINOSUKE *follows* SHŌGEN *through the gate into the garden. Kneeling, he receives the brush from* KITA NO KATA. SHŪRINOSUKE *returns and kneels before the tiger.)*

With this precious brush, Shūrinosuke dips the tip in ink. / He begins at the head of the tiger and slowly moves toward its toes. / Little by little, / he erases the tiger. / It is an inspiring sight to behold. / The tiger disappears like magic.

(Dipping the brush in ink, he "paints" the air in a circular motion. As the large drum plays dorodoro *offstage, the tiger disappears. The* FARMERS *utter exclamations of praise.* SHŪRINOSUKE *crosses into the garden, kneels, and bows to* SHŌGEN.*)*

SHŪRINOSUKE *(Proudly)*: Ohhhh. I have erased the tiger completely.

SHŌGEN: Well done, well done! This is a commendable deed, and with it you have earned the great Tosa name. You will now be known as Tosa no Mitsuzumi and you will be awarded the auspicious brush of the Tosa masters.

SHŪRINOSUKE *(Nearly speechless in gratitude)*: The special brush of the Tosa masters . . . for me? *(He poses.)* I am grateful, master.

*(*SHŪRINOSUKE *bows low in reverence to his teacher and then follows him up the stairs to the residence. The three sit formally, facing front:* SHŌGEN, *left, at the highest position of power;* KITA NO KATA, *center; and* SHŪRINOSUKE, *right.)*

TAKEMOTO:

It is natural that he should be overcome with joy. / The farmers talk among themselves.

SHŌEMON: We have seen several miracles today. This is a story we will be telling our grandchildren. I'd like him to paint ten pictures of famous actors for me. Then I could sell them and get rich!

KAMASAKU: Not me. I'd rather become Shūrinosuke's friend, so he could take a brush and erase all my debts. Ha, ha, ha, ha!

ALL: Yes, yes.

TOYŌZO: To think that he simply erased a tiger! That Tosa no Mitsuzumi is one great samurai!

BEISAKU: It's not just the name. Receiving the master's special brush is a treasure in itself. Now that brush is really something!

SHŌEMON: That's the truth. Well, we should be on our way. Thank you, Master Shōgen.

FARMERS *(Bowing low)*: Thank you.

TAKEMOTO:

The farmers start on their way home.

(Talking among themselves, the FARMERS *hurry off down the* hanamichi.*)*

Shōgen's wife speaks to Shūrinosuke.

KITA NO KATA: You've done well, Shūrinosuke. Your daily effort and dedication have come to fruition. The master will give you a certificate to recognize your accomplishments. Congratulations. *(To* SHŌGEN.*)* Shōgen, why don't you bring him his certificate?

SHŌGEN: Indeed, I will present you with the certificate. Come this way.

SHŪRINOSUKE: Yes, sir.

TAKEMOTO:

They go inside.

(The three exit left, going into the residence, SHŌGEN *leading. A small revolving stage* [yuka] *at left turns, bringing into view a* TAKEMOTO *chanter and shamisen player.)*

TAKEMOTO:

They enter the house. / Tosa's lowest disciple, the absent-minded painter Matahei Shigeoki enters. / Born with a stutter, he is poor, a destitute man, / his only property being the threadbare clothes on his back and the possessions he carries. / Matahei is as pitiable as the tattered papers he keeps in his tinderbox. / So impoverished, he has to burn wood chips not once, but twice, for his meals. / He rents a small place in Ōtsu, and his wife dutifully tends to his shabby, worn brushes and supplies. / Matahei makes his living selling caricatures, / offering his paintings for pennies to passersby wanting cheap souvenirs of their travels.

*(*OTOKU *enters on the* hanamichi, *followed by* MATAHEI. *She wears a plain purple kimono and carries a lantern. She wears a hand towel* [tenugui] *tucked in the front of her obi. Her hair is done up in a high puffed topknot with a purple cloth covering the front.* MATAHEI *wears a nondescript brown kimono, striped* hakama, *and a dark* haori. *He carries a small package wrapped with a cloth.)*

Earning very little, his spirits are as meager as the few cents he earns. / Though husband and wife live a day-to-day existence, / each night they valiantly make the long journey to visit their teacher.

(They pause at shichisan, *tired from the long journey.* OTOKU *motions that it is just a little farther. Onstage, they stop at the gate.)*

OTOKU *(Calling in)*: Excuse me.

SHŪRINOSUKE *(Entering from the house)*: Who's there? Who's calling?

OTOKU: It is Matahei and his wife.

SHŪRINOSUKE *(Pleasantly)*: Ah, you've come to see the master. Of course, come this way, please. *(Kneels and announces their presence.)* Master, master. Matahei and his wife have come to pay their respects.

SHŌGEN: Ah, is that so? Matahei has come?

TAKEMOTO:

Shōgen and his wife come out to meet them.

*(*SHŌGEN *and* KITA NO KATA *enter.* MATAHEI *and* OTOKU *kneel humbly on the ground outside the room while* SHŪRINOSUKE, KITA NO KATA, *and* SHŌGEN *sit within the room.)*

KITA NO KATA: Matahei and Otoku, you are looking well.

TAKEMOTO:

Matahei, who speaks only with his eyes, sits by his wife's side.

*(*MATAHEI *and* OTOKU *bow respectfully to* SHŌGEN *and* KITA NO KATA. MATAHEI *tries to speak but can only mouth a greeting as he bobs and bows helplessly.)*

OTOKU *(Speaks quickly to save the situation)*: Greetings, greetings. Master, madam, as always, it is a pleasure to see you. *(Both bow again. Light shamisen music underscores* OTOKU*'s lines.)* How are you feeling? What strange weather we've had! But the days are slowly getting warmer and longer, and spring is on its way. Soon, everyone will be going up the mountain in droves to view the cherry blossoms. Unfortunately, this mountain retreat is a rather secluded place, and the emperor has forbidden you to work or travel, but perhaps you can still make the most of it. You can raise your spirits by preparing and eating flavorful tofu dishes and drinking the spring sake in its special bamboo flasks. You can go to see the tall statue of the goddess Kannon at the quiet little Seki Temple. We would like nothing more than to welcome in spring with you. In fact, that is all we think about, but our shop is so busy, and there is so much washing to be done. There is always something that needs doing and no time to relax! We feel like eels frantically swimming in circles! Oh! That reminds me! We stopped on the way and bought you some eel, a delicacy of Ōtsu. And we brought a special sake from Ōtsu made with clear water from a celebrated temple to help you have more pleasant dreams. Hopefully, we'll all be happier in the spring. Just as the eel emerges from its hole, perhaps our spirits will emerge, too. *(Pauses.)* Oh dear! I always seem to talk so much, and my husband stutters, so he rarely says a word. I talk, he doesn't, I talk, and he doesn't talk at all! We are certainly a match made in heaven! The two of us talk about as much as one person. Ha, ha. Ha, ha. Ha, ha, ha, ha, ha, ha! Oh dear, now I'm embarrassed!

TAKEMOTO:

She laughs.

(While his wife has been chattering on, MATAHEI *has unwrapped the gift of food.* OTOKU *crosses to the room and passes the gifts up to* SHŪRINOSUKE, *who exits with them through the center doors.)*

And then it is Kita no Kata's turn to speak.

KITA NO KATA: You have come at a good time. *(*MATAHEI *bows deeply.)* A marvelous event happened today. Shūrinosuke received his professional name. He is now

Tosa no Mitsuzumi. Matahei, you should study hard, too, and share in his good fortune.

TAKEMOTO:

Matahei has something to say, and he pushes his wife in front to speak for him. / Putting his hands to the floor, he bows his head in respect. / Otoku knows her husband's heart and voices his feelings.

*(*MATAHEI *gestures for* OTOKU *to speak for him, then takes her hand and pushes her toward center. She is hesitant, but he urges her on. Timidly, she kneels in the garden, facing* SHŌGEN.*)*

OTOKU: Master, please excuse me. I would like to speak for my husband. On our way here, we heard some farmers talking about what happened as we passed them. Shūrinosuke did a miraculous thing today and received the auspicious brush of the masters. Even more importantly, he was awarded the prized Tosa name. We are very pleased for him. *(Quietly, sadly.)* But, my husband, Matahei, is a poor and disabled man. A newer, younger student has earned the Tosa name, while my husband is an older and destitute disciple. He has been studying so long with nothing tangible to show for it. Won't you please consider awarding my husband . . . the great Tosa name?

TAKEMOTO *(A lament* [kudoki] *expressing* OTOKU*'s feelings of sadness)*:

How long must absent-minded Matahei paint scenes of the floating world / such as the actor playing a young maiden posing in wisteria? / Like the painting of the monkey senselessly trying to catch a catfish with a gourd, / despondent Matahei knows his own life plans are futile. / He holds his head tightly in frustration.

*(*OTOKU *points to* MATAHEI, pulls *the hand towel from her obi, and mimes her despondency. Thrusting the towel over her left shoulder and posing, she mimes a wisteria maiden. With the towel, she draws circles in the air and on the ground as if fishing with a gourd in a pool of water. Finally, she grips the towel tightly to her chest in hopelessness.)*

OTOKU: I am always with him and I see what is in his heart. *(Appealing to* KITA NO KATA.*)* I implore, I beg you with my tears, as one wife to another. I know my husband's dearest wish is to receive a Tosa name. Please grant him one, even if it is after his death, so he can claim the Tosa name on his gravestone. *(She realizes what she has just said, and covers her mouth with her towel, as if to silence herself.)* Take pity on my husband, please.

TAKEMOTO:

Longing for his master's compassion, his tears choking in his throat, / Matahei claps his hands together and bows to his teacher. / His tears fall heedlessly to the ground. / The master feels pity, / but his student has done nothing to prove himself. Shōgen speaks harshly.

(Facing SHŌGEN, MATAHEI *bows repeatedly, while* OTOKU *weeps inconsolably.)*

SHŌGEN *(Gravely)*: Listen and listen well. I, myself, have been sent here and forbidden by the emperor to paint because I lost in competition with the painter Oguri Shōtan. If I went to see my competitor and agreed to work for him, then I would certainly regain my former prosperity. But because I refuse to consider such a cowardly option, we have fallen on hard times. I was forced to sell my only daughter, Omitsu, to a brothel in order to survive and to uphold our professional name. *(Strong* TAKEMOTO *shamisen chords.)* Today, Shūrinosuke has proved himself worthy in a remarkable way by erasing a tiger. What have you done to deserve such an honor? Playing the koto, calligraphy, painting, and chess are all things anyone can do by just moving an arm. But painting in the presence of emperors and noblemen is a high art. *(He poses, looking sternly at* MATAHEI.*)* You have done nothing of merit, what right do you have to ask for a name? Instead you paint meaningless pictures of ordinary people! Drink your tea and go home!

TAKEMOTO:

Having no more compassion, he reproaches his student, / Otoku suddenly loses her strength.

OTOKU *(Turning gently to her husband)*: Matahei. After listening to Master Shōgen, I think it will be impossible. It's not your fault that you were born with a stutter that has damned your entire life.

TAKEMOTO:

His request is denied, and Matahei is devastated. / Matahei would like to tear out his throat and reaches in his mouth to pull his tongue out with his hands. / His tears will not cease.

*(*OTOKU *consoles* MATAHEI, *who, weeping, pushes her away.)*

TAKEMOTO:

Just then, a voice is heard from far away.

UTANOSUKE *(Offstage)*: Is the master present? Master? Master Shōgen? Master Shōgen? It is a matter of extreme importance.

TAKEMOTO:

Calling frantically for Shōgen, a young man comes running in at a furious pace / and collapses in the garden.

*(*UTANOSUKE, *a young samurai, staggers onto the* hanamichi *in time to the beating of the* tsuke. *His black kimono has been pulled down and tucked into his obi for battle, revealing a hitched-up, pale blue underkimono. His hair is pulled back in a high topknot. Carrying his sword in front of him, he staggers through the gate and sits cross-legged in the garden.)*

SHŌGEN: This could only be Utanosuke of Kanō. He looks as if he is trying to escape from someone. Quickly, Matahei, go, make certain no one is in pursuit.

MATAHEI: Sir!

*(*MATAHEI *removes his* haori *with* OTOKU*'s help and rushes to the* hanamichi*. Kneeling, he slaps his thighs resolutely and poses to a strong chord of* TAKEMOTO *shamisen music, looking intently into the distance.)*

SHŌGEN: Attend this man immediately.

*(*SHŪRINOSUKE *hands* UTANOSUKE *a cup of tea. He massages* UTANOSUKE*'s neck and chest firmly to two* tsuke *beats and helps him drink the tea.)*

SHŌGEN: Utanosuke, what is of extreme importance? What has happened?

UTANOSUKE *(Groaning and recovering his breath)*: Allow me to explain! *(*UTANOSUKE *thrusts his right foot forward from a kneeling position and poses in a powerful* mie *to two* tsuke *beats. The* TAKEMOTO *shamisen plays a rhythmic melody* [nori] *to which* UTANOSUKE *matches his declamation.)* No doubt, you have heard about the uprising at the mansion where Princess Ichō was staying. You know it was my duty to protect the princess. But the enemy was everywhere. I tried to fight them off and to cover her escape and that of Master Shirōjirō. I hid where I could. But, in the tumult, Master Shirōjirō and I were separated. I don't know what's become of him!

*(*UTANOSUKE *mimes his valorous fighting, extending his right arm forward, as if watching the enemy take captives. He tilts his head left as if wondering what to do.)*

TAKEMOTO *(Continuing* UTANOSUKE*'s speech)*:

"In the moments that I wondered who I should attend to first, the enemy came quickly and with great force. / Summoning my courage, I prepared for battle."

(He slaps his knee and brings his left arm across to the opposite shoulder, as if preparing for a fight. He blows on his sword, cleaning it, then waves it in the air. Stepping forward, he extends his sword, swings it behind his head, and pivots, facing SHŌGEN*.)*

"I thrust my sword out in front, swinging my sword at arms and legs, wherever I could try to strike."

(He pivots front, waving his sword as if preparing for the enemy. He slaps his right knee to the ground, then returns to standing with three leaps, punctuated by a tsuke *beat.)*

"The enemy came from all sides, waving their swords in every direction."

(Pivoting back, he poses, arm in the air, his sword behind his back. He pivots front. He quickly kneels on his right knee demonstrating his preparedness. From a kneeling position, he extends first his right leg, then the left, to the beat of the tsuke*. He jumps to a standing position in time to the* tsuke *and swings his sword left and right.)*

"There were droves of them and one of me. / They easily captured the princess and took her away."

(He moves toward the hanamichi, *his sword extended straight before him. He retreats, parries, then drops his sword. He extends his arms as if watching the princess go, pivots right, and jumps to a sitting position. He thrusts his right leg in front and poses.)*

UTANOSUKE *(Continuing rhythmic speech)*: At Shimo no Daigo, the evil Unkoku's residence, the enemy Banzaemon and other samurai, greatly skilled with swords, lined up guarding the gates. No one could get through.

TAKEMOTO:

"I parried and countered until the blade of my sword / dulled with fighting."

(Rising, UTANOSUKE *strikes with his sword, poses.)*

"Forward, backward, backward, backward. / I don't know what has become of Master Shirōjirō. / I cannot rest until I know he is safe."

(Kneeling on his left knee, he touches the ground and speaks to SHŌGEN.*)*

UTANOSUKE: I must find Master Shirōjirō. Please rescue Princess Ichō, I implore you, Master Shōgen.

TAKEMOTO:

The young man's voice is loud, his feet are fast. / He runs off hurriedly.

(To loud tsuke *beats* [batabata] UTANOSUKE *runs toward the* hanamichi, *where his path is blocked by an unknowing* MATAHEI, *who is still looking intently into the distance. Annoyed,* UTANOSUKE *strikes his sword hilt on* MATAHEI's *shoulder. As* MATAHEI *falls forward,* UTANOSUKE *leaps over him, rushes to* shichisan, *and poses in a strong* mie *to two* tsuke *beats. Beginning with broad and powerful steps, he runs off to* TAKEMOTO *shamisen and rapid* batabata tsuke *pattern. Concerned about* MATAHEI, OTOKU *brings him back to the stage.)*

TAKEMOTO:

Shōgen is deeply worried.

SHŌGEN: We are in terrible trouble. I cannot refuse such a dire request. But I will not receive imperial clemency; I am not allowed to leave the premises. Still, we are obligated to help Utanosuke quell this rebellion against the emperor. I must send someone to rescue the princess. Yet, Shūrinosuke is too young and Matahei is impossible. What can possibly be done?

TAKEMOTO:

Wrinkles form on his brow as he thinks. / Folding his hands, he tilts his head to one side.

(Seeing his master at a loss, MATAHEI *urges his wife to speak but without success. He pulls her, but she escapes.)*

Matahei has something to say, and he pulls his wife by the sleeve. / Thrusting out his hand, he points to Shōgen, / but she is uncertain. / Bravely, he stands in front of Shōgen and tries to speak.

(At last, MATAHEI *approaches* SHŌGEN, *kneels, and bows.)*

MATAHEI: P . . . p . . . p . . . please, . . . s . . . s . . . sir.

SHŌGEN: Ehhhh? You startled me.

MATAHEI: Uh . . . uh . . . uh . . . I know that I am bu . . . bu . . . bumbling, b . . . b . . . but I wo . . . wo . . . wo . . . would li . . . like to g . . . g . . . go, rescue the pr . . . pr . . . princess.

TAKEMOTO:

Shōgen stares at him.

SHŌGEN *(Angrily)*: I almost had a plan, and you interrupted me. Keep quiet!

TAKEMOTO:

Even though Shōgen scolds him, Matahei persists.

MATAHEI *(With great effort)*: I . . . I . . . I ha . . . ha . . . have a request. I am be . . . be . . . begging you on my kn . . . kn . . . knees. I may not be able to speak w . . . w . . . w . . . well, but I have a g . . . g . . . good heart and two good arms and legs. I am not a . . . a . . . a . . . afraid of anything. I know that I . . . I . . . I . . . am con . . . con . . . considered ig . . . ig . . . ignorant, but pl . . . pl . . . please listen to me. I have a sword, and I can c . . . c . . . cut down the enemy or b . . . b . . . be c . . . c . . . cut myself. *(He motions with his sword toward an unseen enemy, then pulls the sword toward his stomach.)* Li . . . li . . . life is a gamble. I am willing to give up my life, for it is not worth m . . . m . . . much. Everyone calls me old absent-minded Matahei, and I have no parents and no children. I h . . . h . . . have no one. M . . . m . . . my li . . . li . . . life is like d . . . d . . . dust and belongs in the d . . . d . . . dustbin. I would gl . . . gl . . . gladly give my life to the g . . . g . . . gods on the high mountain of Shūmisen if that would help. My li . . . li . . . life means nothing. All I have e . . . ever wanted was to inherit the T . . . T . . . Tosa name. *(*MATAHEI *begins to cry.)* P . . . p . . . p . . . please send me to rescue Princess Ichō. If I didn't st . . . st . . . stutter, you would let me do this.

*(*MATAHEI *runs to* SHŌGEN *and tries to get his attention, but his attempts are futile.* SHŌGEN *turns coldly away from him.* MATAHEI *falls to his knees and grips his throat in frustration.)*

TAKEMOTO:

Hatefully, he would like to tear out his throat, the source of his problems.

MATAHEI *(Looking at* OTOKU*)*: D . . . D . . . Dear wife.

*(*MATAHEI *looks at* OTOKU *beseechingly. She nods in sympathy and wipes her eyes with the hand towel as he continues to cry.)*

TAKEMOTO:

Shōgen appears to have no mercy. / Matahei speaks, he cries, he pleads, / but Shōgen does not hear him.

*(*MATAHEI *makes a fist as if to strike* SHŌGEN, *but* OTOKU *motions for him to restrain himself.)*

SHŌGEN: Enough feeling sorry for yourself, Matahei! Shūrinosuke, hurry to Unkoku's mansion, rescue the princess, and bring her back here.

SHŪRINOSUKE: Yes, master.

TAKEMOTO:

Shūrinosuke seizes his sword and plans to leave, / but Matahei stands in his way.

(When SHŪRINOSUKE *comes down into the garden, the kneeling* MATAHEI *grabs* SHŪRINOSUKE*'s* hakama. MATAHEI *shakes his head, urging* SHŪRINOSUKE *to stop.)*

MATAHEI: P . . . p . . . please, wait a minute. Our master does not have any compassion, but please, as a brother disciple, please, sh . . . sh . . . show old Matahei some sympathy. Let me go in your place. Our master won't give his permission, bu . . . bu . . . but please let me go. *(His voice rises with intensity.)* Shūrinosuke, Shūrinosuke, Shūrinosuke!

SHŪRINOSUKE: I do feel sympathy for you, Matahei, but the master has made up his mind and it is my duty to follow his orders. Let go of me, please.

MATAHEI: No. I won't let go.

SHŪRINOSUKE: Let go.

MATAHEI: I won't let go.

SHŪRINOSUKE: Let go.

MATAHEI: I won't let go!

*(*SHŪRINOSUKE *and* MATAHEI *alternate their lines with increasing speed and intensity until they reach a crescendo in unison* [kuriage]*.)*

SHŪRINOSUKE: Let go or I'll cut you down!

*(*SHŪRINOSUKE *holds his sword in his hands. He removes* MATAHEI's *hands. The two pose.)*

MATAHEI *(Slapping his hands against his thighs for emphasis)*: We . . . we . . . well! Go ahead and do it! Cut me down and kill me. I won't let go. *(*MATAHEI *restrains* SHŪRINOSUKE *with both arms around him.)* Strike me, cut me, ki . . . ki . . . kill me. I won't let go!

TAKEMOTO:

Shūrinosuke is at a loss for what to do. / He struggles to get free.

*(*SHŪRINOSUKE *breaks free, but* MATAHEI *grabs* SHŪRINOSUKE*'s sword and holds him back.)*

SHŌGEN: You have annoyed me once too often. I'll cut off your hands myself!

(MATAHEI is startled by SHŌGEN's angry words. He releases SHŪRINOSUKE. SHŪRINOSUKE is surprised, too, and bows to SHŌGEN. MATAHEI pauses in shock, then slowly climbs the stairs to the residence and sits formally on the top step, devastated.)

MATAHEI: We . . . we . . . well. Go ahead and cut me down. If you won't listen to my request, I would just as soon die. I want to die. I want to die. I want to die!

SHŌGEN: In truth, you have become an exasperating nuisance. Shūrinosuke, ignore this imbecile, and hurry on your way.

SHŪRINOSUKE: Yes, sir.

TAKEMOTO:

Shūrinosuke hurriedly leaves to follow his master's orders.

(SHŪRINOSUKE runs to shichisan, *stops, looks, and strikes a* mie *to* tsuke *accompaniment. He moves resolutely down the* hanamichi *to accelerating* tsuke *pattern* [batabata] *and TAKEMOTO shamisen chords while SHŌGEN restrains MATAHEI. When SHŌGEN releases MATAHEI's collar, MATAHEI rolls down the stairs. OTOKU, struggling with MATAHEI, gently pushes him to his knees to prevent him from pursuing SHŪRINOSUKE.)*

OTOKU: Hold on, husband. You heard what the master said. Stop acting like you've gone mad. You must calm down.

(MATAHEI pushes her down and holds her there with one hand.)

TAKEMOTO:

He struggles with her and holds her by the collar.

MATAHEI *(Frantically struggling to speak)*: W . . . w . . . woman! What sh . . . sh . . . should I do? What sh . . . sh . . . should I do? Now you're ca . . . ca . . . calling me cr . . . cr . . . crazy. Even my w . . . w . . . wife has t . . . t . . . turned against me. What k . . . k . . . kind of w . . . w . . . wife are y . . . you anyway?

(While she struggles to get free, he strikes her with his hand again and again, each blow punctuated with a tsuke *beat.)*

TAKEMOTO:

Born with a stutter and a sorrowful fate, / he sits down, his body shaking. / Though he can hardly speak, / sincere feelings in his heart poured forth, / but Shōgen has not listened.

(Falling back, MATAHEI grabs at his throat, then his tongue, in frustration. When OTOKU tries to comfort him, he pushes OTOKU away. He pulls at his hair in rage and collapses in tears.)

TAKEMOTO:

Shōgen speaks again.

SHŌGEN: Matahei, I will tell you one time only. Listen well. In our art, one must demonstrate exemplary skills in painting to receive the prestigious Tosa name. Even a samurai, showing courageous skills in battle, cannot receive the Tosa name on those merits alone.

OTOKU: I understand that you are very angry, but I beg that you give him the Tosa name.

SHŌGEN *(Disgusted)*: Absolutely not.

OTOKU: Under what circumstances might . . .

SHŌGEN: Despicable!

*(*OTOKU *crawls up the stairs and kneels in front of* SHŌGEN. *When he stands, she reaches to hold his sleeve. He pushes her away angrily and stalks off. She then turns to* KITA NO KATA *who shakes her head and dutifully follows her husband off through the sliding doors left.)*

TAKEMOTO:

Barely able to control his anger, Shōgen enters the residence.

(Silence. OTOKU *takes two or three steps as if to follow. She stops, realizes it is futile, and sinks to her knees slowly at the top of the stairs. Music resumes quietly.)*

Otoku's gaze lingers in the distance, / and then she moves to her husband's side.

(All of her usual energy gone, OTOKU *crosses down to* MATAHEI *in the garden.)*

OTOKU: Matahei, dear, it is no use. You will never receive the Tosa name in your lifetime. There is nothing else to do, but . . . give up.

*(*MATAHEI, *utterly without hope and humiliated, slowly reaches for his sword to commit suicide. Silently,* OTOKU *holds his hand in hers, shaking her head "no." Plaintive* TAKEMOTO *shamisen chords underscore their melancholy. Trying to distract him, she looks around. Seeing the water basin, she has an idea.)*

OTOKU: Matahei, dear. Wait. Please wait a minute. Why don't you paint a portrait of yourself on the granite water basin? In front of the master's residence. At least your image will remain there for the master to see. And afterward . . .

TAKEMOTO:

His only hope is for a posthumous name. / Much, much later.

OTOKU: Will you do that?

(He nods. MATAHEI *deliberately and without haste prepares to create his last painting. While he composes himself,* OTOKU *enters the master's room hesitantly. Gathering courage, she selects a brush by testing the tip with her fingers and respectfully bows in the direction of* SHŌGEN. *She brings the brush and* SHŌGEN*'s tray of painting supplies, including his inkstone, to* MATAHEI*'s side. When* MATAHEI, *standing, reaches for the brush, she kneels before him, holding his hands, looks at him lovingly, and speaks in a tear-filled voice.)*

OTOKU: You have two arms and ten fingers. That is enough. Oh, why did you have the unfortunate fate of being born with a stutter?

(They both weep. MATAHEI *wipes his eyes, takes the brush from* OTOKU, *and crosses to the granite basin. He is ready to begin.)*

TAKEMOTO:

Slowly, she prepares the ink.

(While OTOKU *carefully prepares ink, rubbing the ink stick in a pool of water in the inkstone,* MATAHEI *surveys the stone closely, looking it up and down. He walks to the back and to the front and inspects the left and right face of the square granite block. Determining that the back side is the best, he kneels behind the basin, facing the audience, and vigorously rubs the surface clean with paper from his kimono breast.)*

Slowly, deliberately, he begins preparing the stone. / This final painting will be his masterpiece, / his life's work.

(Preparing to paint, MATAHEI *bows in gratitude in the direction of* SHŌGEN. *He rests both hands on the basin and peers deeply into the water. When the ladle falls from the basin, he does not notice. Moving the brush in a large circle, he performs a* mie. OTOKU *places the inkstone by his side. Kneeling behind the basin,* MATAHEI *dips the brush in ink and begins to paint.)*

As he paints his own image, / with his own strokes, he puts his soul into this stone. / And as he paints with all of his heart / on the back of the basin, / The ink does not fade. / Miraculously, his image appears on the opposite side!

*(*MATAHEI *continues to paint, and stroke by stroke, his painted image takes form on the front of the basin. Meanwhile,* OTOKU *tiptoes right so as not to disturb him and spreads his* haori *on the ground.)*

MATAHEI: There!

(Finished, he slumps, exhausted against the stone.)

OTOKU: Oh! You've done a good job. You must be tired. Come rest over here.

(Gently, OTOKU *crosses to* MATAHEI *and leads him away from the basin and has him sit on his* haori. *He tries to set his brush down near the inkstone, but, in a daze, he cannot unclasp his hands.* OTOKU *kindly releases his fingers, one by one, and places the brush back on the tray. Bowing with gratitude to* SHŌGEN, *she returns inkstone and brush to their rightful place inside the residence. In silence,* MATAHEI *drops his outer kimono, takes the swords from his obi, and prepares to commit ritual suicide.* OTOKU *rushes to his side, stopping him. They look at each other, silently thinking of the regrettable task before them.)*

OTOKU *(Trying to prolong the moment)*: Just for a moment, please. You and I. Let's share a final drink together. I'll get some water. Yes, wait right there. *(She crosses to get water from the basin and admires the picture on the back.)* You have done a

Matahei (Onoe Shōroku II) paints on the back of the water basin, watched by Otoku (Onoe Baikō VII). The *takemoto* chanter, right, intones, "As he paints his own image, with his own strokes, he puts his soul into this stone." (Umemura Yutaka, Engeki Shuppansha)

beautiful job, husband. *(Looking for the ladle, she moves to the front of the basin where she sees the image of* MATAHEI *on the front surface. A lone shamisen chord punctuates her astonished disbelief. She falls back, steadies herself, and looks again. Her body trembles with surprise as a single shamisen chord accentuates her movements.)* Aaahhhh!

(To accelerating shamisen chords, she walks back to tell MATAHEI, *her body unsteady with disbelief.)*

OTOKU: Come, come here Matahei! Look! *(*OTOKU *takes* MATAHEI *by the hand and leads him to the back of the basin.)* Now follow my finger.

*(*OTOKU *motions to* MATAHEI *to follow her finger with his eyes. She points first to the image on the back, then slowly moves her finger in an arc to the front side of the basin and back to the opposite side. Disbelieving,* MATAHEI, *following her hand, looks at the back, the front, the back, and finally the front of the basin again. He sinks to his knees.)*

MATAHEI *(Scarcely able to speak)*: Wife! It's real!

TAKEMOTO *(To accelerating shamisen)*:

They are completely overwhelmed!

*(*MATAHEI *stares at the image, kneeling at the front of the basin.)*

Matahei (Onoe Tatsunosuke II) is dumbfounded to see that the painting of himself has magically appeared on the front of the water basin. Otoku (Kamimura Kichiya VI) carefully examines the image. (Umemura Yutaka, Engeki Shuppansha)

Shōgen, has witnessed the whole event. Emerging from the residence, / he carefully inspects the painting and brushes.

*(*SHŌGEN *comes out from the sliding doors and down the steps into the garden carrying a candlestick. Carefully, he looks at the water basin and holds up the brush.)*

SHŌGEN *(His cold demeanor has changed)*: A job well done. Well done! This is truly a miracle! I have heard that in China, two artists painted with such spirit that the soul of one emerged from a tree and the other from a rock, but this is the first time anything like this has happened in Japan! We have witnessed a miracle, and from now on, you will no longer be known as absent-minded Matahei but Tosa no Matahei Mitsuoki.

OTOKU: What? Have you changed your mind and decided to give him the great name of the masters? Truly?

SHŌGEN: Yes. *(*OTOKU *bows in appreciation to* SHŌGEN *and rushes over to* MATAHEI *sitting beside the basin.)* Matahei! You've been granted the Tosa name!

MATAHEI: Ohhhh! To . . . To . . . Tosa no Tosa no Mitsuoki! . . .

OTOKU: Tosa no Mitsuoki. You've earned the name!

MATAHEI: Tosa no Mitsuoki . . .

OTOKU: Tosa no Mitsuoki . . .

(OTOKU and MATAHEI repeat the name to each other several times, overlapping in kuriage *style.)*

MATAHEI: Thank you so very much.

TAKEMOTO:

The couple is overjoyed. / Matahei would like to share his thanks, / but he cannot do so properly with his stutter.

(With great feeling, MATAHEI puts both hands together in gratitude and bows, deeply. OTOKU helps MATAHEI back into his kimono.)

Instead, his appreciation flows down his cheeks in the form of grateful tears. / Dancing and jumping with joy, / his tears of gratitude won't cease.

(He stands and stamps his feet with joy, then drops to his knees, clasping his hands in gratitude.)

SHŌGEN: You have earned your happiness. Take these documents and go to the residence at Shimo no Daigo to rescue Princess Ichō.

MATAHEI: Sir! *(Prepares to leave.)*

SHŌGEN: Hmm, before you go, please consider. This is an important mission. You cannot go looking like that . . . I'll lend you proper clothes. Wife, bring out clothes suitable for Matahei to wear.

KITA NO KATA: Yes, Shōgen. I am coming.

(KITA NO KATA brings out a tray with formal clothing: kimono, kamishimo, *a sword,* tabi, *and a white fan. She hands them to MATAHEI.)*

KITA NO KATA: Congratulations, Matahei. What a marvelous job you have done! Here are formal clothes for you to wear. Change into them quickly.

MATAHEI: Th . . . th . . . thank you, v . . . v . . . very much.

(Offstage shamisen play a lively melody [nichō]. *MATAHEI takes the tray, shows it to his wife, faces the audience, and laughs with pleasure.)*

MATAHEI: Ho, ho, ho. Ha, ha, ha. Ho, ho, ho.

OTOKU: Ha, ha, ha.

MATAHEI: Ho, ho, ho.

OTOKU: Ha, ha, ha.

(MATAHEI's laughter increases in intensity, until, finally, his voice alternates between laughter and tears. With his back to the audience, MATAHEI slips off the kimono he is wearing, while OTOKU drapes the new kimono over his shoulders. Lively shamisen music sets a bright mood. MATAHEI, OTOKU, and SHŌGEN ad-lib as MATAHEI changes. OTOKU helps MATAHEI into his formal garment. At one point, MATAHEI is about to cry into the sleeve of his kimono,

Matahei (Onoe Shōroku II) is dressed in samurai finery by Otoku (Onoe Baikō VII). Matahei adjusts his vest and, holding the brush before him, prepares to exit down the *hanamichi* (Umemura Yutaka, Engeki Shuppansha)

but his wife reminds him not to stain it with his tears. MATAHEI *adjusts his hair and tucks the small sword and fan into his obi. He takes the large sword and poses.)*

SHŌGEN: Matahei, there is one more thing. These are our enemies. You will have to speak to them in order to trick them. What are we going to do about your speech impediment?

OTOKU: Please don't concern yourself with that, sir. He loves *daigashira,* the singing of ballads and stories. I accompany him on the drum, and with my lively rhythm, he hardly stutters at all.

SHŌGEN *(Laughing)*: With a rhythm, he hardly stutters at all. Amazing! Let us try. Bring me the small drum.

KITA NO KATA: I will.

*(*KITA NO KATA *gets the hand drum from the shelves at the back of the room and hands it to* OTOKU*.)*

SHŌGEN: Matahei! Let's have a dance in honor of your deeds today.

MATAHEI: Yes, master!

*(*MATAHEI *bows to* SHŌGEN *and* KITA NO KATA. *He moves to the middle of the stage.* OTOKU *beats the drum. He taps on the ground with his fan to get her attention and proceeds to correct her rhythm. She cheerfully nods and starts again.)*

TAKEMOTO:

Briskly he answers and springs to his feet. / He dances, his body tracing the lines of an ancient dance.

MATAHEI *(Chanting in* nō *style)*: Kamakura's Lord Yoritomo, / should face the punitive armies of Yoshitsune. / Those brave and valiant men were chosen for their military excellence, / among them the priest of Tosa. / And now there is Tosa no Matahei!

TAKEMOTO:

Tosa no Matahei Mitsuoki! / Received the blessings of his teacher.

*(*MATAHEI *begins the dance holding his fan between his hands. With the fan in his right hand, he extends his arms and brings them back to center. He raises his left hand above his head in respect to his teacher.)*

Now, with heavy responsibilities to fulfill, he must part ways with his life in Ōtsu.

(He bows facing front and stands. He flips his right kimono sleeve. Extending his open fan, he dances as if looking off in the distance.)

Pigments applied to a canvas are cheap, / but a name from an esteemed family of painters is priceless. / Matahei's life, seemingly drawn in black ink, suddenly becomes brilliant with color.

(He dances holding the fan over his shoulder, as if carrying a heavy bundle. He dances auspiciously with the fan, turns back to SHŌGEN, *and bows.* MATAHEI *taps the fan on the ground to get his wife's attention and sits at center.)*

His wife hits the drum with more force.

OTOKU *(Tapping the drum and singing in rhythm)*: Now perhaps we should go quickly before he changes his mind.

TAKEMOTO:

She encourages him to hurry.

*(*MATAHEI *and* OTOKU *meet each other's eyes. Tapping his fan in time,* MATAHEI *imitates the sound of the drum as the song comes to an end.)*

MATAHEI: Ho, ho, ho, ho, ho, ho, ho. Let us be on our way.

TAKEMOTO:

He has been a poor artist, an insignificant man, / painting black and white landscapes with brushes and tools tired and decayed. / Suddenly, color and gold dust etch the path to his future. / No longer will he feel inferior to the brightly colored lives of others. / Instead he will bravely charge forward, toward a new life of his own. / Now he will have his brush with greatness.

*(*MATAHEI *dances with the fan, auspiciously, at times stamping his feet in rhythm. He mimes painting as if the open fan were a canvas and his fingers the brush. He points to the brush as if it were the key to his new life and slaps his chest with new self-confidence.)*

OTOKU *(Tapping the drum and singing in rhythm)*: Like the two legendary warriors in Chinese paintings.

MATAHEI *(In time with the rhythm of the music)*: Ta, ta, ta, ta, ta, ta, ta, ta, ta. We must attend to our duty. I must quickly leave.

TAKEMOTO:

Saying this, he prepares to depart.

SHŌGEN: Before you go, I will present you with the scroll you have earned as a master painter.

*(*SHŌGEN *hands* MATAHEI *a scroll and a special brush with the Tosa seal.* MATAHEI *wraps the scroll in a cloth and happily puts it in his sleeve.)*

TAKEMOTO:

Matahei bows his head to his teacher with deep appreciation. / With strength in his steps he moves forward. / His life now has new meaning.

*(*MATAHEI *stamps in time with the music. Reminded by* OTOKU*'s signal, he puts his long sword in his obi. He poses and energetically flips his sleeves. He takes dignified steps in the manner of a distinguished samurai.)*

He will be an inspiration to everyone, and people will learn of his bravery.

(A black-robed STAGE ASSISTANT [kurogo] *brings* OTOKU *and* MATAHEI *their sandals. The couple bows to* SHŌGEN *in gratitude. They stride to* shichisan, *where they pause and bow to* SHŌGEN *once more.* MATAHEI *poses energetically. A* ki *clack signals the curtain to close in silence. Alone on the* hanamichi *for an "outside-the-curtain exit"* [maku soto no hikkomi], OTOKU *and* MATAHEI *gaze happily at each other.* MATAHEI *begins to shuffle down the* hanamichi, *when* OTOKU *urgently stops him. Ad-libbing, "That's no way. You're a samurai. Do it like this," she demonstrates in a comic fashion how to strut with the swinging arms of a samurai. Realizing she must look silly, she stops and chuckles.* MATAHEI *understands and proudly poses in a* mie, *the auspicious brush clenched tightly in his hand, to two* tsuke *beats. He extends his arms and walks, happily and rapidly, down the* hanamichi *to rhythmic* tsuke *beats, drum, and shamisen melody. As* MATAHEI *exits,* OTOKU *dabs at her eyes. With small running steps, she happily follows after him. A single* ki *clack signals the end of the play.)*

Single-panel woodblock print by Utagawa Kuniyoshi (1797–1861). Ichimura-za, Edo, third month 1832. The print identifies "Ichikawa Danjūrō VIII, previously Ebizō, a peddler of the Tora Shop's 'Uirō' medicine." *The Medicine Peddler* was one scene within the longer play *Sukeroku: Flower of Edo.* In a formal stage ceremony *(kōjō)*, the actor's father, Danjūrō VII, announced that he was taking the lesser name of Ichikawa Ebizō VI in order to pass on the Danjūrō name to his

The Medicine Peddler

Uirō Uri

Ichikawa Danjūrō II, with modern contributions by Kawajiri Seitan and Noguchi Tatsuji

TRANSLATED BY LAURENCE R. KOMINZ

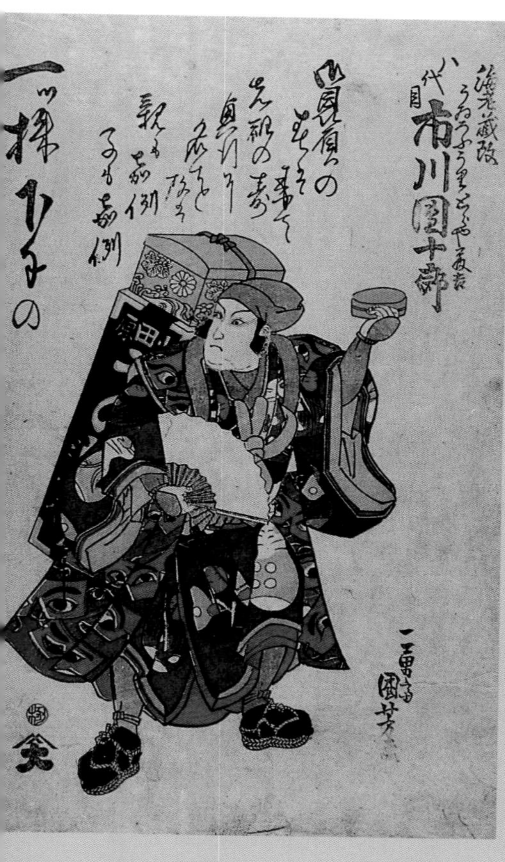

eleven-year-old son. One inscription alludes to the art of the Ichikawa family passing from father to son in this New Year's, or spring, production: "Coming in the favored time of spring, ancestral felicitations, still famed in far Ōshū, celebrated custom of the parents, celebrated custom of the child." A second suggests the peddler's humble status: "One clump, a servant's due, of eggplant seedlings." (Tsubouchi Memorial Theatre Museum of Waseda University)

1718 MORITA-ZA, EDO

The Medicine Peddler

INTRODUCTION

The Medicine Peddler is unique in the repertory of kabuki plays in its display of virtuoso verbal dexterity, containing a remarkable three-and-a-half minute medicine peddler's tongue-twisting spiel. Originally written and performed by Ichikawa Danjūrō II (1688–1758) in the first lunar month of 1718, *The Medicine Peddler*, along with *Sukeroku: Flower of Edo* (Sukeroku Yukari no Edo Zakura, 1713; trans. Brandon 1992)—helped to catapult Danjūrō II to superstar status not only in Edo kabuki but as a national figure. In 1718, *Medicine Peddler* was set within a Soga encounter scene (see the introduction to *The Felicitous Soga Encounter* in this volume). It was presented in the second act of a New Year's play entitled *The High-Spirited Soga Brother Amid the Fresh Green Leaves* (Wakamidori Ikioi Soga). Danjūrō II played Soga Gorō, disguised as a vendor of a famous medicine *(uirō)*. The disguise allows him to approach his father's murderer, Kudō Suketsune, at a gala New Year's celebration at Hakone Shrine. Before revealing his true identity, Gorō regales Suketsune and all of his guests with his playful speech.

Danjūrō II's 1718 New Year's play was a smash hit, running for seven months, one of the longest running New Year's plays on record. The medicine peddler scene is probably the first use of extended tongue-twisting lines in kabuki, but it was not the first popular vendor's role. In 1709, Danjūrō noted in his diary that he had received acclaim as a moxa seller and that all sorts of vendors could be found hawking their wares on the stage: sellers of sweet wine, ice water, fans, crockery, flints, sushi, souvenirs, and many other items. But this medicine peddler's speech was altogether different from anything yet heard. A complete script was published shortly after the play opened, and aficionados from Edo to the Kamigata area were soon memorizing it to recite for fun and at social occasions. When Danjūrō II played the role in 1741 in Osaka, spectators who had memorized the speech began to shout it from the gallery. Danjūrō stopped, waited for the din to subside, and then, in his politest language, thanked the audience for memorizing a challenging family text, whereupon he recited the entire speech backward without mishap, leaving his audience flabbergasted at his dexterity and intuitive powers. Even today, sections from it are used as an oral test when recruiting newscasters and sports announcers.

The medicine seller's monologue begins and ends with what may have been the actual words of peddlers of *uirō*, introducing the medicine, describing its lineage and effectiveness, and exhorting customers to purchase it. Inside this frame are a long series of tongue twisters, full of rhyming and alliteration, and other forms of word play, including puns, free associations, and parodies. Just as English-speaking children love Dr. Seuss' word play, Japanese children enjoy all sorts of word games and tongue twisters, and many of the lines in *Medicine Peddler* derive from children's songs and rhymes. For readers—whether they know Japanese or not—who wish to put their own tongues to the test, here are some lines from the original, beginning with "Raw cod in Kyo" and ending with "you spilled it all."

> *Kyō no nama dara, Nara nama, Nama katsuo, choito shigo kanme. Kuruwa, kuruwa, nani ga kuru? Koya no yama no okokera kozō. Tanuki hyappiki, hashi hyakuzen Tenmoku hyappai, bō happyapon. Bugu bagu, bugu bagu, mi bugu bagu. Awasete bugu bagu mu bugu bagu. Kiku kuri, kiku kuri, mi kiku kuri. Awasete kiku kuri mu kiku kuri. Ano nageshi no naga naginata wa ta ga naga naginata zo. Mukō no gomagara wa . . . sono gomagara ka, magomagara ka? Are koso hon no magomagara. Garapii, garapii kaze guruma. Okiyagere koboshi, okiyagare koboshi yūbe koboshite mata koboshita.*

The monologue is spoken in a monotone, rapidly and loudly, with occasional verbal flourishes.

In this brief play, in addition to his famous speech, Gorō entertainingly teases Chinsai, the tea master buffoon, and has an energetic fight dance *(tachimawari)* with Suketsune's guards. Further, his companion Asahina, Asahina's sister, Maizuru, and two courtesans do a lively dance while Gorō is changing out of his medicine peddler's disguise.

Medicine Peddler, like another enduring Soga play of Danjūrō II, *The Arrow Sharpener* (Ya no Ne), is, to borrow Bakhtin's terminology, a "carnivalistic play, bringing together, combining, and unifying the sacred with the profane, the lofty with the low, the great with the insignificant, and the wise with the stupid."[1] By making Gorō a comical peddler, Danjūrō destroyed the "valorized distance" inherent in Gorō's status as a heroic samurai and virtual deity, bringing Gorō closer to the commoner audience. Because of his humorous qualities, not despite them, Gorō is the most impressive samurai in the play.

Danjūrō II meant to use this role to showcase his acting talent. His approach was to invest elemental play forms that derive from animal behavior, "exhibitions, preenings, showings-off and challenges,"[2] with wit and sophistication through com-

1. Mikhail Bakhtin, *Problems of Dostoevsky's Poetics*, p. 123. Bakhtin uses the term "carnivalesque literature" and I use "carnivalesque drama" in the same vein.

2. Johan Huizinga, *Homo Ludens: A Study of the Play Element in Culture*, p. 47.

plex word play and multiple levels of significance. *Medicine Peddler* is a tour de force that continually verges on metadrama, always asking its audience to delight on two levels, both following the story and consciously watching a virtuoso actor at work.

Uirō was a cure-all patent medicine invented in China, which, according to the family records, dates back 1,400 years. When the Ming dynasty overthrew the Yuan, Chin Uirō left service as court physician to the Yuan emperor and, in 1368, emigrated to Japan. In 1504, his descendants were given land for making and selling their medicine near Odawara post-station on the Tokaidō Road. Thus, travelers of every social station learned of *uirō*.

Danjūrō II is said to have taken *uirō* in 1717 to cure a mucous cough that was preventing him from appearing onstage. The medicine worked so well that Danjūrō traveled all the way to Odawara to thank the maker personally. He "hit it off" with the family patriarch and told the latter that he wanted to thank him by advertising *uirō* on stage. Over the years, successive Danjūrōs faithfully paid calls to the family to ask their permission before performing the scene.

In 1832, *Medicine Peddler* headed the bill when Danjūrō VII (1791–1859) took the name Ebizō and passed the Danjūrō mantle on to his eleven-year-old son, Danjūrō VIII (1823–1854), who performed the medicine peddler. At this performance Danjūrō VII announced the creation of the *Kabuki Jūhachiban* (Eighteen Famous Kabuki Plays) collection, the finest plays and scenes in his family's heritage. *Medicine Peddler* was among them. From the time of Danjūrō VII, a tradition began of having youthful actors perform *Medicine Peddler*. The play celebrates the link between this family heritage and the hero of one of Japan's enduring martial legends.

The first performance of *Medicine Peddler* as a discreet one-act Soga play was staged in 1940 to celebrate the name-taking ceremony of thirty-one-year-old Ichikawa Ebizō IX, who would later become Danjūrō XI (1909–1965). The Soga encounter frame of *The Medicine Peddler* very much resembles *The Felicitous Soga Encounter*. The reader is invited to compare the two plays in terms of narrativity, character development, and the use of dance, music, and monologue arts. The script translated here is the standard present-day version, close to that first performed in 1980, and repeated often since then. The tongue-twisting monologue itself remains very close to the original published in 1718. My translation of it is more free than literal but tries to remain semantically close to the original. Because of the ceremonial nature of *Medicine Peddler*, the lead actor today may present a brief formal address *(kōjō)* within the play. This translation includes the *kōjō* delivered by Danjūrō XII in May 1993 at the Kabuki-za in Tokyo, provided courtesy of Danjūrō XII and the Shōchiku Ōtani Library.

CHARACTERS

KUDŌ SAEMON SUKETSUNE, *powerful minister of state responsible for the death of the* SOGA *brothers' father*

MEDICINE PEDDLER, *actually the nineteen-year-old* SOGA GORŌ TOKIMUNE *in disguise*

ASAHINA SABURŌ YOSHIHIDE, *son of a leading feudal lord, a strong, blustering samurai*

MAIZURU, *younger sister of* ASAHINA

KAJIWARA HEIZŌ KAGETOKI, *villainous feudal lord allied to* SUKETSUNE

KAJIWARA HEIJI KAGETAKA, *son of* KAGETOKI

KEWAIZA NO SHŌSHŌ, *courtesan and* GORŌ*'s lover*

ŌISO NO TORA, *courtesan paramour of* JŪRŌ, GORŌ*'s elder brother*

KISEGAWA, *a courtesan*

KAMEGIKU, *a courtesan*

CHINSAI, *a tea master, dressed as a buffoon with a "catfishlike"* (namazu guma) *makeup*

SIX JUNIOR COURTESANS

EIGHT GUARDS, *wielders of flower spears, menial samurai in the service of* SUKETSUNE

STAGE ASSISTANTS, *formally dressed* kōken

ŌZATSUMA, *chanters and shamisen players heard in* aragoto *plays*

(The draw curtain opens to offstage music [hayakagura] *and a rapid* ki *pattern. This reveals another curtain, the blue drop curtain* [asagimaku], *which conceals most of the stage set. The stage floor is covered with dance platforms* [shosabutai]. SUKETSUNE's GUARDS [hana yakko] *stand in front of the drop curtain, holding six-foot-long flower-decorated staves.)*

FIRST GUARD *(Formally)*: Well now, isn't it wonderful how highly the shogun regards our master, Lord Suketsune?

SECOND GUARD: He was chosen among lords great and small to be marshal of the shogun's hunt at Mount Fuji. The hunt is set for the last ten days in the fifth month, and each participant's camp . . .

(Here begins one of the play's several sequences of passed-along dialogue [watarizerifu].*)*

THIRD GUARD: We have plotted and recorded on a map, following his orders, and since it is now complete, we will present the map to him . . .

FOURTH GUARD: In the hope that all his plans are brought to fulfillment.

FIFTH GUARD: Ceremonies entreating the deity of Hakone . . .

SIXTH GUARD: Were completed today without a hitch.

SEVENTH GUARD: To lighten his fatigue, our master has summoned courtesans, and now he is taking his ease with them.

EIGHTH GUARD: How different that activity is from ours.

FIRST GUARD: It is our duty to straighten out problems, should they arise.

SECOND GUARD: One more time, to increase our vigilance . . .

ALL GUARDS: We shall patrol the grounds.

(They exit right.)

ŌZATSUMA:

Like bamboo shoots, like a jeweled comb, / like the spokes of a fan spreading outward, / his martial glory thrives far and wide. / Inside the shrine, the splendor of / Kudō Saemon Suketsune is unrivaled.

(A ki *clack signals the blue drop curtain to fall, revealing the stage set, which depicts the entrance to Hakone Shrine. A red wooden fence tops the stone boundary of the shrine. At stage center, three stone steps lead under the shrine gate and into the shrine. The interior of the shrine is shaded by a grove of towering cryptomeria trees. Red and white blossoming plum trees can be seen here and there among the evergreens. In the distance, Mount Fuji rises above the mist over a lake choked with reeds. The cryptomerias protrude above a curtain, and red and white sprays of plum blossoms hang down from the top of the proscenium. The* ŌZATSUMA *musicians sit on a dais at stage left. A scarlet rug has been laid on the raised inner stage, and banquet accoutrements are arranged on it. The* JUNIOR COURTESANS *sit in a line in front of the shrine fence.* SHŌSHŌ, TORA, KISEGAWA, and KAMEGIKU *sit side by side in the middle of the stage. They are dressed in gorgeous kimono, with obi tied in bows in the front. To their right are* ASAHINA *and his sister* MAIZURU. ASAHINA's *face is painted in horizontal red stripes* [saru guma], *suggesting a monkey's visage. He has a handlebar mustache; bows of "power paper"* [chikaragami] *protrude from his wig. To the left of the* COURTESANS *is* CHINSAI. *He has a shaved pate, his face is painted in red stripes on white, and he sports a comic mustache that makes him look like a catfish. His striped* hakama *and yellow* tabi *also mark him as a buffoon. To his left are* KAGETOKI *and* KAGETAKA, *their ruddy faces painted with dark lines, marking them as villains.* SUKETSUNE *sits to*

their left on a bench. He wears a black kimono embroidered with his gold "plum blossom in a hermitage" crest. Offstage music plays.)

SUKETSUNE *(Formally)*: The morning sun shines. The white clouds hiding the mountain peak dissolve, and the spring mist spreads out over the plain. My, what a splendid view it is.

ASAHINA: Please let me be the first to express a prayer for your everlasting martial glory. And may I express most humbly how exceedingly delighted I am that today's ceremony has been successfully completed.

KAGETOKI: We are truly thankful for the shogun's reign and this tranquil spring at Mount Hakone.

MAIZURU: When the mountain smiles, we scoop water. Blossoms take the lead on this festive occasion . . .

(Another passed-along dialogue sequence ensues.)

KAGETAKA: The coy denizens of Kewaizaka . . .

TORA: Receiving Suketsune's invitation . . .

SHŌSHŌ: Came here together, wearing sumptuous ceremonial robes—

KISEGAWA: Today we attend in holiday finery.

KAMEGIKU: Sake makes us gay and we frolic . . .

CHINSAI: Young women are fine at flirting and pouring wine.

SUKETSUNE: My goodness, you have so skillfully prepared a fine place for a feast in my honor.

TORA: Now, Lord Suketsune, please . . .

SHŌSHŌ: Be the first to partake of a cup of sake.

KISEGAWA and KAMEGIKU: Yes, please be the first to partake of a cup of sake.

SUKETSUNE: In that case, let all of us drink a cup of sake.

(Offstage shamisen music plays. Served by the courtesans, SUKETSUNE *drinks sake at his banquet seat. A special flute is blown, simulating the song of the bush warbler, a bird said to love sporting amid the plum blossoms.)*

SUKETSUNE *(Reciting a* tanka *poem)*: Is this the fragrance of plum blossoms proclaiming that it is spring? Why, it makes the occasion all the more elegant.

ŌZATSUMA:

Willows on the eastern bank, / the southern branches of the plum / make a fine spring scene, / and composing poems / and listening to the chirping of the birds / are pleasant harbingers of tongue-twisting speech.

*(*SOGA GORŌ*, disguised as a medicine peddler, shouts from inside the* hanamichi *curtain.)*

GORŌ *(Offstage)*: Don't you want to buy the famous Odawara medicine *uirō*? *Uirō*! *Uirō*!

ASAHINA *(In feigned surprise)*: How remarkable. It's the cry of a vendor of *uirō* medicine.

MAIZURU: It has been so long since I heard someone cry out those words.

SUKETSUNE: I have heard of the vendor's tongue-twisting sales pitch. It would be fine entertainment for this occasion. Call him here for a demonstration.

ASAHINA: As you wish, sir. *(Facing the* hanamichi.*)* You medicine peddler over there! Lord Suketsune, he who is resplendent in divine favor, summons you. Today you have more good fortune than you could ever have wished for. So, boldly, fearlessly, and without any shame . . .

(The COURTESANS *each take one step forward as they complete his summons.)*

TORA: Please, quickly, be so kind as to . . .

SHŌSHŌ: Come here, won't you.

GORŌ *(Shouting from inside the* hanamichi *curtain at the same time the women speak)*: Thank you very much.

*(*GORŌ *advances down the* hanamichi *to the accompaniment of offstage shamisen music* [taimen sanjū].*)*

ŌZATSUMA *(Describing the Uirō family compound in Odawara)*:

The establishment bears a proud sign in gold, / a compound with eight buildings, / three facing the main street. / On the gables of these palatial buildings, / the morning sun sparkles on sprinkles of gold leaf. / From the family crest wafts the scent of chrysanthemum— / it is a house with a sterling lineage.

*(*GORŌ *strides down the* hanamichi, *turns with a flourish, and does a* mie *at* shichisan. *He wears a light blue kimono and* haori. *A light blue scarf covers his head down to his sidelocks. On his back, he carries two lacquer medicine boxes, red and black, rigged as a sort of backpack. The larger one says "Uirō from Odawara." The* MEDICINE PEDDLER*'s face has simple lines accentuating his features, and his appearance is that of a strong, handsome youth.)*

GORŌ *(Bowing, but speaking confidently to both characters and audience)*: I humbly beg your indulgence.

CHINSAI: You are dressed just like the vendors in the woodblock prints but are even more handsome. What, may I ask, is your name?

GORŌ: My name is . . . well, that is to say . . .

ASAHINA: Why, I'm flabbergasted. What has come over you? Your name is . . .

GORŌ: My name is . . . Ichikawa Danjūrō XII!

(The actor states his professional name. The audience applauds.)

CHINSAI: Since you have told us your name, we are eager to hear your special sales pitch. Come now, sell your wares, sell your wares!

TORA: Yes, none of us can bear to wait any longer.

MAIZURU: Today, put all of your spirit into it.

ASAHINA: The tongue-twisting patter . . . let it begin, let it begin!

GORŌ: I certainly wish to comply, but this is a great role, far beyond my modest stature, and *(taking in both the theatre and stage audiences)* with an audience composed of such fine people as you . . .

(More pass-along dialogue.)

SUKETSUNE: There's no need for you to hesitate like that . . .

MAIZURU: Exert yourself as you always do . . .

KISEGAWA: With interesting gestures and pantomime . . .

KAMEGIKU: Give it all of your strength . . .

ALL THE WOMEN: And do it for us, please!

GORŌ: In that case, I guess I'll go right over there, right over there.

*(*GORŌ *removes his backpack, which contains his medicine and is labeled in bold letters "Uirō." He proceeds to downstage center to the accompaniment of offstage percussion.)*

KAGETAKA: So, is this peddler someone you girls know?

TORA: Yes, on his rounds he comes often to the Ōiso pleasure district, selling his wares. That's when we see him.

SHŌSHŌ: You might say we know him quite intimately.

(The STAGE MANAGER *strikes the* ki *sticks and shouts,* "East and west, east and west!" *signaling the beginning of the stage announcement. All the actors come forward, kneeling in a single line across the stage, with the actor playing* GORŌ *at the center.)*

GORŌ (ICHIKAWA DANJŪRŌ XII) *(Addressing the audience)*: I beg your forgiveness for interrupting the play and thank you for allowing me to extend these formal greetings. *The Medicine Seller* that you are witnessing today is a play first performed by my father, Ichikawa Danjūrō XI, in 1940. Later, in 1978, I was fortunate to be able to perform *The Medicine Seller* using the same text. Today's play is dedicated to the celebrations accompanying the eight-hundredth anniversary of the Soga brothers' successful accomplishment of their long-sought-for revenge. It is my humble wish that you will sit back, relax, and take great pleasure in viewing this performance. *(Coughs formally to signal the end of the stage announcement.)* Ahem! Ahem!

(All actors return to their previous positions.)

ŌZATSUMA:

Now the *uirō* seller returns to his place and to his business.

GORŌ: As many of you present may already know, my father left Edo and moved fifty miles to the west, and settled in Rankanbashi, Ishikimachi, in the city of Odawara, province of Sagami. His name was Toraya Fujiemon but now he has taken the tonsure and a new Buddhist name, Ensai.

ŌZATSUMA:

Now let me tell of the origin of this miracle drug.

*(*GORŌ *gestures silently, summoning his formally dressed* STAGE ASSISTANT [kōken]. *He mimes giving an order to the* STAGE ASSISTANT, *who bows in obedience and then goes to the pack, which the peddler has placed at stage right, removes a shallow, circular medicine box, and gives it to* GORŌ. *All of this action takes place while the* ŌZATSUMA *chanters sing.)*

Once there was a Chinaman by the name of Uirō / who hailed from the land of Chin. / When he paid a visit to the Japanese emperor, / he revealed the medicine that had been kept a deep secret. / When he used the medicine, / he would remove it a single grain at a time / from a crease in his court cap, / and that is why the emperor bestowed upon the medicine / the name, Tōchinkō, / meaning 'Fragrance Permeating from Above.'

*(*GORŌ *holds the medicine box out in front of him in his left hand.)*

GORŌ: All of this notwithstanding, for those of you present who are still unaware of the powers of this medicine, should you swallow a mouthful of peppercorns or fall asleep with a terrible hangover, just place one grain of this medicine on your tongue . . . *(*GORŌ *mimes putting a grain in his mouth. He rubs his belly and mimes swallowing the medicine.)* Your belly will immediately settle and become calm, and your stomach, liver, and lungs will become healthy and full of vigor. A delicious fragrance will issue from your throat and your mouth will feel cool and refreshed. If taken with fish, fowl, mushrooms, noodles, or any other food, it effects a lasting cure to every illness—as if it were the work of a god. And it has another curious effect . . .

ŌZATSUMA:

Your tongue begins to move faster / than a carriage rolling down a mountain road / and has the strength to outrun, / barefoot, even a spinning top.

*(*GORŌ *dances to the accompaniment of this singing, always holding the medicine box in front of him in his left hand.)*

GORŌ: If it so happens that your tongue spins like this, neither arrow nor shield can stop you. What's this, what's this, what's this? It's starting to spin, it's starting to spin! Now the tongue-twisting patter begins like this *(deliberately)*: *a ka sa ta na, ha ma ya ra wa, o ko so to no, ho mo yo ro otto!* Don't bump into the little Buddha just ahead, don't fall in the gutter or bump into the wall as you stagger along. Raw cod in Kyo, raw in Nara, raw bonito . . . all together thirty-five pounds. It's coming, it's coming, what's coming? A blockhead of a little priest from Mount Koya. A hundred badgers, a hundred chopsticks, a hundred bowls of tea, eight hundred staves. Saber saddle, saber saddle, saber saddle three—all together saber saddle, saber saddle six. Peanut sweetpea, peanut sweetpea, peanut sweetpea three—all together peanut sweetpea, peanut sweetpea six. Whose long lance is it, the long lance lying on the lintel?

Soga Gorō (Ichikawa Ebizō X, later Ichikawa Danjūrō XII), delivers his elaborate pun-filled medicine sales talk. (Tsubouchi Memorial Theatre Museum of Waseda University)

Is the sesame stem there, that sesame stem, a true sesame stem? That surely is a real and true sesame stem. Rattle whee, rattle whee, the pinwheel sings. Roly-poly tumbler doll, roly-poly tumbler doll, you spilled it last night, you spilled it all. Bing, bang, bop. Dingaling, rattatat, bing, bang, bop! Dried octopus—if it falls, we'll boil it and eat it. What can't you eat even if it's boiled or grilled? Iron tripods and grates for the fire. Great bears and stone bears, tigers and bears come bearing stones . . . scariest among them is the ogre Ibaraki Dōji of Rashōmon by Tōji. He gobbled up five whole cups of boiled nuts, but he never ran away from Raikō. Silver carp, kumquats, mushrooms . . . and always for the last course, buckwheat noodles, rice noodles, wheat noodles . . . silly little children's doodles. A little under the little shelf in a little bucket is a little bit of a little bean paste! Little take the little ladle, scoop a little and give a little to me. Okay, that's all right. I understand. If I run through the rice fields of Kanagawa, Kawasaki, Hodogaya, Totsukawa and scrape my moxa cuts, it will be about seven miles. Fujisawa, Hiratsuka, Ōiso in such a rush, Koiso—now I've passed seven stations of the Tokaidō. Rising early, early at dawn, here in the Province of Sō, Odawara's fabulous Tōchinkō . . . known by one and all, high and low, the *uirō* blossom of flowery Edo. There, look at the cherry blossoms, and put your heart at ease. Little newborns, crawling babes, even babes still in the womb, I'm absolutely sure there's not a one who doesn't know how effective *uirō* is. "Dance, dance and get your shells crushed. Raise your horns 'cause here's my stick." Thick, thick eyebrows and the thin mortar in the pestle. Whack, whack! Mercy, mercy! I'll save you from your plight . . . all who have come here today, I must sell you some, I must give you some. Take a deep breath, for I invite the Healing Buddha himself, the master of all the medicine in the whole wide world, to be my witness . . . yes, paying respect to Him, won't you deign to purchase *uirō* from me? *(Spreads his arms, gesturing to the audience.)*

ŌZATSUMA:

So he declaims, never stumbling as his words flow.

CHINSAI *(Enthusiastically, in a high, piping voice)*: My goodness, your tongue was tripping at quite a pace. If I could speak lines as difficult as those just as I please, it should enable me to express just how I feel and win a woman's heart. Why, would you allow me to swallow a grain of your medicine?

GORŌ: It is easy to grant your request. Please give it a try.

*(*GORŌ *mimes giving* CHINSAI *a grain, and* CHINSAI *mimes swallowing it.)*

CHINSAI: There, that should do it. *(*CHINSAI *takes out his fan and holds it as if taking a singing lesson.)* Now, give me some sort of tricky tongue twister so I can test my powers.

GORŌ: Well now, let's see, . . . how would this be? *(He beats out a rhythm with his fan. Very rapidly.)* "Let's make tea, let's make tea, let's make tea standing under the tree, with the green teak tea tray, just you and me." Why don't you give that a try, sir?

CHINSAI: I see, good, good. How is this? . . . "Let's make tea, let's make tea, let's make it we three, sitting here by the teak tree. Silly Gorō dropped the tea bowl right on his knee . . . " Uh, oh . . .

(He chokes, unable to manage the tongue twister.)

ASAHINA: Hey, give it up!

CHINSAI: What have I done? I have embarrassed myself most shockingly!

GORŌ: Don't be so hasty. The medicine needs more time to take effect. Strike your hands together and you'll feel better.

CHINSAI: Will you strike my hands, will you strike my hands?

(He says this eagerly and sidles up to GORŌ *as if eager to be struck by the handsome peddler.* GORŌ *pushes him back to his left and does a* mie, *assuming a defiant posture.)*

GORŌ: No, but maybe I should strike elsewhere! *(Glares at* SUKETSUNE.*)*

SHŌSHŌ: Why, would you please strike a drum rhythm for us?

*(*GORŌ *seems intent on going toward* SUKETSUNE *to strike him, but* SHŌSHŌ*'s verbal intervention stops him.* CHINSAI, *twirling, is drawn to* GORŌ *as if by magical power.* CHINSAI *leans forward, putting his head, baldpate forward, under* GORŌ*'s left arm.* GORŌ *beats on* CHINSAI*'s pate as if it were a hip drum, while a real hip drum* [ōtsuzumi] *is played offstage.)*

GORŌ: And . . . Tap, tap tappety, tappety top, tappety top. Tippety tip, tippety tip, tip, tap, tappety, top.

(During the second sequence of taps, GORŌ *throws* CHINSAI *down and jumps over his supine body twice. He then rolls* CHINSAI *away to stage right.* GORŌ *glares at* SUKETSUNE *and strikes a threatening pose, but* TORA *and* SHŌSHŌ *come forward and stand on either side of him, preventing him from approaching* SUKETSUNE. GORŌ *and the two* COURTESANS *dance briefly, expressing his desire to strike and their stronger desire to prevent him from acting rashly.)*

ŌZATSUMA:

Going beyond Hakone, / Odawara's famous products—*uirō* and fish sausage— / he sells, waving bells, shaking bells.

*(*STAGE ASSISTANTS *hold up a large red cloth upstage center, and* GORŌ *retires behind it to adjust his costume and change his wig. The two* COURTESANS, *joined by* MAIZURU, *continue to dance downstage center, in front of the cloth.)*

Dancing along, swaying along the Tokaidō. / On the road the scent of plum wafts / and the Ōiso pleasure district / is all abustle in a grand banquet.

(The COURTESANS *retire and* ASAHINA *joins* MAIZURU *in a danced duet.)*
The beasts living on the slope of Mount Fuji / have heard—they frolic and gambol about.

*(*ASAHINA *does a humorous, mock heroic solo dance.)*

The snake is the favorite in the zodiac, / the rabbit jumps out of the group, / the deer leaps and prances, / the badger plays his belly drum, his own "eighteen" favorites, /

*(*CHINSAI *joins in and, playing the badger, beats his belly with his fists)*

and the boar is an acrobatic hooligan.

*(*ASAHINA *thrusts* CHINSAI *aside, and all actors clear the area downstage of the red cloth. The red cloth drops, revealing* GORŌ, *who now wears a wig with the elegant forelock sported by handsome adolescents.* GORŌ *struts downstage, stamping loudly. He thrusts both arms out of his overrobe, revealing a bright red underkimono, and poses defiantly, glaring at* SUKETSUNE.*)*

GORŌ *(Loudly)*: Suketsune, prepare to die!

SHŌSHŌ: No, wait! *(She rushes forward and grips* GORŌ*'s right sleeve.)*

ŌZATSUMA:

There's no need to be in such a rush. / Having done every tongue twister / in one of Danjūrō's renowned eighteen, / the wind of heaven blows in retribution after eighteen years; / splendid clouds of blossoms . . . / the *uirō* flower in full bloom.

(Near the end of this choral passage, GORŌ *does a strong sidling movement* [jirijiri] *and a* mie, *demonstrating his resolution to avenge his father's murder.)*

KAGETAKA *(Loudly, and with a flourish of his right arm)*: Seize him!

EIGHT GUARDS *(Shouting from offstage)*: Yes, sir!

*(*EIGHT GUARDS *enter from stage right. They do an energetic fight dance* [tachimawari] *with* GORŌ *to the accompaniment of offstage flute and percussion.* GORŌ *prevails and the combatants pose in a concluding* mie.*)*

SUKETSUNE: All of you, move back!

EIGHT GUARDS: Yes, sir!

(They move away toward the upstage wings, in two groups of four each.)

SUKETSUNE *(Intently)*: From your actions just now, would I not be mistaken in thinking that I am in the presence of the orphaned son of Kawazu no Saburō Sukeyasu?

GORŌ: I have nothing to hide any more. *(He produces a series of guttural snorts associated with* aragoto *acting.)* I . . . I . . . I . . . I . . . am Gorō Tokimune. Murderer of my father, prepare to die!

ASAHINA *(Shouting)*: Now, wait just a minute Gorō, don't be rash. *(Emphatically.)*
You must cooperate with your brother, wait for the proper time, and then attack.

Group pose at the final curtain *(hippari mie)* showing the fierce antagonism between Soga Gorō and Kudō, the man who murdered Gorō's father. Each character strikes a unique pose at the same moment. From left to right, Gorō's retainer Asahina (Bandō Hikosaburō VIII), Soga Gorō (Ichikawa Shinnosuke VII), courtesan Tora (Nakamura Shibajaku VII), courtesan Shōshō (Kataoka Hidetarō II), and the Soga family's enemy, Kudō Suketsune (Kataoka Nizaemon XIII). (Umemura Yutaka, Engeki Shuppansha)

GORŌ: If my older brother were here with me now, we would not go home empty-handed. How frustrating!

SUKETSUNE *(Commandingly)*: No, by no means will I send you home empty-handed. For you brothers who are so filial in spirit, I have a parting gift, a small token of my esteem.

(He throws a small packet onto the stage, wrapped in gauzelike material. GORŌ *picks it up and examines it.)*

GORŌ: Why, look at this! It's a map of where the camps will be set up at the hunt. We'll be looking for the one with the "plum blossom in a hermitage" crest.

(A passed-along dialogue sequence follows.)

KAGETOKI: Strung aloft, all over the hunting grounds . . .

KAGETAKA: Will be the familiar crest of Lord Yoritomo of Kamakura.

TORA: And, finally, the day will come when you can realize your hopes.

SHŌSHŌ: You'll perform remarkable feats, for you were raised as samurai.

KISEGAWA: To ensure the divining hairpin will indicate good fortune . . .

KAMEGIKU: And await your success in happy anticipation . . .

ASAHINA: We will set the living creatures free—

MAIZURU: The butterfly and the plover.

GORŌ: So, until that day . . .

SUKETSUNE: When we meet again at the hunting ground . . .

GORŌ: Farewell!

ALL: Farewell!

(When the flute plays a shrill note, all the actors move to their final positions and face upstage. GORŌ *and* SUKETSUNE *nod to each other as a signal, and all actors except the* GUARDS *turn to face downstage.* ASAHINA *and* SHŌSHŌ *stand on either side of* GORŌ, *restraining him from attacking his enemy.* GORŌ *holds out the map triumphantly in his left hand. The* EIGHT GUARDS *stand behind the rest of the cast holding their flower spears diagonally, replicating the slope of Mount Fuji, painted on the backdrop. As the tempo of the* ki *clacks increases, the curtain is pulled shut and the play ends.)*

Two-panel woodblock print by Utagawa Toyokuni III (1786–1864). Probably Ichimura-za, Edo, first month 1850. "Kajiwara Heizō Kagetoki" (Arashi Kichisaburō III) strikes a *mie*, holding an open fan overhead as he prepares to authenticate a valuable sword. The sword's owner, the elderly "mother- of-pearl craftsman Rokurōdayū" (Ōtani Tomoemon IV) and his "daughter Kozue" (Onoe Baikō IV) watch expectantly. (Tsubouchi Memorial Theatre Museum of Waseda University)

The Stone-Cutting Feat of Kajiwara

Kajiwara Heizō Homare no Ishikiri

Hasegawa Senshi and Matsuda Bunkōdō

TRANSLATED BY WILLIAM LEE

1730 TAKEMOTO-ZA, OSAKA

The Stone-Cutting Feat of Kajiwara

INTRODUCTION

The Stone-Cutting Feat of Kajiwara, known for short in Japanese as *Ishikiri Kajiwara* (Stone-Cutting Kajiwara), is a kabuki adaptation of what was originally a much longer history play *(jidaimono)* written for the puppet theatre by Hasegawa Senshi (dates unknown) and Matsuda Bunkōdō (dates unknown), better known simply as Bunkōdō. The puppet play was first performed in Osaka at the Takemoto-za in the second lunar month of 1730 and was adapted for kabuki the same year in Osaka. Its first Edo production was in 1795. The original play was entitled *The Plum-Blossom Reins of Miura no Ōsuke* (Miura no Ōsuke Kōbai Tazuna) and consisted of five acts. The present kabuki play is the final part *(kiri)* of the third act. It is set in 1180 and deals with the beginning of the Genpei War between the Genji (or Minamoto) and Heike (or Taira) clans. The emphasis in the puppet play is on the attempts of Genji leader Minamoto Yoritomo to raise an army and win converts from the Heike side, including Kajiwara Heizō Kagetoki. The play's principle sources are the *Mirror of the East* (Azuma Kagami) and *An Account of the Genpei Wars* (Genpei Jōsuiki), two chronicles of the Kamakura period (1185–1333), which, although covering much the same ground as the more famous *Tale of the Heike* (Heike Monogatari), contain additional historical and anecdotal information.

The play is characteristic of eighteenth-century puppet drama and contains many of the standard twists or dramatic devices *(shukō),* including surprising revelations of identity, the "return" *(modori)* or disclosure of a supposedly evil character's good intentions, and character substitution *(migawari).* While the overall theme of the original full-length play is Minamoto Yoritomo's effort to raise troops to attack the Heike enemy, *Stone-Cutting* consists of interwoven subplots involving characters other than Yoshitsune. The humble craftsman Rokurōdayū and his daughter, Kozue, who are sympathetic to the Genji, attempt to raise three hundred gold coins in war funds, and the play's title character, Kajiwara, shifts his allegiance from the Heike to the Genji while pretending otherwise. Three of the four action units turn on the sword of the play title, yet the real drama of the kabuki play centers on Kajiwara's personal conflicting loyalties. Kajiwara, who is mentioned in many historical accounts and appears in other kabuki plays, is usually portrayed in a negative light, due to both his shift in allegiance and his alleged slander of Yoritomo's younger brother, Yoshitsune. In the present play, he is treated rather sympathetically: the Heike are portrayed as villains and Kajiwara's decision to go over to the Genji is shown to be justified and not mere opportunism. The plot requires the actor to portray Kajiwara as a man struggling to maintain his composure and prevent the Heike generals from sensing his change of allegiance.

The play's four performance highlights are the inspection of the famous returned sword, during which Kajiwara realizes but is careful not to reveal the sword's significance; the test of the sword on two human bodies; Kajiwara's mimed narrative *(monogatari),* in which he explains his reasons for switching his allegiance to the Genji cause; and Kajiwara's demonstration of the sword's quality by cutting through the stone water basin. Kajiwara is at the center of all four of these moments, and his role clearly dominates the play. At the same time, a degree of variety is provided by the other roles, including—in addition to Rokurōdayū and Kozue—the villains and the prisoner.

The play is now a kabuki standard and has been performed more than seventy times since the end of the Second World War. This was not always the case, however. Records indicate that the play was very rarely performed during the nineteenth century. Although Ichikawa Sadanji I (1842–1904) occasionally acted Kajiwara during the Meiji era, Ichikawa Danjūrō IX (1838–1903), the leading actor of the day, considered Kajiwara a double-dealing samurai because of his change of allegiance and refused to play the part. Subsequently, however, the role became a favorite of such important actors as Nakamura Ganjirō I (1860–1935), Ichimura Uzaemon XV (1874–1945), and Nakamura Kichiemon I (1886–1954), and their portrayals—including a number during the war years themselves, despite the theme of switched allegiance—have given the play a firm place in the present repertory. Today, actors follow performance patterns, or *kata,* that were created by Uzaemon and by Kichiemon. The most striking difference between the two traditions occurs during the climax, the severing of the water basin. In the Kichiemon *kata,* Kajiwara slices the basin from in front, placing his back to the audience. In the Uzaemon *kata,* he stands behind the basin, facing the audience, and after cutting the basin in two, jumps forward between the two halves.

The translation is based on the text published in Toita Yasuji et al., eds., *Meisaku Kabuki Zenshū,* Vol. 3. Also consulted was Koike Shōtarō, ed., *Kabuki On-Sutēji,* Vol. 4. Stage directions were adapted and a few minor cuts to the text were made based on the January 1999 production of the play at the Kabuki-za in Tokyo. The opening sequence between the good lords and the villainous lords is often cut and many productions begin after Ōba and Matano already have entered.

CHARACTERS

KAJIWARA HEIZŌ KAGETOKI, *a Taira general, secretly in sympathy with* YORITOMO, *leader of the Genji forces*

ŌBA SABURŌ KAGECHIKA, *a Taira general*

MATANO GORŌ KAGEHISA, *brother of* ŌBA, *also a Taira general*

GOOD LORDS, *four in all, followers of* KAJIWARA

VILLAINOUS LORDS, *four in all, followers of* ŌBA *and* MATANO

ROKURŌDAYŪ, *an elderly mother-of-pearl inlay worker*

KOZUE, *daughter of* ROKURŌDAYŪ

NOMISUKE, *a prisoner condemned to death*

SAMURAI

ATTENDANTS

TANIYAMA HAYASUKE, *a messenger; the name is often changed to* KIKUBEI *when played by a leading actor*

STAGE ASSISTANTS, *black-garbed* kurogo

TAKEMOTO, *narrator and shamisen player who accompany the action*

(The curtain opens to offstage music [geza] *to reveal the entrance to the Tsurugaoka Hachiman Shrine in Kamakura. At center stands a large shrine gate through which can be seen the painted backdrop representing the shrine. A stone wall runs left and right from the gate. In front of the wall stand several plum trees in bloom, while a border of hanging plum blossoms* [tsurieda] *frames the set overhead. In front of the wall to the right of the gate is a stone water basin, and on the extreme left a bamboo lattice fence, before which a target has been set up. Two long benches covered with red cloth are on either side of the stage. In front of the right bench stand the* VILLAINOUS FEUDAL LORDS, *and in front of the left bench are the* GOOD FEUDAL LORDS. *All are dressed in formal garments* [kamishimo] *but with the vest part of their costumes slipped down over one shoulder. Each maintains a bowing position.)*

FIRST GOOD LORD: Well, gentlemen, the present is said to be a time of peace, but now Yoritomo has left Hirugakojima and gone into hiding . . .

SECOND GOOD LORD: Waiting for his opportunity, he has not yet raised his banner and will not be taken in . . .

THIRD GOOD LORD: Therefore we diligently spend our time in target practice . . .

FOURTH GOOD LORD: For with our enemy's whereabouts unknown, we must not be negligent in our preparations for battle.

(The four VILLAINOUS LORDS *step forward.)*

FIRST VILLAINOUS LORD: Don't fall into a panic! There is no need to worry about Yoritomo and his men . . .

SECOND VILLAINOUS LORD: Even if he tries, he will not be able to muster more than a trifling force . . .

THIRD VILLAINOUS LORD: As the saying goes, it would be like throwing straw against the wind; if he dares do battle . . .

FOURTH VILLAINOUS LORD: Our well-trained archers will show their mettle and . . .

ALL VILLAINOUS LORDS: Raise the victory cry!

TAKEMOTO:

Just at that moment, / striding slowly, / enter Ōba no Saburō / and Matano no Gorō.

*(*ŌBA SABURŌ KAGECHIKA *and* MATANO GORŌ KAGEHISA *enter on the* hanamichi *to the accompaniment of offstage music. Both are dressed in elegant formal attire,* ŌBA *in gold and* MATANO *in green, red, and gold.* MATANO *wears a wig with a pompon-shaped forelock, and his face is made up in red to emphasize his villainous character. His manner is pompous and arrogant. They are accompanied by two* SAMURAI *and two* ATTENDANTS *each.)*

FIRST GOOD LORD: Lord Ōba! Lord Matano! Men, be on your best behavior!

MATANO: So, I see you have been doing archery practice, hoping no doubt to receive the blessings of this shrine as you prepare for illustrious exploits in battle.

FIRST VILLAINOUS LORD: Whether we will receive the blessings of the gods, I cannot say. But Yoritomo, who was exiled to Hirugakojima, is biding his time, waiting for an opportunity to start a rebellion. Therefore, we have been diligently doing target practice.

ŌBA: That is well and good, but an exile like Yoritomo will not be able to muster more than three hundred horsemen. Attacking us would be like a mole trying to dig up Mount Fuji. Were I to capture him alive, I would bake him in the sun and then skin the rogue. How mortifying that he managed to slip through my grasp.

FIRST VILLAINOUS LORD: We will soon discover his hiding place, and when we do, we will quickly engage him in battle.

SECOND VILLAINOUS LORD: Just as you, Lord Matano, slew Sanada no Yoichi at Ishibashiyama, we are also looking forward to achieving honor on the battlefield.

SECOND GOOD LORD: But that was a night battle, and, as they tried to pin each other down in the total darkness, it was impossible to see whether it was Lord Matano or Sanada on top. It was a very dangerous bout . . .

FIRST GOOD LORD: And Lord Matano was fortunate to be the victor.

FIRST VILLAINOUS LORD: Good heavens! Are you reproaching Lord Matano for his valiant deed?

FIRST GOOD LORD: No, that's not what I meant.

FIRST VILLAINOUS LORD: But what you said just now! If you take your words and examine them one by one, what else could they mean?

THIRD GOOD LORD: Gentlemen! What is this quarrel? Lord Matano's defeat of Sanada has already met the approval of Lord Kiyomori in Kyoto, and everywhere people are speaking of it as an unparalleled act of valor.

ŌBA: It's just as you say. The fact is, the defeat of Sanada was my brother's work. You others should try to emulate his feat.

FIRST GOOD LORD: Yes, indeed, we should all strive to be his equal in battle.

VOICE: Lord Kajiwara Kagetoki!

ŌBA: What!?

ALL: Kagetoki!

(The TAKEMOTO *chanter and shamisen come into view, seated on a small platform at left.)*

TAKEMOTO:

As the music plays, / entering down the runway, / comes Kajiwara Heizō Taketoki, / a valiant warrior / of uncommon strength.

(To offstage shamisen and hip and shoulder drum music [daishō iri], KAJIWARA *enters along the* hanamichi. *He is dressed in elegant formal attire with a gold and black arrow feather pattern and wears both a large and small sword. He is followed by three* samurai, *also dressed formally, and two* ATTENDANTS *carrying carpets, tea implements, and lunch boxes. They stop at* shichisan. KAJIWARA *strikes a* mie.*)*

MATANO: Lord Kajiwara! If we had known you meant to make a pilgrimage to the shrine today, we would have insisted on coming together.

ŌBA: But since we didn't know your intentions, we have come on our own.

KAJIWARA: Lord Ōba, Lord Matano. Your presence here at the shrine bespeaks your faith and devotion. *(Looks around at the others.)* And gentlemen, the archery practice you are engaged in, that is also most laudable.

FIRST VILLAINOUS LORD: Lord Kajiwara!

ALL VILLAINOUS LORDS: Please, this way!

KAJIWARA: Thank you.

TAKEMOTO:

Accepting the invitation, / Kajiwara approaches the party, / bowing to all.

*(*KAJIWARA *bows to those assembled and takes a position at center.)*

KAJIWARA: The recent victory at Mount Ishibashi was no doubt due to the divine grace bestowed on our archers by the gods of this shrine. Truly, there is nothing like faith in the power of the gods.

MATANO: Lord Kajiwara, attributing a victory to the power of the gods is unbefitting a warrior. Neither my brother nor I, for instance, have ever read the Kannon Sutra. The slaying of Sanada, the so-called demon warrior, was the result of my own physical strength. Likewise, it was fear of the wrath of Heike swords that caused Yoritomo to take to his heels. And I hardly need to mention my brother's unsurpassed knowledge of military tactics. Even though one might think of it as a divine blessing, it is not. Our pilgrimage here today is simply a diversion, a means to pass the time. For a warrior to say that victory was achieved only through the grace of the gods is a disgrace. I would suggest you refrain from voicing such sentiments.

TAKEMOTO:

Kajiwara laughs derisively.

KAJIWARA: Ho, ho, ho. I see I've injured your pride with my inconsiderate words. I humbly beg your pardon. Nonetheless, I, Kajiwara—let Hachiman, the god of war, be my witness—have never believed that praying to the gods for divine assistance means dishonor to a warrior. Were we to think so, then that would mean that Sakanoue Tamuramaro, who long ago defeated the demon of Suzukasan through the divine grace of the goddess of mercy, would also lose his reputation, and that would be most regrettable, would it not? Ha, ha, ha.

TAKEMOTO:

His polished words / ring true with wisdom.

KAJIWARA: In any case, because of your great military exploits, we have won the recent battle. But now, in this tranquil setting, we have a beautiful view of plum blossoms. Fortunately, I have brought along some refreshments. Men, get them ready.

SAMURAI: Yes, my Lord.

TAKEMOTO:

Swiftly obeying, / they bring out the boxes, / beautifully adorned / with gilt lacquer work.

(The ATTENDANTS *spread out two red carpets and bring out the boxes of food and drink.* KAJIWARA *sits on the carpet on the left, and* ŌBA *and* MATANO *sit on the carpet on the right.)*

KAJIWARA *(Taking a sake cup)*: Now, let's have a drink!

(He passes the cup to the ATTENDANTS, *who serve* ŌBA *and then* MATANO. *Ad-lib dialogue* [sutezerifu].*)*

TAKEMOTO:

Like unto the scattering blossoms, / an old man, his youth spent, / holds onto a treasure, / a blessing in an hour of need. / Like a placid river / or a well-tempered blade, / deep and hardened / is his resolve. / Accompanied by his daughter, / the two enter, / bearing a sword.

*(*ROKURŌDAYŪ *enters along the* hanamichi. *He carries a sword wrapped in a cloth. He is followed by his daughter,* KOZUE.*)*

ROKURŌDAYŪ: Look! There's his lordship over there. Hurry up, hurry up!

TAKEMOTO:

Joyfully they approach.

(ROKURŌDAYŪ and KOZUE come onto the stage, where the LORDS notice them.)

FIRST VILLAINOUS LORD: Here are some unfamiliar townspeople. Why have you come . . .

ALL VILLAINOUS LORDS: Before Lord Ōba?

(ROKURŌDAYŪ and KOZUE advance and kneel.)

ROKURŌDAYŪ: Forgive us for intruding, but I have a favor to ask of his lordship. I am Rokurōdayū, a mother-of-pearl inlay worker from Katabiragatsuji. I have learned that Lord Ōba is interested in a sword in my possession, and since I am suddenly in need of money, I have come to the shrine today in hopes of selling it. If his lordship were to buy it, I would be most grateful.

TAKEMOTO:

Fervently, / he makes his entreaty.

ŌBA: So you are Rokurōdayū, the inlay worker I have heard about. And you want to sell the sword? Excellent! I have long been interested in buying just such a sword. Fortunately, we have with us today Lord Kajiwara, a noted connoisseur of fine blades. What a fortuitous coincidence. If the sword meets his approval, I will pay the price you demand.

ROKURŌDAYŪ: Thank you, my lord. Daughter, what are you doing? Hurry up and take the sword to his lordship!

KOZUE: Yes, father.

(She unwraps the sword and is about to take it to ŌBA.)

ŌBA: Woman, give the sword to Lord Kajiwara. Lord Kajiwara, may I call upon your excellent judgment?

TAKEMOTO:

An obedient girl, / she does as she is told.

KOZUE: Oh, father, what a blessing. Just think! How fortunate we are to have someone like Lord Kajiwara inspect our sword!

TAKEMOTO:

Full of gratitude / and happiness too, / she bows innocently, / and Kagetoki himself / cannot suppress a smile.

(KOZUE places the sword on the carpet next to KAJIWARA and bows.)

KAJIWARA: The sword of Rokurōdayū, or whatever his name is, is his family's heirloom. To pass judgment on it would be most impertinent on my part. Please allow me to decline.

ŌBA: But if you refuse, what will we do? Unless you judge the sword, I can't grant him his request and buy it. Therefore, please, I entreat you.

Kajiwara Heizō Kagetoki (Matsumoto Kōshirō IX) begins to examine the sword, sliding it from its protective cloth wrapping, while Rokurōdayū (Nakamura Kichiemon II) and Kozue (Nakamura Fukusuke IX) carefully watch. (Umemura Yutaka, Engeki Shuppansha)

MATANO: That's right. This is a sword my brother has long been hoping to get his hands on. Humbly, I beg you.

KAJIWARA: If you put it that way, it would be rude of me to refuse. Very well, I will look at the sword.

TAKEMOTO:

Suddenly he stands / and, as he approaches / the water basin, / Rokurōdayū calls out.

(KAJIWARA *stands and walks slowly toward the water basin.*)

ROKURŌDAYŪ: Lord Kajiwara! It is enough that you deign to examine our sword. There is no need for you to wash your hands.

KAJIWARA: Whoever's sword it is, if it is a work of fine craftsmanship it deserves a samurai's respect. A sword is the military symbol, as the mirror represents civil authority. They are both the gods' gifts to Japan, and one must not be disrespectful of either.

TAKEMOTO:

Standing on decorum, / he purifies himself at the basin, / then raises the sword / in a sign of reverence.

(KAJIWARA washes his hands at the stone basin. He then returns to the carpet, kneels, and raises the sword reverently to his forehead before unwrapping it. He reaches into his kimono and pulls out a sheet of paper, which he places in his mouth to prevent his breath from spoiling the blade. He then slowly unsheathes the sword and begins to examine it from various angles and with growing excitement. The intensity of his focus on the blade is one of the play's acting highlights.)

The unsheathed sword / shines without a blemish / like a raging waterfall / lit by the midnight moon / on a cloudless night. / Oh wondrous blade, / perfect in every way / from hilt to tip.

KAJIWARA *(Shouting, as the paper drops from his mouth)*: Amazing!

TAKEMOTO:

In spite of himself, / he cannot take his eyes / from the remarkable blade.

KAJIWARA *(Keeping his eyes fixed on the blade)*: An uncommonly splendid piece of work! Incompetent though I be, I, Kajiwara Heizō no Kagetoki, have in-spected many swords in my day, but never before have I held in my hands one as fine as this. There does not appear to be a signature, but there can be no doubt but that it is the work of a great master. *(He seems lost in thought for a moment but then returns to his senses.)* Lord Ōba, buy this sword and cherish it as a family treasure.

TAKEMOTO:

Like a true expert, / he does not mince words. / And the verdict / is much to Ōba's liking.

(KAJIWARA picks up the paper, wipes the blade, returns the sword to the sheath, and wraps it. An ATTENDANT takes the sword and places it beside ŌBA.)

ŌBA: It is surely a fine sword to have received such praise. I am delighted. Old man, I will grant your request and buy the sword. What is your price?

ROKURŌDAYŪ: Thank you very much. As for the price . . . *(He hesitates and turns toward KOZUE.)* Daughter?

KOZUE *(Gesturing to ROKURŌDAYŪ to speak up)*: Tell him!

ROKURŌDAYŪ: Yes, well . . . if you were to pay me 300 gold pieces, I would be most grateful.

ŌBA: Three hundred gold pieces? That's a steep price. But since I have had Kajiwara's expert opinion, I will agree. Retainer! Hand over the money to this man.

SAMURAI: Yes, my lord. *(Prepares to take out the money.)*

MATANO: Wait! Excuse me brother, but aren't you being a bit hasty? Though the workmanship may appear superior even to the legendary Kusanagi sword, for all we know, its edge may be no better than that of a common fish knife.

SECOND VILLAINOUS LORD: Indeed, it is just as Lord Matano says. Until its cutting edge is tried, the sword cannot be judged a masterpiece. You would do well . . .

ALL VILLAINOUS LORDS: To test it thoroughly!

ROKURŌDAYŪ: Lord Matano, in all deference, the quality of a sword's edge should be apparent on inspection. What's more, it has been said that this sword can cut through two bodies laid one on top of the other easier than a knife slicing through bean curd.

MATANO: Be quiet! Old man, you want the money so bad I don't doubt you would try to swindle us by making up such a story. I find your pushy sales tactics abominable.

TAKEMOTO:

Kajiwara cannot / let this scolding go by / unchallenged.

KAJIWARA *(Growing indignant)*: Lord Ōba, Lord Matano! I have inspected the sword as you have requested. You will disappoint Rokurōdayū now if you don't buy it.

FIRST GOOD LORD: Yes, indeed, you slight Lord Kajiwara by doubting his judgment.

SECOND GOOD LORD: But if proof be needed, and there are two prisoners condemned to death . . .

THIRD GOOD LORD: Then, why not have them brought here, so you can see for yourselves . . .

FOURTH GOOD LORD: How easily the sword can cut through two human bodies?

ŌBA: Yes, that's the answer. Somebody, go to the prison and bring back two convicts sentenced to death!

SAMURAI: Yes, my lord. *(Exits upstage left.)*

TAKEMOTO:

Swiftly obeying, / he goes off running, / while at the same moment, / a messenger arrives, / panting for breath.

*(*TANIYAMA HAYASUKE *enters along the* hanamichi, *carrying a letter case, and proceeds onto the main stage.)*

TANIYAMA *(Kneeling)*: I am Taniyama Hayasuke, in the service of Lord Sukechika, the lay priest of Itō. Having gone first to your lordship's residence, I was informed that you had come to this shrine. I therefore rushed here in all haste, for I bear an urgent message.

TAKEMOTO:

Making his introduction, / he hands over the letter.

*(*TANIYAMA *removes a letter from the case and hands it to* ŌBA.*)*

ŌBA: You are to be commended for your haste on the long journey. *(Reads the letter.)* Well! Yoritomo has called on Miura no Ōsuke for support and taken refuge at Miura's castle in Kinugasa.

FIRST VILLAINOUS LORD: We had heard that Yoritomo somehow secretly withdrew from Sugiyama in Doi . . .

SECOND VILLAINOUS LORD: And with only seven men left made good his escape via Manazurugasaki. As everyone knows, Lord Sukechika bears a grudge toward Yoritomo.

THIRD VILLAINOUS LORD: And now this urgent message from him. Let us be off quickly, so that we too might have a chance to strike the rogue Yoritomo.

FOURTH VILLAINOUS LORD: Indeed, the time has come for us to earn our fame as warriors.

ALL VILLAINOUS LORDS: To battle! *(They stand and are about to leave.)*

FIRST GOOD LORD: Now is not the time . . .

SECOND GOOD LORD: For hotheaded indiscretion.

ALL GOOD LORDS: Wait!

VILLAINOUS LORD I: We will not!

ŌBA: Men, don't get into an uproar. If you want my opinion, I, too, think we should wait.

TAKEMOTO:

As he restrains his men, / just then . . .

(The SAMURAI *who had gone to the prison returns.)*

SAMURAI: My lord. I checked the prison records carefully, but there is only one convict who is sentenced to death. How shall we manage the test of the sword?

ŌBA: I am interested in this sword, but if we can't conduct a proper test, the deal is off. I won't have one prisoner cut in half for no good reason. Old man, take the sword and go home.

TAKEMOTO:

Rokurōdayū receives the dismissal / with doubt and confusion. / Seeing the look on his face, / his daughter, Kozue . . .

KOZUE: Father, please get up. Our efforts have been to no avail. Your request will not be granted. Therefore, as we discussed earlier, I will go into service in a brothel and soon raise the money. Don't worry yourself sick. Please, let's go back home and talk things over.

(Seeing the sadness on ROKURŌDAYŪ *'s face, she begins to weep. She dries her tears on the hand towel* [tenugui] *tucked into her obi.)*

TAKEMOTO:

How moving the sight, / as she tries to dissuade her father / for his own peace of mind. / But then Rokurōdayū, / who just a short time ago, / turned down his face in dejection, / suddenly . . .

ROKURŌDAYŪ *(Raising his head)*: Oh, how foolish of me. I completely forgot. Some ten years ago, Lord Itō had one of his men inspect the sword. At that time, the test on two human bodies was performed and a certificate was issued verifying the sword's quality. It is usually kept with the sword, but in my haste to come here, I grabbed the sword and forgot about the certificate. I will send my daughter for it, and when your lordship has inspected it, we can complete the sale.

ŌBA: What is that? You say Lord Itō had the test performed and made out a certificate? Well, hurry up and get it!

ROKURŌDAYŪ: Yes, at once. Daughter! It s a nuisance, but I want you to go home quickly and bring back the paper.

KOZUE: Yes . . .

ROKURŌDAYŪ: It's in the drawer in the cabinet under the Buddhist altar. Be careful on your way back. Make sure you don't drop it!

KOZUE: Don't worry. I will go at once and be right back.

ROKURŌDAYŪ: I m sorry for having to make you do this.

KOZUE: Father, please wait for me.

TAKEMOTO:

As she stands, / tucking up her kimono . . .

(She rises and heads toward the hanamichi, *stumbling on the way.)*

ROKURŌDAYŪ: Careful! Are you all right?

KOZUE: Yes, I think so.

ROKURŌDAYŪ: Take your time if you have to. Sorry . . .

KOZUE: Yes, yes . . .

TAKEMOTO:

Heading for home, / she hurries off, / while Rokurōdayū / stretches to catch a glimpse / of her retreating form.

*(*KOZUE *leaves by the* hanamichi. ROKURŌDAYŪ, *silently sobbing, rises and steps forward to watch her as she leaves. Removing a handkerchief from his kimono, he wipes away his tears. He then returns to his earlier position, kneels, and turns toward* ŌBA.*)*

ROKURŌDAYŪ: Lord Ōba, I have another request to make of you. Please conduct the test right away. Use the one prisoner available, and I will provide the second body. If you will then pay the three hundred gold pieces, I will be much obliged.

TAKEMOTO:

The surprising request / causes Ōba / to raise his voice / in anger . . .

ŌBA *(Angrily)*: Old man, are you out of your mind? Do you realize what you are asking? Perform the test like that and you will be a dead man!

MATANO: So, the old man doesn't mind if he loses his life, as long as he gets the money! Not a very discriminating fellow, is he? Ha, ha, ha.

ROKURŌDAYŪ: Your surprise is well founded. *(To offstage shamisen music* [meriyasu].*)* Life may be more precious than a thousand, or even ten thousand, pieces of gold. But in times of honor or loyalty, it can be as easy to dispose of as the most worthless rubbish. The white hairs on my head are the snows of the seventy-nine winters I have seen. Whether it will be tonight or tomorrow, death will surely come soon. And now, out of duty, my daughter is facing hardship. Though I am an old man, I cannot sit by calmly and do nothing. In exchange for my life, and as a token of my compassion, I offer this sword, the price of which has been fixed at three hundred gold pieces. When I think of how much it will benefit my daughter, I do not regret losing my life. But I have a further request to make to you. Please, conduct the test at once, before my daughter returns. I said earlier that Lord Itō had issued a certificate of the sword's quality. That was a lie. If my daughter were here, she could not stand to see me die before her eyes. I therefore made up the story about the certificate in order to send her home. But it is for her that I so desperately need the money. When my daughter returns, please explain to her what happened and make payment to her. Now, Lord Ōba, Lord Matano. You have heard my request. Please use me for the test. I entreat you . . . *(Puts his hands together in prayer.)* I beg you.

TAKEMOTO:

He has had his say / and stated his reasons. / Yet the request, / however unavoidable, / is pitiable all the same. / As for Ōba, / his desire for the sword / makes him resolute, / and his resolve, / though a virtue of sorts, / makes him blind to pity.

ŌBA: I have heard your request and am prepared to carry out the test as you wish. I will make sure your daughter gets the money. I can see your heart is set on getting the three hundred gold pieces, which, no doubt, represents a great sum for a man in your station. It is good that you have contrived to have your daughter absent. For her sake, if the sword cuts through two bodies, I will not mind paying five hundred or even one thousand.

ROKURŌDAYŪ: Then you will grant my request? Thank you. I am most grateful.

TAKEMOTO:

Hearing Ōba's decision, / Rokurōdayū pours out his gratitude, / then stands and proceeds / to the site of his execution.

(ROKURŌDAYŪ bows deeply, while an ATTENDANT spreads out a straw mat at center. ROKURŌDAYŪ removes his haori *and kneels down on the mat.)*

ROKURŌDAYŪ: Now, men, if you please, the ropes!

MATANO: Tie up the old man!

ATTENDANT: Yes, my Lord.

TAKEMOTO:

Quickly obeying, / Rokurōdayū is bound / from head to foot.

(ATTENDANTS bind ROKURŌDAYŪ with ropes, tying his hands behind his back.)

MATANO: Bring out the prisoner.

SAMURAI: At once, sir.

TAKEMOTO:

On the order, / the prisoner is brought out. / He is bound with ropes / and walks with unsteady steps.

(GUARDS bring out the prisoner, NOMISUKE, from upstage left. He is dressed in a simple, pale blue kimono, and his upper body and arms are bound with ropes. His head is unshaven and he has a beard. He is led to center and made to kneel on the mat next to ROKURŌDAYŪ.)

ROKURŌDAYŪ *(Turning to NOMISUKE)*: Unusual circumstances have made you my companion on the road to death. Let us be friends as we depart this world.

TAKEMOTO:

His voice quivers / as he speaks . . .

(The following comical monologue is spoken to shamisen accompaniment.)

NOMISUKE: Oh, woe is me. I have been undone by a pint of sake. I just had the one drink, but that was enough to arouse my wrath. And then I killed my master. It's the sake's fault: it was stronger than I thought. And now I'm like one of those sake casks wrapped up in a reed mat. I've been aging in prison and have been brought out now to be the toast on this ceremonial occasion. Or am I just the chaser to ward off a hangover? Actually, my insides feel more like chilled sake, and these tears that I shed are the dregs. If I were the drink of the Immortals, I might yet be saved, but I'm more like the sake from Itami, which some call Itami-ache—I can feel the pain already—for I'm about to be cut in half to test a sword. What a cruel fate.

TAKEMOTO:

His distress is evident, / as he awaits his execution.

(NOMISUKE begins to weep and then is led away by the GUARDS to prepare for his death.)

ŌBA: Brother, let us see your skill. Test the sword! *(Hands the sword to MATANO.)*

MATANO: Yes, brother. We shall now see if this sword really can cut two bodies in half.

TAKEMOTO:

He takes the sword / and stands . . .

(MATANO takes the sword, stands, and begins to walk toward the execution mat.)

KAJIWARA *(Angrily)*: Lord Matano, wait! Earlier you and your brother asked me to inspect the sword. But now, without any further ado, you have taken it upon yourselves to perform the test. I consider that an insult.

TAKEMOTO:

His face shows his anger . . .

(KAJIWARA rises on one knee and strikes a mie.*)*

MATANO: Lord Kajiwara, don't lose your temper. For having inspected the sword, I'll gladly turn the job over to you. I'm sure you will give us a fine example of how the test is done.

TAKEMOTO:

He presents the sword / to Kajiwara.

*(*MATANO *poses in a* mie *as he offers the sword to* KAJIWARA.*)*

KAJIWARA: Good, that is as it should be.

TAKEMOTO:

Taking the sword, / Kajiwara proceeds / with deliberate steps . . .

*(*KAJIWARA *receives the sword from* MATANO, *stands, and approaches* ROKURŌDAYŪ. *The* ATTENDANTS *remove the carpets. Black-robed* STAGE ASSISTANTS [kurogo] *place stools* [aibiki] *for* KAJIWARA, ŌBA, *and* MATANO *to sit on.)*

KAJIWARA: Rokurōdayū, I have heard your story and understand. In old age, a man naturally cares more about his children than his own life. I have volunteered to carry out your request in order to make your end as dignified as possible. Your worries about your daughter have led you into darkness, but just as the light of the moon can illuminate the darkest night, so will the truth of this sword shine forth, thus ensuring a brighter future. Rest assured of that and cast aside the gloom that clouds your heart.

ROKURŌDAYŪ: I am much obliged. To know that my end will be by the hand of Lord Kajiwara, the greatest samurai in the entire Kantō region, brings me more comfort than could the most venerable priest with all his sutras. I have only one more thing to ask of you. Please receive the money from Lord Ōba, and when my daughter returns, kindly give it to her. If you will agree to that, I can go to my death with a light heart. And please, don't have any qualms about performing the test.

TAKEMOTO:

A single teardrop / wells up in his eye, / more moving / than a flood of tears. / Kajiwara turns away / and, raising his sleeve, / wipes away his own tears.

*(*KAJIWARA *stands and goes to the rear of the stage. He sits on a stool and pushes the upper part of his formal garment down over both shoulders.)*

Meanwhile Kozue, / having failed to find / the precious document, / has returned / and come upon this scene.

*(*KOZUE *comes running onto the* hanamichi.*)*

KOZUE: Who tied up my father? What crime could he have committed?

(She attempts to go to him but is stopped by the GUARDS.*)*

GUARD: Don't come any nearer! Stand back!

KOZUE: Whoever you are, I won't stand back until you tell me what's going on.

TAKEMOTO:

She bursts out crying.

(The GUARDS *block* KOZUE *'s way with their staffs. She kneels down and weeps.)*

ROKURŌDAYŪ: It's natural that you should be surprised, but whatever happens next, try to stay calm. You will understand later. Lord Kajiwara, you must find my daughter's lamentations bothersome. I'm sorry to hold things up with this inconvenience. Now, without any further delay, please enjoy what you have to do.

TAKEMOTO:

He tells him to enjoy it, / but at that moment, / his daughter realizes / what is about to happen / and is overcome with sadness.

KOZUE: So, you are throwing away your life in order to test the sword? You must be greedy to want to sell the sword so badly. But think about my own feelings. What value has a sword that kills a beloved parent? Lord Kajiwara, please don't strike him. Try the sword on my body instead. Please have mercy on him.

TAKEMOTO:

She pleads in tears / for his ropes to be untied. / Rokurōdayū / raises his voice in anger.

ROKURŌDAYŪ *(Angrily)*: Quit carrying on with your unreasonable request. Three hundred gold pieces is a good price for this worn-out body of eighty years. Trying to protect me goes against filial piety. Besides, to fail now when the money is as good as in our hands would not be doing your duty to your husband. Don't be a childish coward!

TAKEMOTO:

She sees her father's anger / but does not heed his words.

KOZUE: Whatever the circumstances, I cannot see how turning my back when my father is about to be killed can be called fulfilling my duty to my husband. If I had known you were going to do this, I would have secretly sold myself to a brothel to raise the money. That's the way a woman's mind works. But you didn't even think of that. Instead, in your greed, you decided to deceive me by sending me to get the certificate so that you would buy yourself a chance to die, leaving me to grieve later. I won't hear of it. Lord Kajiwara, please forgive me.

(She attempts to go to KAJIWARA*'s side but is stopped by one of the* GUARDS *holding a staff.)*

KOZUE: Please let me pass. *(She turns to face* ŌBA, MATANO, *and the other* LORDS, *but they all look away.)* Oh, there are so many of you. Is there no one who will intercede on my behalf? My lord, I beg you!

TAKEMOTO:

How pitiable the sight / as she pleads in vain, / first to one then another / of the samurai leaders.

(In a dancelike stylized struggle, KOZUE *attempts to get past the* GUARDS, *who block her way with their staffs.)*

Now Rokurōdayū / has had enough.

ROKURŌDAYŪ: Oh, how embarrassing! Please, take the girl away.

TAKEMOTO:

The guards swarm / around the poor girl / and push her away.

(The GUARDS *attempt to drive* KOZUE *away with their staffs. She resists, is struck, and collapses in a heap.)*

ŌBA *(Striking a* mie*)*: Lord Kajiwara!

MATANO: If you will, sir?

KAJIWARA: Certainly!

*(*KAJIWARA, *who all this time has had a look of concern on his face, suddenly changes his mood. He resolutely draws the sword and motions to an* ATTENDANT. *The* ATTENDANT *brings a bucket and ladles water on the blade in order to purify it.)*

TAKEMOTO:

Kajiwara gives the signal, / and the two bodies are prepared. Rokurōdayū / closes his eyes / in resignation, / while the Ōba brothers / and all the others / watch with rapt attention. / There is a flash in the air / as Kajiwara raises / the sword of polished steel.

(On KAJIWARA*'s signal,* ROKURŌDAYŪ *is laid down and a dummy representing the prisoner is placed on top of him by the* GUARDS, *who squat down in front of the pair of bodies, their backs to the audience.* KAJIWARA *stands behind, raises the sword, and poses in a* mie. ŌBA *and* MATANO *fix their eyes on him.* Tsuke *beats, followed by large bell* [hontsurigane] *and wind pattern* [kaze no oto] *drumbeats. Plum blossoms fall.)*

TAKEMOTO:

Then with a loud cry, / he brings the sharp blade down / with a powerful swing. Suddenly a sound / and a cloud of dust. / Behold, / Kozue comes running.

*(*KAJIWARA *lets out a cry as he brings down the sword. The dummy is cut in two, but only the ropes binding* ROKURŌDAYŪ *have been severed. The* GUARDS *carry away the two parts of the dummy. The audience chuckles at seeing red paint where the dummy has been cut in half. All are amazed at the outcome. Meanwhile,* KOZUE, *having regained her senses, also has witnessed the scene. She rushes to her father's side, weeping. Examining his body, she is surprised to discover that he has not been cut.)*

Kajiwara Heizō Kagetoki (Nakamura Karoku V) prepares to test a famous blade by cutting through two stacked bodies with one stroke. A prisoner, Nomisuke (actually a dummy), lies on top of Rokurōdayū. (Umemura Yutaka, Engeki Shuppansha)

KOZUE: Father, you're not wounded, are you? *(She attempts to get him to sit up.)*

ROKURŌDAYŪ: Nonsense, I've been cut clean through and I'm dying. I was a test for the sword, and now I'm finished.

(He sits up and runs his hands over his body, feeling for a wound.)

KOZUE: No, you haven't been cut.

ROKURŌDAYŪ *(Bewildered)*: How can that be?

TAKEMOTO:

The sword's failure / proves Kajiwara's judgment wrong, / and his look of consternation / is greeted by derisive laughter.

MATANO: Ha, ha. Well, this is how I thought it would turn out.

FIRST VILLAINOUS LORD: It is just as you suspected, Lord Matano. Is it a masterpiece or a fake?

SECOND VILLAINOUS LORD: Is he an expert or a blind man? There is a world of difference . . .

THIRD VILLAINOUS LORD: Between Kajiwara's reputation and what we have actually seen.

FOURTH VILLAINOUS LORD: The whole thing was a ridiculous affair.

ALL VILLAINOUS LORDS: Ha, ha, ha.

(In the meantime, an ATTENDANT *has ladled water on the sword.* KAJIWARA *wipes the blade, sits on a stool, and returns the sword to its sheath. As he readjusts his upper garments, an* ATTENDANT *wraps the sword and returns it to* ROKURŌDAYŪ.*)*

MATANO: Well, we were almost swindled out of three hundred gold pieces. But now, brother, shouldn't we be returning to our posts?

ŌBA: If you had not advised me to test the sword, I would have bought it, trusting Lord Kajiwara's judgment, and thus become a laughingstock.

How would I have been able to face my men? To think of it! That damned swindler!

MATANO: You are quite right, brother.

ŌBA: Well, then, men.

ALL: Yes, sir.

TAKEMOTO:

And with that / they take their departure . . .

(To offstage drumbeats, ŌBA *and* MATANO *exit upstage right. The* VILLAINOUS *and* GOOD LORDS *and the rest of* ŌBA *and* MATANO*'s party follow them.* KAJIWARA *and his* SAMURAI *and* ATTENDANTS *remain onstage, along with* ROKURŌDAYŪ *and* KOZUE.*)*

Rokurōdayū remains, / gnashing his teeth / in vexation.

ROKURŌDAYŪ: Oh, how mortifying. I won't be able to live down the shame.

TAKEMOTO:

Much to Kozue's distress, / Rokurōdayū attempts / to take his own life.

*(*ROKURŌDAYŪ *tries to kill himself with the sword. He is stopped by* KOZUE.*)*

KOZUE: Father, what are you doing? You're lucky to be alive, and now you want to kill yourself? Have you gone mad? Are you possessed by some evil demon? *(Grips his arm.)*

TAKEMOTO:

She clings to him . . .

ROKURŌDAYŪ: For some strange reason, I have escaped death, but as far my honor is concerned, I might as well be dead. *(Offstage shamisen and flute accompaniment begins.)* I am determined not to live any longer, but let me try to explain why. I have cherished this sword since I was a child. Many people praised it, and I was foolish enough to believe I was in possession of a rare and priceless piece of workmanship. I know nothing about swords but was proud of it all the same and bragged about it to my son-in-law. I told him not to worry, that I would get the money he needed for Yoritomo's war chest. Now my only answer to him will be my death. Farewell.

(Pushing KOZUE *away,* ROKURŌDAYŪ *tries to kill himself again.* Tsuke *beats. He is stopped by* KAJIWARA, *who kneels beside* ROKURŌDAYŪ.*)*

KAJIWARA: It would be a shame to defile such a blade with the blood of suicide. The test on the two bodies was of no import. This is indeed a rare sword, one that even demons and spirits would fear. What saved your life was not the dullness of its blade: I purposely cut only the ropes that bound you, a feat which could only be done with the most finely made and balanced blade. Put away your doubts and set your mind at rest. If you will let me have the sword, I will pay the price you demand.

TAKEMOTO:

Father and daughter / are surprised / at the words.

*(*KAJIWARA *takes the sword away from* ROKURŌDAYŪ. ROKURŌDAYŪ *and* KOZUE *look at each other in disbelief.)*

ROKURŌDAYŪ: You mean you want the sword?

ROKURŌDAYŪ and KOZUE *(Together)*: Thank you, thank you.

TAKEMOTO:

Their joy is evident . . .

*(*ROKURŌDAYŪ *and* KOZUE *bow to* KAJIWARA *in gratitude.)*

KAJIWARA: I wanted to keep it a secret from Ōba and Matano and therefore purposely didn't say anything about it, but the name Hachiman is written on the back of the scabbard. I assume that means you are in some way related to the Genji family, whose tutelary god is Hachiman. I thought there might be something like that behind this business. Come now, you needn't have any scruples about telling me. Who are you?

TAKEMOTO:

His courteousness / pleases Kozue.

KOZUE: Since you have been so kind to us, I see no reason to keep any secrets from you. Actually, my husband . . .

ROKURŌDAYŪ *(Agitatedly)*: What are you saying?! Lord Kajiwara knows we're on the Genji side, so there's no point in denying it. But he is a Heike general! It would be the height of indiscretion to tell him about your husband. After all, we have our own obligations, and an enemy is an enemy. If Lord Kajiwara takes offense at that and wants to kill us, so be it! *(Defiantly.)* Whatever happens, don't tell him anything.

TAKEMOTO:

He spits out his words / and stands firm.

KAJIWARA: Oh, a splendid example of unflinching loyalty. Now that you've shown me where your heart lies, let me make my own confession. *(He addresses his* SAMURAI *and* ATTENDANTS.*)* Men, you may go.

SAMURAI: Yes, sir.

TAKEMOTO:

They get up and / prepare to leave.

(The SAMURAI *and* ATTENDANTS *leave upstage left.)*

Kajiwara looks around / and lowers his voice.

KAJIWARA: Come closer. *(*KAJIWARA *stands up and casts a glance around.* ROKURŌDAYŪ *and* KOZUE *approach.* KAJIWARA *sits on a stool at center. Sections of the following narrative* [monogatari] *are taken over by the* TAKEMOTO *as the actor mimes the action with his fan, but these are not indicated here.)*

Recently at Sugiyama in Doi, while we were routing the last of the Genji forces, I caught sight of Lord Yoritomo, the head of the Genji clan, hiding in a hollow tree. I gave chase, thinking how fortunate I was to have spotted such a prize. Without any trouble, I caught him and, holding him down with one knee, was going to strike off his head. And then—and how strange it was—suddenly my whole body froze and I could not move. When I looked upon him I was struck by his noble appearance, which defied even the accounts I had heard. Here, I thought, was a personage of unsurpassed character, one blessed by nature with the qualities of a great samurai leader and endowed with the three virtues of wisdom, benevolence, and valor. I could see by the brilliance in his eyes that this was a man destined to lead Japan into a new era of samurai glory. For a humble soldier like me to strike him, I thought, would be sacrilegious.

TAKEMOTO:

How awe-inspiring his tale.

KAJIWARA: When I think about that moment, I am reminded that my family formerly served the Genji. At the time of the battle, I was fighting on the side of the Heike, but what held me back was a sense of loyalty to my ancestors' former lords. I thought it best to bide my time and wait for Lord Yoritomo's fortunes to rise. I therefore spared his life and steered Lord Ōba away from him. Now, outwardly I serve the Heike, but in my heart I am a samurai whose life is devoted to the protection of Lord Yoritomo. And I am ready to throw my life away for his sake. Such is the sense of loyalty and devotion I feel. The world may shun me and label me a traitor or slanderer, and after my death my reputation may be defamed, but I don't mind. Now that I have told my story, I hope that you at least will understand what really lies in my heart.

TAKEMOTO:

Leaving nothing unsaid, / he has told his tale.

ROKURŌDAYŪ: Now that I have heard your story, I am greatly relieved. The only thing that troubles me is the sword. Since I still don't have any proof of its quality, I am loathe to force it on you. And without proof, how can I be sure that I really owe my life to your skill?

KAJIWARA: I will show you proof. Now, let me see . . . of course! That's just the thing!

TAKEMOTO:

Saying "Just the thing," / he rises, and, / taking them by the hand, / leads them to the basin, / where they see their reflections / in the water.

*(*KAJIWARA *looks around and spots the stone water basin. He leads* ROKURŌDAYŪ *and* KOZUE *to the basin and has them sit beside it.)*

KAJIWARA: Now look, both of you. *(He slips his upper garment down over his right shoulder. During the following,* KAJIWARA *speaks his lines in time to the rhythm of* TAKEMOTO *shamisen music* [nori]*.)* They say a dead man has no reflection, but you can clearly see yours in the water. I shall now give you proof of this magnificent sword's cutting edge. *(Draws the sword and crosses to the front of the water basin.)*

TAKEMOTO:

One foot thick / is the stone basin, / and, if cut in half, / so too will be / the reflections / of father and daughter . . .

*(*KAJIWARA *stamps his feet and raises the sword above his head. To* tsuke *beats, he brings the sword down, slicing the basin, which falls apart in two pieces.* ROKURŌDAYŪ *and* KOZUE *are amazed.)*

KOZUE: Oh, Father!

KAJIWARA: Truly, a remarkable sword!

Kajiwara Heizō Kagetoki (Ichikawa Shinnosuke VI, later Ichikawa Danjūrō XII) cuts through a stone water basin with a single stroke to prove the sword's unique quality. (Tsubouchi Memorial Theatre Museum of Waseda University)

Kajiwara Heizō Kagetoki (Ichimura Uzaemon XVII), having severed the stone basin with one stroke, steps forward triumphantly and strikes a pose with the sword held overhead. (Tsubouchi Memorial Theatre Museum of Waseda University)

ROKURŌDAYŪ: And no less remarkable, the man who wields it!

*(*KAJIWARA *strikes a* mie. *He then wipes the sword on his sleeve and returns it to the sheath. He hands it to* ROKURŌDAYŪ.*)*

TAKEMOTO:

Kajiwara Kagetoki, / a true samurai / of the Genji line, / one destined / to rise to eminence / and serve as protector / of the Kamakura shogun / with this rare / and matchless sword. / Truly, he is / the very model / of a samurai.

ROKURŌDAYŪ: Now I am truly relieved.

KAJIWARA: Rokurōdayū, you and your daughter accompany me to my house. There I will pay you for the sword.

ROKURŌDAYŪ: Thank you, we will gladly follow you.

*(*KOZUE *helps* KAJIWARA *readjust his garments.)*

KAJIWARA: Come!

TAKEMOTO:

As his name suggests, / Kajiwara—or "blacksmith field"—can be likened / to a splendid sword / forged by a master smith. / And to this day / his family crest / with its arrow notch design / has served to remind us / of this great warrior / and the way of the samurai.

*(*ROKURŌDAYŪ *puts on his* haori, *while* KOZUE *wraps up the sword in the cloth.* KAJIWARA *stares at the water basin and strikes a* mie. *He then moves to the* hanamichi, *followed by* ROKURŌDAYŪ *and* KOZUE. Ki *beats. Offstage curtain-closing drum pattern* [dangire] *and the sound of temple bells* [teragane]. *The curtain is drawn, leaving the three characters isolated on the* hanamichi *for an "outside-the-curtain" exit* [maku soto no hikkomi]. KAJIWARA *looks at* ROKURŌDAYŪ *and* KOZUE *and smiles. He then exits, striding slowly down the* hanamichi *to the accompaniment of offstage shamisen and drum music.* ROKURŌDAYŪ *and* KOZUE *follow him at a distance. A single* ki *beat, followed by ceremonial drum and flute music* [shagiri].*)*

Two-panel woodblock print by Utagawa Kunisada I (later Toyokuni III, 1786–1864). Nakamura-za, Edo, ninth month 1827. "Abe Yasuna" ("Onoe Kikugorō" III) kneels contritely before his wife, Lady "Kuzunoha" ("Segawa Kikunojō" V). (Tsubouchi Memorial Theatre Museum of Waseda University)

Lady Kuzunoha
Kuzunoha

Takeda Izumo II

TRANSLATED BY CODY M. POULTON

THE ABENO WEAVING HOUSE
Abeno Hataya no Ba

THE INNER ROOM
Oku Zashiki no Ba

THE SHINODA FOREST JOURNEY
Shinoda no Mori Michiyuki no Ba

1734 TAKEMOTO-ZA, OSAKA

Lady Kuzunoha

INTRODUCTION

Lady Kuzunoha is part of a five-act, puppet theatre history play *(jidaimono)* by playwright Takeda Izumo II (1691–1756), first performed under the title *A Courtly Mirror of Ashiya Dōman* (Ashiya Dōman Ōuchi Kagami) in 1734. The full-length play is about the dynastic struggle *(ōdaimono)* between two court families during the reign of the Emperor Suzaku (930–946). The rarely performed Acts I, III, and V show Dōman, traditionally dramatized as a court villain, transformed by Izumo into a hero. Act II concerns Dōman's opponent, Yasuna, who goes mad with grief when his lover Sakaki dies. This is the source of the popular kabuki dance piece *Yasuna* (translated in Volume 3 in this series). Act IV is about Yasuna and his love for Sakaki's sister, Kuzunoha, whose form miraculously has been taken by the spirit of a white fox.

Lady Kuzunoha takes up the story at its climactic point, where Fox-Kuzunoha must give up her young son, Dōji, so the child can be properly raised by its human mother, Lady Kuzunoha. In events prior to this, court diviner Kamo Yasunori dies and Yasuna and his rival, Dōman, both aspire to be appointed his successor. But the secrets of his art of divination are passed on to Dōman, and Yasunori's adopted daughter, Sakaki, in love with Yasuna, kills herself in despair. Yasuna, driven mad with grief, wanders in the forest of Shinoda, where he meets and falls in love with Sakaki's little sister, Kuzunoha, a girl who so resembles Sakaki that Yasuna almost believes that his beloved has come back to life. Yasuna marries Kuzunoha and begets a child, Dōji. Unknown to Yasuna, however, Kuzunoha's place has been taken by the spirit of the white fox of Shinoda.

The scene translated here begins six years later. Yasuna and Fox-Kuzunoha are living in rural retirement when the real Lady Kuzunoha arrives with her parents. Fox-Kuzunoha's rapid appearances and disappearances soon make it evident that Yasuna has in fact taken up with Kuzunoha's double. Realizing that she can no longer keep up the pretense, Fox-Kuzunoha regretfully leaves her husband and child. In one version of the final scene, Dōman encounters Dōji, who has gone to Shinoda Forest with his father in search of his mother. Impressed with the boy's unearthly wisdom (Dōji is secretly prompted in his answers by his fox-mother), Dōman passes the secrets of divination to the boy and renames him Seimei.

Abe Seimei (921–1005) was a historical personage, and tales of his magical feats were recorded in such late-Heian period works as *The Great Mirror* (Ōkagami) and *The Tales of Uji* (Uji Shūi Monogatari). Seimei established a venerable line of court magicians who specialized in a form of divination based on the Chinese classic *I-Ching*, renamed *Tsuchimikado*. The family was still in charge of practicing divination at court during the Tokugawa period. Legend had it that Seimei's mother was a fox. Foxes are typically portrayed in Japanese folklore as shape-shifters, tricksters, and spell casters. There is still a shrine to Kuzunoha in Shinoda Forest, and within its precincts is a well in which, it is said, she gazed on her reflection while on her flight from Yasuna and her boy.

The story of the fox of Shinoda was already a conventional theatrical "world" *(sekai)* when Izumo wrote his play. A puppet drama entitled *The Shinoda Wife* (Shinodazuma) was staged in 1674, and the famous puppet theatre dramatist Ki no Kaion (1663?–1742) wrote a play on the same subject. Izumo's play incorporates a legend from Izumi province about a hunter who saved a wounded vixen; the vixen returned the favor by assuming the form of a beautiful woman and marrying the man. Some years later, she disappeared, leaving a poem, "If you long for me, / Come seek me in Izumi, / where, in the forest of Shinoda, / you'll find your Kuzu / of the clinging vine." The hunter goes to Shinoda Forest, where he finds the body of a fox who had committed suicide. This poem serves as a kind of lyrical climax in Izumo's play. The phrase "Kuzu of the clinging vine" is an attempt to render *urami no kuzunoha*. The leaves of the kudzu *(kuzunoha)* were a poetic epithet for jealousy and regret *(urami)*, but the word *"urami"* can also be written to mean "seeing the future," underscoring the prophetic powers of the fox-mother and her son.

Japanese folklore is rife with tales of animals who, assuming the form of women, marry and beget children, and this motif is frequently employed in plays. Its appeal has much to do with the way in which it illustrates not only an important link for the Japanese between the human and the natural world but also the erotic otherness of the opposite sex. Izumo returned to the fox motif again with the character of Fox-Tadanobu in *Yoshitsune and the Thousand Cherry Trees* (Yoshitsune Senbon Zakura, 1747; trans. Jones 1993).

The story of Yasuna, Fox-Kuzunoha, and their son highlights the private pathos of maternal love, a theme far more appealing than the arcana of Heian politics, the subject of Dōman's "world." Edo-period audiences, composed largely of commoners, could identify with the high and mighty only if their problems were brought down to earth, and the fox-mother motif was an excellent emotional device for leveling social differences. Twentieth-century novelist Tanizaki Jun'ichirō, in his story *Arrowroot,* notes that folk songs associated with the fox of Shinoda were still sung by Meiji-period maids and apprentices in Osaka, their lyrics evoking the keen homesickness these country folk felt for their mothers back home. Many scholars also suggest that Izumo's play expresses a veiled critique of feudalism. Kabuki women and children, who are frequently sacrificed according to the harsh code of duty *(giri),* serve to throw into high relief the contradictions and cruelty of the feudal system. The expendability of Tokugawa women is summed up in the phrase "wombs are on loan," meaning that a woman's sole function was to bear children. In the play, once she has fulfilled this office, Fox-Kuzunoha is no longer essential to the institutions that will determine her boy's fortunes. Yet she cannot abandon her abiding love for her child or for her husband.

Over the years, both text and staging have undergone numerous changes. In particular, the motif of doubling is cleverly exploited, providing opportunities to display the special effects *(keren)* unique to each. The play's first production was noteworthy for featuring, for the first time, the use of three-man puppets in a scene in which two identical retainers of Yasuna (one a fox-spirit) save the lives of Lady Kuzunoha, Yasuna, and Dōji. A kabuki version was staged the next year in Kyoto, and the first production in Edo was in 1737. A dance play *(shosagoto)* based on Fox-Kuzunoha's flight to Shinoda, *The Wild Chrysanthemums by the Forest Where I Dwell* (Waga Sumu Mori no Be no Rangiku) was staged in 1804. The version of *Lady Kuzunoha* translated here is similar to this dance play in that it presents her journey *(michiyuki)* in song and dance. The original puppet play and other kabuki versions feature the more vigorous action of the loyal retainer Yokanbei and his fox double Yakanbei. In some versions, a female retainer (yet another fox) saves Yasuna and the child.

The role of Fox-Kuzunoha is technically demanding, involving a number of quick changes. Nakamura Baigyoku III (1875–1948) initiated the practice of playing the two roles of Lady Kuzunoha and Fox-Kuzunoha in 1894. The special effects scene where the fox-wife writes her poem on the paper screens holding the brush in her mouth while cradling her child—first staged in 1802—provides considerable scope for virtuoso acting. There are also special vocal requirements for this role: Kuzunoha betrays her nature through so-called "fox talk" *(kitsune kotoba).*

Balancing the play's reputation for trickery, the beautiful *takemoto* lyrics—especially during the child separation sequence *(kowakare)*—help evoke enormous sympathy for the tragic fox-mother. Though this scene and its lament *(kudoki)* is a showpiece for her, the drama also provides tragic magnitude to Yasuna: his passions drive him to the edge of madness and death, and his dilemma—torn between his love for three identical women (one of whom is a fox)—makes for powerful drama.

This translation is based on the script for a June 1998 production at the Kokuritsu Gekijō (National Theatre of Japan) in which much has been trimmed away that would divert attention from the story of Fox-Kuzunoha and her separation. Dōman is erased entirely, as are Akuemon and his henchman. Similarly, Yasuna's groping of Kuzunoha to determine whether she is human or a fox has been deleted (as it commonly is in performance) because of its distracting lewdness. Other texts consulted include the puppet text in Tsunoda and Uchiyama, eds., *Shin Nihon Koten Bungaku Taikei,* Vol. 93; a kabuki version in Toita Yasuji et al., eds., *Meisaku Kabuki Zenshū,* Vol. 3; and Koike Shōtarō, "*Kuzunoha* Saiken" (A Close Look at *Kuzunoha*).

CHARACTERS

ABE YASUNA, *a gentle, romantic man, a disciple of the court diviner Kamo Yasunori*
SHINODA SHŌJI, *a samurai, father of* LADY KUZUNOHA
SHIGARAMI, SHŌJI*'s wife*
LADY KUZUNOHA, *daughter of* SHŌJI *and* SHIGARAMI
FOX-KUZUNOHA, *a fox who assumes the identity of* LADY KUZUNOHA
ABE DŌJI, *son of* YASUNA *and* FOX-KUZUNOHA
SAMURAI ATTENDANTS
PALANQUIN BEARERS
STAGE ASSISTANTS, *black-garbed* kurogo
TAKEMOTO, *narrator-chanter and shamisen player who accompany the action*

The Abeno Weaving House

(A humble cottage with straw-thatched roof in Abeno, south of Osaka. The room at left is a workshop with a loom, its walls covered with bamboo latticework. A three-foot square window with paper screen is open to reveal a red clay wall inside and an entrance to the workshop; at left is a Shinto altar with doors decorated with ritual paper streamers, a sprig of holy evergreen, and a flask of sacred sake. Down left is a thatched gate, and, at right, a shed and an entrance to the house with a rope curtain. The curtain opens to the song "A Persimmon Grows Next Door," sung offstage by FOX-KUZUNOHA. Ki *clacks are heard, signaling the beginning of the play. The stage is empty as the* TAKEMOTO *sings.)*

TAKEMOTO:

In Abeno, / by a reed fence hard by the hallowed / Sumiyoshi Shrine and Tennō Temple, / a scene where father makes his rounds / to pray for his child's rising star, / while mother minds the boy, / her flying shuttle a toy to while away the hours / as she spins her heart's colors into her loom. / Her cares and sorrows are the warp and weft of her weave.

(The sound of the loom comes from the room at right. Enter DŌJI. *The child runs down the* hanamichi *to rapid* tsuke *beats and stops at* shichisan. *He strikes a* mie, *then moves to the stage and enters the door of the residence, stopping at the straw matting that denotes the floor of the interior. He is wearing a child's kimono and obi. In one hand, he carries a small pouch with a drawstring; in the other, a bamboo pole on which is tied a dragonfly. He trips and falls at the gate, then strikes another* mie, *to two* tsuke *beats.)*

DŌJI: I'm home now, mama!

TAKEMOTO:

No sooner has he called / than his mother rushes out from the weaving house.

(Enter FOX-KUZUNOHA. *She is dressed in a rustic kimono with apron and sashes to tie back her sleeves. She is holding a cotton towel* [tenugui]. *An offstage shamisen plays.)*

FOX-KUZUNOHA *(Scolding gently, with motherly concern)*: Are you up to your tricks again, boy? Look at you! All covered in mud! Why, just yesterday your papa scolded you for this bad habit of yours, spending all your time killing bugs. "You'll never amount to anything if taking life is what gives you pleasure now," he said. Have you forgotten? What would your mother do if you were to hurt yourself while your father's out? I forbid you leaving the garden and getting into trouble! Come now, come here!

*(*DŌJI *obediently goes to his mother, who takes him in and brushes off his kimono.)*

DŌJI *(In a high-pitched voice)*: Mama, I'm sleepy.

FOX-KUZUNOHA: Come, I'll give you some milk. Then to bed with you.

(To offstage singing, FOX-KUZUNOHA *lifts the child in her arms and takes him behind a low screen up left center to put him to sleep.)*

TAKEMOTO:

Suckling at his mother's breast, / what dreams will the boy encounter?

(The child having fallen asleep, she comes out and kneels center.)

FOX-KUZUNOHA: Children are such thoughtless creatures. Look at him now, would you—fast asleep already. *(Pause.)* Now, back to the kimono I was weaving you.

(Rises and exits to room at left, looking back with concern at her child.)

TAKEMOTO:

She sets to work at the loom again. / "A persimmon grows next door." / Sweet thing she is, at first sight, / scarcely sixteen, or seventeen, perhaps. / And now, an elderly couple in travel dress, / *(singing)* through flowers and withered grasses, / they make their way.

*(*SHŌJI *enters from the* hanamichi, *dressed in field-*hakama, *two swords, and sedge hat, followed by* SHIGARAMI, *in travel dress, carrying a cane and sedge hat. They are followed in turn by two* BEARERS *carrying a closed palanquin in which* LADY KUZUNOHA *is riding. An offstage shamisen plays during their dialogue.)*

SHŌJI: I'm dead on my feet, wandering all over the country like this. You must be feeling worse for wear, too.

(They proceed to the main stage.)

SHIGARAMI: Aye. I thought it'd be just a little further, but there's no getting past the fact that I'm not as young as I used to be. The man said we're almost there. *(*SHŌJI *goes to the palanquin to get* LADY KUZUNOHA.*)* That house yonder must be Lord Yasuna's place. Go call on him for us.

(The same actor playing FOX-KUZUNOHA *enters as* LADY KUZUNOHA *via a trap underneath the palanquin. Dressed as a "red princess"* [akahime], *she alights from the palanquin and kneels center.)*

LADY KUZUNOHA *(Eagerly)*: Then, that is Lord Yasuna's house? Hurry, let me see him!

SHIGARAMI *(Shamisen continues)*: Old man, I can well understand our daughter's haste. I, too, would have words with him. Go to the house and call for him.

SHŌJI: I see what you mean. Come to think of it, it's been six years already since he left. Not a single word all this time whether he lived or no, and though our hearts haven't changed, it's hard to fathom what's been on Yasuna's mind. Let me go speak to him first, then I'll call you both. *(Pause.)* Till then, hide yourselves in that shed over there.

LADY KUZUNOHA: We'll hide ourselves for just a little while, papa, but hurry. Let me see him.

SHŌJI: That's a good girl. Quickly now, inside.

*(*SHIGARAMI *and* LADY KUZUNOHA *hide in the shed up right and close the sliding wooden door behind them. The actor playing* LADY KUZUNOHA *then descends down another trap underneath the shed and proceeds with yet another quick change to reappear as* FOX-KUZUNOHA.*)*

SHŌJI *(Enters the house and calls out)*: I say, is anyone home? Heavens! Seems no one's here. *(Paces back and forth, then goes to the window at right.)* I say! Is anyone home?

*(*FOX-KUZUNOHA *peers out through the interior window, a white cotton cloth covering her hair and hiding the actor's princess wig. Only the front half of her costume has been changed, and a black-garbed* STAGE ASSISTANT [kurogo] *holds it in place from behind. Shamisen music plays offstage.)*

FOX-KUZUNOHA: Hello? Who is it?

SHŌJI *(Seeing her)*: Why, how did you manage that? *(Stares.)*

FOX-KUZUNOHA: Excuse me?

(Slams shut the window and quickly returns to the shed. SHŌJI *runs around to the front of the house.)*

SHŌJI: Old woman, daughter! Come out, quick.

(She comes out of the shed with LADY KUZUNOHA, *who kneels between her parents.)*

SHIGARAMI: What now, old man?

SHŌJI *(Agitated)*: What now, you say! This is most strange. Our daughter's in that room, weaving!

SHIGARAMI: Eh? Nonsense. What are you talking about? How could Kuzunoha be over there, too, weaving cloth? In this wide world, surely there's any number of look-alikes.

LADY KUZUNOHA *(Anxiously)*: Someone like me, at Lord Yasuna's . . . ?

SHŌJI: Aye, but look-alikes are, generally speaking, like crows and crows, or snow and snow. This is of another order altogether. I swear to you, our daughter was there—in very name and form. If you doubt me, go to that window and see for yourself.

LADY KUZUNOHA *(Agreeing)*: Mama, the way papa talks, perhaps it's the truth after all.

SHIGARAMI *(With a touch of finality)*: As you say, your father wouldn't lie to us.

TAKEMOTO:

The three gaze at each other, nodding in agreement. *(The women return to the shed.)* / As they hide themselves, Yasuna returns.

(To the accompaniment of an offstage song, YASUNA *enters onto the* hanamichi. *He is dressed simply in a black and grey kimono, with a single sword in his obi. He carries a round, reddish, lacquered sedge hat. A pinwheel is tucked into his obi at the back and peeks out over his shoulder.)*

SHŌJI: Why, isn't that Lord Yasuna I see?

*(*YASUNA *stops at* shichisan.*)*

YASUNA: Oh, is that really you, Lord Shōji? *(Bows respectfully.)*

SHŌJI: You came at just the right time. How good it is to see you again!

YASUNA *(Surprised and delighted, he approaches* SHŌJI*)*: Indeed, it is. You haven't changed at all! I'm so glad.

TAKEMOTO:

It is no wonder they are overjoyed.

YASUNA: You've found my house, I see. Come, come in, please.

TAKEMOTO:

He makes to enter, but Shōji grasps his sleeve.

SHŌJI: First, I've something to give you.

YASUNA: Give me?

SHŌJI: Our daughter, your betrothed. Shigarami, bring out the girl.

SHIGARAMI *(To* LADY KUZUNOHA*)*: Come, come. No need to be shy.

*(*SHIGARAMI *leads* LADY KUZUNOHA *out of the shed, the latter acting bashful at the sight of* YASUNA. *As their eyes meet, she shyly turns away, moves toward him, and then away, but her mother urges her back again.* LADY KUZUNOHA *gracefully kneels, hiding her face behind her sleeves. She is between* YASUNA *on her left and her parents on her right.)*

TAKEMOTO:

Dragged out against her will to meet him, / and though bereft of speech, / Kuzu's countenance betrays her heart.

(Both LADY KUZUNOHA *and* YASUNA *look embarrassed.)*

YASUNA *(Thinking this is some kind of prank)*: Well, well! You've gone quite out of your way for me. It would seem she met up with you while I was out. Did you have her change and bring her back here so that you could have a little joke on me? You should know better, Kuzu. What's the meaning of dressing up so that you'd look like you just arrived with your parents? Ha, ha, ha! *(Taps* LADY KUZUNOHA*'s shoulder playfully. She rises and moves away to her mother.* SHŌJI *countercrosses to* YASUNA, *who kneels.)* Well, what can I say? What a stroke of luck for the old couple! Listen, let me tell you our tale. *(*YASUNA *places his hat and pinwheel on the floor as he begins his narrative. An offstage shamisen plays.)* She came to my rescue in Shinoda Forest when I was about to put an end to my life after my run-in with that villain, Akuemon. It's been six years now since we fled that place. We made a home for ourselves here and gave birth to a son as well, our boy, Abe no Dōji. I've been meaning all this time to go beg your forgiveness, thinking I'll do it today or perhaps tomorrow, that telling you what a fine grandson he's grown up to be might give you some small consolation for the shameless liberty I took with your daughter. Easier said than done, however. Eking out the living of a *rōnin*, I've not been able to do as I please. In deference to your grandson, I'd be eternally grateful to you were you to forgive me for all my indiscretions. *(Gesturing toward* SHIGARAMI, *who is seated at right with* LADY KUZUNOHA.*)* Mother, please put in a kind word for me to your husband.

TAKEMOTO:

He bows deeply and begs forgiveness.

*(*YASUNA *bows gracefully, with deep humility.)*

SHŌJI: Why, Lord Yasuna, this is no time for apologies! The fact of the matter is, something very, very strange is going on. When I arrived here a moment ago, somebody was weaving. Go look for yourself.

(All the while, one can hear the loom at work in the weaving house. YASUNA *rises and moves toward the house.)*

YASUNA: I truly hadn't paid it any attention, but if my wife is here *(wonderingly)*, who's weaving?

(He stealthily crosses to the window, left, and peeks in. Suddenly, reacting to what he sees, he reels back in shock. To TAKEMOTO *singing, he moves distractedly from side to side at center. In perfectly timed movements, he returns to the gate, puts on his straw sandals* [zōri], *stumbles against the gatepost, steps in a spinning motion out the gate, closes the gate, and poses in perplexity against the post, right hand in kimono at his chest.)*

TAKEMOTO:

So muttering, he rises and goes to look. / Pale with shock, he quickly returns.

YASUNA: A Kuzu there, and a Kuzu here as well. What's this?

TAKEMOTO:

What, indeed? He is astounded. / Looking inside, he is amazed; gazing at the girl before him, / he is dumbfounded and cannot speak, nor stand, nor sit. / This unexpected shock has left him quite baffled. / Yasuna considers the matter carefully.

YASUNA: Whichever, forgive me, but please hide in the shed . . . till I decide on a proper course of action.

SHŌJI: Indeed, there must be something behind all this. *(To* LADY KUZUNOHA.*)* Now, go with your mother, and wait where you were.

SHIGARAMI: We'll wait, but you get some answers from Lord Yasuna. Come, girl! Into the shed with you.

LADY KUZUNOHA: No! No! I'll stay here and cry myself to death!

SHŌJI *(Sharply)*: Have some sense, child! Are you not the daughter of a samurai? You're too fond by half! If you've no sense of your own, I'll give you something to think about.

SHIGARAMI: Listen to what your father says. Come, I'll join you.

TAKEMOTO:

Mother gently coaxes her daughter back into the shed. / Shōji watches them go.

(To TAKEMOTO *singing,* LADY KUZUNOHA *and* SHIGARAMI *rise. The girl, exchanging longing glances with* YASUNA, *is led off into the shed by her mother, as the latter bows to* YASUNA *and closes the door. The men kneel opposite each other.)*

SHŌJI: Imagine our shock, Lord Yasuna, when we discovered two Kuzus here. It's no wonder you, too, were amazed. Surely this is the work of some kind of goblin, perhaps a long-nosed *tengu.* This is no time for the faint of heart. Take courage, then, Lord Yasuna. Go find out what it is.

YASUNA: Aye, you needn't concern yourself there. A disciple of the wizard Kamo Yasunori, I'll bring what's obscure to the light of understanding. I know what to say and do. I'll be sure to give you a sign.

SHŌJI: Take care . . . I wouldn't have you fail.

(Offstage shamisen plays.)

YASUNA: I'll not fail you.

TAKEMOTO:

With doubtful heart, Shōji hides himself inside the shed.

*(*SHŌJI *rises, crosses to the shed, and enters it as* YASUNA *bows deferentially to him.* YASUNA *rises and crosses into the house, picks up the pinwheel, stumbles against the folding screen, and sees his sleeping child.)*

YASUNA *(Shocked)*: This won't do. Look at the poor lad, all tired out from his pranks! You've thrown off your covers in your sleep. We can't have you catching cold. Wife! *(Steps forward, and realizing that the child's mother is not there, calls to her more forcefully.)* Kuzu, where are you? Kuzu!

(The last word is drawn out emotionally for emphasis. YASUNA *poses, holding the pinwheel against his raised upstage hand, suggesting his concern for the child. He kneels forward.)*

TAKEMOTO:

Calling "Aye!" his wife comes to the curtained doorway, / still in her apron, with her sleeves tied back with cords.

*(*FOX-KUZUNOHA *enters the room from left and moves to* YASUNA*'s right, kneeling while speaking. The offstage shamisen plays.)*

FOX-KUZUNOHA: Did you just get home? It was rather windy today. You must be chilled to the bone.

(There is something strange in her intonation of the last word, a slight hint of her fox nature.)

YASUNA *(Not noticing the change)*: No, being out in the world kept me warm today. I made my rounds to Sumiyoshi and Tennō Temple. *(Hands her the pinwheel.)* Look, I've brought the lad a toy.

FOX-KUZUNOHA: Why, how thoughtful of you! The boy will be delighted. Give it here—I'll surprise him.

(She rises to go over to the boy, but YASUNA *stops her with a gesture, and she resumes kneeling.)*

YASUNA: Wait, we'll give it him when he wakes.

FOX-KUZUNOHA: Aye.

YASUNA: Which reminds me . . . I've got some happy news for you.

FOX-KUZUNOHA: Yes?

YASUNA: On my way home today, I happened to meet your father, Lord Shōji, with your mother, at the temple's Hall of Hours.

FOX-KUZUNOHA *(Agitated, she turns to him)*: Is this true?

YASUNA: Indeed, I did. *(Offstage shamisen begins.)* I felt so remiss for not getting in touch that I was loath to go up to them, but they came over looking as if they didn't in the least resent me. Having heard where we were living, they'd hurried to see their daughter . . . They said they'd come around sundown. It's been a long time for you, too. You must be pleased you'll see them.

FOX-KUZUNOHA *(Feigning happiness)*: Sundown, you say? That's soon. I really ought to fix something special.

YASUNA *(Reassuring her)*: Why, just showing off their grandson would be a feast in itself for them. And seeing you will be the next best treat. Go comb your hair, and get out of that shabby kimono and into something brighter. Make yourself beautiful . . . Ah, visitors from long ago, and plenty of tales to tell. We'll not get far if we don't have a bit of a nap first. Get me that pillow.

FOX-KUZUNOHA: Aye.

*(*FOX-KUZUNOHA *rises, crosses behind the screen, puts the pinwheel by the child, and returns with a hard pillow on which* YASUNA *rests his neck, his back to her, head toward the audience. She kneels at his side, right.)*

TAKEMOTO: Yasuna pretends to fall asleep.

FOX-KUZUNOHA *(Looks around, worried)*: But there's a draft in here. Let's go inside. Get yourself a good sleep till sundown. *(Looks at* YASUNA*, who appears to have fallen asleep. Tentatively, she calls him.)* Hello? Are you asleep already? Come, you don't want to catch cold. I'll throw something over your legs. Goodness, what snoring! He must have been quite exhausted. I'll go dress up my hair.

TAKEMOTO:

Her heart darkening, the wife wraps her thoughts in a coverlet, / embraces her child, and regretfully goes within.

(She adjusts the pillow under his head and covers his legs with a coverlet. She begins to go inside, then returns once, twice, three times, hesitating. As TAKEMOTO *begins, she turns front, rises, crosses to the sleeping child, lifts him, and stands with him in her arms. She turns upstage, looks down at her sleeping husband, and slowly exits up center. As soon as she is gone,* YASUNA *raises his head, pushes the pillow aside, and rises sharply to his knees.)*

Yasuna's doubtful eyes follow her leave-taking.

(He rises, lifts his sword, and takes a step backward. Then, slowly and cautiously, he crosses up to center doorway, pushes open the split curtain, and peeks inside.)

YASUNA *(Perplexed)*: It makes no sense whichever way I look at it. She wasn't shocked in the least when I told her about her parents, but even so . . . what if it is her?

TAKEMOTO:

So saying, he watches her in the inner room, putting up her hair.

YASUNA *(Peering in)*: It's my wife Kuzu and no other, I'll be bound. *(He turns front, thinking, and takes the scabbard cord in his right hand.)* My wife of six years . . . *(He steps forward, distractedly.)* I've no reason to doubt her, surely. But what about the girl Lord Shōji and his wife brought here? *(He looks off into the distance, thoughtfully.)*

TAKEMOTO:

Yes, what of her? he wonders. So he steals a look / into the perplexing darkness of his heart, / into the depths of the house.

(He crosses up to the shrine altar at the back wall, puts down his sword, and, facing upstage, claps three times to pray. He picks up the ritual paper streamers by the shrine and crosses downstage a few steps to center, whisking the streamers side to side, then poses resolutely with the streamers as a sharp ki *clack signals the end of the scene. The large offstage drum* [ōdaiko] *plays under the* TAKEMOTO *music as the stage darkens and the set revolves, bringing on the next scene. The drum continues to beat* [tsunagi] *as the new scene, showing the inner room, comes into view. The drum gets louder and more rapid. A single* ki *clack signals the lights to come up and the scene to begin. The* TAKEMOTO *musicians, previously hidden behind bamboo blinds at left, now are in view, wearing formal attire* [kamishimo] *and seated on their dais* [yuka].*)*

The Inner Room

(The cottage's inner room. At left, an alcove with a scroll, and beyond, a wall, and an exit with a split curtain. To right, a partition with a latticed transom on top. Far right is a bamboo thicket. Down left is a gate made of woven sticks, which is operated by a hidden mechanism. At center, DŌJI *is lying within a screened partition. The scene revolves to wind-pattern drumbeats* [kaze no oto]. *To* TAKEMOTO *singing,* FOX-KUZUNOHA *reenters, sadly, wearing a pale gold formal kimono with black lining, and a wide black obi. She stands upstage center in front of the divided curtains, looks over at her child, crosses to him, and staggers back tearfully. She falls to her knees, anguished.)*

TAKEMOTO:

Yasuna spies in upon his wife. Now in a fresh change of clothes, / she enters from within to see her child, and with a heavy heart looks down / upon their sleeping son. She is about to speak, / but her voice is stopped with tears, and she sobs.

FOX-KUZUNOHA *(To lyrical shamisen melody* [meriyasu], *she pauses, lost in thought)*:

Ah, how wretched, how ashamed am I! All these years and months, the secret I have hidden has been in vain. That it should come to such a pass, that my true form has been revealed and I must now leave, breaking my ties as wife and mother! I would tell your papa, but I'd bow my head in shame were I obliged to confess my past. Hear me with your sleeping ears, then, and remember . . .

TAKEMOTO:

Tell your papa this . . .

(As she draws her outstretched left hand slowly toward her body, the hand curves unconsciously into a paw. She notices it and quickly hides it in her sleeve. Both hands, hidden in their sleeves, are held across her body, then placed on her raised knee.)

FOX-KUZUNOHA: In truth, I am not human. Six years ago, in Shinoda Forest, I was in the clutches of the wicked Akuemon and on the verge of death when Lord Yasuna saved me. Orchids and chrysanthemums bloomed again! A thousand years upon this earth . . .

(Unable to restrain her fox nature any longer, she makes a sharp, animallike movement of her head, scurries downstage a few steps, gestures to the gate with her paw as it magically opens and closes, scurries back into the room, facing the screen, and gestures with her paw again as the screen flips over upstage, revealing the sleeping boy. She faces front, posing in a foxlike attitude, in profile on one knee, slowly raising one leg backward into the air, suggesting a tail under her kimono. Eerie drum and flute music, "lightning" [raijo], *underscore this business.)*

TAKEMOTO:

I've lived. In truth, I am a fox.

(The strange intonation of the word "fox" *conveys her real nature. She turns front, becoming more human in attitude, but with hands still formed as paws.)*

FOX-KUZUNOHA: But your father, too, had been sorely wounded because of me. Wishing to repay the favor he had shown me, I took on the form of Lady Kuzu, and just as he was about to take his own life, I stayed his hand and nursed him back to health.

TAKEMOTO:

As I kept him company, mercy turned to passion, / and our hearts desired to join as man and wife. / Since that time we made our vows . . .

FOX-KUZUNOHA: I've honored and treasured my husband.

*(*FOX-KUZUNOHA *turns upstage and expresses her longing, then turns back and mimes her grief to* TAKEMOTO *singing.)*

TAKEMOTO:

Truly a hundred times more devoted / than any mortals are the beasts!

FOX-KUZUNOHA: Above all now, since I gave birth to you.

TAKEMOTO:

Sweet words I'd exchange with my man and child, / each fast in my embrace as I lay between you of a night.

(She rises and crosses to the curtain, and looks off. She turns back, but turns upstage again, drawn powerfully by her husband's offstage presence. She tries to break the spell but stumbles against the screen and sees her child.)

But never again will I share your bed!

(She scurries on her knees to center, rises, crosses above child to left, and, as TAKEMOTO *becomes very emotional, poses in agony, then drops to her knees, weeping loudly. She twirls on her knees and bows in the direction of* YASUNA, *then turns to her child.)*

With all her magic, has this unwitting fox / lost her dear, beloved ones?

(Arms crossed in front of her, she weepingly addresses the boy. TAKEMOTO *music underscores her words.)*

FOX-KUZUNOHA: That we must now part is not your papa's fault. Indebted as I am to him, I bear no grudge. Lord Shōji and his wife are your grandparents now, so love Lady Kuzu as your own true mother. Do not think ill of her, but end, once and for all, your foolish pranks. Throw yourself into your studies and master what you learn, so that you may be praised as your father's son. Ah! Truly, there's nothing now I can do for you . . .

(Moving like a fox, she scurries on her knees to the other side of the child and smoothens his hair, her hands held like paws. She hugs herself to restrain her feelings.)

TAKEMOTO:

Do not call out your mother's name, / lest you be scorned and reviled as a wicked fox-child.

FOX-KUZUNOHA *(Speaking in increasingly agitated tones, her voice rising to a wail)*: Though I must leave you now, you have a new mother to look after you in all the years to come. So I say, but how can I abandon you, returning to my native place? Our parting is like a dream; surely, when I'm gone you'll cry out for my breast! Oh, my sweet, beloved child!

(She moves backward a step, beckons toward the child with her paw, and, via a special effect sure to produce a chill in the spectators, he and the small mattress on which he is sleeping suddenly slide to her side. She moves to his other side, then turns to the right side and places herself across him protectively. She takes his hand and sinks down over him, weeping.)

TAKEMOTO:

"Come, I cannot leave you!" she would cry, / but she breaks down weeping. / Presently, she wipes away her tears.

FOX-KUZUNOHA *(Composing herself)*: My tears cannot change anything now . . . At least a message I could leave . . . Yes . . .

(To the accompaniment of an offstage solo [dokugin], *sung slowly and mournfully, she touches her cheek to the child's face, arranges his bedclothes, and wipes her tears away with her back to the audience. Then, she takes a tray with writing utensils of brush and ink from a low table right, kneels, rises, crosses left, and walks along the veranda as the stage revolves.)*

OFFSTAGE SINGER:

The reeds of grief lie thick as dew in Shinoda Forest. / Alas, though I yearn for dreams entwined with you, / weeds will be my bed, grass my pillow. / The dew will tell my brush to speak: / tears on my sleeves are white chrysanthemums.

(The stage revolves and a new set comes into view, showing the outside of another raised room with four simple sliding paper doors on the upstage wall. FOX-KUZUNOHA *begins to write a verse on the one at right, her brushstrokes moving from above to below and right to left. For the first line, however, she begins at the top and then, indicating her supernatural nature, finishes it by writing it from the bottom up.)*

DŌJI *(Entering from right)*: Mama! Mama!

(Mother and child embrace as TAKEMOTO *music resumes. As she continues writing, she ad-libs with the distraught child, whom she must console as he plaintively calls for his mother's arms. Holding his hand in her right hand, she is forced to write on the final panel, at left, with her left hand.)*

OFFSTAGE SINGER:

The insects crying so confusedly in the fields, / burn with a love as bright as fox fires. / Come look for me, Kuzu of the clinging vine.

(The child insists on being held, and she must finish the verse by holding the brush in her teeth. Yet she still manages to produce excellent calligraphy.)

FOX-KUZUNOHA: Ah!

(She falls weeping, then turns on her knees and embraces the child.)

TAKEMOTO:

Yasuna bolts in when he hears / Kuzu burst into reckless tears.

*(*YASUNA *enters from right, outside the house.)*

YASUNA: I heard everything now. Why must you leave the boy?

TAKEMOTO:

Loath to let her go, he tries to hold her fast. / Then, suddenly abandoning the boy, she vanishes from sight.

*(*FOX-KUZUNOHA *crosses down to center, where* YASUNA *tries to prevent her from leaving. They move from one side to the other and pose with the child between them.* YASUNA *takes the boy, and* KUZUNOHA *moves like a fox to the right, where she drops to her knees. A* STAGE ASSISTANT *helps to loosen her hair and make a rapid costume change* [bukkaeri], *revealing a white inner kimono patterned with red flames. She rushes in foxlike leaps to* shichisan, *turns back and faces* YASUNA, *then rapidly disappears into the* hanamichi *elevator trap* [suppon] *as piercing flute and loud* dorodoro *drum pattern play.* YASUNA, *holding the child on stage, has not seen this because his back is turned to her. He now turns front, holding the child in his arms and sinking to his knees.)*

One-panel woodblock print by Utagawa Toyokuni III (1786–1864). Nakamura-za, Edo, fifth month 1850. "Fox-Kuzunoha" (Bandō Shūka I, posthumously Bandō Mitsugorō V) writes a farewell poem to her husband, "Abe no Yasuna" (Ichikawa Danjūrō VIII), shown in the inset. Her child cradled in her arms and with the brush held in her teeth, she begins to write on the paper screen: "If you long for me, come seek me in Izumi. . . ." (Tsubouchi Memorial Theatre Museum of Waseda University)

Abe Yasuna (Sawamura Sōjūrō II) looks on as Fox-Kuzunoha (Nakamura Shikan VII), having written a farewell poem on the screen, cradles her beloved son whom she must leave. (Tsubouchi Memorial Theatre Museum of Waseda University)

YASUNA *(In rhythmic cadences to the* TAKEMOTO *shamisen accompaniment)*: Can you not hear, wife? Though you have a vixen's body, surely you can take pity on creation, can't you? Can I not repay the debt I owe you for these six years you lived with us? And what of the child you bore? Let them laugh, those who'd laugh at me for taking a fox as wife. I'm not in the least ashamed. If indeed you have to leave us, then tell me to my face, let it be with my consent. Only then have done with it and be gone. I'd never leave you like this! *(Rising, he holds the final vowel in emotional torment.)* Hear me, Kuzu! (He looks left and right for KUZUNOHA as he carries the child in his arms. When he cannot find her, he kneels center in despair. Then, turning upstage, he notices the message on the paper doors.)

YASUNA *(Reading)*: "If you long for me, / Come seek me in Izumi, / where, in the forest of Shinoda, / you'll find your Kuzu / of the clinging vine." *(He turns front.)* Would you abandon your child with nothing more than a poem as a keepsake? Very well, then. I'll bring your boy, and together we'll follow these thirty-one syllables that trace . . . *(emphasizing his anguish on the final word, he sinks to his knees, still embracing the child,)* the twisting path of your regrets. (YASUNA *releases the child, who climbs on his back. He rises.)*

TAKEMOTO:

"If you long for me, / Come seek me in Izumi . . ."

(As TAKEMOTO *finishes the line,* YASUNA *runs to* shichisan, *to accelerating* tsuke *beats, then stumbles.)*

YASUNA: Mother of this boy!

*(*YASUNA *calls out to* KUZUNOHA. Ki *clack. Pose. He speaks his last line, then, beginning slowly, he gradually accelerates in speed as he moves off down the* hanamichi, *the accompanying* tsuke *accenting his movement with rapid beats. Loud* dorodoro. *A sharp* ki *clack signals the beginning of the scene change. The stage darkens to the sound of rhythmic offstage drums, gong, and shamisen as the previous scene descends on a trap* [seri] *to reveal Shinoda Forest.* Ki *clack.)*

TAKEMOTO:

And so, to the forest of Shinoda.

The Shinoda Forest Journey

(Lights up. Banks of chrysanthemums and pampas grass dress the stage and back the group of three TAKEMOTO *singers and three shamisen players who appear onstage* [degatari] *on a platform at left. Overhead hang two lines of lights suggesting fox fires.)*

TAKEMOTO:

She who would put an end to her sorrows here / is Abe no Dōji's mother. / Go, then, return to your ancestral home!

(Loud, rapid dorodoro. *Eerie flute music* [netoribue]. *Lights darken.* FOX-KUZUNOHA *rises into view on* suppon, *her strange entrance highlighted by two black-robed and masked* STAGE ASSISTANTS *who crouch on either side of her, holding long, flexible black poles* [sashidashi] *on the ends of which are candles used to light her face in a reminder of an old-time kabuki convention. She wears a black-lined silver kimono with a black obi, a lacquered sedge hat, and carries a walking stick in her hand. Covering her face is a white fox mask with an extended snout. As the* TAKEMOTO *plays, she slowly dances on the* hanamichi *in foxlike fashion, manipulating her stick and raising her head at one point to clearly indicate her facial transformation. Her dance expresses the pain she feels after having been separated from her child.)*

TAKEMOTO:

Her native village no more / than a passing abode of autumn mists, / and bright chrysanthemums beguile her way, / ashamed that those she left would know her as she truly is. / On nimble feet, she scurries, / scurries, now here, now there, / her apparel and hair disheveled / in the clover and pampas grass.

(Sound of flute, stick drum, dorodoro. *She poses suddenly, wheels about, and, through a trick, her mask disappears into her hat, revealing the actor's face. Lights*

up. She runs to the main stage, center, where she kneels on one knee as a STAGE ASSISTANT *takes her sandals and stick and replaces her trick hat with another. She scurries left on her knees and poses, then moves back to center.)*

With a sharp intake of breath, / she stops and straightens her dress. / Under her sedge hat, / the slanting sun's rays glare.

(She slowly crosses upstage center, moving up a sloped platform there to a higher level and looking around.)

Danger on all sides for one in flight: / here a village, there some passersby . . .

(She comes back down again and kneels on one knee as a STAGE ASSISTANT *takes her hat. Through all this, intermittent* dorodoro.*)*

Above all, the howling of dogs . . . *(rises and expresses alarm)* / chills her bones / and her spirits drenched by a sudden shower, / a burst of rain, then sun, then rain again . . .

(She begins dancing her feelings as the TAKEMOTO *sings to shamisen accompaniment.)*

What folk call a fox's wedding / is her body turning back to its old nest. / "But what of my boy?" *(Sinks to one knee and rises again.)* / "The dear, sweet boy I left behind?"

(She turns back to wipe away her tears, then turns front. She looks around, crosses to chrysanthemum bush left, takes a flower, and cradles it as if it were a child. She crosses to center with it.)

"Poor child, he'll surely grieve / without my breast to comfort him," / and her tears eclipse her way.

(She crosses left several steps. Posing, she sees her fox image reflected in the imaginary water. Dorodoro *as she ruffles the surface of the "water" to disperse the image. She crosses rapidly to center and sinks to one knee, holding her arms across her breasts.)*

Reflected in the pool, she sees her real form. / It is well that she makes this trek through the fields alone.

(Rises and executes slow movements expressing grief.)

"Though we had to part, / we truly had to part, / I'll cling to you like your very shadow, / I'll watch over you in all the years to come!"

(Kneeling, she wipes away her tears. Light dorodoro. *She rises and crosses left a step.)*

"I've no regrets, I'll not grieve," she says . . .

(Two low-ranking SAMURAI ATTENDANTS [yakko] *appear at left and right, their trousers tucked up to expose their legs. They wear a fringed apron and red kimono patterned in white. Seeing them,* FOX-KUZUNOHA *rushes upstage to loud* dorodoro *and sinks to her knees. She does a backward bending "prawn-shaped"* mie [ebizori no mie] *to* tsuke *beats. She rises and, to rapid drumbeats,*

Fox-Kuzunoha (Nakamura Ganjirō III), transformed into her true fox shape, poses on a red, cloth-covered platform in the final scene. (Umemura Yutaka, Engeki Shuppansha)

poses in a group mie *with the* SAMURAI, *who hold out their hands to either side as if to prevent her escape. A choreographed combat* [tachimawari] *ensues to the sounds of the* TAKEMOTO *shamisen, swelling* dorodoro, *and* tsuke *beats that punctuate the more vigorous movements. During the dancelike battle, the* SAMURAI *try to seize* FOX-KUZUNOHA, *but she holds them off with fox movements. Every few moments, the group strikes a new* mie. *After a minute or two, she breaks away and rushes to downstage right, where she disappears through a secret door in the wall—painted with foliage—next to the offstage musicians' room* [geza]. *Four more* SAMURAI *appear from each side, whirling and tumbling on the ground under the fox's spell. They leap and fall to their bottoms, facing upstage.* KUZUNOHA, *now represented by a white puppet, peeps out through a small trap in the dais on which the* TAKEMOTO *musicians sit. She looks about and disappears. A black-robed puppeteer holding the fox enters from camouflaged doors set in front of the* TAKEMOTO *dais and moves upstage among the flowers, manipulating the fox to suggest its prancing movements. With a flick of the fox's tail, the six* SAMURAI *tumble backward, legs in the air. In the following sequence, the fox, upstage, seems to control the* SAMURAI*'s movements, making them look foolish as they rhythmically execute her commands. Now they look here, now they look there, now they turn one against the other in comic poses and attitudes. They move with foxlike leaps and pounces, jumping, tumbling, and whirling about. As they pose, the fox moves from left to right, touching each in turn, causing them to fall to the ground, stunned. The fox-puppet exits right and the actor playing* FOX-KUZUNOHA, *hair hanging loosely, instantly appears from the same place, dressed in a kimono of white furlike material.* FOX-KUZUNOHA *poses on her knees at center and the fight resumes. The* SAMURAI *lift her into the air and assume a group* mie. *The stage darkens as the* SAMURAI *surround her in a pose on the center ramp.* Ki *clack. Loud* dorodoro.*)*

But her thoughts are confused, / like the tangled blooms of the wild chrysanthemum / borne aloft upon the wind.

(A STAGE ASSISTANT *attaches a wire to the actor's hidden harness and* FOX-KUZUNOHA *rises into the air as the* SAMURAI *fall back in amazement, three to either side, each holding up a hand for protection. Rapidly accelerating* tsuke *beats. The* SAMURAI *turn toward the audience and pose in a group* mie. *Lively offstage musical accompaniment plays as the curtain closes, and* FOX-KUZUNOHA, *suspended in the air at center, leaps about in fox movements surrounded by fox fires. The curtain closes.)*

One-panel woodblock print by Utagawa Toyokuni III (1786–1864). Ichimura-za, Edo, sixth month 1855. Matsuemon (in reality "Higuchi Jirō Kanemitsu"; Nakamura Fukusuke I, later Nakamura Shikan IV) brandishes an oar overhead as he repels a Genji attacker. (Tsubouchi Memorial Theatre Museum of Waseda University)

The Secret Art of Rowing
Sakaro

Matsuda Bunkodō, Miyoshi Shōraku, Sen Zensuke et al.
TRANSLATED BY MATTHEW JOHNSON

Matsuemon's Home
Matsuemon Uchi no Ba

The Secret Art of Rowing at the Fukushima Pine
Fukushima Sakaro no Matsu no Ba

The Large Pine on Shore
Sakaro no Matsu no Ba

1739 TAKEMOTO-ZA, OSAKA

The Secret Art of Rowing

INTRODUCTION

In Japan's puppet theatre, the span between the death of Chikamatsu Monzaemon (1653–1725) and the golden days inspired by the writing team of Takeda Izumo II (1691–1756), Namiki Senryū (1695–1751), and Miyoshi Shōraku (1696–1772) at Osaka's Takemoto-za was dominated by the playwright Matsuda Bunkodō (dates unknown), usually referred to only as Bunkōdō. Despite his success, many of Bunkodō's plays were ignored in the puppet theatre after their premieres. This was mostly because, while Bunkodō wrote innovative plots, his characters were not deep enough to stand up well in the narrative-driven puppet theatre. Bunkodō's plays, however, took on a new life when adapted to kabuki, as with *The Stone-Cutting Feat of Kajiwara,* translated in this volume. The lack of character development allowed kabuki actors to fill out the roles in their own ways. An exception is *A Beginner's Version of the Rise and Fall of the Heike and Genji Clans* (Hiragama Seisuiki), which has remained equally popular on both the puppet and kabuki stages and is the source of *The Secret Art of Rowing.*

The well-rounded characters and excellent script of *Secret Art* mark it as one of Bunkodō's finest works and have kept it a principal part of the puppet and kabuki repertoires since its premiere in the fourth month of 1739. Its strongly contrasting characters include the powerful warrior, Higuchi Jirō, whose real nature is set against his disguise as the simple commoner Matsuemon. Also, Ofude, a maidservant in a high-ranking household, is contrasted with the commoner Oyoshi, while the wise general Shigetada stands out against the rough-mannered Higuchi.

A Beginner's Version freely dramatizes events described in *An Account of the Genpei Wars* (Genpei Seisuiki), one of the many medieval accounts of the war among the rival Genji and Heike clans in the late twelfth century. The play begins with the famous crossing at the Uji River and ends on the eve of the battle of Ichinotani (an event that forms the subject of the great puppet and kabuki play *Chronicle of the Battle at Ichinotani* (Ichinotani Futaba Gunki, 1751; trans. Brandon 1992). This was a time when the Genji clan was preoccupied with fighting among rival factions; one especially threatening faction was commanded by Kiso Yoshinaka. Yoritomo, head of the Genji, fearing Yoshinaka's growing power, sent his younger brother Yoshitsune to crush Yoshinaka, thereby earning the enmity of Matsuemon, Yoshinaka's retainer and the hero of this play.

The five-act play has two main story lines. The first tells of Kajiwara Genta's failure to be the first to cross the Uji River and the aftermath of that failure. Genta's story comprises the majority of the play. Act II, in which Genta returns home to receive punishment for his failure, shows this handsome young man who, though a warrior, is cultured enough to place plum blossoms in his arrow case. The story is famous in both *nō* and nondramatic literature. The scene of Genta's disinheritance ("Genta no Kandō") is still often seen in kabuki. Act IV, closely modeled on *The Courtesan at Asamagatake* (Keisei Asamagatake, 1698), a landmark play in the history of female-role specialization in kabuki, shows how Genta's lover, Chidori, is willing to sacrifice herself—even risk falling into hell—to raise the money necessary for Genta to join the battle at Ichinotani. The second story line of the play tells of the attempt of Kiso Yoshinaka's retainer, Higuchi Jirō, to take revenge on Yoshitsune for his lord's death. Higuchi's story, dramatized in *Secret Art,* occupies the latter part of Act III. The title refers to a method of rowing backward that was considered important for naval maneuvers.

The role of Higuchi/Matsuemon is among kabuki's greatest challenges for leading men *(tachiyaku)* who specialize in history play *(jidaimono)* characters. Entering with a confident swagger, Matsuemon tells of his visit with Kajiwara no Kagetoki (see this character's idiosyncratic depiction in *The Stone-Cutting Feat of Kajiwara,* which shares the same background world [*sekai*]). Such storytelling sequences, known as *monogatari,* are important in plays adapted from the puppet theatre; the actor, confined to a limited space and using only a simple prop, such as a fan or hand towel, must reenact an event through mime and depict others' voices and behavior. This narrative-performance tradition is typically delivered by a warrior. In this scene, Matsuemon performs the *monogatari* in the guise of a commoner, so the audience has the pleasure of discerning his performance on two levels simultaneously. When Matsuemon appears again later and is forced to reveal his true identity as Higuchi, he changes from a commoner boatman into a powerful samurai. The actor must express the valiant Higuchi's commanding presence in a way that strikingly contrasts with the actor's earlier incarnation as the everyday Matsuemon. Yet even this high-ranking samurai must bow his head to Gonshirō, a common fisherman, to ask his forgiveness. Here the actor must show Higuchi's true feelings without losing his martial poise and stature.

Though Matsuemon is the center of the play, Gonshirō is almost as important. This proud fisherman has shown great compassion by taking the child Komawaka into his household. Further, the playwright uses Gonshirō as a sounding board for criticizing the samurai class. His scathing rebuttal of Ofude's tale of the death of Tsuchimatsu and of her request for the return of Komawaka is deeply rooted in the commoners' feelings that the privileged samurai class used people for their own needs, no matter the consequences. Perhaps an even greater swipe at samurai values comes later, when Gonshirō feels it would be unsightly to be seen grieving over Tsuchimatsu's vest. Though Matsuemon, speaking as a samurai, tells him he is wrong, it reveals the playwright's ridicule of the vaunted stoicism associated with the samurai class.

The play is a famous example of a "substitution drama" *(migawari mono)* in which the life of a lord's child is saved by substituting someone else's son for him. Such dramas, which were especially popular in the puppet theatre, were based on the playwrights' imaginings about the ultimate sacrifice possible under the feudal system; no such actual substitutions in which a parent killed a child for some lord's sake are known to have occurred. The original substitution occurs accidentally in the present drama, but the results force Matsuemon—and later, Gonshirō—to make important decisions about the child based on loyalty to a superior. Deceptions in which a child or adolescent is forced to play the role of another because of circumstances stemming from the hidden loyalties of an adult fill numerous puppet-derived plots. Among them are such classics as the "Kumagai's Battle Camp" (Kumagai Jinya) act from *Chronicle of the Battle of Ichinotani,* mentioned above, and "The Village School" (Terakoya) act from *Sugawara and the Secrets of Calligraphy* (Sugawara Denju Tenarai Kagami, 1746; trans. Ernst 1959, Jones 1985, and Leiter 2000).

The kabuki script of *Secret Art* rarely veers far from the original puppet version, but because the play has been extremely popular in kabuki over a long period of time, performance has accrued many distinct kabukiesque aspects. For example, a number of long speeches do not rely on the *takemoto* narrator. Traditionally, in plays adapted from the puppet theatre, the narrator either shares long speeches with the actors or dominates them. Edo actors and audiences generally did not like the intrusion of narrators into plays and, by taking over sections traditionally performed by the *takemoto,* actors were able to greatly enhance and develop their roles. Another kabuki contribution to this play is the large-scale choreographed fight *(tachimawari)* that begins the third scene. The scene is considered a masterpiece of *tachimawari* choreography, with its use of oars and boat images. Kabuki's complex fighting conventions, capable of far more spectacular choreography than is possible in the puppet theatre, reach their apogee in this great example of a full-scale *tachimawari,* with a single hero doing combat with a host of attackers.

Productions of this play in both kabuki and the puppet theatre share the unusual convention of distant perspective *(tōmi),* used to show action supposedly set far out in the bay. To convey a sense of distance, child actors take the place of adults. Dressed identically to the adults, the smaller figures appear to be far away.

This translation is based on the script used for a production at the Kokuritsu Gekijō (National Theatre of Japan) in March 1998, featuring Ichikawa Danjūrō XII (b. 1946) as Matsuemon and Nakamura Matagorō II (b. 1914) as Gonshirō. A videotape of that production also was helpful.

CHARACTERS

MATSUEMON, *actually* HIGUCHI JIRŌ KANEMITSU, *high-ranking retainer of* KISO YOSHINAKA, *disguised as a commoner*

GONSHIRŌ, *fisherman and father-in-law of* MATSUEMON

OYOSHI, *wife of* MATSUEMON

TSUCHIMATSU, *actually* KOMAWAKAMARU, young *son and heir of* KISO YOSHINAKA, *now in the care of* MATSUEMON

TOMIZŌ, *boatman sent to learn secret rowing strategy from* MATSUEMON

KUROSAKU, *boatman sent to learn secret rowing strategy from* MATSUEMON

MATAROKU, *boatman sent to learn secret rowing strategy from* MATSUEMON

UNNEN, *priest*

PARISHIONERS

SERVANTS

SAILORS

BODYGUARDS, *high-ranking retainers of* SHIGETADA

OFUDE, *a lady-in-waiting of the Kiso household*

HATAKEYAMA SHŌJI SHIGETADA, *prominent Genji general*

STAGE ASSISTANTS, *black-garbed* kurogo

TAKEMOTO, *shamisen and narrator combination that accompanies the actors*

Matsuemon's Home

(The curtain opens to drumbeats pounding out the sound of waves [nami no oto] *against the house of* MATSUEMON *in the village of Fukushima. The house has a door at right and two levels. The lower level is covered with straw runners suggesting* tatami *mats. The upper level, a platform about eighteen inches high, has a split-curtained entrance at center. A simple step center leads from one level to the other. In the right corner is a folding screen with two folk paintings* [Ōtsu-e] *on it. To*

the left of the curtained doorway is a Buddhist altar, and to its left is a Shinto altar with a formal stand and scroll containing the name of the god of sailors. To the left is a separate room closed off by paper sliding screens [shōji]. *Outside the house, a painted backdrop of a rocky cliff demarcates the edge of the stage. A small pine, indicative of the large tree used later in the play, stands next to the house. The sea is visible in the background. As the play opens, a prayer group is sitting in a semicircle in the middle of the upper room, facing the Buddhist altar. All wear plain kimono in drab colors and hold Buddhist rosaries. Among them is* UNNEN, *a priest with a shaved head.)*

UNNEN: Well, everyone, you have done a good job reciting the prayers. Let's take a rest and have a drink.

(The group breaks the circle and the PARISHIONERS *divide into two groups. They speak quickly and casually.)*

FIRST PARISHIONER: Recently Oyoshi invited us over.

SECOND PARISHIONER: She asked us to recite prayers for her.

THIRD PARISHIONER: Inviting everyone in our prayer group along . . .

FOURTH PARISHIONER: We all came here.

FIFTH PARISHIONER: The members of this household have always been helpful.

SIXTH PARISHIONER: We are very fond of them.

UNNEN: The prayers we recite are not just for the benefit of others. They are also for us.

FIRST PARISHIONER: That certainly . . .

ALL: Is true.

(Wave drum pattern is heard again as GONSHIRŌ, OYOSHI, *and* TSUCHIMATSU *enter through the curtained doorway and sit.* GONSHIRŌ *is a white-haired old man who wears a checkered kimono and a heavy, blue robe. He carries a Buddhist rosary.* OYOSHI, *a commoner's wife, wears a simple purple kimono tied with a black obi from which a white hand towel* [tenugui] *hangs. Covering the crown of her wig is a purple cloth* [boshi]. TSUCHIMATSU, *a boy whose white makeup suggests his refinement, wears a green checkered kimono and has his hair in a child's unshaven topknot.* OYOSHI *distributes tea to the prayer group and opens a small box of food.* GONSHIRŌ *sits at center, with* TSUCHIMATSU *at his right and* OYOSHI *to the boy's right.)*

GONSHIRŌ: Hello, everyone. Thank you all for your help today. Oyoshi, I know we don't have much to offer them, but please pass out what there is.

OYOSHI: It isn't very good, but I hope you enjoy it.

ALL PARISHIONERS: There was no need to go to the trouble, but thank you very much.

UNNEN: By the way, Gonshirō, what is the occasion for the prayers today?

ALL PARISHIONERS: Yes, what is it?

GONSHIRŌ: Today is the third anniversary of the death of Oyoshi's first husband. Usually we would offer you a proper meal for your trouble, but, as you know, we have just returned from the western pilgrimage to sacred sites of Kannon. Traveling with my weak-legged daughter and grandson used up most of our savings. But please have some tea and enjoy yourselves.

OYOSHI: We have no household help, and this boy takes up all my time. It is not much, but please have some.

FIRST PARISHIONER: Has it already been three years? My, how time passes. It hasn't been that long since you married your current husband, Matsuemon, and since we haven't had many chances to speak with him, we're not sure what type of man he is.

SECOND PARISHIONER: But we remember what a good man Tsuchimatsu's father was.

THIRD PARISHIONER: We do have a question, though. Before you left on the pilgrimage, Tsuchimatsu was somewhat plump.

FOURTH PARISHIONER: He was big for his age and quite a robust young boy.

UNNEN *(At right)*: He was as sturdy as a pine and was always playing outside. Even I was jealous of his abundance of energy. But now his complexion is much paler and he's gotten skinny. His face seems different, his body is smaller, and he seems very weak. *(With a touch of irony.)* Could your pilgrimage really have been the cause of such a blessing?

ALL: Could this be the case?

GONSHIRŌ: There is actually a good reason for this. This is not Tsuchimatsu.

UNNEN: What?

ALL PARISHIONERS *(Surprised)*: What do you mean?

GONSHIRŌ: There is a story behind it all. Have a listen. *(He thinks a moment. Background shamisen music begins.)* Let's see. Just when did it all begin, Oyoshi?

OYOSHI: On the night of the twenty-eighth.

GONSHIRŌ: Oh yes, that's right. On the twenty-eighth of last month, we donated our votive cards at Mii Temple and spent the night at an inn in Ōtsu. Suddenly, from out of nowhere, a large group of soldiers ran in yelling, "Halt" and "I've got you." We couldn't see and we didn't dare say anything. It's true what they say, "If you panic, you will even knock your child over." I don't know how we did it, but we managed to escape and ran without looking back. When it finally seemed as though we were out of harm's way, we were in O'okame Valley. Thinking we were still being followed, we were spooked even by the sound of the valley stream, and the wind blowing through the pines was easily mistaken for pursuing samurai. We ran until Fushimi as though our lives depended on it. *(Pats boy on the back.)* Once there, I looked at the face of the child on my back for the first time, and to my surprise I found that I had mistakenly grabbed the child of the group staying in the adjoining room. My daughter pleaded with me to run back and exchange him for her child, but my fear was far greater than my desire to do so. I couldn't even take one step in that direction. I tried to calm her, saying that there would be other chances to exchange the children. The other group had probably already discovered that they had the wrong child as well. If we were to care for this child, everything would work out. *(Bowing slightly.)* After all, they say that the grace of Kannon can make flowers bloom on a dead tree. We decided to wait until we could return home and calm down before doing anything. Catching the afternoon boat down the river, the child began to fuss, wanting to be breast-fed. Oyoshi gave him her breast and, since then, the days have passed. Not knowing his name, we began calling him Tsuchimatsu. *(Affectionately.)* He seemed to take to it and even began calling me grandpa. I have come to love him as much as our own Tsuchimatsu.

OYOSHI: Though we were brought together through such circumstances, I can't help but feel that somehow it was meant to be, and thus I've done my best to take care of him. How could I treat him as a stranger? He calls me mother and drinks from my breast. I offer my breast and think of him as my own child. I have no ill feelings toward him, but if possible I'd like things to return as they were. Perhaps your prayers will help.

FIRST PARISHIONER: That answers all of our questions. We are certain that Kannon . . .

SECOND PARISHIONER: Will bring your Tsuchimatsu back to you.

THIRD PARISHIONER: There is no need to fret.

UNNEN: Well, everyone, we've had some tea and filled our stomachs. It's just about time to go.

GONSHIRŌ: There's no hurry.

OYOSHI: Please stay and have a chat.

FIRST PARISHIONER: We'll save that for another day. For now . . .

ALL: We'll take our leave.

(The bustling prayer group steps down into the lower room and exits the house. OYOSHI, GONSHIRŌ, *and* TSUCHIMATSU *see them off at the door.)*

UNNEN: Give my best to Matsuemon when he returns.

ALL: And for us as well.

*(*UNNEN *closes the door and the group walks to the* hanamichi.*)*

TAKEMOTO:

As they exit, / from the distance . . .

(To two loud beats of the backstage drum and background song, MATSUEMON *swaggers confidently onto the* hanamichi. *He wears a light blue formal kimono and*

carries over his left shoulder an oar wrapped in his hakama. *He meets the prayer group at* shichisan.*)*

UNNEN: Matsuemon. We were just at your place while you were gone and were treated to tea and snacks.

MATSUEMON: Are you already heading home? Today is the third anniversary of my wife's first husband's death. I'd hoped to meet with you all, but, unfortunately, I was called away on business. This role of being a husband is still new to me, and I rarely have time to rest.

FIRST PARISHIONER: We stayed quite a while and drank a whole pot of tea . . .

SECOND PARISHIONER: But they say there's fortune in leftover tea.

THIRD PARISHIONER: Have a drink . . .

ALL PARISHIONERS: And a rest.

MATSUEMON: Well then, everyone.

ALL PARISHIONERS: Matsuemon.

MATSUEMON: Until later.

ALL PARISHIONERS: Until we meet again.

(Background shamisen music. Prayer group continues single file down the hanamichi *and exits. After bowing to them from the stage,* MATSUEMON *enters the house. Those within come to the door to greet him.)*

MATSUEMON *(Happily)*: Father, I'm home.

GONSHIRŌ: Son-in-law. Welcome home.

OYOSHI: You certainly are late getting back.

*(*OYOSHI *takes the oar from* MATSUEMON *and they all sit on the lower level of the room.* MATSUEMON *is at center,* GONSHIRŌ *at his left,* TSUCHIMATSU *at his right, and* OYOSHI *to the boy's right.)*

MATSUEMON: Even though I was hoping to rush home as soon as possible, my meeting was with a samurai lord who lives a much more relaxed life-style. That's why I'm so late. You must be tired as well. I'm sorry to have kept you waiting, Oyoshi.

OYOSHI: Not at all. You must be very hungry. Would you like dinner?

MATSUEMON: I don't need anything yet. I'll tell you when I'm ready.

OYOSHI: Just tell me when.

GONSHIRŌ *(Somewhat apprehensive)*: Tell me, son-in-law, why were you called to the mansion today? Is it something we need to worry about?

MATSUEMON: Not at all. I'll tell you all about it. *(Grandly.)* Father, Oyoshi, listen to this. This is what happened. *(Offstage shamisen music sets the mood as* MATSUEMON *delivers his famous narrative* [monogatari]. MATSUEMON *gestures with a hand towel* [tenugui] *as he speaks.)* You know, father, among the many daimyo, Lord Kajiwara is said to be an exceptionally thorough man, and, believe me, it's just as they say. *(Bowing.)* I announced myself saying, "Boatman

Matsuemon appearing as ordered." After a short wait, his retainer, Banba no Chūta, appeared and said *(speaking as* CHŪTA*)*, "Matsuemon? Thank you for coming. My lord will meet with you right away. Follow me." I followed meekly behind him, not knowing what to expect. *(Putting down the towel, he gestures with his hands.)* The mansion was magnificent, sparkling everywhere, just like the inside of a Buddhist altar. *(Picks up the towel.)* I was told to wait, and after doing so for six hours, the sliding screens opened to the side like this *(puts down the towel and motions with his hands)*, and Lord Kajiwara entered, saying *(speaking slowly, like a high-ranking samurai)*, "So you are Matsuemon the boatman." I answered, "Yes, I am Matsuemon," and Lord Kajiwara continued. "Our general Yoshitsune is a skilled strategist, but even though I tried to tell him about a secret rowing technique I knew of called '*sakaro*,' he would not listen. Have you ever trained anyone to use this strategy in battle?" I was at a loss for an answer, but said *(picks up the towel and bows)*, " I sail commercial boats and have never seen a naval battle even in my dreams. Still, that secret art of rowing is handed down in my family and I do know it." He replied right away, saying, "I understand. I want you to invite fellow sailors over tonight and secretly teach them how to use that technique in battle. When you are done, send word to me. If things go well, I will make you the captain of Yoshitsune's vessel." *(*GONSHIRŌ *and* OYOSHI *show their surprise.)* I was overjoyed. I returned home as quickly as possible, but it was as if I were in a dream. Mataroku of the ship *Hiyoshi,* Kurosaku of the *Nadayoshi,* and Tomizō of the *Myōjin* will come at dusk to practice. *(Happily.)* Rejoice, father. I am to be the captain of the great Yoshitsune's private vessel! Oyoshi, come tomorrow, I'll be able to provide you with a comfortable life. Rejoice my lad. You'll have a fine kimono to wear and toys to play with. *(Bowing.)* I'm so happy. This promotion was all thanks to you, father. How can I ever begin to express my gratitude?

GONSHIRŌ: This is wonderful. *Sakaro* is so difficult that you could teach it to someone for one thousand or ten thousand years, but if they weren't talented, they'd never catch on. When you married Oyoshi, you were nothing more than a rank amateur, and now you've been commissioned to be the captain of the boat of a great general. *(Happily.)* This can't all be due to my teaching, but, by golly, it must have everything to do with your excellent talent. *(Laughs.)* This calls for a celebration. Daughter, run and get us a bottle.

*(*OYOSHI *bows and begins to leave, but* MATSUEMON *stops her.* TSUCHIMATSU *falls asleep on* MATSUEMON*'s knee.)*

MATSUEMON: Don't bother. I had some sake at Kurosaku's place on the way home. It was the experience of a lifetime talking with a real lord. *(Rubs knee.)* My knees were wobbly and I couldn't walk straight. *(Shaking his arms as if trying to keep his balance.)* It was as if I'd come across a south wind on Harima Bay. *(Noticing* TSUCHIMATSU.*)* The boy has also fallen asleep. *(Affectionately.)* I'll take a nap with him.

TAKEMOTO:

He stands and turns / toward the inner room . . .

(As OYOSHI *goes into the upper room at left to prepare the bed,* MATSUEMON *puts his hand towel in his kimono breast, picks up* TSUCHIMATSU, *and steps into the upper room.)*

MATSUEMON: Father. *(Bowing.)* Please excuse me for a while.

TAKEMOTO:

He heads within.

*(*MATSUEMON *carries* TSUCHIMATSU *into the room at left.)*

GONSHIRŌ *(Moving to the upper level and calling inside)*: You must take care after this important promotion. Be sure not to catch a cold. *(To* OYOSHI, *who returns from within.)* Let's light a candle to the patron god of sailors to celebrate.

OYOSHI: It's already lit.

GONSHIRŌ: Then offer some sake.

OYOSHI: I already have.

GONSHIRŌ *(Lightheartedly)*: Oh? Then give some of that sake to this old sailor.

OYOSHI: How silly you are, father.

(As requested, OYOSHI *brings over a container of sake and motions that she will heat it as he rests. She takes it with her as she enters the curtained doorway.)*

GONSHIRŌ: What a filial child.

TAKEMOTO:

The room is filled / with the light of the candle.

*(*GONSHIRŌ *sits in front of the Shinto altar at upstage left and prays. He then goes to the Buddhist altar at left center and prays. He steps down into the lower room and stands to the left of the step.* OYOSHI *returns with a small wooden pillow and crosses to* GONSHIRŌ. *Helping* GONSHIRŌ *take off his outer robe, she covers him with it as he lies down for a rest.)*

Like a deer searching for its love, / Ofude has traveled treacherous mountains and waters / and faced hardships / that have made her life as black as ink. Having asked around after arriving in Fukushima, / she knows to look for the name on the gate and the large pine. / Finding the house, / she approaches.

(Wave pattern. OFUDE *enters on the* hanamichi. *She wears a black kimono with a short sword in her obi, and her hair is in the style of a samurai household maid-servant. She carries a round straw hat, indicating that she has been traveling. After stopping briefly at* shichisan, *she comes to the front door.)*

OFUDE: Pardon me. Is this the house of the boatman Matsuemon? I've come a long way to meet him, and I would be grateful if he would see me.

TAKEMOTO:

She speaks in a graceful manner.

(Somewhat warily, OYOSHI *goes to the front door to answer.)*

OYOSHI: Yes, this is Matsuemon's house. Please come in. *(Seeing* OFUDE, OYOSHI *quickly slams the door and runs to her father. Flustered, she sinks to her knees at center.)* Father, it's happened.

GONSHIRŌ *(Awakening)*: What's happened?

OYOSHI *(With a touch of jealousy)*: A beautiful young woman has come and asked to meet with my Matsuemon. *(She rises and crosses above* GONSHIRŌ, *where she kneels again and forces him to get up.)* I just knew it was too good to be true.

TAKEMOTO:

She can't tell her right from her left, / and her words reveal the jealousy / that has already surfaced.

*(*OYOSHI *rises, stamps her foot, and cocks her head toward the door in a show of defiance toward* OFUDE. *She then kneels by* GONSHIRŌ *again.)*

GONSHIRŌ *(Getting up and fixing his kimono)*: A woman has come calling for Matsuemon? What if it happens to be his sister? Calm down. *(Walking to the door.)* Who is it? Matsuemon is home. Please feel free to come in. *(*GONSHIRŌ *opens the door.)*

OFUDE: Then you are Matsuemon? I don't know your face, since I've never met you.

GONSHIRŌ: Then why have you come?

OFUDE *(Somewhat hesitantly)*: I was led here by this vest. It bears the name Tsuchimatsu, son of Matsuemon of Fukushima, Settsu province.

GONSHIRŌ: Then you were the one at the inn in Ōtsu on the twenty-eighth?

OFUDE: Yes, I am the one who mistakenly took your child.

(Hearing this, OYOSHI, *who has taken the pillow and* GONSHIRŌ*'s robe offstage, enters though the upstage curtains, runs to the door, and sits next to her father.)*

GONSHIRŌ *(Excitedly)*: I knew I had seen your face before. Oyoshi, rejoice. This is the woman who took Tsuchimatsu. Please come in.

OFUDE: Thank you.

TAKEMOTO:

She unties her hat / and takes it off as she enters.

*(*OYOSHI *helps take* OFUDE*'s hat and sandals, and* GONSHIRŌ *excitedly shows her inside.* OFUDE *sits left,* GONSHIRŌ *center, and* OYOSHI *right.)*

GONSHIRŌ *(Bowing)*: Thank you so much for coming. We should have searched for you to return your child, but we had no idea where to begin. *(Taking out his hand towel, he wipes his eyes.* OYOSHI *does the same.)* We only had our tears. *(Clearly making the point.)* We hope you will be happy that in return we have made sure the child has not received a scratch or suffered from a stomachache. My daughter is still able to breast-feed, so he needed only simple meals. The breast milk was usually enough.

OYOSHI: We did our best to make sure that he didn't even catch cold. *(Bowing.)* But I am sure my child caused you all sorts of trouble. Thank you for bringing him home.

*(*GONSHIRŌ *and* OYOSHI *turn toward the door as if* TSUCHIMATSU *were waiting outside.)*

GONSHIRŌ *(Calling out)*: Tsuchimatsu, have you forgotten your own home? Why haven't you come in?

OFUDE *(Sadly)*: I'm afraid he's not at the gate.

GONSHIRŌ *(So excited that he does not notice her tone)*: So you're having someone bring him by later? You didn't have to go to all that trouble. Thank you very much. *(Scolding.)* Oyoshi, thank the woman quickly.

OYOSHI: Don't be silly father. Do you think my gratitude could be expressed so easily? *(Somewhat worried.)* Why hasn't Tsuchimatsu come yet?

GONSHIRŌ: I can't wait to see him again.

TAKEMOTO:

They take turns looking out the door, / waiting for Tsuchimatsu, / and thanking Ofude. Watching them rejoice in such a way, / Ofude feels as though / she were being branded in the heart. She looks down, / not knowing how she is going to explain things now, / and for a while cannot find the right words to begin.

(As OYOSHI *bows in gratitude to* OFUDE, GONSHIRŌ *goes to the gate and looks out. He takes a doll of the legendary warrior-priest Benkei, one of* TSUCHIMATSU*'s toys, and carries it outside as if to beckon the boy, but the head falls off. This momentarily disturbs* GONSHIRŌ, *who thinks it might be an omen, but his joy quickly returns and he goes back inside.* OFUDE, *unable to watch, turns her back and closes her eyes in mourning.* GONSHIRŌ *and* OYOSHI *take turns bowing to* OFUDE, *and in their excitement they end up bowing to each other. They resume their former places.* OFUDE *tries to settle them down.)*

OFUDE: There was a favor I needed to ask of you and have come here in secret carrying my shame. Seeing you rejoice in such a way, I find it difficult to say what must be said. Please listen to my story. *(Offstage shamisen music plays in the background.)* At the sudden disturbance that night, the fact that you were able to escape quickly and hide must have been the blessing of your pilgrimage. There was a sick woman in my group.

TAKEMOTO:

"It did not help / that we had a retainer / because he was too old to protect us. / We were unable to escape / or hide as we had hoped."

*(*OFUDE *points off into the distance and then crosses her arms across her chest.)*

OFUDE: The child we mistakenly took . . .

GONSHIRŌ *(As if expecting good news)*: What about the child?

OFUDE: The child . . .

GONSHIRŌ: The child . . .

OFUDE *(Breaking down in tears)*: Died that same night.

TAKEMOTO:

They are so shocked hearing this, / understandably they forget to ask why or how, / or even to cry.

*(*GONSHIRŌ *and* OYOSHI *fall back in horror.* GONSHIRŌ *looks off into the distance as if he cannot believe what he has heard, and* OYOSHI *falls forward in tears.)*

OFUDE: Though we are all fated to die, the events of that night were too sad. I find myself lucky to still be alive. I will tell you the story as I try to explain myself.

TAKEMOTO:

"Please listen / and then feel free / to take out your anger on me."

*(*GONSHIRŌ *and* OYOSHI *sit motionless, unable to look up.)*

OFUDE: Though I cannot reveal her identity, the lady with me that night was my mistress. Getting caught up in the commotion *(cradling her arms as if holding a child),* I grabbed my young lord and fled from the inn, not noticing that I had taken the wrong child.

TAKEMOTO:

"Though we were able to escape without injury . . ."

(Pointing off into the distance.)

OFUDE: We were followed by a large group of soldiers. Our retainer fought them off like the famed Chinese general Hankai, but he was too old to be of much help and was killed in the battle. My young lord was stolen from me, and I searched about madly trying to retrieve him.

(Mimes fixing her obi and searching in the darkness. Taking out her sword, she shows how she pushed through the thick bamboo.)

TAKEMOTO:

"I searched deep into the night / made darker due to the lack of moonlight. / Then, within a grove of bamboo . . ."

OFUDE: "What luck. My young lord is here," I thought. But as I picked up his body and looked closely, I saw that it had no head. *(She takes out a cloth-wrapped package and opens it. Taking out the vest, she holds it as though holding a child.)* Looking closer, I noticed it was not my young lord. The proof is this vest. *(Places the vest in front of* GONSHIRŌ.*)* I realized I must have taken the wrong child in the commotion and felt relief that my young lord might still be alive. Then my lady and I realized we were responsible for the death of this child. What would we have now to exchange for our young lord? The pain of this was enough to push my lady beyond endurance. *(She begins to cry.)* She died soon after. *(Regaining composure.)* While it is very difficult for me to say so, what is done is done. I ask that you realize nothing can be done for your own child and that you return our young lord to me. When I heard you tell how well you took care of him, I didn't know whether to feel happy or sad. I ask your forgiveness for what has happened.

(OFUDE *brings her hands together, pleading. The others have their faces pressed to the ground in grief.)*

TAKEMOTO:

She falls flat to the ground in her tears. / Gonshirō does not let out a word, / but the tears flowing into his mouth / through gritted teeth get caught in his throat. / He sobs incessantly/ and cries enough tears to float his whole body.

(GONSHIRŌ *takes the vest and bites down on it to contain his overwhelming grief.)*

His daughter loses control / and she takes the vest of her lost son / in her hands.

(OYOSHI *rises to her knees and holds her chest as though she has a sharp pain. Cradling the vest, she gazes at it as if it were her child.)*

OYOSHI *(Sobbing)*: Tsuchimatsu. It's your mother. I'm here. *(Her words are drowned in tears.)* Just last night you were in my dreams. Your father was carrying you in his arms as we went to Tennō Temple. Perhaps I had this dream because you were both on my mind, as it was the third anniversary of your father's death.

TAKEMOTO:

"I was certain I would hear word of you today, / the anniversary of your father's death."

(OYOSHI *points off into the distance and then hugs the vest close to her chest.)*

OYOSHI: Such is the disgrace of attachments in this world. Each day I asked myself, "Will somebody bring him home today? Will he return tomorrow?" I continued to wait, but even the invocations I wrote on your vest were unable to save you. *(Looking at the vest.)* The pilgrimage was supposed to give us peace in both this world and the next.

TAKEMOTO:

"But it did not help at all. / Kannon showed no mercy. / I am so angry, / so lonely."

(OYOSHI *slaps the vest in anger.)*

OYOSHI: Why couldn't this have all been a dream?

TAKEMOTO:

She holds the vest to her face / and writhes in agony, / falling in tears so intense / that she becomes unaware of anything around her.

(She affectionately rubs the vest to her cheek and then appeals to her father as if asking how this could have happened. With nothing else to do, she drops her head to the ground, weeping.)

GONSHIRŌ *(Scolding)*: Stop crying, Oyoshi. Do you think your tears will bring Tsuchimatsu back? Will your useless complaints allow you to meet him again? Will you ignore all the times I taught you not to complain?

TAKEMOTO:

Encouraged by these words . . .

OFUDE: It is just as your father says. No matter how much you mourn, it will not bring Tsuchimatsu back. Yet if you were to give up on your son and return my young lord to me, it would do more to comfort his spirit than creating one thousand statues of Buddha or building one thousand temples, writing ten thousand sutras, or having ten thousand priests say prayers . . .

GONSHIRŌ *(Before* OFUDE *can even stop speaking)*: Shut up! I don't want to hear anything else out of you! Do you realize what you've been saying? Have you no shame? When you raise your own child, if you should cause it harm, at least you can take responsibility as a parent. But we are also responsible for the children of others. *(The end of his sentence is punctuated by a sharp note from the* TAKEMOTO *shamisen.)* You talk about your mistress and your young lord. It's obvious you are not from a common household. *(Looking toward the sky and bringing his hands together in prayer.)* I and my father and his father before him have taken the rudder, living day to day, but the sun never fools you. Shall I show you your child, the child we took great pains to take care of? *(He begins to stand, but stops.* OFUDE *shows a moment of hope in his words.)* No. No, I won't. If I do, your eyes will probably turn in their sockets. *(He throws down his hand towel to emphasize his words.)* When you take care of someone's child, you expect them to take equal care of yours as well. That's why we took such good care of him. But you probably still won't be satisfied. You'll probably make a face and ask why we didn't search for you. Even if we wanted to, we wouldn't have known where to begin. You had the address written on the vest. *(Beginning to sob.)* We waited each day, wondering each morning and each evening if someone would bring Tsuchimatsu back today, or perhaps tomorrow. *(Points to the screen with the* Ōtsu-e *paintings.)* Here, look at these pictures. Our dear Tsuchimatsu begged me to buy them as we left Mii Temple, but I said no. When I finally gave in, you should have seen how happily he walked through the streets. I bought pictures of the demon's prayer and the priest Geho having his head shaved by a man on a ladder. I bought the painting of Geho instead of the woman holding a branch of wisteria blossoms in the hope that it would be a lucky charm and that he, too, would live long enough to have grey hair and a long beard *(the tears begin to flow, and his voice becomes clouded)* or that he would become as strong as a demon and be able to get the best of anyone, making them crawl around like hungry ghosts begging for mercy. Thinking of how happy he'd be to see the pictures when he got home, I pasted them to the screen. But now I know that the ladder on Geho's head . . .

TAKEMOTO:

"Only led to his descent into Hell."

*(*GONSHIRŌ *places his hand on his head and then slips it down his face until it falls to the ground.)*

GONSHIRŌ: And he has turned into the hungry ghost beaten by demons. Were prayers to Amida enough to save him? The more I think about it, the more I go out of my head. *(Accusingly and gradually becoming more and more angry.)* How could you have allowed this to happen? Now you want us to forget about Tsuchimatsu and return your young lord? How can you have the audacity? Oh, I'll give him back all right. *(*OFUDE *is again filled with hope at his words.)* We may be simple commoners, but your young lord is the enemy of my grandson. *(Rising to one knee.)* I'll give you back his head!

*(*OFUDE *and* OYOSHI *fall back in shock as* GONSHIRŌ *rises.)*

TAKEMOTO:

He stands that instant. / Crying out "You cannot," / Ofude tries to stop him, / but he merely pushes her away.

*(*OFUDE *tries to keep* GONSHIRŌ *from going, grabbing his sleeve, but he pushes her aside. When he gets past her,* OYOSHI *tries to hold* OFUDE *back as* GONSHIRŌ *opens the sliding screens to the left room and stands ready, holding the hem of his kimono in his hands.)*

Opening the screens to the inner room, / he is surprised to find Matsuemon / with the young lord at his side. / His sword in his hand, / Matsuemon stands like a strong warrior. / Seeing this . . .

(Inside the room, MATSUEMON *sits boldly on a stool* [aibiki] *holding* TSUCHIMATSU *by his left side. The boy stands on a small black stool.* MATSUEMON *now wears a thick green kimono with yellow stripes and a yellow obi tied in a large bow in front. Underneath, there is a hint of a black kimono with silver and gold trim. He wears a sword in his obi, and running to his temples from the edge of his eyebrows is a slight red line in the* kumadori *makeup style.* MATSUEMON *grips a white hand towel in his right hand.)*

OFUDE *(Shocked)*: Higuchi.

MATSUEMON *(Warning)*: Careful, young woman. You resemble someone I saw by the canal gate. The young lord is in my care. You need not worry. I will announce my name when the time is right. Until then, you must make certain not to accidentally open the canal gate.

TAKEMOTO:

Seeing the silent signal in his eyes, / she nods her agreement / and says no more. / Gonshirō has noticed none of this.

*(*OFUDE *quietly sits at right.* OYOSHI *sits to her right.)*

GONSHIRŌ: Well done, Matsuemon. I knew you wouldn't have been able to sleep through all the commotion. You surely heard everything. That child is the enemy of Tsuchimatsu. Cut up the brat and hand him over to this woman.

MATSUEMON *(Sternly)*: I will not.

GONSHIRŌ: Will not? What do you mean "will not"? *(*MATSUEMON *hesitates.* GONSHIRŌ *falls to the ground in tears.)* How can you be so unfeeling? *(Becoming angry.)* I see. You do not consider him your enemy because Tsuchimatsu was only your stepson. I won't let you get away with it. *(Angrily.)* All bets are off! I no longer consider us father and son. Oyoshi, run and call a group of young men to throw him out of the house.

TAKEMOTO:

He hurriedly sends her on her way.

*(*GONSHIRŌ *ties up his hand towel into a headband. Rising, pulling his right sleeve to his shoulder, and taking the hem of his kimono in his hands, he stumbles slightly as he plants his foot in a* mie *to* tsuke *beats. He stands, glaring threateningly at* MATSUEMON*.)*

MATSUEMON *(Calling out)*: Oyoshi, wait. There's no need to call anybody. Father, are you really that determined to take revenge on this boy as the enemy of Tsuchimatsu?

GONSHIRŌ *(Emphatic)*: You bet.

MATSUEMON: Then I have no choice. I will reveal my identity and explain everything.

TAKEMOTO:

Placing the young lord in Ofude's care . . .

(Carrying TSUCHIMATSU, MATSUEMON *crosses right and enters the main room.* OFUDE *crosses up to take the boy. She leads him to sit on the left as* MATSUEMON *slowly comes downstage and looks outside to make sure no one is listening. As he places his foot outside the gate, and then puts his hand on the gatepost, his movements are punctuated by sharp notes from the* TAKEMOTO *shamisen.)*

MATSUEMON *(Slowly)*: Gonshirō. Your head is too high.

GONSHIRŌ *(Incredulously)*: You must be joking.

MATSUEMON *(Closing the door and posing inside, he speaks commandingly)*: Bow down low! *(He slowly crosses to center.)* Lightning in the heavens may not be visible, but it announces its presence with a great thunder. This child is Komawaka, the son of the Asahi Shogun Kiso Yoshinaka. *(Shocked,* GONSHIRŌ *loses his balance. Replacing his sleeve and taking off the headband, he meekly walks to the*

Matsuemon (Nakamura Kōshirō IX) poses powerfully with one foot planted on the center step. Gonshirō (Kawarasaki Gonjūrō III) and his wife, Oyoshi (Sawamura Tanosuke VI), left, react with amazement as they hear that the child, Tsuchimatsu, right, protected by Lady-in-Waiting Ofude (Onoe Baikō VII), is actually the son of Lord Kiso Yoshinaka. (Umemura Yutaka, Engeki Shuppansha)

right past MATSUEMON. MATSUEMON *brings his right fist to his chest and stretches his left arm out, begins to speak slowly, and builds into a crescendo.)*

I am Higuchi Jirō Kanemitsu!

TAKEMOTO:

At his words / Gonshirō and Oyoshi forget their anger / and can only stand in shock.

*(*GONSHIRŌ *and* OYOSHI *fall back in surprise.* MATSUEMON *returns to the upper level. With one foot on the step, he suddenly turns back and glares at* GONSHIRŌ *in a* mie *emphasized by two* tsuke *beats. On the upper level, he turns to glare at* GONSHIRŌ *while he poses again.* GONSHIRŌ *puts his right arm around a kneeling* OYOSHI *as if to protect her, unable to hide his shock at* MATSUEMON*'s revelation.)*

Higuchi turns to Ofude.

*(*MATSUEMON *sits center on a stool placed by a black-garbed* STAGE ASSISTANT [kurogo]. *His dynamic pose, with widespread legs, and his slow, powerful speech indicate his transformation into his true identity as a powerful warrior.)*

MATSUEMON: I commend your diligence. Despite your best efforts, Lady Yamabuki passed away, and your father also met his end in battle. How you must grieve. *(*OFUDE *drops her head in sorrow.)* Still, you must wonder what I am doing here. My lord ordered me to assassinate the traitor Tada no Kurandō Yukiie, even though he was the granduncle of the young lord. While I was away on this mission, Yoshinaka's forces were defeated at the battle of Kuritsu. Though innocent, my lord Yoshinaka was forced to kill himself. Hearing of his death, I rushed to the battlefield, but I then considered how important the task of avenging his death would be. I married into this family as part of an elaborate plan to kill Yoshitsune and Noriyori.

TAKEMOTO:

"I was able to approach Kajiwara / by saying I knew the art of *sakaro*."

*(*MATSUEMON *mimes rowing a boat. He points off into the distance and glares in a* mie *emphasized by two* tsuke *beats.)*

MATSUEMON *(In time to the rhythm of the* TAKEMOTO *shamisen* [nori]*)*: Now I have been named the captain of Yoshitsune's boat. *(Laughs triumphantly.)* With my goal in hand, I turned my attention to the whereabouts of our young lord.

TAKEMOTO:

"I could not help but worry / if he was safe."

(Places both hands out wide as if searching left and right, and then bows.)

MATSUEMON: Hearing your story from inside the *shōji* screens, I looked into the face of the boy *(looks toward* KOMAWAKA*)*, and the more I looked, the more I was convinced that he truly was Komawaka. It wasn't planned, and I hadn't even dared to hope that it could be true. *(Crossing his arms back and forth.)* But the fact that you should both stay at the same inn on the same day and mistake each other's child was the good fate of our young lord. *(Raises his hand in a sign of praise toward* KOMAWAKA *but suddenly stops, and his voice becomes filled with regret.)* And yet . . .

TAKEMOTO:

"Tsuchimatsu was my stepson."

*(*MATSUEMON *points to the vest and closes his eyes as tears begin to well up.)*

MATSUEMON: Offering his life in place of Komawaka, he showed his true loyal heart. He was able to discern the wishes of the gods and Buddhas. Though he was not my child by birth, he showed his loyalty.

TAKEMOTO:

"There is nothing / that could make me happier."

(Despite his words, MATSUEMON *throws his head back in sorrow.)*

MATSUEMON: And to whom do I owe all of this? *(Placing his hand towel in his kimono,* MATSUEMON *crosses down to* GONSHIRŌ *and helps him to stand.)* Please.

(Taking both of GONSHIRŌ's *hands and keeping his head bowed low as a sign of respect,* MATSUEMON *leads* GONSHIRŌ *to the seat of honor, left.* MATSUEMON *kneels center, facing* GONSHIRŌ.*)* Father, I owe this all to you. You set the example by treating me as your own child. Seeing this, Tsuchimatsu treated me as his own father. How can I hope to repay you? If it were only some other child, were you and Oyoshi to order me to take revenge, I would not hesitate. But I cannot take the life of the son of my lord. Tsuchimatsu called me father, but that was possible only because you were kind enough to call me son. The love you have shown me is higher than the highest mountain and deeper than the deepest sea, but by right of birth the benevolence of the son of my lord is still greater. How can I allow you to kill him as the enemy of your grandson? *(Grappling with his inner conflict.)* Do you expect me to bear the burden of being known as the murderer of my lord? There is nothing I can say that can take away your anger and your pain, but I ask that our relationship as father and son, as the husband of your daughter, can allow you to pass this tragedy off as fate. Allow me to fulfill my duty as a samurai. *(Bowing.)* Father, please.

TAKEMOTO:

"Father, please hear my words." / Higuchi's manner, / devoted in loyalty to his lord, / is greater than that of either fellow retainers Kaneie or Tomoe. / As one of Kiso's bodyguards, / he is a samurai among samurai.

*(*MATSUEMON *crawls on his knees toward his father-in-law, and, placing his hand on* GONSHIRŌ*'s right knee, looks into his eyes, pleading. Looking off into the distance, he takes two steps back on his knees, and, after first raising his hands above his head, bows low to* GONSHIRŌ.*)*

Gonshirō clasps his hands together.

*(*GONSHIRŌ *lifts his head and fixes the collar of his kimono.)*

GONSHIRŌ *(Resigned)*: If my son is a samurai, then I must be one as well. My son's lord is my lord. Son-in-law, lift your hands. Please, lift your hands. *(*GONSHIRŌ *motions to* MATSUEMON *with his hand, and* MATSUEMON *sits upright.)* Praise to the god of sailors. I am no longer angry, no longer sad. I will cry no more. *(He begins to sob.)* Oyoshi, you must do your best to bear another Tsuchimatsu.

MATSUEMON *(Hopefully)*: You have changed your mind?

GONSHIRŌ: Yes.

MATSUEMON *(Filled with gratitude)*: You have? I am eternally grateful. *(Bows deeply.)*

TAKEMOTO:

They release the feelings / in their hearts / and show as much joy as those / afloat and lost on the waves, / who spy a port in the distance.

*(*MATSUEMON *and* GONSHIRŌ *approach each other on their knees and, taking the other's hand, gaze deeply at each other. Separating, they face forward and bring their hands together in a sign of gratitude.)*

Ofude happily hands the young lord / over to Higuchi Jirō.

*(*MATSUEMON *crosses to the upper level and sits center.* OFUDE *places* KOMAWAKA *in his care and sits at right.)*

OFUDE: Higuchi, there is no more reason to worry about the child. I have heard that my sister is currently working nearby in the city of Kanzaki. I would like to search for her as well as offer services for my father, who was killed in Ōtsu. I will be on my way.

TAKEMOTO:

As she stands . . .

*(*OFUDE *crosses below and takes a seat at right center.)*

MATSUEMON: Hearing your reasons, I will not try to stop you. You may go as you please.

GONSHIRŌ: You cannot let her leave so easily. Please stay for two or three days. Isn't that so, Oyoshi?

OYOSHI: It's just as you say. Having expressed our feelings in such a way, even though we just met, it's difficult to say farewell so soon. Please stay at least the night.

OFUDE: Thank you very much, but, as I've just explained, there is important business I must attend to. I ask you to please take care of my young lord.

OYOSHI: We are so close, there's no need to ask. Once your task is complete, I hope you will come again.

OFUDE: Until then . . .

GONSHIRŌ: Young woman on the road . . .

OFUDE: Farewell.

*(*GONSHIRŌ, OFUDE, *and* OYOSHI *bow.)*

TAKEMOTO:

Saying farewell themselves, / they see her off at the door, / and watch Ofude go / as she disappears into the distance.

(Offstage drum plays wind pattern [kaze no oto] *as* OFUDE *bows to* GONSHIRŌ *and* OYOSHI *and then turns to bow to* KOMAWAKA. OFUDE *takes her traveling hat from* OYOSHI *and exits the house, walking toward the* hanamichi. *Reaching* shichisan, *she turns back and bows. Then, with* GONSHIRŌ *watching from the door, she looks off into the distance and exits down the* hanamichi *at a gradually quickening pace.)*

GONSHIRŌ: There's just something about women raised in samurai households. You could learn a lot from her, Oyoshi. *(Coming back into the house,* GONSHIRŌ *spots the vest and quickly turns away. Mournfully.)* Oyoshi, that troublesome vest is over here. Throw it away.

MATSUEMON: That would be disrespectful. You should at least place it on the altar, offer incense, and say a prayer.

GONSHIRŌ: But wouldn't people laugh at me as being too sentimental now that I'm the father of a samurai?

MATSUEMON: Why would anybody laugh?

GONSHIRŌ *(As if a great weight has been lifted)*: That is just what I wanted to do. *(Sitting down, he picks up the vest and holds it as if it were* TSUCHIMATSU.*)* I wanted him to live one thousand or a hundred thousand years, but he barely made it to six. Hail, Amida Buddha. Tsuchimatsu, may the bodhisattvas show your spirit the path to enlightenment. Son-in-law, daughter, you pray as well.

TAKEMOTO:

They look into each other's face / and shed tears / as the sound of the evening bell / is heard in the distance.

*(*MATSUEMON *places his sword in his obi, stands with* KOMAWAKA *in his arms, and exits through the curtained doorway.* GONSHIRŌ *takes* OYOSHI*'s hand and they follow. The stage is empty as the sound of the temple bell* [kane no oto] *is heard three times. The pace quickens and the mood lightens.)*

It is dusk, / time for the boatmen to come. / Kurosaku and Mataroku arrive, / led by Tomizō,/ and call in immediately from the gate.

*(*KUROSAKU, MATAROKU, *and* TOMIZŌ *run down the* hanamichi *and stand before the front door. They wear short work jackets and orange coats tied with simple obi. Each holds a large oar.)*

THREE BOATMEN *(Briskly, in time to the* TAKEMOTO *shamisen)*: Matsuemon. Matsuemon. Are you inside or out, or perhaps in the boathouse? Just as promised . . .

TOMIZŌ: Tomizō . . .

KUROSAKU: Kurosaku . . .

MATAROKU: Mataroku . . .

TOMIZŌ: All three of us have come . . .

THREE BOATMEN: To learn the secret art of rowing.

*(*MATSUEMON *enters from the curtained doorway, crosses to the door, opens it, and motions them in.)*

MATSUEMON: Thank you for coming. Please come in and have a smoke.

THREE BOATMEN: No. This is a very important and urgent matter. We can have a leisurely smoke after we have worked up a sweat.

MATSUEMON: If that's the case, let's head to the dock.

THREE BOATMEN: Matsuemon . . .

MATSUEMON *(Calling out and raising his hand to beckon them)*: Come on.

TAKEMOTO:

He leads them out back.

(Taking an oar, MATSUEMON *leads them through the curtained door as the accelerating clack of the* ki *is heard. Curtain.)*

The Secret Art of Rowing at the Fukushima Pine

(The curtain opens to a drum wave pattern, revealing a light blue curtain [asagi-maku] *that covers the full stage, hiding the scene behind it.)*

TAKEMOTO:

Aboard a boat in famous Fukushima Bay / are the sailors who have come / to perform *sakaro.*

(Wave pattern crescendos. One ki *clack signals the blue curtain to drop, revealing a scene of waves lapping the seashore. Left and right, large stones represent the shore. Standing in a three-dimensional boat at sea are* MATSUEMON, MATAROKU, KUROSAKU, *and* TOMIZŌ, *played by child actors to make the scene seem farther away by a trick of perspective* [tōmi]. *Each has removed the top layers of clothing for work, revealing stylized octopus-leg patterns on his undergarments.* MATSUEMON*'s dress is a striking gold and silver on black. The sailors' kimono are light blue, and they have hand towels tied like bandannas around their heads.)*

THREE BOATMEN *(In rhythm to* TAKEMOTO *shamisen)*: Matsuemon, we have supported our families by working on boats, but we have never heard of *sakaro.*

MATSUEMON: That is no surprise. Leave everything to me and I will teach you. Tomizō, stand here. Kurosaku, stand like this. Mataroku should be here. *(He places them in position at three corners of the boat.)* This is how *sakaro* is done.

TAKEMOTO:

"On land, / both ally and enemy forces / ride on horseback / and are free / to move back and forth / as they please."

*(*MATSUEMON *raises his hand and looks right and left. He then looks down at both his right and left sleeves. He places his oar in the water and moves his head in a traditional three-step movement from back to front on both the left and right. Lifting his oar from the water, he waves his hand left and right and then in a beckoning motion.)*

MATSUEMON: But it is different on a boat. As you know, boats are pulled by the tide . . .

TAKEMOTO:

"And can be subject / to movements of the wind. / Move your oars in rhythm."

(Wave pattern. MATSUEMON *waves his hand while moving his arm from the upper right to the lower left to symbolize the wind, then stamps his foot on the side of the boat and pretends to spit on his hand. With both hands on the oar, he performs a* mie *emphasized by two* tsuke *beats.)*

MATSUEMON: Starboard!

THREE BOATMEN: Port!

TAKEMOTO:

"Watch the wind and tide."

(Placing his oar in the water and his right arm straight out above and behind him, MATSUEMON *poses in a* mie *emphasized by two* tsuke *beats.)*

MATSUEMON: All together now.

THREE BOATMEN: Yes, sir.

ALL: Row, row, row!

(All four place their oars in the water and row alternately, first the two in front and then the two in the rear.)

TAKEMOTO:

They row farther out into the bay. / Seeing their chance, / Tomizō and Kurosaku take up their oars / and hit Matsuemon in the knees. / They swing left and right.

*(*KUROSAKU, MATAROKU, *and* TOMIZŌ *lift their oars and turn threateningly on* MATSUEMON, *who, keeping one hand on his oar, throws his left arm straight out above and behind him in a* mie *emphasized by two* tsuke *beats. They swing their oars at* MATSUEMON, *but he is able to hold off their blows. When* TOMIZŌ *hits him on the forehead, he seizes* TOMIZŌ*'s oar, forces him down, and holds off* KUROSAKU *and* MATAROKU *with his own oar. At the clack of the* ki, *he stamps his foot on the side of the boat, raises his oar into the air, and performs a* mie *emphasized by two* tsuke *beats. At the clack of the* ki, *a curtain with a painting of the sea drops in from above to hide the stage and the large drum beats a loud wave pattern.)*

The Large Pine on Shore

(After a few moments, one ki *clack signals the curtain to fall, revealing the shore behind* MATSUEMON*'s house. The rear entrance to the house is visible to the left. Next to it stands a large anchor with a long, thick rope attached to it. Center is a large pine with a stump into which steps are built just downstage of it. Two groups of* SOLDIERS *dressed as boatmen run onstage, perform coordinated somersaults* [tonbo] *center, and then stand waiting, looking to the left. Another large group enters, carrying oars, until twenty-five or thirty men fill the stage. They all wear short jackets* [hanten], *leggings in a similar pattern, and loincloths. They hold their oars ready to attack as* MATSUEMON*—a large scar on his forehead—enters from left. As he brandishes his oar left and right, half the* SOLDIERS *run past him. Reaching center, he extends his hand and poses in a* mie *emphasized by two* tsuke *beats as* TOMIZŌ, MATAROKU, *and* KUROSAKU *confront him.)*

MATSUEMON: What do you think you are doing?

TOMIZŌ: You should know. You are the traitorous warrior Higuchi Jirō, retainer of Kiso Yoshinaka.

KUROSAKU: Lord Kajiwara knew it from the beginning. He ordered us to learn the secret art of rowing from you . . .

MATAROKU: And to take the opportunity to capture you. We order you . . .

THREE BOATMEN: To surrender!

TAKEMOTO:

Hearing their insulting demands, / Higuchi gives a loud, / cheerful laugh.

(With a loud cry, they raise their oars threateningly. Bringing his fist in front of him, MATSUEMON *looks left and right.)*

MATSUEMON *(Laughs)*: If you wish, I will announce my name. Listen well.

TAKEMOTO:

"Kiso Yoshinaka, / the General of the Rising Sun, / called me one of his four bodyguards."

*(*MATSUEMON *jumps out, spreading his legs, and edges forward in a shuffling movement* [jiri-jiri]. *Spreading his arms wide, he steps forward in a bounding "six-directions" movement* [roppō]. *He throws down his oar.)*

MATSUEMON *(Loudly)*: I am Higuchi Jirō Kanemitsu. *(He spits on his hand and snorts, bringing his fist in front of his chest, and performs a* mie *emphasized by two* tsuke *beats.)* Trying to fight me would be like an ant trying to pull the largest of anchors. I dare you to attack.

TAKEMOTO:

He opens his long arms, / waiting for them.

(Stamping boldly with his foot, he spreads his arms wide to the staccato rhythm of the TAKEMOTO *shamisen and poses in a* mie *emphasized by two* tsuke *beats.)*

TOMIZŌ: Get him!

(A large-scale choreographed fight [tachimawari] *follows. To the loud beats of the backstage drum and rhythmic* tsuke *that emphasize their movements, the* SOLDIERS *divide into two groups, flanking* MATSUEMON. *They swing their oars in the "mountain shape"* [yamagata]. MATSUEMON *spins them into a large circle and they surround him with their oars on their shoulders. The* SOLDIERS *form a boat, from stern to bow, extending across the stage, with* MATSUEMON *standing on the backs of men in the middle, holding up an oar and posing in a* mie *to two* tsuke *beats. The* SOLDIERS *split into two groups. The group on the right rushes at* MATSUEMON, *swinging oars like swords, but he easily deflects their blows and the* SOLDIERS *fall to the left. The group on his left repeats this futile attack. Both groups run offstage, returning to attack in groups of three or four. When they strike with their oars,* MATSUEMON *is able to hold them off, either with an oar or empty-handed. Defeated, the* SOLDIERS *flip in somersaults while* MATSUEMON *performs a* mie *to two* tsuke *beats. The* tachimawari *is also marked by acrobatic stunts. Three men kneel to form an interlocking circle as one lies on top with his legs spread upward, imitating an octopus. The man on top then stands and flips off the others' backs. Men flip over their partners' backs or jump over their heads while standing. One group of six performs somersaults and then does headstands flanking* MATSUEMON *as he performs a* mie *emphasized by two* tsuke *beats. The entire*

Matsuemon (Onoe Shōroku II), a warrior in disguise, strikes a *mie* as he seizes the oars of attacking Genji soldiers. (Tsubouchi Memorial Theatre Museum of Waseda University)

group of SOLDIERS *reenters, seizing the thick anchor rope and unwinding it until it reaches halfway down the* hanamichi. MATSUEMON *lifts the anchor in a great feat of strength and, swinging it back and forth, makes them fall. Breaking off the end of the rope, he lifts the anchor above his head and glares at the fallen* SOLDIERS *menacingly.)*

TAKEMOTO:

They are hesitant to attack him / and flee when faced with his great strength. *(*MATSUEMON *throws the anchor at the* SOLDIERS, *who carry it off.* MATSUEMON *chases the others down the* hanamichi. *Stopping at* shichisan, *he glares fiercely. From behind, two* SOLDIERS *attack with oars, but* MATSUEMON *takes control and forces them to kneel. Standing on their backs and holding onto the upright oars, he poses in a* mie *that resembles the bow of a boat. Pressing down with his weight, he crushes the men below his feet. They rise listlessly, and he throws them aside by flinging away the oars. Back on the main stage, men flip and lie motionless.* MATSUEMON *poses in a* mie *facing the stage. Spying the large pine, he runs to it in a stylized "flying-in-six-directions"* [tobi roppō] *movement, hopping alternately on each leg while his arm movements simulate swimming.)*

The sound of a battle drum / can be heard in the distance. / He spots a large pine / that should give him a good view. / Taking a perch, he gazes out in the four directions.

(Standing at the foot of the pine, MATSUEMON *looks off to the left.)*

MATSUEMON: From Ebie and Nagara in the north . . .

TAKEMOTO:

"To Kawasaki and Tenma village / in the east . . ."

(He looks off to his right.)

MATSUEMON: From Tsumura and Mitsu Beach in the south . . .

TAKEMOTO:

"To the Genji camps in the west, / there are people as far as the eye can see."

(His view is blocked by a large pine branch, so he lifts it and, looking off into the distance, poses in a mie *emphasized by two* tsuke *beats.)*

MATSUEMON: They have all come to capture me. What a cunning scheme.

TAKEMOTO:

Seeing this, / he jumps down.

(Leaping down, he calls out toward the house.)

MATSUEMON: Wife!

*(*OYOSHI *runs out from the house carrying* MATSUEMON*'s swords.)*

OYOSHI: Father broke a hole in the wall of the back room and has disappeared.

MATSUEMON: He must have gone to sell me out. I can't believe I trusted a simple boatman. It's as if my own dog had bitten me.

TAKEMOTO:

He tightens his fists / and cries tears of regret.

(Reacting as described, he strikes at each arm in turn. Stamping with his foot, he crosses his hands before his chest, and his chest heaves with his heavy breathing.)

Suddenly there is a voice / in the distance.

SHIGETADA *(From offstage)*: Higuchi Jirō Kanemitsu! I, Hatakeyama Shōji Shigetada, would meet with you!

MATSUEMON *(Looking off into the distance)*: What is going on?

*(*OYOSHI *hands* MATSUEMON *his swords and hides behind his back. Putting his swords through his obi,* MATSUEMON *spreads out his arm to hide and protect her.)*

TAKEMOTO:

His authority as a great samurai / shining like the large lamps of his procession, / Hatakeyama Shōji Shigetada enters, / led by Gonshirō.

*(*SHIGETADA, *the opposing Genji general, enters with his entourage, including a pair of* SERVANTS *carrying two large lanterns printed with his crest, one* SERVANT *carrying his stool, and his four* BODYGUARDS. SHIGETADA *wears a white kimono with black formal overvestments* [kamishimo] *and a lacquered hat* [eboshi] *with a metal crest on the front. The* BODYGUARDS *wear armor over gold*

kimono tied at the arms and legs. The SERVANTS *wear striped* hakama *over bright yellow kimono. Those carrying the lanterns have flat, cone-shaped caps with a large red circle on the front.* GONSHIRŌ *follows, carrying* KOMAWAKA *on his back. The servants carrying the lanterns sit in front of the offstage music room* [geza], *right.* SHIGETADA *and his* BODYGUARDS *countercross with* MATSUEMON, *going to the right as* MATSUEMON *moves left. The* SERVANT *places the stool on which* SHIGETADA *sits, while his* BODYGUARDS *take seats on the ground behind him. A large group of* SOLDIERS *dressed as boatmen enters from the left and right and sits on the ground at rear.)*

Seeing this . . .

OYOSHI: Father, how could you?

*(*GONSHIRŌ *sits at left and lets* KOMAWAKA *down off his back.)*

GONSHIRŌ: Are you also angry at Tsuchimatsu?

OYOSHI: If you call him Tsuchimatsu, Matsuemon will become angry.

GONSHIRŌ: Why should he? I became worried that my grandson would be taken away because of his relationship to Higuchi. This is not the son of Higuchi, but of your former husband. When I pleaded for mercy for my grandson in exchange for giving the location of Higuchi, they listened to my request. The heavens have opened and Tsuchimatsu has been saved, but it was I who saved him. Why should Higuchi be angered? The boy is not his child, and he is not the young lord. He is my beloved grandchild. Am I supposed to let him be killed just so I can fulfill my duty as a samurai? Can those large eyes of yours not see how I struggled to find a solution? How could you be angry at me? Rather, your words are angering me.

TAKEMOTO:

His voice clouds with emotion. / Higuchi would say "Well done," / and express his gratitude, / but he is unable to speak/ lest the deception become known. / His tears, though, / express his thoughts / better than one hundred times as many words. / Still, he does not show this openly / and approaches Shigetada.

*(*MATSUEMON *slaps his knees and raises his hands with his palms facing outward in a sign of praise and then uses his hands to hide his tears as he throws his head back in sorrow. He sits on a stool placed center by a* STAGE ASSISTANT.*)*

MATSUEMON: If I were facing Kajiwara, I would cut him down with such fierceness that my sword would break at its hilt, but I cannot turn my sword on someone who opposes me with compassion. I will slit open my stomach and present my head to you.

TAKEMOTO:

Before he can even finish his words . . .

SHIGETADA: I have no intention of gloating over my victory by taking your head. Since you have accepted your defeat, prepare to be bound.

MATSUEMON: It is the way of the warrior to commit ritual suicide when fate turns against him. I have no intention of living out my days in shame, bound as a prisoner.

SHIGETADA: Don't be foolish, Higuchi. *(Background music sets the mood.)* You were known as bodyguard to Kiso Yoshinaka and did your best to avenge his death. I have no intention of insulting such a fine man. I will bind you because I know it is the will of my great leader, Yoshitsune, who also sees you as a loyal, brave warrior.

TAKEMOTO:

Approaching Higuchi, / he twists his arm and smiles broadly.

*(*SHIGETADA *hands his tassels to his servant and lifts* MATSUEMON*'s hand by the wrist.)*

MATSUEMON: Throughout the eight provinces of Kanto, no warrior is as brave and strong as Shigetada. But I am just as strong, and though it would be easy enough to tear your arms from their sockets, I am no match for the power of your wisdom and honor. You may bind me.

TAKEMOTO:

He places his hands / behind his back.

*(*MATSUEMON *puts his free hand behind his back.)*

SHIGETADA: Lord Noriyori attacks in the fore and Lord Yoshitsune defends in the rear. The rope that binds Higuchi is as strong as their wise rule and their scholarly and military learning.

TAKEMOTO:

Both captor and prisoner / are brave warriors: / loyalty holds the rope / that binds Higuchi.

*(*SHIGETADA *puts* MATSUEMON*'s other hand behind his back. His* BODYGUARDS *surround* MATSUEMON *and bind him with a thick rope.)*

SHIGETADA: Woman. Tsuchimatsu is a very important child for Higuchi. Let him say his farewell.

TAKEMOTO:

At his words, / Oyoshi approaches Higuchi in tears.

(Bowing, OYOSHI *leads* KOMAWAKA *to* MATSUEMON*'s side.)*

OYOSHI *(To* KOMAWAKA*)*: Even though your time together was short, this will be your final opportunity to call each other father and son. Show him your face.

TAKEMOTO:

She pushes the child forward.

*(*OYOSHI *backs away and bows.* MATSUEMON *turns to the boy and gazes into his face.)*

MATSUEMON: Tsuchimatsu. Say your farewell, but don't call me father.

KOMAWAKA *(In the high, slow tones of a child role)*: Higuchi, farewell.

TAKEMOTO:

The young child calls out / like a young chick / being separated from its parent.

*(*MATSUEMON *expresses both his joy and sadness at these words and closes his eyes in tears. Facing front, he throws his head back, overcome with sadness. A sequence of passed-along dialogue* [watarizerifu] *follows.)*

SHIGETADA: Though some may pray for long life . . .

MATSUEMON: The impermanence of this world is difficult to bear.

GONSHIRŌ: The old remain . . .

OYOSHI: While the young die . . .

SHIGETADA: In this backward world.

MATSUEMON and SHIGETADA: A lesson taught by the Sakaro Pine.

(The large offstage drum [ōdaiko] *is heard. All stand.* MATSUEMON *turns and bows to* SHIGETADA, *who turns his back to the audience.* MATSUEMON *gazes into* KOMAWAKA*'s face, then crosses right with the* BODYGUARDS. GONSHIRŌ, OYOSHI, *and* KOMAWAKA *move behind* MATSUEMON *and* SHIGETADA.*)*

TAKEMOTO:

Even today / this pine remains in Fukushima, / its branches unwithered.

(A clack of the ki. SHIGETADA *faces forward, and* MATSUEMON *and* SHIGETADA *turn to face each other in a tableau pose* [hippari mie]. *The curtain closes to the pounding of the backstage drum and continuous clacks of the* ki.*)*

Three-panel woodblock print by Toyohara Kunichika (1835–1900). Shintomi-za, Tokyo, July 1883. "Danshichi Kurōbei" ("Ichikawa Danjūrō" IX), his naked body covered with tattoos, is about to kill his evil father-in-law, "Giheiji" ("Ichikawa Sadanji" I). Danshichi looks over his shoulder at approaching festival dancers, while Giheiji tries to fend off the coming blow with an outstretched hand. Danshichi's sworn brother, "Issun Tokubei," shown in the inset, wears a distinctive large-striped kimono, On alternate days the role was played by "Ichikawa Sadanji" I (pictured) and Onoe Kikugorō V. (Tsubouchi Memorial Theatre Museum of Waseda University)

Summer Festival: Mirror of Osaka
Natsu Matsuri Naniwa Kagami

Namiki Sōsuke, Miyoshi Shōraku, and Takeda Koizumo

TRANSLATED BY JULIE A. IEZZI

BEFORE THE TORII AT SUMIYOSHI SHRINE

Sumiyoshi Torii Mae no Ba

HOUSE OF SABU THE BOATMAN

Tsurifune Sabu no Uchi no Ba

BACK STREET OF NAGAMACHI

Nagamachi Ura no Ba

1745 TAKEMOTO-ZA, OSAKA

Summer Festival: Mirror of Osaka

INTRODUCTION

Summer Festival was penned by the trio of playwrights Namiki Sōsuke (Senryū) (1695–1751), Miyoshi Shōraku (1696–1772), and Takeda Koizumo (Izumo II) (1691–1756), who would become famous as the authors of the "Three Masterpieces" of the puppet theatre: *Sugawara and the Secrets of Calligraphy* (Sugawara Denju Tenarai Kagami, 1746), *Yoshitsune and the Thousand Cherry Trees* (Yoshitsune Senbon Zakura, 1747), and *The Treasury of Loyal Retainers* (Kanadehon Chūshingura, 1748). *Summer Festival,* a nine-scene domestic play *(sewamono),* written for the puppet theatre, was the team's first successful collaborative work, debuting in the seventh month of 1745 at the Takemoto-za in Osaka. The play caught the audience's fancy immediately, and it ran through the end of the year. A month after it opened, two Kyoto kabuki theatres adapted the play, and in the twelfth month, all three of Osaka's large kabuki theatres staged competing productions.

Unlike the historical worlds *(sekai)* of the subsequent "masterpieces," this all-day play *(tōshi kyōgen)* is set in the everyday world of the Osaka merchant and contrasts the driving force of money against the samurai virtues of obligation and honor, which the commoner class increasingly emulated. Honor wins out over greed, though at the cost of a samurai's sacrifice for his lord.

Translated here are the three scenes of the original play most commonly staged today in both kabuki and the puppet theatre: "Before the Torii at Sumiyoshi Shrine" (scene iii of the original), which dramatizes the pact of brotherhood between Danshichi Kurōbei and Issun Tokubei, two gallant street knights *(otokodate),* and their vow to sacrifice everything to care for the disowned young samurai Isonojō; "House of Sabu the Boatman" (scene vi), in which Tokubei's wife, Otatsu, scars her face with a hot iron, sacrificing beauty for honor; and "Back Street of Nagamachi" (scene viii), which graphically depicts Danshichi's murder of his scheming father-in-law, Giheiji, epitomizing kabuki's beauty of cruelty *(zankoku no bi)* aesthetic.

In recent years, Ichikawa Ennosuke III (b. 1939) and Nakamura Kankurō V (b. 1955) have staged longer productions, including scenes from the original that set up the conflict between Isonojō, his prostitute lover, Kotoura, and the jealous older samurai, Sagaemon; show Danshichi rescuing Isonojō from the hands of a devious pawnshop clerk conspiring with Danshichi's greedy father-in-law; and end with a grand fight scene *(tachimawari)* as the police surround Danshichi on the roof of his home.

One reason for the popularity of *Summer Festival* was the adventurous staging of puppeteer Yoshida Bunzaburō I (d. 1760) in the 1745 premier. Arguably the most influential puppeteer in Japanese puppet theatre history, he increased puppet expressivity by inventing movable eyes, fingers, and hands. For the scene in which Danshichi murders Giheiji, Bunzaburō utilized real mud, providing a realistic touch as the puppets became covered in it during the struggle. Bunzaburō then used real water to wash the mud from Danshichi's body. When *Summer Festival* was adapted to kabuki, the mud and water came along, too, giving the scene its popular title, the "Mud Scene" (Doro Ba). It is also said that kabuki audiences found Danshichi's nearly naked body, covered with tattoos, erotically exciting.

A chilling murder and cooling water are two elements typical of a kabuki play produced in the summer. Summer is also a time when the distinctive flute melodies and percussion patterns of festival music drift through the streets of Japanese towns and cities. Particularly effective in building tension during the murder, the festival music that underscores the final scene serves as a constant reminder of the approaching festival revelers. They burst on stage in a frenzy, shouldering a portable shrine and singing and dancing, mere seconds after Danshichi desperately manages to wash the mud and blood from his body, put his kimono back on, and resheath his sword.

The female characters in *Summer Festival* are as brazen and bound by honor as the males, to the extent that they are referred to as *onnadate,* the female counterpart of the *otokodate.* Danshichi's wife, Okaji, shies away from no challenge and is instrumental in obtaining her husband's release from prison. Otatsu's sacrifice is so courageous that Sabu admiringly remarks she should have been "born a man."

Two years after *Summer Festival* took Osaka and Kyoto audiences by storm, the play made its way to Edo, opening in the fifth month of 1747 at the Morita-za. To some extent, present-day stagings can be seen as a result of two and a half centuries of cross-fertilization between Edo and Kamigata area styles. Among the many distinctions between the two styles—such as the number and form of Danshichi's *mie* during the murder scene—the most characteristic differences are in the music. The play's climactic murder is set during the summer festival of Osaka's Kōzu

Shrine, which takes place on the eighteenth day of the sixth month of the lunar calendar. Osaka theatre audiences know the percussive festival music, *danjiri,* that is specific to Kōzu Shrine, and they consider its special sound essential in the creation of the proper festival atmosphere. Edo-style productions, however, use music that includes flute as well as percussion, following the tradition of music performed at summer festivals in Edo.

The Kamigata method of performing *Summer Festival* is preserved primarily in the performance traditions *(kata)* of Kataoka Nizaemon XIII (1903–1994), carried on today by Ennosuke III. Less commonly seen are the *kata* of Jitsukawa Enjaku II (1877–1951), an Osaka actor who eliminated *takemoto* music and narration of the puppet theatre from the play, believing it interfered with realistic acting, and who portrayed Danshichi with a dark, sandy skin color, reflective of the character's original rough nature.

The earliest play featuring Danshichi was *Homeless Danshichi* (Yadonashi Danshichi) in 1698, supposedly based on an actual incident in which a fishmonger killed his father. In the 1745 production of *Summer Festival,* Danshichi was rewritten as a gallant street knight, which was all the rage at the time, and over the years he has come to sport a white face *(shiro nuri)* to emphasize his upstanding chivalrous nature. Later puppet productions adopted kabuki's transformation of Danshichi's nature by using a rather refined puppet head with a white face, known as Bunshichi, for the character.

The *kata* of Nakamura Kichiemon I (1886–1954) and of Onoe Kikugorō VI (1885–1949), representative of the Edo tradition, are carried on today by Kichiemon II (b. 1944) and Matsumoto Kōshirō IX (b. 1942), and by Nakamura Kankurō V (b. 1955), respectively. Kankurō's father, Nakamura Kanzaburō XVII (1909–1988), was particularly known for playing the contrasting roles of Danshichi and Otatsu.

A testament to the popularity of *Summer Festival* is that, since its debut 250 years ago, rarely have three years passed without the play being staged, and never has the gap been more than five years. *Summer Festival* arguably ranks as the fourth "masterpiece" of Sōsuke, Shōraku, and Koizumo and is the only domestic play among this illustrious group.

This translation is based on unpublished scripts (daihon) used for a July 1997 production starring Ennosuke III and a June 1999 production starring Kōshirō IX, both at the Kabuki-za. Also useful were videotapes of productions starring Kankurō V at the Kabuki-za and the Kanamaru-za, the restored Edo-period theatre in the town of Kotohira, Shikoku.

CHARACTERS

DANSHICHI KURŌBEI, *fishmonger by trade and gallant commoner by nature*
OKAJI, *his strong-willed wife*
MIKAWAYA GIHEIJI, *her greedy father*
ICHIMATSU, *young son of* OKAJI *and* DANSHICHI
TSURIFUNE SABU, *tough old fisherman friend of* DANSHICHI
OTSUJI, *his wife*
ISSUN TOKUBEI, *gallant commoner and sworn brother of* DANSHICHI
OTATSU, *his spirited wife*
TAMASHIMA ISONOJŌ, *young dismissed samurai protected by* DANSHICHI
KOTOURA, *a former courtesan, ransomed by* ISONOJŌ
ŌTORI SAGAEMON, *evil samurai in love with* KOTOURA
GOOD-FOR-NOTHIN' GON *and* SLIMY HACHI, *thugs who do anything for money*
SANKICHI, *a barber*
TSUTSUMI TONAI, *an official*
SHRINEGOERS
PRISON GUARDS
PALANQUIN BEARERS
FESTIVAL DANCERS
STAGE ASSISTANTS, *black-garbed* kurogo
TAKEMOTO, *shamisen and narrator who accompany the actors*

Before the Torii at Sumiyoshi Shrine

(The curtain opens to continuous ki *clacks* [kizami] *and a cheerful song accompanied by shamisen and stick drum* [taiko] *from offstage. A large stone torii at left marks the entrance to Sumiyoshi Shrine in Osaka. A low stone wall cuts across upstage. The pine forest of the shrine grounds and several shrine buildings are visible beyond. At right a large, colorful curtain, incorporating the crest of the actor playing* DANSHICHI KURŌBEI, *hangs in front of a small barbershop. Two plain wooden benches for passersby are at center. Between them stand two signposts.* SHRINEGOERS *are passing through the torii, going to and from the shrine. As music fades, a final* ki *clack signals the action to begin. Music resumes as* TSURIFUNE SABU, *an elderly boatman, enters on the* hanamichi. *His hair is grey and he wears a yellow, striped summer kimono and low clogs. He carries a bundle of clothes. He is followed by* OKAJI, *wife of* DANSHICHI, *who is leading their young son,* ICHIMATSU, *by the hand. She wears a thin summer kimono of*

dark blue linen, a plain, woven obi, and simple sandals. The child is dressed in knee-length cotton kimono fastened with a soft sash. They stop at shichisan. *Music stops.)*

OKAJI: Well, Sabu, why don't we stop over there and rest a while?

SABU: Yes, let's. *(Encouraging* ICHIMATSU.*)* Son, right over there is Sumiyoshi Shrine. C'mon, hurry. Let's go.

ICHIMATSU: Okay.

(Song resumes. They cross to the benches and sit, SABU *left,* OKAJI *and* ICHIMATSU *right. Shamisen continue softly.)*

SABU: The boy really did a fine job of walking. When we stopped at Tenka Teahouse, I thought I'd have to fork out twenty-five coppers and hire a palanquin. But three coppers worth of crackers did the trick, so I'm ahead twenty-two! Ha, ha, ha, ha.

OKAJI: He's probably excited about seeing his father after so long.

SABU: Me, too. Last night after I heard Danshichi was getting out of jail today, I couldn't sleep a wink.

OKAJI: I know exactly what you mean. I was overjoyed when I heard about the pardon. It couldn't have happened without help from you and all of our neighbors. Sabu, I sincerely thank you.

SABU: Indeed, I imagine you are happy. Say, isn't Giheiji coming?

OKAJI *(Ashamed)*: No, this morning father said his lower back hurt.

SABU: He's faking it.

*(*SABU *laughs lightheartedly. Music fades.)*

OKAJI: No, really, it's not like that.

SABU: Ah, forget it. Nobody likes coming out to meet a jailbird.

OKAJI: Sabu, since we're here, I'd like to pay respects at Sumiyoshi Shrine.

SABU: That's a good idea. I'll stay here and keep my eyes peeled for Danshichi.

OKAJI *(Rises)*: Well then, Sabu . . .

SABU: Okaji . . .

OKAJI: We'll be back soon.

(The song resumes. SABU *watches* OKAJI *lead* ICHIMATSU *off through the torii. Music stops.)*

SABU: Well, I guess I'll take a little break.

(Music resumes. SABU *saunters toward the barbershop, but stops when he hears* HACHI *and* GON, *who enter from left with a palanquin, set it down, and open the flap, revealing* TAMASHIMA ISONOJŌ. *Singing stops. Shamisen continue.)*

GON *(Respectfully)*: Listen, sir, you'll have to take another palanquin from the rest area ahead. Get off here, and we'll take our fare.

ISONOJŌ: What's the meaning of this? When I got in, you said you'd take me to Nagamachi.

GON: But road conditions aren't good, so we'd like you to pay us here.

(ISONOJŌ, a handsome, gentle young man, steps out of the palanquin. Recently dismissed from his rank as a samurai, he is dressed in the simple white cotton kimono and traveling sandals of a commoner.)

ISONOJŌ *(With dignity)*: I would like to pay you, but unfortunately I am not carrying any money at the moment. I can give it to you when we reach Nagamachi.

GON *(Growing angry)*: What? You don't have money? Why, you're trying to cheat us!

ISONOJŌ *(Posing proudly)*: Here now. Do not speak so rudely to a samurai.

HACHI *(Derisively)*: What's that? Why, you aren't even carrying a sword!

GON: He's a cheat!

HACHI: Let's teach this guy . . .

GON and HACHI: A thing or two!

(Tsuke beat as they grab ISONOJŌ and jostle him. SABU pushes them off and stands defiantly between them, center.)

SABU: You guys do something rash and you'll regret it.

GON: Hey, old man, you don't know anything about this.

HACHI: What makes you think . . .

GON and HACHI: You can interfere?

SABU: Hey, you can't go around stealing people's money! *(To ISONOJŌ, kindly.)* I'm sure there is a reason for this. So, how much is the fare?

ISONOJŌ *(Apologetically)*: We settled on two hundred fifty coppers.

SABU: Two hundred fifty? *(Glaring at HACHI and GON.)* That's mighty steep! All right you guys. This old man will have to fight you for it.

GON: You think you . . .

GON and HACHI: Can fight us?

SABU: No problem! But I am willing to negotiate first. *(He confidently points to the Buddhist prayer beads on his ear.)* If I used these beads to count the number of fights I've won, I'd get nine hundred ninety-nine. Beating you guys to a pulp would make it an even thousand. But I'm going to give you a break and let you go.

GON: What? Let us go? Interesting prospect. How are you . . .

GON and HACHI: Gonna' make us go?

(GON rushes SABU from right and HACHI from left. SABU knocks GON to his knees and throws him off right. HACHI flees to the palanquin.)

SABU: You shouldn't have asked for so much. I'll give you half. Take this and get the hell out of here!

(He throws a packet of money on the ground near GON. Music stops. GON cautiously picks it up and runs for the palanquin, skirting SABU's path.)

GON: We gave him the ride! We earned this fare!

GON and HACHI *(Angrily)*: We'll remember you!

(Shamisen play as they hurriedly shoulder the palanquin and exit left.)

ISONOJŌ *(With decorum)*: With your assistance, this dangerous situation was settled without incident. I am extremely grateful. *(Bows.)* At present I am a masterless samurai, but I wish to have your address so I may properly express my appreciation in the future.

SABU: Don't worry about it. Have a seat. *(They sit down,* SABU *left and* ISONOJŌ *right.)* I heard you say you're heading for Nagamachi. What part of Nagamachi?

ISONOJŌ: I am not sure, but I wish to visit Mikawaya Giheiji.

SABU *(Supressing his surprise)*: Hmm, business with Giheiji. Well, you know some unusual people!

ISONOJŌ: No, we haven't met. I wish to see his daughter, Okaji.

(Music fades.)

SABU: By any chance would you be Isonojō?

ISONOJŌ: Yes, indeed, I am.

SABU: I know all about you. This is what happened. *(Shamisen resume.)* I heard Danshichi was getting out of jail today, so I came here with his wife, Okaji, and little boy to meet him. Okaji told me about you on the way over. Anyway, Danshichi will take good care of you, so don't worry about a thing. Okaji is at the shrine praying right now, so why don't we do this? We're planning to have lunch at a restaurant in Shinke called Kobuya. Why don't you just go ahead and wait for us there? Tell them Sabu sent you.

ISONOJŌ *(Standing)*: What good fortune! All right, I will do that. *(Music stops.* ISONOJŌ *speaks as he dreamily crosses right to the* hanamichi.*)* Yesterday I spent the day in Sakai, and today, on my way to Osaka, I came across you at precisely the right time.

SABU: We can talk at leisure later. Please go ahead

ISONOJŌ *(Turning back at* shichisan*)*: Well then, Sabu, we shall talk later.

(Offstage song begins. ISONOJŌ *composes himself and exits gracefully down the* hanamichi. SABU *watches, pleased. Music stops.)*

SABU: That gentleman is lucky he ran into me when he did. Hmm, I wonder why Danshichi's so late. Hey there, barber! Barber!

SANKICHI *(Offstage)*: Coming. Coming.

(Shamisen play as SANKICHI *enters through shop curtain.)*

SABU: I came from Osaka to meet a prisoner being released today. I'll just borrow one of your benches until he comes.

SANKICHI: Sure, no problem. Say, why not come and rest inside?

SABU: Well, then *(flips his fan open)*, if I may.

(Stick drum joins shamisen as they go in through the curtain. Offstage music stops. From behind a bamboo blind on the second story musicians' box offstage left, TAKEMOTO *musicians begin narration.)*

TAKEMOTO:

No time at all passes when, clanging noisily / Danshichi toils along, straight down the road.

*(*DANSHICHI KURŌBEI *hobbles on from left, his arms bound by ropes, dressed in a convict's pale blue kimono. He has an unshaven pate and bushy eyebrows and beard. He is followed by a samurai official,* TSUTSUMI TONAI*, and two* GUARDS. SHRINEGOERS *stop to watch.)*

FIRST GUARD *(Forcing* DANSHICHI *to kneel)*: Bow down!

TONAI: In accordance with the law, remove the criminal's bonds.

BOTH GUARDS: Sir.

(They untie DANSHICHI*'s ropes and retreat to the rear.* DANSHICHI *faces* TONAI*, bowing humbly.)*

TONAI: Attention, Danshichi! These are the details as presented by the presiding official, Tamashima Hyōdayū, at his manor. Last year on the thirteenth day of the ninth month, you injured a retainer of the samurai Ōtori Sagaemon, and both of you were jailed. The other man's injury was minor and healed, but when he died in prison, this investigation was closed. You are hereby absolved of a death sentence but banished from the town of Izumi Sakai. Show your gratitude.

DANSHICHI *(Bowing deeply)*: I humbly thank you.

TONAI *(To the guards)*: Come!

GUARDS: Sir.

TAKEMOTO:

Passing judgment, he turns and takes his leave. / Danshichi watches as they disappear.

*(*TONAI *turns away, flips his fan open, slowly raises it overhead, and exits left.* GUARDS *follow.* DANSHICHI *watches them go. The* SHRINEGOERS *stare at* DANSHICHI*, murmur to each other, then disperse, exiting through the torii.)*

DANSHICHI *(In a tired, weak voice)*: Ah, I'm so happy. So happy! It was horrible being accused of killing one of Sagaemon's worthless underlings, but now my life has been spared, thanks to the good graces of Tamashima Hyōdayū. *(Looks out as if speaking to* HYŌDAYŪ.*)* To show my appreciation, I'll make sure no harm comes to your son Isonojō, though I be killed or chopped into a million pieces. With this pledge, please accept my gratitude. *(Bows deeply.)* Thank you so much. Thank you so very much.

SABU *(Calling from inside)*: Danshichi! Danshichi!

*(*DANSHICHI *comically looks around, trying to find the source of the voice.)*

DANSHICHI: Yes? Yes? Yes, yes, yes? Where are you? Where are you? Where are you?

SABU: Danshichi! Danshichi!

DANSHICHI: All right! I hear you calling, but where are you?

SABU: Not where . . . *(Accented by rhythmical percussion, he playfully pokes his head through the curtain.)* Here!

(Shamisen, stick drum, and flute play a bright melody.)

DANSHICHI *(Overjoyed)*: Old man, it's good to see you! I really appreciate you coming!

(SABU and DANSHICHI clasp hands and hug, ad-libbing greetings.)

SABU: I'm glad to see you back! C'mon, let's have a seat. *(They sit on right bench. Drum and flute stop. Shamisen continue.)* You know, I was thinking, someone as good-natured as you must have been pushed to the edge to get in a fight and land in jail. Well, anyway, everything turned out fine. Just fine. And don't be ashamed. They say you're not really a man until you've been in jail and visited Edo. *(Taps DANSHICHI on the shoulder with his fan, laughing.)* Your wife and little boy came to meet you. They're waiting for you.

DANSHICHI: My wife and boy are here?

SABU: They're praying at the shrine right now, so you . . . *(Catches a whiff of DANSHICHI's stench, fans the odor away, and notices DANSHICHI's constant scratching.)* That kimono is ripe! And look at your long hair! I brought you a change of clothes. *(Indicates the bundle.)* Have the barber shave your head and trim your hair, get cleaned up, and run off to see your wife.

DANSHICHI: Really, Sabu, thanks for all your help. *(Pointing to the prayer beads hanging on SABU's ear.)* By the way, you picked up some serious prayer beads while I was away.

SABU *(Pointing to the beads)*: Nowadays, this is the way. This right here. When I get angry, instead of fighting, I count my beads and it's "Hail, Lord Buddha." When people laugh at me it's "Hail, Lord Buddha." Why, I'm busier chanting than a believer at a prayer meeting! Ha, ha, ha, ha, ha. Oh, I've got something important to tell you. Isonojō is here.

DANSHICHI: Isonojō? You don't know how much I owe him.

SABU: Yes, I heard. Okaji told me all about it. Anyway, I sent him ahead to Kobuya. We should hurry over to meet him. *(Music fades.)* Hey barber! Barber!

(SANKICHI enters through curtain, dressed in a plain dark kimono and apron.)

SANKICHI: Yes, coming.

SABU: Give Danshichi's head and face a good close shave.

SANKICHI: Yes, sir.

DANSHICHI: Well then Sabu . . .

SABU: Danshichi . . .

DANSHICHI *(Proudly)*: I'll go get polished into a first-rate gentleman.

(Lively shamisen play as DANSHICHI enters the barbershop. SANKICHI follows, carrying the bundle of clothes. Music stops.)

SABU: Ah, well that's done. Good, good. *(Remembering the contents of the bundle.)* The kimono and obi . . . clogs and tobacco pouch. Oh, I can't believe it! I forgot the most important thing—his loincloth! That was stupid! *(Looking down at himself.)* Well, what the devil, ha, ha. This was brand new this morning. *(Lifts up the hem of his kimono in front, revealing the red loincloth below.)* And I haven't been wearing it long. Hey, barber! Barber!

SANKICHI *(Poking his head out from the shop curtain)*: What can I do for you?

SABU: Barber, would you mind giving this a little tug? Ready? One, two, three, pull!

(Standing profile to the audience, SANKICHI *grabs the loose end of* SABU*'s loincloth through the front of his kimono and pulls in time to rhythmical shamisen and percussion, slowly drawing the three-yard-long scarlet loincloth from underneath* SABU*'s kimono, folding it as he pulls. When finished,* SABU *ad-libs, "Good, good. Take it inside," as* SANKICHI *exits into the shop. Music ends.)*

SABU *(Calling inside)*: Danshichi, I'm going ahead. I'll wait for you there.

TAKEMOTO:

"Kobuya, I'm on my way!"

*(*SABU *stops at* shichisan *to hike up his kimono. Remembering his missing loincloth, he shyly covers his groin area with a fan.)*

SABU: Here I go.

TAKEMOTO:

He hurries away!

(Offstage percussion plays a lively pattern as SABU *exits. Percussion stops.* TAKEMOTO *becomes melodic and gentle.)*

Thoughts only of her lover, she has no eyes for the road. / Tripping as she hurries, Kotoura runs on.

*(*KOTOURA *rushes on from left to quick* batabata *beats of the* tsuke*. She has long tortoiseshell hairpins decorating an elaborate hairdo in the manner of a courtesan. She is holding up the trailing hems of her light blue, figured kimono so she can run more easily in her black lacquered clogs.* TAKEMOTO *shamisen continues.)*

KOTOURA: I've been running in a daze. I wonder where I am? *(Looking around, she sees the* torii.*)* Why, this is Sumiyoshi Shrine. In the past, Isonojō and I often came here from the Naniwa Brothel. Perhaps he's here . . .

*(*ŌTORI SAGAEMON*, wearing a chic white kimono and black summer* haori*, sneaks up behind* KOTOURA *and covers her eyes. A samurai's two swords are thrust in his obi. Music stops.)*

SAGAEMON: I found you. I found you!

KOTOURA: Who is it? Who is it?

SAGAEMON: It's me. It's me!

KOTOURA: But who is "me"?

SAGAEMON: Right here next to you . . . *(Wraps* KOTOURA's *arm around his shoulders and cuddles up to her.)* Sagaemon.

KOTOURA *(Trying to run away)*: It's you!

SAGAEMON: Now, hold on! Hold it right there. *(Grabs* KOTOURA *and forces her to sit.)* Kotoura, you are so cruel! So heartless! *(Background shamisen begins.* SAGAEMON *sits next to her on the right bench.)* You managed to give me the slip at the Otai Brothel! I had my eyes on you, but that Iso fellow bought your contract and boxed you up where I couldn't lay a finger on you. I got our lord Hyōdayū to dismiss his foolish young snip of a son—all for you. So Isonojō is finished as a samurai, washed up. Remain faithful to a drifter and you'll end up fodder for the birds and dogs of Tobita execution grounds. *(Illustrates a severed head by resting his chin on his arms.)* Give up Isonojō . . . *(takes her hand)* and marry me.

*(*KOTOURA *tries to run away, but* SAGAEMON *grabs her sleeve.)*

KOTOURA: How can you say such horrible things? Let go of me! Let go of me!

SAGAEMON: Struggle all you want, but I've got you and won't let go!

KOTOURA: Oh, get away from me!

(Breaking away, she runs into the barbershop. SAGAEMON *follows. Music stops. Two* tsuke *beats accent the unseen action of* DANSHICHI *grabbing* SAGAEMON *behind the curtain.)*

SAGAEMON *(Inside)*: Ouch! Ouch! Who are you? Who do you think you are?

DANSHICHI *(Inside, in a booming voice)*: Not just anyone. You're talking to me!

TAKEMOTO:

Emerging from the curtain, now freshly shaven / hair styled like a dandy, his crown gleaming brightly.

(Transformed, DANSHICHI *is shaven and dressed in a crisp white cotton kimono patterned in red and blue. Exuding strength and confidence, he swaggers out, stamping loudly with his tall clogs, forcing* SAGAEMON *ahead of him. He twists* SAGAEMON*'s wrist and poses in a* mie, *accompanied by two* tsuke *beats.)*

SAGAEMON: Hey, you're the guy that got out of jail today.

DANSHICHI: Danshichi Kurōbei is my name.

SAGAEMON: So, Danshichi, what makes you think you can interfere?

DANSHICHI: I'm not interfering . . . But a samurai shouldn't be chasing after women. You should show . . . *(releases* SAGAEMON, *who cringes in pain)* a bit more respect.

(Background shamisen play slowly as KOTOURA *emerges from the barbershop.)*

KOTOURA: You must be Okaji's husband.

DANSHICHI: Ah, and you are Kotoura, freed from the Otai Brothel. Have you seen Isonojō yet?

KOTOURA: No. I came here hoping to meet him, but . . .

DANSHICHI: Don't worry about a thing. Isonojō happens to be . . . *(pointing down the* hanamichi*)* right over there.

SAGAEMON: Where?

DANSHICHI: Here, lend me your ear. *(Whispers to* KOTOURA.*)* Got it? Well, get going. Go on!

KOTOURA *(Joyfully)*: I will.

*(*KOTOURA *rushes down the* hanamichi. SAGAEMON *tries to follow, but* DANSHICHI *pins him on the ground.)*

DANSHICHI *(Calling after her)*: Do you know the way?

KOTOURA *(Turning back at* shichisan*)*: No, I don't.

DANSHICHI: Then I'll have to show you. Go straight down this road and . . . *(using* SAGAEMON *as a prop,* DANSHICHI *gives directions: he lifts* SAGAEMON *to his feet and spreads his arms wide)* you'll see a black wall. From behind the black wall . . . *(twists one of* SAGAEMON*'s arms high into the air)*, there's a pine tree poking out. Opposite the pine . . . *(trips* SAGAEMON *into a sitting position, facing front, hands clasped in a Buddha-like* mudra *position)*, look for a stone statue of Jizō. Next to Jizō . . . *(kicks* SAGAEMON, *who falls on all fours.* DANSHICHI *poses, one foot on his back)*, there's a stone bridge. Cross the stone bridge and . . . *(*DANSHICHI *removes his foot.* SAGAEMON *jumps to his feet and is spun three times)*, it's the first . . . second . . . third building. *(Knocks* SAGAEMON *over and pushes him out of the way.)*

KOTOURA *(Turning to go)*: I see. I see.

TAKEMOTO:

Buoyantly rejoicing she . . .

DANSHICHI *(Calling after her)*: Oh, wait, wait! It's on the east side!

KOTOURA *(Calling back)*: Yes, I understand!

TAKEMOTO:

Hu-u-u-rries on her way.

(Her first slow steps are timed rhythmically to the syllables of the TAKEMOTO *narration. Strong* tsuke *beats gradually quicken as* KOTOURA *exits. Music stops.* SAGAEMON *stands, confronting* DANSHICHI.*)*

SAGAEMON: Wise men avoid trouble, so you'd be smart to run. I'll show you!

(Shamisen play. SAGAEMON *raises his sword.* DANSHICHI *glares back, cowing* SAGAEMON. *Dropping the sword to his shoulder,* SAGAEMON *flees left, accompanied by* tsuke *beats. Music stops.)*

DANSHICHI *(Laughing)*: What a weakling. *(Background shamisen begin.)* I should visit the shrine, but that guy is nasty enough to cut off Kotoura down the road. And no telling what awful things he might do to her. I'll pay my respects from here. *(Facing Sumiyoshi, he briefly folds his hands in prayer.)* Okay, I'm ready.

"Street knights" Issun Tokubei (Ichikawa Danzō IX), standing, and Danshichi Kurōbei (Onoe Tatsunosuke II), kneeling, fight with sign-posts. Behind them is the curtain of a barber shop, dyed with the crest of the Onoe acting family. (Umemura Yutaka, Engeki Shuppansha)

(He starts down the hanamichi, *as* GON *and* HACHI, *wearing their kimono hiked up in back, and* ISSUN TOKUBEI *enter from left.* TOKUBEI *wears a dark, patterned kimono and plain wooden clogs.)*

GON and HACHI *(Calling* DANSHICHI*)*: Hey! Hey! *(*DANSHICHI *ignores them.)* Hey! Hey! Hey you!

TOKUBEI: Can't you hear us calling you?

DANSHICHI *(Stops at* shichisan*)*: Are you calling me?

TOKUBEI: Stop right there.

DANSHICHI *(Turning around)*: Why? You got something to say to me?

TOKUBEI: Why else would we be calling you? Come back over here.

DANSHICHI: You guys are a stinkin' nuisance. *(Shamisen and stick drum play as* DANSHICHI *returns and stands brashly facing away from them.)* Well, what do you want? Hurry up and spit it out.

(Music stops.)

TOKUBEI *(Calling)*: Good for Nothin' Slimey. Take care of him. In the meantime, I think I'll finish . . . *(emphasizing each syllable)* plucking my beard.

TAKEMOTO:

Tobacco pouch unrolls, out come his tweezers / as thick and plucky as his interrogation.

*(*TOKUBEI *sits on left bench, crosses one leg over the other, and strikes a gallant pose, arm thrust out through the front of his kimono, exaggeratedly plucking his whiskers with oversized tweezers.* GON *and* HACHI *confront* DANSHICHI. *Music stops.)*

DANSHICHI: So, you're in the mood to fight. Well I'm not, so go on. Get outa here!

GON: No way, we ain't leavin'. We came for that girl who was just here. Are you gonna stop wastin' time and turn her over?

DANSHICHI: If I won't give her to you, what the hell can you do about it?

GON: Quit beatin' around the bush. Good-for-Nothin' Gon . . .

HACHI: And Slimy Hachi, will use these fists . . .

GON and HACHI: To take her from you.

(Rapid percussion and flute play as GON *and* HACHI *pick up sticks from the ground and rush* DANSHICHI. *He dodges their blows, knocks* HACHI *down, takes his stick, and beats them both. They flee right. Music stops.)*

DANSHICHI: What a couple of weaklings.

*(*DANSHICHI *tosses the stick off right and starts walking down the* hanamichi.*)*

TOKUBEI *(Calling after him)*: Danshichi, wait a minute.

DANSHICHI *(Turning back)*: Are you talking to me?

TOKUBEI: Let's sit down and handle this like men.

DANSHICHI *(Impressed)*: You're a man of some experience, I see. *(Shamisen play slowly in background.* DANSHICHI *returns, squatting on the ground casually, his back to* TOKUBEI.*)* Okay, I'm sitting. What is it?

TOKUBEI: A certain samurai asked a favor, and once Issun Tokubei agrees to something, he doesn't back off—not an inch!

(He squats back-to-back with DANSHICHI *and grabbing* DANSHICHI*'s obi, knocks him off balance.)*

DANSHICHI: Ah, this bit is interesting! Then I'll try this . . .

(Returns the move, leaving his hand on TOKUBEI*'s obi.)*

TOKUBEI: Then I'll do this . . .

(Puts his hand on DANSHICHI*'s obi so their arms are crossed.)*

DANSHICHI: And I'll do this. *(Punctuated by* tsuke *beats, they stand, stamp, and engage in a game of one-upmanship, turning and stepping in tandem. Losing balance, they split.* TOKUBEI *hops right, in front of the barber's curtain, and* DANSHICHI *hops left, losing a clog along the way. He stands on right bench.)* Over here! Over here!

TOKUBEI: So you are!

(Both turn forward, pull up the hems of their kimono, and pose. An offstage song, accompanied by shamisen, stick drum, and flute begins. DANSHICHI *and* TOKUBEI *tuck up their kimonos, grab signposts, and engage in a stylized fight* [tachimawari] *as* tsuke *beats accent the action. They alternately swing and grab the end of each other's signpost, moving right to left and back to center. They strike a* mie, DANSHICHI *standing in back,* TOKUBEI *kneeling in front, the signposts crossed between them.* OKAJI *enters from left with* ICHIMATSU *and ushers him into the barbershop. The men strike another* mie, DANSHICHI *standing left and* TOKUBEI *kneeling right.* OKAJI *tries to stop the fight, but they push her aside. She rips a signboard off the side of the barbershop and, standing between them, uses it to wrestle the men's signposts to the ground. Music stops.)*

OKAJI: Stop! Stop! Stop this right now!

(The three strike a mie, DANSHICHI *and* TOKUBEI *kneeling on either side, right legs thrust powerfully forward. Their signposts form a V shape, with* OKAJI *kneeling at the center.)*

DANSHICHI *(Surprised)*: What's that, my wife? . . .

TOKUBEI *(Impatient)*: Before you get hurt . . .

DANSHICHI: Move away!

TOKUBEI and DANSHICHI: Move away!

OKAJI: I will not! I will not move away! *(Background shamisen begin. The men lay down the signposts and* OKAJI *the signboard.)* Now listen to me, dear. Let me remind you that the pardon you received today was for fighting. And now you're doing it again, before you've even seen the happy faces of your wife and son. Now please, stop this. *(Turning to* TOKUBEI.*)* And you, sir, I don't know what this is all about, but forgive . . . *(Music fades. She recognizes* TOKUBEI.*)* Ah! Aren't you the beggar I hired just yesterday?

TOKUBEI *(Surprised and embarrassed)*: And you're the lady from the manor!

OKAJI *(Furious)*: Stand back! Stand back! *(*TOKUBEI *retreats, bowing apologetically.)* How dare you lift a hand against my husband. You . . . monster!

DANSHICHI: Hey, hey, hey! How do you know this guy?

OKAJI: Please, let me tell you. *(Background shamisen begin.)* To make a long story short, I had the idea to hire this man to stage a mock fight and make up a story about his wayward life. This was done to convince young master Isonojō to leave the Otai Brothel and return home. As a reward, I gave him that kimono from Lord Hyōdayū's wife, our mistress *(points to the one* TOKUBEI *is wearing)*, and money so he could give up his life as a beggar.

(Music stops.)

DANSHICHI *(Rises, ready to fight)*: That's even more despicable—wearing a gift from our lord, Tamashima Hyōdayū, and fighting against his son, Isonojō, at the same time. It's inexcusable!

TOKUBEI: Wait a minute. Are you talking about Isonojō, son of Tamashima Hyōdayū, the lord from Bitchū province?

DANSHICHI: I certainly am.

TOKUBEI *(Humbled and apologetic)*: I had no idea. Truly, no idea! *(Shamisen begin.)* I was born in Bitchū myself, and so my wife and I consider Tamashima Hyōdayū our lord. When my buddies and I were hired by Sagaemon, I didn't know what a big mistake I was making. Instead of fighting, let me serve Isonojō with you. Please, please.

(Bows deeply. Music stops.)

DANSHICHI: We'll make a firm pledge and seal it.

TOKUBEI: Name it. Should we slit our arms? Drink blood?

DANSHICHI: No, no, why do that? The important thing is what's inside. *(Hits his chest.)* Without that, it's meaningless. *(Ponders momentarily, then nods with conviction.)* Hmph. Let this symbolize our pledge.

TAKEMOTO:

Acting with full resolve, Danshichi now / tears free a single sleeve of his kimono.

(Accented with light taps of the tsuke, DANSHICHI *rips off a sleeve.)*

DANSHICHI: This sleeve was worn next to my skin. It is proof of my vow to serve Isonojō. Accept it.

TOKUBEI *(Rips off a sleeve)*: I, too, present this as a pledge. I will be a shoulder of support for Isonojō. Accept it.

(Placing the sleeves on the ends of the signposts, each extends his pole, offering his sleeve to the other. Each accepts and covers his bare arm with the other's sleeve.)

DANSHICHI: By taking this sleeve and placing it thus on my shoulder, I pledge my support. And you, Tokubei?

TOKUBEI: Now that I hang this from my shoulder, let there be no doubt. I accept all risks.

DANSHICHI: From now on . . .

TOKUBEI: We will act . . .

DANSHICHI and TOKUBEI: As brothers!

OKAJI: Now that you understand each other, we can all relax.

DANSHICHI: It's decided. Tokubei, you should come to Kobuya with us. Isonojō is there, and I can introduce you.

TOKUBEI: I'll do that.

*(*DANSHICHI *and* TOKUBEI *let down their kimono hems and put on their clogs while* OKAJI *brings* ICHIMATSU *out of the barbershop.)*

ICHIMATSU *(Running to* DANSHICHI*)*: Father!

DANSHICHI *(crouches, looking into* ICHIMATSU*'s eyes)*: Son. My, you've grown so much!

ICHIMATSU: Give me a piggyback ride!

(Laughing, DANSHICHI *lifts* ICHIMATSU *onto his back.)*

DANSHICHI: Oh, you've gained weight!

*(*DANSHICHI, *carrying* ICHIMATSU, OKAJI, *and* TOKUBEI *move onto the* hanamichi, *ad-libbing as they go.)*

OKAJI: Dear, the barber left a piece of paper in your hair.

*(*DANSHICHI *stops at* shichisan. OKAJI *affectionately removes the paper.)*

TOKUBEI: Okaji, you don't miss a thing!

OKAJI *(Embarrassed)*: Oh, now, really.

DANSHICHI: Well then, Tokubei!

TOKUBEI: Danshichi!

DANSHICHI: Shall we go?

(The curtain closes to the lively song that opened the scene, accompanied by shamisen and stick drum and rapid ki *clacks* [kizami] *as all stroll happily off down the* hanamichi.*)*

House of Sabu the Boatman

(To lively offstage festival music [danjiri], *the curtain opens on the main room of* SABU*'s house, a curtained doorway at back, a closet with an altar above it, and sliding doors leading to an inner room left.* SABU*'s kimono, painted with a fierce dragon, hangs on the wall. A sake barrel sits in the corner with a charcoal brazier next to it. Thickly painted letters on the outside wall beyond the doorway right read "Fishing Boats." A small festival lantern hangs from the eaves.* SABU*'s wife,* OTSUGI, *fans herself as she grills skewered mackerel on the brazier. She wears the plain dark kimono and wide obi of a middle-aged woman. Two men in a lion costume enter the house, dance about inside, and exit. Closing the door,* HACHI *and* GON *remove their costume. Using the pretext of performing the lion dance in*

people's homes during the summer Bon festival, they have been searching for KOTOURA. *They nod knowingly to each other and exit right. Music stops.)*

OTSUGI: Those two smell fishy. This is no time to let down my guard.

(Shamisen play. She exits through the curtain.)

KOTOURA *(Offstage)*: How could you? How could you, how could you?

*(*KOTOURA *enters from the sliding doors left and sits center, followed by* ISONOJŌ.*)*

ISONOJŌ: Stop this!

KOTOURA *(Angry)*: No matter what you say, it's obvious you had a fling with that Onaka!

ISONOJŌ *(Sits fanning himself, irritated)*: All you can say is Onaka, Onaka. I don't know what you're talking about. You're jealous! Well, I've given you no reason to mistrust me.

KOTOURA *(Furiously fanning herself)*: Oh, you make me so angry!

OTSUGI *(Enters and sits between the two lovers)*: What is going on with you two?

KOTOURA: Otsugi, you'll listen to me, won't you? The daughter of the antique dealer where Isonojō was staying fell in love with this creature. Oh, it makes me so angry.

ISONOJŌ *(Defensively)*: That's ancient history. Thanks to Danshichi, we are being well cared for here at Sabu's. If you're dissatisfied, then tell me.

KOTOURA: I know your tricks. Trying to change the subject by getting me to complain.

ISONOJŌ *(Snidely)*: To be a man, one mustn't refuse when delicious fruits are offered!

KOTOURA: What a horrible thing to say!

(She pinches him. Music stops.)

ISONOJŌ: Ow, ow, ow!

OTSUGI *(Scolding them)*: Now, now. Please stop this! Really, young people can be so childish!

(An offstage song accompanies SABU *as he enters right, going directly inside.* OTSUGI *crosses to the door, kneeling to greet him. Singing stops. Shamisen continue.)*

SABU: Wife, I'm home. Did you get things ready for the festival while I was gone?

OTSUGI: Yes, yes, just like you said, grilled, salted mackerel, fresh fish, even the vinegared octopus, it's ready and waiting.

SABU: Oh, good. Good. *(Seeing* KOTOURA *and* ISONOJŌ, *he shakes his head disapprovingly.)* We can't have this. Why are you letting Isonojō and Kotoura sit out here? Danshichi's worried and says we shouldn't keep Isonojō in Osaka, but at the moment, there's no place else to hide him. As for Kotoura, that samurai is looking everywhere for her.

OTSUGI *(To* ISONOJŌ *and* KOTOURA*)*: See what you've done! *(Music stops.)* Quickly, Kotoura, take Isonojō into the back.

KOTOURA *(Affectionately taking* ISONOJŌ*'s arm)*: Well then, dear Iso . . .

ISONOJŌ *(Pulls his hand away, embarrassed)*: Hey, Sabu is watching.

KOTOURA: Oh, stop that. *(Stands, taking his hand.)* Come with me.

(A song accompanies KOTOURA *as she leads a mildly protesting* ISONOJŌ *into the room left. Music stops.)*

SABU: Young people don't understand anything. *(Laughs.)* Well, I think it's time for a nap. Would you bring me a pillow?

OTSUGI: Yes, right away.

(Ad-libbing, OTSUGI *lays a pillow and straw mat in the lower room, left.* SABU *lies down to sleep.)*

TAKEMOTO:

Now comes a woman of twenty-six or -seven, / an unfamiliar face beneath a parasol.

(Offstage musicians continue with a song for the entrance of TOKUBEI*'s wife,* OTATSU, *on the* hanamichi. *Dressed in a chic summer kimono, she carries an open parasol and has an air of dignity about her. She stops briefly at* shichisan *and looks about before continuing to* SABU*'s. Singing stops. Shamisen continue.)*

OTATSU *(Calls out politely)*: I would like to inquire if this is the home of Sabu the boatman, who ferries goods to the market?

OTSUGI *(Going to the door)*: Yes, yes, Sabu is my husband, and who might you be? *(Opens the door, but upon seeing a beautiful woman, quickly slams it shut. Music stops.)*

OTSUGI *(Shaking* SABU *awake)*: Dear, there's . . . somebody . . . there . . . there . . .

SABU: There! There! Who the devil is there?

OTSUGI: A beautiful young woman is there. Asking for you!

SABU: What are you talking about? You act like it's the first time a young woman ever came here. *(Getting up and crossing to the door.)* Okay, okay. I'm Sabu. Who is it? *(Opens the door.)*

OTATSU: It's me.

SABU: Otatsu, it's you!

OTATSU: Sabu, I'm glad you're home.

SABU: It's good to see you. Good to see you! *(To* OTSUGI.*)* Look here, this woman is Tokubei's wife, Otatsu.

OTSUGI *(Embarrassed)*: Oh, you're Tokubei's wife. *That* Tokubei's wife. *(To* SABU.*)* That's what I've been trying to tell you.

SABU: Well, well, come in. Come in.

OTATSU: If I may, please excuse me.

(Shamisen play. All ad-lib greetings as OTATSU *enters and sits center in the lower room.* SABU *settles down to smoke his pipe while the women get acquainted.* OTSUGI *brings a smoking tray and sits right of* OTATSU.*)*

OTATSU: I am Tokubei's wife, Tatsu, from Tamashima. *(Bows.)*

OTSUGI: How rude of me not to introduce myself sooner. I am Sabu's, wife, Tsugi. I'm pleased to make your acquaintance. *(Bows.)* My, it certainly is a hot time of day to be out.

OTATSU: Well, where should I begin? After Tokubei committed some petty crimes, he had to leave our hometown. Thanks to your help, he came to Osaka. Tokubei was born with a temper. He's the first to jump in at the word "fight" and the first to draw a blade. I'm sure he's been a handful, so I wanted to come and express my thanks.

OTSUGI: No need to thank us. As for a wild temper, it's the same here. Until recently, my husband loved brawling so much he couldn't sleep at night unless he'd been in a fight. But now the little Buddha wouldn't harm a mosquito.

SABU: Like my wife said, when I get angry now, these beads are the answer. Right here. *(Proudly points to the prayer beads hanging on his ear. Music fades.)*

OTATSU: A fine solution, indeed.

SABU: By the way, Otatsu, didn't you say earlier that you were going back home to Tamashima? Isn't Tokubei going with you?

OTATSU: Well, things don't always go the way a wife would like. Ah, please listen to my story. *(Background shamisen begin.)* When Tokubei was pardoned for his crimes and allowed to return home, I went to meet him. I was overjoyed, but I didn't have a moment to enjoy the feeling before Tokubei blurted out *(imitating* TOKUBEI*)*, "I'll be along in four or five days, so you . . . go ahead of me." Just like that. So, I had no choice but to start home before him.
(Offstage music stops.)

TAKEMOTO:

During the conversation, Sabu's wife suddenly has the idea / of asking Otatsu a favor. / Creating a chance to speak, she serves tea to her guest.
*(*OTSUGI *finishes making tea in the upper room, serves* OTATSU*, and sits to her right. Offstage shamisen play in the background.)*

OTSUGI: Otatsu, I would like to ask a favor of you. Would you mind?

OTATSU: I may live in the Tamashima countryside, but I am the wife of Issun Tokubei, a spirited man who would never back away from a request. As his wife, I live up to that spirit. Ask me anything.

OTSUGI: How wonderful. Let me first thank you. *(Bows.)* Perhaps Tokubei told you that Danshichi asked us to look after Isonojō. But it is awkward for him to be in Osaka, and we were wondering what to do. Would you be willing to take him with you? You'd be doing us a great favor.

OTATSU: Of course, I'll take him. He can accompany me back to Tamashima.

OTSUGI: Then you'll take care of him for us?

Tokubei's wife, Otatsu (Nakamura Kanzaburō XVII), angrily listens as boatman Sabu (Ichikawa Sadanji III) asserts that he will lose his honor as a man if she is seen with the young samurai Isonojō. (Tsubouchi Memorial Theatre Museum of Waseda University)

OTATSU: Certainly. Tokubei's wife will never go back on her word. I will be happy to look after Isonojō.

(Offstage music fades.)

OTSUGI: This is truly wonderful!

TAKEMOTO:

But Sabu stops her angrily.

SABU: Stop right there! Wife, being too clever can get you into trouble. If it were a good idea, I would have asked her. I can't send Isonojō off with her. I'd lose my honor as a man. Leave us!

TAKEMOTO:

Sharply scolded, Otsugi hesitatingly retreats. / Tokubei's wife simply cannot believe her ears.

(Clearing OTATSU *'s teacup and tobacco tray,* OTSUGI *moves to the upper room where she quietly sits facing the wall.)*

OTATSU *(Offended)*: Listen to me, Sabu. I didn't force anyone to ask me anything. Will you explain how taking the gentleman into my care will sully your honor?

Are you afraid because I'm a woman, I'll be useless in an emergency? I won't be ridiculed and mocked! Someone here asked a favor, . . . and I accepted. *(To stress her point, she demonstrates by holding out one index finger, then the other.* SABU *sits fanning himself, ignoring her.)* I have promised to take him in my care. Have I, a woman, no honor? Has Tokubei, too, no honor? Have we no honor? *(*TAKEMOTO *shamisen strikes two notes, punctuating the growing tension.)* No honor at all? Give us honor . . . hear me . . . Sabu! *(Poses strongly, leaning in* SABU*'s direction.)*

TAKEMOTO:

The woman's sharp tongue speaks words peppered with hot spices. / Now is the time for his bald head to take action.

*(*SABU *rapidly fans himself and swats at flies, trying to ignore her.)*

SABU: No matter what, I cannot put Isonojō into your care, Otatsu. It wouldn't be honorable.

OTATSU: And why wouldn't it be honorable?

SABU: It wouldn't be honorable, Otatsu, because you . . . are too beautiful.

OTATSU: What?

(Background shamisen begin. OTATSU *sits in disbelief.)*

SABU: Now, listen. I'm just a bungling old man, but I'd be an idiot—an absolute idiot—to put that young man in the care of an attractive young woman. I'm sure Tokubei would agree. *(He softens, trying not to offend* OTATSU.*)* Of course, I know nothing would happen with you, but . . . you know the expression "with love there is always the unforeseen." If your face was lopsided, or your cheeks hollowed, neither Tokubei nor the rest of society would have any reason for doubt. *(*OTATSU *ad-libs protests.)* I swear on these prayer beads I'd like to entrust him to someone of your spirit. However, it's that one-in-a-million chance, you see. *(Music ends.)* Otatsu, please try to understand.

TAKEMOTO:

This point of reasoning presented to her / unlike before, Otatsu now has no words to answer. / She sits bowing her head, gazing intently.

*(*OTATSU *repeats to herself the words* honor *and* society's gaze, *emphasized by an occasional note on the* TAKEMOTO *shamisen. At a loss,* OTATSU *looks around, wondering how to respond, when she sees the brazier. She nods resolutely.* TAKEMOTO *shamisen strikes a punctuating note.)*

She rises to her feet, roused by an idea. / Lying in the embers, a flaming rod of iron, hot as fire. / Reaching out, squeezing tightly in her hand, she lifts it to her face, / firmly pressing the branding iron to her flesh.

*(*OTATSU *crosses right to the brazier. Taking a hot iron in her hand, she blows ash from the glowing end, then presses it to her cheek, searing the skin. She cries out in pain but quickly suppresses it.* TAKEMOTO *shamisen plays a rapid, tense melody*

as OTATSU *replaces the iron and covers her wound with a handkerchief.* OTSUGI *rushes over with a cup of tea. In great pain,* OTATSU *drinks, glimpsing her reflection in the tray. Music stops. Slowly she stands the tray on end, leans on it and poses in a* mie. OTATSU *stares at her reflection, punctuated by sparse, poignant strikes of the* TAKEMOTO *shamisen.)*

OTATSU: Well, Sabu. The face that beckons the unforeseen is now scarred. Do you still find it . . . beautiful?

(She poses boldly, leaning on the tray. SABU *stands, raising his arms in praise.)*

SABU: Admirable! I'll put Isonojō in your care!

OTATSU: You'll entrust him to me?

SABU: Take him all the way to China if you like!

OTATSU: Now I, too, can preserve my honor. *(She dabs at her tears. Brief* TAKEMOTO *interlude.)* Tokubei and I think of Isonojō's father, Hyōdayū, as our master. If I failed to care for Isonojō, both my husband and I would have lost honor. So I decided to scar this face . . . *(a tinge of sadness in her voice)* given to me at birth by my parents. Sabu, please understand what this means to me.

TAKEMOTO:

Hearing her story, Otsugi is moved to tears. / Sabu, too, is tearful, so greatly moved is he.

*(*OTSUGI *dabs at her eyes.* SABU *stoically fights off tears.)*

SABU: What can I say? Thank you. Thank you! *(Folds his hands and bows.)* Otsugi, take Otatsu, introduce her to Isonojō, and prepare for their journey to Tamashima.

OTSUGI *(Coming to* OTATSU*'s side)*: Yes, yes, by all means. Let us go in the back . . .

OTATSU: And talk . . .

OTSUGI: And listen . . .

BOTH: To each other.

OTATSU *(Standing)*: Well, then, Sabu.

SABU: Otatsu.

OTATSU: We shall speak later.

(Offstage musicians sing a short song [tada uta]. SABU *stands, looking after* OTATSU *in admiration.)*

SABU: My, my, Tokubei is fortunate to have such a spirited wife. Someone like that—why wasn't she born a man? Maybe she had one . . . and it fell off. *(Chuckles.)* Well, I should say my prayers.

(Taking the beads off his ear, SABU *crosses upstage and kneels facing the altar to pray.)*

TAKEMOTO:

Two gang buddies burst in, interrupting Sabu. / Good for Nothin' Gon and Slimey Hachi.

(Festival percussion and shamisen play as GON *and* HACHI *enter from right and sit in the lower room, fanning themselves. Percussion stops. Shamisen continue.)*

GON: Sabu home?

HACHI: Is he here?

SABU *(Without turning around)*: You two want to see me? I have my hands full of prayer beads at the moment. See that sake cask there? Help yourselves to a drink. *(Strikes a prayer bell.)*

GON *(Impatient)*: Listen, Sabu. We came because you got somethin' we want. Turn over the flower.

GON and HACHI *(In unison)*: Turn over the flower!

SABU: What? Give you a flower? How did you earn a bouquet while I was gone—carry a festival float or something?

HACHI: We did a lion dance here earlier, and laid eyes on a beautiful flower.

GON: A certain samurai asked us to come pick it for him.

SABU *(Turns around)*: What's that? Would that samurai be Ōtori Sagaemon, by any chance?

GON and HACHI *(In unison)*: Yeah, you got it.

SABU: Listen to me! Kotoura already has a respectable man named Isonojō. Tell that to Sagaemon!

GON: Old man, don't treat us like a couple of kids.

SABU: Children are children. You guys look more like a couple of pests.

HACHI: What's that? Pests?

GON *(To* HACHI*)*: If we're pests, let's pester him. Pester him. Pester him!

GON and HACHI *(Snidely)*: Pester him! Pester him! Pester him! Pester him!

*(*HACHI *and* GON *leap around the room several times, then smugly sit, fanning themselves.* OTSUGI *enters left.)*

OTSUGI: Dear, I heard. Don't let them treat you like this!

SABU: You're right. Bring me a change of clothes!

OTSUGI: With pleasure. Right away.

*(*OTSUGI *takes the colorful kimono off the wall. She and* SABU *ad-lib as he changes.)*

SABU *(To* OTSUGI*)*: I'm throwing away all those years of prayer for the next life. I'm going to rip them up.

OTSUGI: That might be going too far.

SABU: If there were ever a time, it's now!

GON: This is getting interesting. Just try to rip us up. Well, rip away!

GON and HACHI: Rip away! Rip away! Rip away!

(Music stops. GON *and* HACHI *challenge* SABU, *striking poses on either side of him.)*

SABU: That's enough! I'm talking about ripping apart my prayer beads!

TAKEMOTO:

With a vengeance he breaks the string, / tossing the beads aside.

SABU *(Hiking up his kimono)*: Now, I'm the sailor I used to be. *(Looking condescendingly at* HACHI *and* GON.*)* I won't even need a blade with you fellas.

(Kicks them, sending them flying onto their backs.)

TAKEMOTO:

Kimono hem tucked up high, he stands tall and proud.

*(*Tsuke *beat as* SABU *poses in a display of strength. Festival music and flute begin offstage.)*

SABU: Wife, bring me my sword.

OTSUGI: I thought you said you wouldn't need a sword?

SABU: It's not for those idiots, but I'm going after a born and bred samurai. An unarmed man would be a laughing stock! Bring it. Now.

*(*SABU *motions* GON *and* HACHI *out the door while* OTSUGI *retrieves his sword from the back room. Kneeling, she hands it to him.)*

OTSUGI: Your sword.

SABU: Well then, wife. *(Music stops.)* I'll be off.

TAKEMOTO:

Sabu follows, prodding mercilessly. Toward the shrine they go.

*(*SABU *glares, forcing the men to back down the* hanamichi. GON *rushes* SABU *at* shichisan. SABU *grabs* GON*'s arm, twisting it into the air.)*

SABU: You guys! *(Throws* GON *down.)* I've got you where I want you!

(Offstage song is sung as they exit. OTSUGI *watches with admiration. Music ends.)*

OTSUGI: Say, dear, don't let them get the best of you! Do you hear? *(Proudly.)* Ah, really, that husband of mine may have aged, but his years of experience certainly do show. The way he twisted that young man's arm and said, "I've got you where I want you!" Ha, ha! Three cheers for Matsushimaya! *(She raises her arms in praise, and, in a typical moment of metatheatricality, calls out the "shop name"* [yagō] *of the actor playing* SABU. *Bending over laughing, she notices her feet.)* Oh my goodness, I'm out here in bare feet!

(She goes inside. Offstage shamisen play. ISONOJŌ *and* OTATSU *enter from left.)*

ISONOJŌ: Otsugi, I will be leaving now. Please send news from Kotoura soon.

OTSUGI: I most certainly will. Don't worry.

ISONOJŌ: I go, but my heart remains.

OTATSU: Leave everything to me. *(*ISONOJŌ *starts out the door. Music stops.)* Ah, wait. Use this to conceal yourself. *(Gives* ISONOJŌ *her parasol.)*

ISONOJŌ: Otsugi, please take care of Kotoura for me.

(Offstage song begins as ISONOJŌ *exits slowly down the* hanamichi, *shielding his face with the parasol.* OTATSU *remains inside, ad-libbing with* OTSUGI. *Music stops.)*

OTATSU: Please give my regards to Sabu when he returns. I'll be going now. *(Hurries toward the* hanamichi.*)*

OTSUGI: Oh, wait, Otatsu! *(*OTATSU *turns back at* shichisan.*)* Now that your beautiful face is scarred, won't Tokubei's feelings toward you change?

OTATSU: Don't be ridiculous. What my husband loves is not this . . . *(points delicately to her face)*, but this right here.

(Pats her heart and nods proudly. Offstage song resumes. She exits. Music stops.)

OTSUGI *(Looking admiringly after* OTATSU*)*: Yes, indeed. Otatsu is a most exemplary woman. *(Exits into the back room.)*

TAKEMOTO:

Heading toward the door comes Mikawaya Giheiji.

(Festival music begins. GIHEIJI *enters on the* hanamichi. *He wears a light brown kimono, hiked up to his knees, and a* haori, *and his face is hidden within a folded straw hat tipped low over his head. Two* PALANQUIN BEARERS *carrying a palanquin follow. He calls inside. Music softens.)*

GIHEIJI: Ahem. Excuse me!

*(*OTSUGI *enters through curtain, crosses to the door and kneels.)*

OTSUGI: Yes, who's there? Oh, is it you, Giheiji?

GIHEIJI *(Steps inside doorway)*: Ah, Sabu's little lady. Haven't seen you for a long time. You haven't changed a bit.

OTSUGI: What brings you here?

GIHEIJI: Danshichi says a group of good-for-nothin's were hired to keep their eyes on Kotoura and steal her away. They'll never think to look right under their noses, so we'll keep her at our place for a while and give you and Sabu a break. He sent a palanquin to pick her up.

OTSUGI: You know, a pair of ruffians were here this minute looking for her. My husband went to have it out with them. Yes, it would be good to put Kotoura in your care. Just a moment, I'll get her. *(*OTSUGI *crosses left, retrieves* KOTOURA *from her room, and gently guides her to the door.* KOTOURA *has changed to a modest striped kimono, and her hairdo is plain, indicating her new status outside the brothel.)* Kotoura, Danshichi sent his father-in-law, Giheiji, to get you.

KOTOURA: Then I'll be going to Danshichi's house?

OTSUGI: For a few days. Don't worry about a thing.

KOTOURA: What if a letter comes from Isonojō?

OTSUGI: I'll handle it. Giheiji, make sure you take good care of Kotoura.

GIHEIJI: You can count on me.

(Music grows louder. KOTOURA *gets in the palanquin and* GIHEIJI *rushes it down the* hanamichi *and off, never once showing his face. Music stops.)*

OTSUGI: Well, well, well, how fortunate! Isonojō is off to Tamashima and Kotoura is going to stay with Danshichi. I think I'll light a candle at the altar and relax. *(Crosses to altar, kneels, and lights a candle.)*

TAKEMOTO:

Returning from the shrine come excited voices.

DANSHICHI *(Offstage)*: Listen, old man . . .

TOKUBEI *(Offstage)*: Let him go!

DANSHICHI and TOKUBEI *(Offstage)*: Let it go!

(A song from offstage accompanies TOKUBEI, SABU, *and* DANSHICHI, *who enter on the* hanamichi, *ad-libbing about* SABU*'s fight.* DANSHICHI *and* TOKUBEI *wear matching large plaid print kimono, in red and blue, respectively. Removing their sandals inside the door, they sit comfortably on the edge of the upper room, fanning themselves.* SABU *goes into the upper room to greet his wife. Singing ends. Shamisen continue.)*

TOKUBEI: So, Otsugi, your old man is back in one piece.

OTSUGI: Is he, now? Danshichi, Tokubei, how nice to see you. So that husband of mine didn't get hurt?

DANSHICHI: No matter how old he gets, you don't have to worry about him losing a fight. Right, Tokubei?

TOKUBEI: That's the truth. He's as fit as ever. He sent Gon and Hachi into the lotus pond—splash!—no trouble at all. And Sagaemon ran for his life! From the looks of things, Otsugi, he's still got quite a few years in him.

OTSUGI *(Obviously pleased)*: Oh, you're just saying that! *(To* SABU.*)* Well, we have a festival to celebrate today. Why don't you offer them a drink inside?

SABU: That's a great idea. Let's go.

(Music fades.)

DANSHICHI: I need to talk to Otsugi. Go ahead, I'll be right in.

SABU: If you say so. Come on, Tokubei. Let's get started.

(Shamisen resume. SABU *and* TOKUBEI *exit through the curtain.)*

DANSHICHI: So, Otsugi, have Isonojō and Kotoura been in good spirits?

OTSUGI: Well, it's like this. As Tokubei probably told you, for Isonojō's safety, we sent him to Tamashima with Otatsu. She was going home and fortunately happened to stop here on her way.

DANSHICHI: That was the right thing to do. Ah, that's great. Just great. I suppose Kotoura is feeling lonely left here all alone.

OTSUGI: What are you talking about? The messenger you sent just picked her up.

(Music stops.)

DANSHICHI: What's that? A messenger from me? Came to get Kotoura?

OTSUGI: Yes.

DANSHICHI: Come on, don't joke. It's too hot for that today.

OTSUGI: Your father-in-law came with a palanquin, saying you sent him. He just left with her.

DANSHICHI *(Alarmed)*: What? Giheiji said I sent him? He took Kotoura?

OTSUGI: Yes.

(Rhythmical festival music of drums and flute begins offstage. DANSHICHI *jumps up and runs to the door and then back again.* OTSUGI *frantically runs after him.)*

DANSHICHI: Which way did they go?

OTSUGI: Due south. You mean, you didn't know about this?

DANSHICHI: We can discuss that later. Just get out of my way!

OTSUGI: No, I won't. Not until you answer me.

DANSHICHI: Out of my way, out of my way! Get out of my way! *(Music grows louder. They jostle each other in rhythm to the music.* DANSHICHI *accidentally hits* OTSUGI *in the stomach with the handle of his sword as he runs out the door.* OTSUGI *doubles over, crying out in pain.* DANSHICHI *runs first toward her and then toward the* hanamichi, *unable to decide whether to run after* GIHEIJI *or help* OTSUGI. *He stops, slaps his knee decisively, and music stops. He tosses his tobacco pouch in through the open door.)* Otsugi, there's medicine in my tobacco pouch. Take it, please!

TAKEMOTO:

Nagamachi straight ahead!

*(*DANSHICHI *tucks his sandals in his obi and hikes up his kimono. Thrusting a leg forward, he strikes a* mie *at* shichisan. *Festival percussion and flute music resumes, and* tsuke *beat rapidly as* DANSHICHI *charges down the* hanamichi. *The curtain closes to a continuous* ki *pattern. Festival music continues softly during the scene change.)*

Back Street of Nagamachi

*(*Ki *clacks join the festival music as the curtain opens. A dirt road rises gradually from the end of the* hanamichi *to form an embankment that runs the width of the stage. Behind it is a row of shrubbery and a high wooden fence with rooftops visible beyond. Along the road, left, is a well with a bucket and in front of it a pond, the surface of which is a blue "water cloth"* [mizu nuno] *containing a flap through which a body can fall. Festival music stops. A final* ki *clack signals the* TAKEMOTO *music to begin.)*

TAKEMOTO:

Marching around shouldering gods and Buddhas, / Kōzu Shrine festival eve crowds celebrate. / Hoping to hide among them, in rushes Giheiji.

(Festival music resumes. Two PALANQUIN BEARERS *trot onto the* hanamichi *with the palanquin carrying* KOTOURA. GIHEIJI *hurriedly totters down the* hanamichi *after them.)*

DANSHICHI *(Offstage)*: Hey! Wait!

(To rapid beats of the tsuke, DANSHICHI *runs on, shouting. Catching the palanquin at the top of the embankment, he pushes* GIHEIJI *aside and strikes a* mie, *his arm held out to stop the palanquin. Festival percussion stops. Softer flute and drum continue.)*

BEARERS *(Protesting as they back off, left, with the palanquin)*: What are you doing? That's dangerous!

DANSHICHI: I kept yelling for you to stop. Why didn't you? *(Turning to* GIHEIJI.*)* Come on now, pop.

GIHEIJI: What!

DANSHICHI: Pop, where are you taking Kotoura? You're probably planning to sell her to some good-for-nothin'. You tried to cheat Isonojō out of money before this. Pop, this is wrong! This is really stooping too low. *(*GIHEIJI *clears his throat, waving his fan at* DANSHICHI *to be quiet.)* All right, I won't say any more. I've said it over and over, and you never change.

(Music fades. DANSHICHI *sits left, while* GIHEIJI *stands right.)*

GIHEIJI: What's that? I never change? I've stooped too low, you say? I've been waiting to hear you say that. *(*GIHEIJI *slowly removes his hat and poses, glaring at* DANSHICHI. TAKEMOTO *shamisen begins in the background.* DANSHICHI *sits on one knee, wiping sweat from his face.* GIHEIJI *gives his hat and jacket to the* PALANQUIN BEARERS.*)* Hey, you guys, I've got to talk to this guy for a minute, so take a break. And hold on to these for me. *(Turning back to* DANSHICHI.*)* You're the one who married my daughter and left her with me to take care of for the last six years. Should I charge for her keep? You don't know gratitude! So, Danshichi, you think you're quite a man, do you? *(To* BEARERS.*)* Hey, you guys listen, too. This no-good tries to look important, but you know why people called him "homeless Danshichi"? Kept company of the finest tramps, ate only what he could beg . . .

DANSHICHI: Pop, do you have to talk about that?

GIHEIJI: It's true, isn't it? I'm just telling the truth. Yep, kept company of the finest tramps and ate what you could beg—until I saved you. Set you up selling fish down at the Sakai seashore. That debt of gratitude you forgot all about. You started flirting with my daughter, Okaji, and she ended up birthin' that brat Ichimatsu. Well, that's okay, I thought—you gave me a little bit every month so I closed my eyes. But then you got in that big fight in Chimori town and got tossed in Izumi jail for a hundred days.

DANSHICHI: C'mon pop, do you have to keep talking about all that?

GIHEIJI: What if I do? What's the matter? You got put in jail for a hundred days, and, hey, who in the hell do you think was takin' care of your wife and kid?

DANSHICHI: I have you to thank for that.

GIHEIJI *(Making a show of his disgust)*: Don't talk to me! Don't talk to me! I had to do something to get the extra money we needed. Things were finally happening until you screwed it up! So I filched Kotoura for Sagaemon. He's in love with her and will give me a big bundle of cash when I deliver.

DANSHICHI: But if you do that, I'll completely lose face.

GIHEIJI: What? You'll lose face? Exactly what face are you talkin' about? Is it this face you'll lose? *(Hits* DANSHICHI *'s cheek with his fan.)* This face? *(Hits the other cheek.)* This face? *(Laughs derisively at* DANSHICHI *'s surprise.)* You're quite a man! The man who lets someone else feed his wife and kid. Is that the "man" who's gonna lose face? Don't give me any of your bull!

TAKEMOTO:

Kicked and beaten by his father-in-law, Danshichi / Endures his wrath quietly. / Suppressing resentment, clenching his teeth tightly, / he realizes there is nothing to do but apologize. / Clasping his hands together, he goes on bended knee.

(Kicked over by GIHEIJI, DANSHICHI *uses every ounce of strength to control his temper.* TAKEMOTO *shamisen and flute continue in the background.)*

DANSHICHI *(Trying to placate* GIHEIJI*)*: Pop, I don't blame you for being mad. You helped me over and over again, and I interfered in your moneymaking scheme. I see why you're riled, and I promise never to do it again. But please, do this one favor and take Kotoura back to Sabu's. Okay, pop? I'm asking you. I'm begging you. I was wrong and I apologize. *(*DANSHICHI *bows humbly, but* GIHEIJI *turns away, fanning himself.)* I was wrong and I'm begging. Pop, don't do this. C'mon, have a heart. It's not like I'm some stranger—we're father and son. Please, I'm begging you, begging you. *(*DANSHICHI *bows again, apologizing.* GIHEIJI *turns away, sticks his bare backside contemptuously into* DANSHICHI *'s face and fans between his legs.* DANSHICHI *turns away, swallowing his humiliation.)* C'mon pop, all you ever think about is money, money, money. *(Inadvertently picking up a stone as he speaks,* DANSHICHI *gets an idea. He quickly wraps several rocks in a cloth and puts the bundle in the breast of his kimono while* GIHEIJI *is busy ignoring him.)* Oh, yeah, pop. I completely forgot. You know, when I got in that fight in Sakai and was sent up to Izumi jail? . . . I mean, when I *went* up to Izumi that time. A bunch of friends pooled some money for me to get started again. And I got that money right here. Three . . . I mean thirty gold pieces. *(*GIHEIJI *is suddenly attentive.)* It's yours if you take Kotoura back to Sabu's. If you don't, my honor as a man is lost. *(Music stops.)*

Have mercy. Please pop. Just this once. Please! *(Clasps his hands and bows, pleading.)*

TAKEMOTO:

He kneels, clasping his hands and waving his arms. / He has no choice but to plead; he is compelled. / Giheiji, too, thinking of the money he will soon have, begins to soften a little.

(Counting on his fingers, GIHEIJI *stands, thinking it over.* TAKEMOTO *shamisen and flute continue softly in the background.)*

GIHEIJI *(Turning to face* DANSHICHI*)*: You're tellin' me that while you were in jail, your friends got some money together, and you've got that money—thirty gold pieces—right now?

DANSHICHI: Yes, I do. Right here.

GIHEIJI: You've really got thirty gold pieces? Thirty gold pieces. Thirty gold pieces. He, he, he. *(Laughs.)* Well, what d'ya know? Actually, if I bring Kotoura to Sagaemon, he'll put a stack of gold pieces right in front of my eyes. *(Dangles his fan to illustrate the point.)* But, seeing as we're related through my daughter . . . *(Hesitates. Music fades.)* Okay, I'll knock the price down and send her back for thirty.

DANSHICHI: You will? Oh, thank you. Thank you! *(Starts toward* PALANQUIN BEARERS.*)*

GIHEIJI: Stop it, boy. Do you really have thirty gold pieces?

DANSHICHI: Yes, I do.

GIHEIJI: Where are they?

DANSHICHI: Right here.

GIHEIJI: Where? Why don't you show them to me?

DANSHICHI: Pop, I'll let you feel them. Okay? Here they are. Okay? Here, right here. *(He places* GIHEIJI's *hand on the bundle of rocks tucked in his kimono.)* Thirty gold pieces. They're all right there.

GIHEIJI *(Pleased)*: He, he, he. They sure are. Well, then, I'll send her back. *(To* BEARERS.*)* You, there!

*(*GIHEIJI *and* DANSHICHI *stumble over each other as they shout instructions.)*

DANSHICHI: Pop, that's okay, I'll tell them. Take this palanquin back to Sabu's where you came from.

BEARERS: Sure thing.

GIHEIJI: And make sure to collect your fare and tip over there.

DANSHICHI: Okay, they'll take care of everything at that end. Now be careful, and get her back quickly. Tell them Danshichi will be over later. Don't let me down.

(Festival music plays as the palanquin is carried out the hanamichi. DANSHICHI *sees it off, then crosses and sits in the center of the road, looking off in the distance.*

GIHEIJI *hovers, standing to his left. Festival music slows, softens.* TAKEMOTO *shamisen plays softly underneath.)*

GIHEIJI: Okay, son. I sent the palanquin back just like you said. Now are you happy?

DANSHICHI: Nothing could make me happier.

GIHEIJI: That's good. That's good. Me, too. Now if you're really happy, hurry up and spread the joy.

DANSHICHI: Spread the joy?

GIHEIJI *(Growing impatient)*: Remember what you said before. If I sent the palanquin back . . . you know . . . the promise . . . you know.

DANSHICHI: Promise?

GIHEIJI *(Fanning furiously)*: Ah, son, you're getting hot! Really hot!

DANSHICHI: Oh, yes, it's hot, isn't it.

GIHEIJI: Cut it out. C'mon. I sent the palanquin back, just like you said. I sent it back, see? Just like you asked, right? And you promised the . . . mon . . . mon . . . mon . . . C'mon, son, you're so hot!

DANSHICHI: Oh, yes, it's really hot, isn't it?

GIHEIJI: For somebody so young, you got a helluva bad memory. The thirty gold pieces you promised! *(Music stops.)* Hand 'em over now!

*(*DANSHICHI *freezes.)*

DANSHICHI: Uh, the thirty gold pieces . . .

GIHEIJI *(Expectantly)*: The thirty gold pieces . . .

DANSHICHI: The money . . .

GIHEIJI: The money . . .

DANSHICHI *(Defeated)*: The money . . . *(taking the bundle from his breast pocket, the rocks fall to the ground, one by one)* isn't here.

GIHEIJI *(Mindlessly repeating)*: The money . . . isn't here. *(Pause.)* No! *(*GIHEIJI *falls back in surprise. Offstage festival music begins. He runs down the embankment after the palanquin.)* Hey, you guys, come back! Come back!

(Accented by tsuke, DANSHICHI *and* GIHEIJI *run toward the departed palanquin, yelling and waving their arms, repeatedly overtaking each other.)*

DANSHICHI: No, don't! Keep going! Keep going!

GIHEIJI: Come back! Come back!

DANSHICHI: No, don't. Keep going!

(Enraged, GIHEIJI *grabs* DANSHICHI*, drags him up the slope, throws him down, and beats him.* DANSHICHI *covers his head but doesn't resist.)*

GIHEIJI: I'll teach you!

DANSHICHI: I was wrong! I'm sorry.

GIHEIJI: I'll teach you! I'll teach you to trick your saintly father! Damn, you make me mad! Damn you! I'll teach you! Take that! And that! And that! *(As he strikes,* GIHEIJI *pulls out one of* DANSHICHI*'s sandals, tucked in his obi.)* What's this?

Leather soles? You wearin' these fancy things? In all my years, I wore nothin' but cheap straw sandals! You dude up and talk about losing face? This face here? *(Rubs* DANSHICHI's *face with the sole of the sandal.)* This face? *(Rubs again.)* This face? *(Rubs again.)* I'll give you what you deserve!

(He spits on the sandal, rubs it in the dirt, and continues hitting. DANSHICHI *sits up and* GIHEIJI *delivers a final blow, cutting* DANSHICHI *on the forehead.)*

DANSHICHI: Ow, that hurts! Ow! Pop, you didn't have to do that! I told you I'd get you the money. Okay, I was wrong, but I apologized didn't I? Ow, that hurts. *(*DANSHICHI *sits up and puts his hand to the wound. Lowering his hand, he sees blood on it and instantly is enraged. Music stops.)* How dare you . . . *(turns menacingly to* GIHEIJI, *thrusts his leg forward, and poses)* mar my face!

GIHEIJI: So, I cut it. I cut it! *(Squats in front of* DANSHICHI, *returning his glare.)* So wh-wh-what!

*(*DANSHICHI *reaches for his sword to strike.* GIHEIJI *runs, hiding behind the well.* Tsuke *beats accent their* mie *pose. Festival music begins.)*

GIHEIJI *(Taunting)*: What? So what about your face? Don't forget I'm your father. Your father! Glare at your father like that and you'll go cross-eyed! I see you fingering that sword. Plannin' to kill me?

DANSHICHI *(Fights to control his anger)*: No, no. I wouldn't kill you. You know that.

GIHEIJI: Ha! At this age, I'd be happy to die at your hands. Go ahead, kill me. C'mon. Do it quickly! What do you want to cut first? *(Inches closer to* DANSHICHI, *taunting.)* Slice my arms? Cut my shins? Well, hurry up and kill me! Kill me, kill me, kill me! *(Grabs* DANSHICHI *and poses cross-eyed.* DANSHICHI *pulls away, and* GIHEIJI *falls over on purpose.)* Ow, ow, ow! You knocked your father down. Knocked me right over!

DANSHICHI: Pop, don't be ridiculous. You did that yourself and you know it.

GIHEIJI *(Standing)*: I'd rather you kill me right now than treat me so badly. Don't you know how to do it? Here, I'll show you.

*(*GIHEIJI *presses against* DANSHICHI *and pulls the sword from its sheath.)*

DANSHICHI: Hey, that's dangerous! What the hell are you doing? Somebody could get hurt. Be careful!

*(*Tsuke *beat as* GIHEIJI *swings the sword awkwardly. Wrestling for the sword,* DANSHICHI *falls into a sitting position, facing upstage.* GIHEIJI *stands over him, holding the sword on* DANSHICHI*'s neck.)*

GIHEIJI *(Taunting)*: I'm your father. Your father! Hear me? If you even scratch me, you'll wind up with a foot-long bamboo saw slicing . . . your . . . neck. *(Illustrates by moving the sword back and forth with each syllable.)*

DANSHICHI *(Passionately, crying out)*: I know that! Forgive me, please! *(*DANSHICHI *rises, pushes* GIHEIJI *back, and, as he wrests the sword away, unknowingly cuts*

GIHEIJI *across the shoulder.* GIHEIJI *clasps his shoulder, still unaware of what has happened. Music stops.)* Oh, come on, stop being so rough. What if somebody gets hurt? Now where'd the sheath go?

GIHEIJI: Ow, it hurts! *(Slowly draws his hand away and sees blood.)* Aagh! You sliced me! Murderer! Parent murderer! *(Runs around shouting.)*

DANSHICHI *(Frightened)*: C'mon, pop, you can't go around yelling that. *(Grabs* GIHEIJI *and puts him in a headlock, covering his mouth.)* You've gone too far. Some things are okay to say out loud and some things aren't. What will people think if they hear you? Why would I . . . *(feels a dampness on his hand)* want to . . . kill you?

(Notices the blood on his sword blade. Temple bell rings. Shocked, DANSHICHI *loosens his grip on* GIHEIJI*'s mouth.)*

GIHEIJI *(Screams)*: Murderer!

*(*DANSHICHI *quickly covers* GIHEIJI*'s mouth. The sword in his hand shakes.)*

DANSHICHI *(To himself, horrified at the thought of what he must do)*: You don't give me a choice! *(Crying out.)* Pop, forgive me!

*(*DANSHICHI *releases* GIHEIJI *and rushes at him with the sword.* GIHEIJI *dodges, grabs* DANSHICHI*'s topknot, pulls, and* DANSHICHI*'s hair falls loose down his back.* DANSHICHI *pierces* GIHEIJI *in the side and dashes to* shichisan. *Pulling down the top of his kimono, revealing his tattooed arms and torso, he strikes a frightening* mie, *holding his sword overhead. Offstage shamisen begin playing slowly, accompanied by flute and stick drum. A procession of lantern-covered festival floats crosses the stage in the distance behind the fence.* Tsuke *accent the movements and poses in the following stylized, eerily beautiful murder scene.* DANSHICHI *looks to see that no one is coming and returns to the embankment to attack* GIHEIJI, *who feebly throws rocks and sticks in self-defense.* GIHEIJI *grabs and pulls* DANSHICHI*'s obi, slowly spinning him around and around until obi and kimono fall away, leaving* DANSHICHI *dressed solely in a red loincloth and body tattoos.* DANSHICHI *strikes a picturesque* mie, *standing profile, balanced on one leg, sword raised ready to strike.* GIHEIJI *swings the obi at* DANSHICHI, *who becomes entangled, and it stretches taut between them as they pose in a* mie. GIHEIJI *stumbles and cowers behind the well.* DANSHICHI *glares, pointing his sword. They strike a* mie. DANSHICHI *rushes at* GIHEIJI *and stabs him. Falling, the old man grabs* DANSHICHI*'s leg.* Mie. *In the struggle,* GIHEIJI *falls into the pond.* DANSHICHI *follows, dragging him out. Wet and muddy, both struggle until* DANSHICHI *delivers a final stab in the chest.* GIHEIJI *falls, center. Music stops.* DANSHICHI *stands astride the body and pierces* GIHEIJI*'s neck with the tip of his sword.* Mie. *Loud festival drums begin. In time with the offstage cheers and voices,* DANSHICHI *jumps, turning to face upstage, straddling the body. He looks both ways and again jumps to face front, still standing over the body. Voices of villagers*

Danshichi Kurōbei (Matsumoto Kōshirō IX) is desperate to show a normal appearance to approaching festival dancers. Using buckets of water, he washes Giheiji's blood from the blade of his sword and mud from his torso and legs. (Umemura Yutaka, Engeki Shuppansha)

carrying the portable shrine grow louder and closer. DANSHICHI *rolls the body into the pond. He frantically washes mud and blood off his body, using bucket after bucket of water from the well. Slipping and sliding in the mud, he shakes violently as he tries to resheath the sword. He has barely tossed his kimono on when the revelers, dressed in identical festival kimono, enter left, shouting loudly and stepping rhythmically with the festival calls.)*

ALL: Yo ho, heave ho. Yo ho, heave ho. Yo ho, heave ho.

(Men waving fans shout, cheering on those shouldering the portable shrine. The group crosses right, loops once around the stage, and parades down the hanamichi. DANSHICHI *follows, pulls a hand towel* [tenugui] *from the obi of one of the men, unfolds it, and puts it on his head, tying it underneath his chin. Following at a distance,* DANSHICHI *pretends to be part of the cheering group until they are gone. Shouts and music fade. Left alone,* DANSHICHI *falls at* shichisan, *grief-stricken.)*

DANSHICHI: Even if he is evil, a father-in-law is still a parent. *(Clasping his hands,* DANSHICHI *cries out in pain and regret.)* Father, please. *(Temple bell rings.)* Forgive me!

TAKEMOTO:

On to Hatchōme, the crossroads of destiny!

(Forceful TAKEMOTO *narration and music pull* DANSHICHI *to his feet. As festival percussion and voices fade in, a dazed* DANSHICHI *stumbles off down the* hanamichi. *Accelerating* ki *pattern accompanies the curtain as it closes. Music stops.)*

Three-panel woodblock print by Utagawa Kunisada I (1786–1864). Ichimura-za, Edo, ninth month 1824. In the final scene of the play, Nan Yohei ("Nanpō Jūjibei, Ichikawa Danjūrō" VII), bearing a samurai official's two swords, poses, listening outside the gate. "Nuregami Chōgorō" ("Bandō Mitsugorō" III) kneels center, ready to escape. Yohei's "wife Ohaya" ("Iwai Shijaku" I, later Iwai Hanshirō VII) poses beside the lamp. The lengthy inscription consists of the last fifteen lines of the play, spoken by Oko, Ohaya, Yohei, and Chōgorō: "I have caught Nuregami. Good work . . . I owe you so much. No more words! Just go!" (Tsubouchi Memorial Theatre Museum of Waseda University)

The Skylight
Hikimado

Takeda Izumo II, Namiki Senryū, and Miyoshi Shōraku

TRANSLATED BY MATTHEW JOHNSON

1749 TAKEMOTO-ZA, OSAKA

The Skylight

INTRODUCTION

The Skylight is a scene in *Chōgorō and Chōkichi: A Diary of Two Butterflies in the Pleasure Quarters* (Futatsu Chōchō Kuruwa Nikki), part of one of the greatest winning streaks in either kabuki or puppet theatre history. During the 1740s at the Takemoto-za in Osaka, the writing team of Takeda Izumo II (1691–1756), Namiki Sōsuke (Senryū) (1696–1751), and Miyoshi Shōraku (1696–1772) produced a string of plays that were both popular and critical hits. Today, they constitute a major segment of the canon for history plays *(jidaimono)* and combined history-domestic plays *(jidai-sewamono).*

Chōgorō and Chōkichi came toward the end of this remarkable streak and did not at first achieve great acclaim. Critics and audiences tended to think that it was too much of a regurgitation of *Summer Festival: Mirror of Osaka* (Natsu Matsuri Naniwa Kagami), translated in the present volume. Despite its lukewarm reception in the puppet theatre, the play did rather well in kabuki. Kabuki performances were mostly limited to the "Sumo" scene, in which sumo wrestlers Chōgorō and Chōkichi confront each other outside a temporary arena. The role of Chōgorō was usually played by the head actor *(zagashira)* of the troupe, someone capable of capturing the stature and poise of a high-ranking wrestler, and Chōkichi by a popular younger actor, showing a newcomer's youthful and somewhat explosive energy. The audience would be thrilled by the heated intergenerational exchange.

In the scenes preceding this long play's other commonly performed scene, *Skylight,* translated here, Chōgorō, an established sumo champion, has lost his first match with the newcomer Chōkichi. The patrons of both wrestlers are vying for the affections of the courtesan Azuma. Elated by his surprise victory, Chōkichi meets with Chōgorō and is surprised to find that the latter threw the match so the other wrestler would owe him a favor and have his patrons give up on Azuma. The news, however, wounds Chōkichi's pride and, instead of understanding Chōgorō's well-meant intentions, he vows to do everything in his power to help his patrons in their attempt to buy out Azuma's contract. This, in turn, leads to the tragic murder of Chōkichi's patrons by Chōgorō and the fugitive status the latter finds himself in at the beginning of *Skylight.*

The play as a whole is centered on these two wrestlers, and the formal title—*Futatsu Chōchō Kuruwa Nikki*—is a pun on their names. Combining the first syllable from each wrestler's name forms the word *chōchō,* or butterfly. Though much of the play does take place in the pleasure quarters *(kuruwa),* accounting for the title's second half, these scenes are rarely, if ever, performed, making the title seem inappropriately colorful for the subdued tone of *Skylight.*

The original script of *Skylight,* which was the responsibility of playwright Takeda Izumo II, would have looked very similar to that performed today, but its feeling would have been quite different in the Edo period. Its main focus is currently Nan Yohei, but in the pre-Meiji period, his mother, Oko, would have been played by a higher-ranking actor and therefore viewed as the principal character. This is more in keeping with the theme of the puppet version; it is much more common for puppet play scenes to be built around the laments of elderly characters. In the early nineteenth century, when stars such as Ichikawa Danjūrō VII (1791–1859) attempted the role, more attention was given to Yohei, but this failed to raise the scene's popularity and the emphasis on Yohei slipped into oblivion.

Skylight was reinstated in the repertory in 1894 when Nakamura Ganjirō I (1860–1935) of the Kamigata area revived it. Ganjirō succeeded in making Yohei central again by altering the script and imposing on it his own brand of acting gentle, upright young men *(wajitsu).* His performance was well received and restored interest in the scene in both kabuki and the puppet theatre. *Skylight* became a regular part of Ganjirō's repertoire and was picked up by Tokyo actor Nakamura Kichiemon I (1886–1954), who further developed the role by intensifying its psychological aspects, using the style of interiorized acting, or "gut acting" *(haragei),* pioneered at this time by Danjūrō IX (1838–1903). Today, these two chief acting styles—the Ganjirō and the Kichiemon—remain, and Yohei is one of the few roles acted in both Tokyo and Kamigata patterns *(kata)* on a regular basis.

With only six roles, two of them minor, *Skylight* has a simple structure but a powerful emotional effect. As in many scenes attributed to Takeda Izumo II, there is a complicated web of duty *(giri)* and desires driven by personal feelings *(ninjō).* Oko is torn between her duty toward her stepson, Yohei, and her love for her true son, Chōgorō. Yohei's duty in his new position as magistrate—which involves his promotion from commoner to samurai status—is to capture Chōgorō, but, for the sake of his mother, he wants to let him escape. Chōgorō, certain that his life is near its end, is drawn to visit his mother one last time but feels honor-bound to allow Yohei to capture him. Throughout all of this, it is the simple skylight in the roof that symbolizes the societal constraints that bind them. When closed, the characters act on their duty as expected in the heavy darkness of a strict feudal society. When open, they are free to express their true feelings with open hearts.

It is interesting that, though all the characters choose personal feelings and compassion over duty, none have to face the consequences. Usually, the escape of Chōgorō would require someone to take responsibility, especially since Yohei—even though under strict orders from the local lord—has allowed it. In most kabuki plays, some tragic sacrifice would have to be made to make up for Chōgorō's escape, with either Oko or Yohei obligated to commit suicide. Yohei is yet another example of the ambivalent kabuki samurai, drawn between two allegiances and responding to the one that most touches his emotional, rather than his moral, fiber.

Having been reworked in the Meiji period, with new trends and tastes taken into consideration, the strong psychological portraits and the characters' rejection of feudal restraints make *Skylight* a very modern play that continues to appeal strongly to today's audiences. It is a good example of how the efforts of actors in this actor-centered theatre can bring popularity where even the greatest writing team of the eighteenth century could not.

This translation is based on the unpublished script (daihon) produced at the Kabuki-za, Tokyo, September 1994, and on a videotape of a November 1984 performance at the same theatre.

CHARACTERS

NAN YOHEI, *later* NANPŌ JŪJIBEI, *a commoner newly promoted to samurai status as the local magistrate*

OHAYA, *his wife*

OKO, *his mother*

HIRAOKA TANPEI, *a samurai with a vendetta*

MIHARA DENZŌ, *a samurai with a vendetta*

NUREGAMI CHŌGORŌ, *a sumo wrestler and son of* OKO

STAGE ASSISTANTS, *black-garbed* kurogo

TAKEMOTO, *shamisen and narrator combination who accompany the actors*

(The curtain opens to offstage shamisen music, evoking the mood of the countryside, and to an accelerating ki *pattern. The house of* OKO *is visible. It is quite large for a commoner and is surrounded by a grove of bamboo. Hills of the surrounding countryside can be seen in the distance. The first floor contains a raised entrance, a curtained doorway in the center, and sliding* shōji *screens leading to a room within.*

The curtain is decorated with a grass design closely associated with rural settings. A short hallway and three steps lead to a second-floor room hidden by closed shōji *screens. In the roof of the corridor is an open skylight with a pull-rope tied to a pillar below. In front of the house is a small garden with a stone basin. It is afternoon on the fourteenth day of the ninth month. The fifteenth is known for the Moon-Viewing Festival, and in this region it is also the day of the Ritual of Release, in which people release caged animals, often birds, to improve their karma for the next life.)*

TAKEMOTO:

It is mid-autumn / in the household of the village magistrate of the Yawata area, / in which only the wife now remains. / The time has come for the Ritual of Release. / Her daughter-in-law has prepared / a decoration on a small wooden stand for the Moon-Viewing Festival. / On the stand are twelve rice dumplings / placed there as a wish to the moon for children. / Oko comes out from within.

*(*OHAYA *enters through curtained doorway at center. She wears a kimono, decorated with a simple black and white pattern, and an apron. Her hair is covered with a cotton hand towel* [tenugui], *indicating that she has been doing housework. She climbs the steps to the second-floor room. Opening the front sliding screens, she places the flower arrangement on the balcony, clasping her hands in prayer and looking to the sky with anticipation.* OKO *comes through the same curtained entrance as* OHAYA *returns to the lower level.* OKO *wears a plain brown kimono and has grey hair. The cloth covering her forehead, usually purple for a female-role specialist* [onnagata], *is brown, indicating her advanced age. They sit together,* OHAYA *at right and* OKO *at left, and talk.)*

OKO: Here now, daughter-in-law. The decorations for the Moon-Viewing Festival shouldn't be put out until tomorrow night. It's a day early and still light out.

OHAYA: But, mother, you've been making preparations for the Ritual of Release even though it doesn't take place until tomorrow. I thought it was customary to make preparations the night before. That's so silly.

(She laughs. OHAYA *removes the hand towel from her head and folds it into a triangle, tucking it into her obi. Offstage shamisen music begins in the background.)*

OKO *(Scolding)*: Watch what you say. That phrase is particular to the pleasure quarters. You're no longer the courtesan Miyako in the Shinmachi pleasure quarters of Osaka. You are the wife of Nan Yohei and go by the name Ohaya. If neighbors should drop by, you would offer them tobacco, sake, and light refreshment, as a good wife should. We may have fallen somewhat, but my husband was Nanpō Jūjibei, a man whose position others were jealous of. After my husband's death, Yohei began a life of reckless pleasure. The title of magistrate was taken away, and we lost all of our possessions. I was forced to bear one embarrassment after another. But there's been a change of lordship, and new magistrates are to be named. As the son of the former magistrate, Yohei was suddenly called to appear at the lord's mansion. I've offered simple fare to the gods in the hope that things will return to how they once were. Though my voice is no more than a flea's breath, I hope it will reach the heavens. I can't wait to hear what the lord had to say.

OHAYA: Please don't worry. I'm sure your wish will be granted and Yohei will be promoted.

*(*OHAYA *removes their tea tray and helps* OKO *as she stands on a stool to place offerings before the household altar on the wall at right.)*

TAKEMOTO:

Unable to hold their excitement, / they look out the front gate. / Hiding his face with a cloth tied around his cheeks, / Chōgorō approaches the house cautiously, / all the while looking around to see if he is being watched.

*(*CHŌGORŌ *enters quickly on the* hanamichi. *He wears a large-striped kimono typical of kabuki sumo wrestlers. He is padded, and the kimono is made of heavy cotton to make him seem large and muscular. He holds a straw mat around his body to hide his identity. He rolls up the mat, revealing his striking appearance, with the youthful forelock of the premodern wrestler and a prominent mole on his right cheek. He hastily approaches the house.)*

CHŌGORŌ: Mother, are you home?

*(*CHŌGORŌ *opens the door and enters, standing below the interior platform at right.)*

TAKEMOTO:

She is startled by the words.

OKO *(Crossing to him, surprised)*: Chōgorō, is that you?

CHŌGORŌ: Good, you're here.

OKO: How wonderful to see you again. Please come in.

*(*OHAYA *enters and prepares a bucket of water with which* CHŌGORŌ *can wash his feet at the entrance. He sits on the edge of the platform as* OHAYA *steps down to assist him.)*

CHŌGORŌ: Please excuse me.

OHAYA *(Surprised)*: Chōgorō, is that you?

CHŌGORŌ: Miyako. I'm glad to see you're doing well.

OHAYA: It certainly has been a long time.

*(*OHAYA *dumps the remaining water outside as* OKO *invites* CHŌGORŌ *to have a seat inside.)*

OKO: You seem to be doing well.

CHŌGORŌ *(Bowing)*: I'm glad to see you haven't changed. It's Miyako who's changed.

*(*CHŌGORŌ *sits center, placing his sword on his right.* OKO *sits on his left.*

OHAYA *brings* CHŌGORŌ *a tobacco box and then returns to sit on the right.)* Were you able to marry Yohei, just as you'd hoped?

OHAYA *(Modestly)*: Yes, luckily everything worked out. Gonkurō was jailed for using counterfeit money to buy out my contract, and it was found that the entertainer Yohei murdered was actually a thief and the killing was justified. We married, and I've changed my name to Ohaya. I have so much to thank you for. *(Music stops.)*

CHŌGORŌ *(Heavily)*: What happy news. It seems for those who kill, there is both good and bad luck.

OKO: What do you mean?

CHŌGORŌ *(Changes tone and acts as though he has said nothing)*: But this is very good news indeed.

OKO: You two talk as if you know each other.

OHAYA: Yes, we met in the pleasure quarters.

OKO *(Curious)*: Does Yohei know him as well?

OHAYA: No, just me. Why did Chōgorō call you mother?

OKO: I understand your confusion and knew I'd have to tell you someday. Please listen. *(Shamisen music plays offstage.* CHŌGORŌ *takes out pipe and begins to smoke.)* I was forced to put Chōgorō up for adoption when he was five-years-old. When I married into this family, my husband already had Yohei by his prior wife. Though Yohei knew I was his stepmother, he always ignored the fact and treated me as his true mother. I'd lost touch with Chōgorō, but I happened to come across him last year when I traveled to Osaka for the festival. Though it had been many years, I recognized him because he had a mole on his upper cheek just like his father. *(Pointing to her right cheek.)* I asked if he wasn't Chōgorō, who had been adopted by Chōemon. We talked of old times, and he told me how his adoptive parents had passed away and how he'd become a sumo wrestler. I thought about telling Yohei of our encounter, but I was afraid he'd think I'd purposefully sought out my son in an effort to reclaim the past, so I hid it from him. *(Happily.)* But now that Chōgorō has come here, we can unite the brothers and drink a toast when Yohei returns. If you count my daughter-in-law, I now have three children. I must be the luckiest person in the world.

(OHAYA *rises and crosses right to get tea for* CHŌGORŌ.)

TAKEMOTO *(Slowly)*:

The more he thinks about how happy his mother is, / the more Chōgorō worries that he may not even be alive come tomorrow. / He does his best to hide his tears.

(Contemplating his mother's words and his own situation, CHŌGORŌ *unconsciously drops his pipe and chokes on tea brought to him by* OHAYA, *who*

resumes sitting at right. She offers him a hand towel to cover his mouth. Music stops.)

CHŌGORŌ *(Seriously)*: Mother, you should continue to keep my identity a secret from Yohei.

OKO: Why?

CHŌGORŌ: I'll tell you. *(Shamisen music resumes.)* Sumo wrestling is a profession where you fight for a living. Sometimes when you get into a real fight, whether it be with a commoner or a samurai *(rising slightly as if agitated)*, you get caught up in it as if it were a match and things can get out of hand, or someone can even end up dead.

OKO: What are you saying?

CHŌGORŌ *(More calmly, to keep her from worrying)*: Of course, I have done no such thing, but there's always the chance that I might, and that may cause trouble for you. Until I retire, you must treat me as a stranger. Do not even act like you have a son. Nobody knows when his time will come. *(With deep feeling.)* This may be the last time we ever meet. *(In a lighter tone.)* Ohaya, please tell Yohei to take care of my mother. I'm leaving for a tournament in Nagasaki and won't be able to see you for a long time. *(Sadly, deliberately.)* I hope you both live long and healthy lives.

TAKEMOTO:

He hangs his head dejectedly.

OKO *(Mollifying him)*: Chōgorō, must you continue being a wrestler? You don't have to go to Nagasaki or anywhere else. Why don't you stay here and talk it over with Yohei? Together you should be able to come up with a solution. Isn't that so, Ohaya?

OHAYA: Of course. Yohei is sure to be pleased to hear you are brothers. Why don't I fix some tea porridge while you wait?

OKO *(Happily)*: This is his first visit. We should make him something special to eat. Some fish or some boiled burdock root. And didn't you used to like octopus? While we're preparing them, you can think about what we've discussed. Have a drink upstairs. The room has an excellent view of the Yodo River.

CHŌGORŌ: Mother, you needn't worry about me. I'll be fine with a simple bowl of rice and then be on my way.

TAKEMOTO:

Rising, he can only think of his mother's food / as if it were his final meal before execution. / Taking the tobacco box, he sullenly heads upstairs.

*(*OKO *goes to prepare the upstairs room. She soon returns and resumes her seat.* CHŌGORŌ *rises as if to leave, pauses in a dramatic pose, then, thinking the better of it, takes the tobacco stand offered by* OHAYA *and heads upstairs.* OKO *rises and playfully mimics his bulky walk. The women exit up center.)*

TAKEMOTO:

You never know when your chance to get ahead will come. / His ship having come in, / Nan Yohei heads home with his new kimono and swords / accompanied by two samurai. / *(In a powerful staccato rhythm.)* Their identities are unknown, / but they are full of youthful strength.

(As an offstage [geza] *song accompanies them, the samurai* TANPEI *and* DENZŌ *enter on the* hanamichi, *followed by* YOHEI. *All wear formal black kimono,* hakama, *and* haori. YOHEI *stops the two at* shichisan, *and the song softens.)*

YOHEI: Gentlemen, we have arrived.

TANPEI: So that is your house?

DENZŌ: Please lead us there.

YOHEI: This way, please.

(Song resumes. They move on, pausing near the house for YOHEI *to take the lead. They stop outside the door, where* YOHEI *turns to address the samurai. The song ends and is replaced by offstage shamisen music.)*

YOHEI: Gentlemen, I know the topic you brought up with my lord is secret. Please forgive me, but could you please wait over there in my mother's prayer hut until I call you in?

TANPEI: That would be prudent. We don't want others to hear our discussion.

DENZŌ: Until you call . . .

TANPEI: Sometime soon . . .

YOHEI: Please wait.

(Offstage music stops.)

TAKEMOTO:

After bowing to each other, / Nan Yohei cheerfully opens the front door.

*(*YOHEI *leads the two offstage right. Returning, he gleefully fixes his hair and kimono. He pokes his head in through the door.)*

YOHEI *(Excitedly)*: Mother, wife. *(Straightening up and speaking with an air of authority.)* I have returned.

*(*OHAYA *enters through curtained doorway.)*

OHAYA: Welcome home, dear. *(Calling excitedly.)* Mother, mother.

(Offstage shamisen music resumes. OKO *enters through the curtained doorway.* YOHEI *crosses to center and kneels, placing his swords to his side.)*

OKO *(Excitedly)*: What is it? Oh, Yohei, you've returned. And what a sight you are.

*(*YOHEI *bows low to his mother. The women sit on either side of him.)*

OHAYA: He's returned as an impressive samurai.

OKO: Things must have gone well. That's the case, isn't it?

YOHEI *(Excitedly)*: I have great news. Things couldn't have gone better. Aren't you happy for me, Ohaya?

OHAYA *(Proudly)*: I'm overjoyed. There's nothing that would make me happier. Mother, look at what an impressive samurai he's become.

(Music ends.)

OKO: Isn't it wonderful? It must all be thanks to my prayers. *(Urging him on.)* Tell us what happened.

YOHEI: I shall tell you then. Mother, wife, this is what happened. Please listen. *(He bows. Offstage shamisen and hollow "fulling block" percussion play* kinuta *pattern, which creates a rural atmosphere by creating a sound resembling that of cloth being beaten by a mallet.)* I was so worried about why I had been called today. When I arrived at the government office, I was told that the lord had ordered me to appear before him right away. This made me even more scared. *(Worriedly rubbing his hands.)* I proceeded with more than a little hesitation into his presence, and this is what the lord said *(speaking as the lord)*: "In the case of the son of Nanpō Jūjibei, who had jurisdiction over seven villages in this district, I have heard that he led an excessive lifestyle after his father's death. Since the position of magistrate had formally been in his family for many generations, I hereby return the title of magistrate of the seven villages to him. May he serve this position without negligence." *(Out of breath.)* I cannot begin to tell you how surprised I was. I was thankful for our lord's mercy, though I can't help but feel more than a little unworthy. Just look. *(Spreading the sleeves of his new* haori.*)* I was given these clothes and swords. *(Taking out his handkerchief and wiping his forehead.)* I was so taken by surprise that I began to sweat heavily. When I think of how this is all due to the help of my parents, I can't help but shed tears of joy. Mother, I hope you understand just how happy I am. *(Weeping, he bows deeply.)*

OKO: But, of course, you are. Congratulations. Maybe it's just the musings of an old woman, but you seem to resemble your father in your new clothes.

OHAYA: Mother, I never had the opportunity to meet my father-in-law, but did he look like just like my dear husband does now in his samurai attire?

OKO: He's the spitting image.

OHAYA *(Embarrassed)*: Then my father-in-law was surely a very handsome man.

OKO: Go ahead and sing his praises. This is all thanks to my belief in our ancestral gods. Yohei, you should thank them as well.

(All three turn upstage to a small Shinto shrine hanging on the wall. Clapping their hands twice, they pray and then face front. Music ends.)

OKO: Thank you.

YOHEI *(Seriously)*: In all my happiness, I forgot about important business I have to attend to. I've been assigned a mission and have brought men home with me to discuss it. It's a secret matter, so you two should go in back and stay there. Wife, if I need you, I will call.

OHAYA: Yes, my dear.

OKO: It must be very important. We will do as you say. Daughter-in-law, beginning today you are the wife of a samurai. You must learn to stay in your place.

OHAYA *(With an air of importance)*: Yes, mother. Beginning today I am the wife of a samurai. Now, when we travel to the family shrine, you'll ride in a palanquin and I in a fancy robe on the back of a horse. *(Playfully grasping her apron as if it were a bridle.)* Giddyap, giddyap, giddyap, whoa!

OKO: Women don't ride horses, even the wives of samurai.

OHAYA: Of course, they don't. That's so silly.

(Both YOHEI *and* OKO *slap their hands on the straw matting in admonishment.)*

OKO: There's that phrase again.

OHAYA: Anyway, dear, I mean, my honorable husband. *(Bowing exaggeratedly.)* I'll return later to receive your orders.

TAKEMOTO:

Mother and daughter-in-law go into separate rooms. / Afterward, Yohei heads outside.

(The women mime their pleasure and excitement. OHAYA *exits through the curtained doorway and* OKO *exits through the* shōji *screens upstage.* YOHEI *crosses outside and calls to the two samurai, who enter from right.)*

YOHEI: Gentlemen, thank you for waiting.

DENZŌ: You are certain we can speak alone?

YOHEI: Please come this way.

BOTH: Thank you.

TAKEMOTO:

Leading the samurai in, / he places them in the seat of honor.

(They enter the house and, removing their sandals, sit left. YOHEI *joins them at center, and they all remove their swords and set them at their sides.)*

YOHEI *(Bowing)*: Now, as for the matter you brought up with my lord and which I have been ordered to assist in, please tell me the details.

(Offstage music begins.)

TANPEI: I am Hiraoka Tanpei. This is Mihara Denzō. Your lord is acquainted with our lord. This spring our brothers were killed in Osaka, and we are searching for the culprit, but, despite our efforts, we still do not know his whereabouts.

DENZŌ: Recently, we heard the murderer had relatives here in Yawata and that he was visiting them. We approached your lord for permission to search for the murderer of our brothers and take our revenge.

TANPEI: But since we are unfamiliar with the area, we were told to gain the assistance of a local person. That is why we have come to you.

DENZŌ *(Pretentiously)*: This is why . . .

BOTH: We have come.

(OKO slips open the shōji *screens and eavesdrops, while OHAYA peers in from behind the curtain.)*

TAKEMOTO:

As they speak, / Yohei's mother and wife become uneasy. / Yohei does not notice their eavesdropping.

(Offstage shamisen music resumes.)

YOHEI: It sounds just like a vendetta. I thought this might be the case, so I asked my mother and wife to leave so we could discuss it in private. Please tell me the names of those who were killed.

(OHAYA, mindful of OKO's instructions on behaving as a proper samurai wife, enters and crosses to the right, where she begins to make tea for the guests.)

TANPEI: My brother, Hiraoka Gozaemon.

DENZŌ: And my brother, Mihara Ariemon.

YOHEI *(Thoughtfully, as if recognizing the names)*: Hiraoka Gozaemon and Mihara Ariemon?

BOTH: Yes.

(Music ends.)

YOHEI: Hmm.

BOTH: You know them?

YOHEI: I have heard of them. And who is the murderer?

TANPEI: He is the famous sumo wrestler . . .

DENZŌ: Nuregami . . .

BOTH *(Drawing out the word)*: Chōgorō.

(DENZŌ hands YOHEI a portrait of CHŌGORŌ.)

TAKEMOTO *(Rapidly)*:

Hearing this, / Yohei's mother slams the sliding screens shut, / and Ohaya spills the tea she is carrying.

(OHAYA, having risen, stumbles and falls at YOHEI's right, spilling the tea.)

YOHEI: You clumsy fool!

TAKEMOTO:

Though understanding why she is scolded by her husband, / Ohaya sits at the back of the room / and continues to listen.

(OHAYA returns to the rear of the room at right. Apologizing for his wife's actions, YOHEI examines the portrait.)

YOHEI: So then, what are your plans?

TANPEI: I will search the houses of the district.

YOHEI: And Denzō, what will you do?

DENZŌ: I will post portraits like this one throughout the neighboring villages. If anyone seems suspicious, I will force my way into their barns and wood houses and even search the second floor of their houses or underneath if necessary.

YOHEI: Yes, but he's such a big man, I doubt he'll be hiding under a house. *(Looking toward the second floor of the house.)* The second floor is much more probable. Why don't you start searching around Kuzuha and Hashimoto? When night falls, I will take up the search. *(Strongly and confidently.)* He may be a sumo wrestler and difficult to overcome, but if I find him, I will tie him up and hand him over. You need not worry.

DENZŌ: We are encouraged by your words. Tanpei, let's make our way to Kuzuha.

TANPEI: During the day, we will work. At night, we leave the search up to you. This is a most important request. Now if you will excuse us, we will take our leave.

(The two samurai take their swords, rise, and quickly exit the house, crossing directly to the hanamichi.*)*

YOHEI: Gentlemen . . .

TANPEI: Until we meet at the lord's mansion . . .

ALL: Let us do our best.

(They exit by the hanamichi.*)*

TAKEMOTO:

The two samurai leave. / Throughout, Ohaya has been deeply worried, / keeping her head lowered.

(Having seen the samurai off, OHAYA *meekly returns inside. Standing for a long moment at the door before stepping up on the platform, she sits on* YOHEI*'s right.* YOHEI *takes out his magistrate's truncheon* [jitte] *and begins to polish it.)*

OHAYA *(Deeply worried)*: Yohei, this is an interesting job you've been asked to do, but are you truly planning to catch Chōgorō and turn him over as requested?

YOHEI *(Laughing)*: What a silly thing to ask. *(Offstage shamisen music plays.)* I have no relation to the samurai, and I have no grudge against Chōgorō, but I was ordered by my lord to help the men. Perhaps my lord did so because he had heard I was somewhat familiar with the Sekiguchi style of sword fighting. In these circumstances, it would be normal procedure for the case to be handed over to the provincial authorities, but they've just arrived here and are unfamiliar with the area. That's why it was deemed necessary to assign them the help of a local. They'll conduct their search during the day, while I will conduct a thorough search at night. If I'm able to capture Chōgorō and hand him over, I'll be the pride of the province. This is the chance of a lifetime. If I succeed in this mission, I'm certain my mother will also be overjoyed.

OHAYA: She will not.

YOHEI: And why is that?

OHAYA: Until today, you've been nothing but a commoner from Yawata. They say that a little knowledge of fighting techniques is a dangerous thing. Think of how much she would grieve if you should be injured. Please stop now before something happens. *(Bowing.)*

YOHEI *(Laughing)*: The worries of a woman. You would have me give up before I even try?

OHAYA: I'm only thinking of you.

YOHEI *(Suspiciously)*: Why are you trying to protect this man? If I succeed in finding Chōgorō and capturing him, it would be the greatest form of filial piety.

OHAYA *(Desperately)*: On the contrary, you would be the most unfilial son there is.

YOHEI: You say it would be unfilial to tie up Chōgorō?

OHAYA: Well . . .

YOHEI: Well? Well? Just why is that?

OHAYA *(Hesitating)*: Well, I mean, . . . I know. You're weaker than Chōgorō.

YOHEI *(Demanding)*: What?

*(*YOHEI *shakes his truncheon, showing his dissatisfaction at being admonished by his wife.)*

OHAYA *(Chastened)*: If you should be lucky enough to capture him, you cannot imagine how sad your mother will be. You should stop now before either of you gets hurt. *(Pleading, she bows low.)*

YOHEI: Why are you still trying to protect him? *(Shaking his truncheon threateningly.)* Perhaps you're in league with Chōgorō?

OHAYA: How could you think that?

YOHEI *(Threatening)*: I'm now a man with responsibility. It will take more than mere words to convince me.

TAKEMOTO:

He turns the hilt of his sword.

*(*YOHEI *adjusts the position of his sword as* OKO *enters hurriedly from the screened room upstage. She sits between* YOHEI *and* OHAYA*.)*

OKO: Young couple, wait. *(Slowly, cautioning* OHAYA*.)* Say nothing more, daughter-in-law. Nothing more. *(*OHAYA *turns upstage, weeping.)* Yohei, I have heard everything from the other room, and I was wondering if you know what this Nuregami Chōgorō looks like.

YOHEI: Yes, I once saw him at the tournament at Horie, and I also ran into him in the pleasure quarters. *(Pointing to his scalp.)* He has the forelock of a sumo wrestler that makes him hard to miss plus a prominent mole on his right cheek. *(He points to his cheek.* OKO *is startled.)* And if there's anyone who doesn't know what he looks like, I have this portrait to pass around the villages. Have a look.

TAKEMOTO:

Taking the portrait from his kimono, he shows it to her.

*(*YOHEI *removes the portrait and passes it to his mother. As* OKO *and* OHAYA *look at it,* YOHEI *rises, proudly gazes at his new* haori, *and shakes off some dust. He then kneels.* CHŌGORŌ *slightly opens the sliding screens at the front of the upper room, and, kneeling on one knee, listens to the conversation below.)*

Nuregami Chōgorō (Jitsukawa Enjaku III) opens a second-floor window to reveal his presence. Nan Yohei (Nakamura Ganjirō II), kneeling, sees Chōgorō's reflection in the water basin. (Tsubouchi Memorial Theatre Museum of Waseda University)

As she looks at the portrait, / Chōgorō peers down from the second floor, / not knowing his image is reflected in the water basin, / a fact that does not escape Yohei. He looks up toward the room.

(YOHEI, glancing into the stone water basin in the garden, notices CHŌGORŌ's reflection in the water. Holding his haori *open to mask his intentions, he deliberately leans forward to take a closer look. As he quickly turns to look upstairs, their eyes meet and CHŌGORŌ slams the sliding screens shut. Throwing off his* haori, *YOHEI goes for his long sword. OKO and OHAYA try to stop him, but he throws them aside and retrieves the portrait, putting it in his kimono.)*

Ohaya, understanding what has happened, / quickly closes the skylight. / It becomes as dark as night inside.

(YOHEI has taken out his truncheon and a rope, preparing to go upstairs, when OHAYA does what the TAKEMOTO chanter describes, plunging the room into darkness. YOHEI stops and poses in a mie *to two* tsuke *beats. OHAYA kneels to his left, holding the skylight rope.)*

YOHEI *(Loudly)*: What have you done?

OHAYA *(Meekly crying)*: It was beginning to rain, and, besides, it is almost night. I will go get the lamp.

YOHEI *(Amused by her attempt to throw him off)*: How interesting. If the sun has set, it is time for me to go to work. I shall arrest the man who has sneaked inside the house. *(He faces the upstairs room.)*

OHAYA: But the sun is still high in the sky.

*(*OHAYA *releases the rope, opening the skylight. Following kabuki convention, the stage lighting does not change but remains bright throughout the scene.)*

TAKEMOTO:

She opens the skylight, / and Yohei is touched by his wife's actions, / even though she is unable to utter her true intentions with words.

*(*YOHEI *is determined to go upstairs but is held back on either side by* OKO *and* OHAYA. *He tosses them off, and, unfurling his rope and gripping the truncheon in his mouth, poses in a determined* mie *to two beats of the* tsuke.*)*

OKO *(Kneeling at left and seeing that* YOHEI *is still of a mind to go upstairs)*: Yohei, I have the favor of a lifetime to ask of you.

YOHEI *(Surprised)*: You have a favor to ask of me, your son?

OKO: Will you hear me out?

YOHEI: Please go ahead.

(Quietly, YOHEI *puts the rope in his sleeve, kneels at center, places his sword at his side, and turns respectfully to his mother.)*

OKO: Please wait a moment.

TAKEMOTO:

His mother goes to the box and, / opening it with care, / takes out a package of money.

*(*OKO *goes through the upstage sliding screens and returns with a wooden box. Opening it, she takes out a sheet of paper and begins to place money on it from a small purse.)*

OKO: This money . . . I was planning to donate this very important money to the temple to commission a reading of sutras to secure my future in the next world. But I have found another use for it. Would you please sell me that portrait?

(Having placed all the money on the paper, she folds it and places it in front of YOHEI.*)*

YOHEI: What? You want to buy the portrait?

OKO *(Crying)*: Yes.

*(*YOHEI *takes the portrait from his kimono. Thinking about why she might be doing this, he realizes the answer.)*

YOHEI *(Crying slightly and in a somewhat hurt tone)*: Mother, why are you hiding things from me? I'm your child. I've heard that you gave away your true son for adoption twenty years ago in Osaka. Is this son still alive?

OKO: That's why I want you to sell me the portrait.

YOHEI: You've been pinching pennies for years and years to save that money. Are you sure you want to use it to buy the portrait instead of making an offering to the Buddhas?

OKO *(Through her sobs)*: I will not change my mind even if it means I fall into hell.

YOHEI *(Closing his eyes and shaking his head in realization of the problem he now faces)*: That much . . .

TAKEMOTO:

He throws aside his swords.

(Putting away the portrait, YOHEI *takes up his long sword and removes his short sword, holding the pair across his lap.)*

YOHEI *(With authority)*: When I wear these swords, I am Nanpō Jūjibei. *(Putting down the swords and speaking lightly, like a commoner.)* When I do not, I am Nan Yohei, a commoner of Yawata, as I have always been. If you want to buy an item from a merchant, I shall accommodate you. *(Places portrait in front of her.)*

OKO: Then you will forsake . . .

YOHEI *(Crying)*: No. It is not my duty during the day.

OKO: I cannot express how thankful I am.

TAKEMOTO:

Receiving the portrait, / both mother and daughter-in-law wipe tears from their eyes.

OHAYA *(Moving closer to* YOHEI*, she speaks intimately)*: Yohei, you have just successfully completed a very important task by understanding the deep pain in your mother's heart. She has always loved you more than her own true son, and it has taken all of her strength to hide what is in her heart. I hope you will understand that as well.

(All three cry, and YOHEI *takes the money from his mother. He motions to* OHAYA *for his* haori *as his mother takes the portrait into the next room.)*

TAKEMOTO:

As she sheds her tears, / time passes. / The ringing of the temple bell / counts off their sorrows as well as the time. / It is the eve of the full moon, / and the light reflected from its large disk / fills every corner.

*(*OHAYA *brings the* haori *and places it over* YOHEI*'s shoulders.* OKO *emerges from upstage and kneels.)*

YOHEI: Night has come. I must leave to search the villages.

TAKEMOTO:

Standing, / he comes up with an idea.

YOHEI: Mother, this murderer is certainly no longer in the area. *(Loudly, so* CHŌGORŌ *can hear.)* There is an escape route to Kawachi province if you follow the Kitsune River on the left bank and then turn to the right and cross the mountain pass. *(He gives his mother a meaningful look.* OKO *clasps her hands in gratitude.)* But I am sure he would not have taken that route.

TAKEMOTO:

His compassion is as thick / as the bushes growing outside.

(As YOHEI *steps into the doorway to leave the house, he calls* OHAYA *and gives her the money received from his mother, silently nodding to her.)*

OHAYA: So I should . . .

(Crossing outside, YOHEI *slams the door in a sign to be silent.)*

YOHEI *(Calling out loudly)*: Hey! Chōgorō! Where are you?

TAKEMOTO:

Though the moon be hidden by clouds, / that does not mean it is not in the sky. / Yohei hides himself nearby.

*(*YOHEI *runs to* shichisan, *where he pretends to search about. He then returns to the main stage and stealthily hides behind the house.)*

Chōgorō is no longer able to restrain himself. / He flies out of the second floor room / and runs to the front door, / but his mother stops him.

*(*CHŌGORŌ, *running down from the second floor, tries to leave, but* OKO *stops him by kneeling in his path.)*

OKO *(Angrily)*: You fool. Where do you think you're going?

CHŌGORŌ: Do I really have to explain? I was certain my time had come, but I was graciously saved by your actions. I didn't want to show you my tears and tried hard to hold them back until I left, but out of consideration for Yohei, I'm ready to give myself up. Please forgive me.

TAKEMOTO:

Ready to run out, / Oko grabs him and forces him down.

OKO *(Angrily, through her tears)*: You ungrateful fool. *(He bypasses* OKO, *but she runs behind him and grabs him. His sudden movement causes her to fall to her knees. She grabs his left hand and forces him down.)* It wasn't just me who saved you. It was Ohaya, too. And the compassion of Yohei. Would you ruin all of our efforts? Not trusting my stepson, I asked him to sell me the portrait to determine whether he would allow you to escape or not. *(Clasping her hands in gratitude.)* I was so happy when he agreed to sell it to me that I will thank him even though he isn't here. He was also generous enough to tell you of an escape route to Kawachi. It is as if he were allowing a caged animal to escape during the festival. Dying isn't the only way to save your honor.

TAKEMOTO:

What kind of unfilial child kills men in a fight / when he has a mother near the age of seventy?

(Sobbing, OKO *crosses her hands across her chest and then mimes cutting with a sword.* CHŌGORŌ *is visibly moved.)*

OKO *(Sobbing)*: Since you only asked for a simple bowl of rice when you came, it is obvious you knew you could be caught at any time. How could I let that happen? If you feel any filial duty toward me, the least you can now do is escape for as long as possible, to live for as long as possible. What fate . . .

TAKEMOTO:

"Caused you to become a wanted man," / she asks as she throws herself to the ground, / sobbing so intensely that all around becomes a blur. / Ohaya wipes the tears from her eyes.

(OKO slaps CHŌGORŌ on the leg again and again in helpless anger, in the end collapsing in tears.)

OHAYA: This is no time for crying. Come dawn, the villages will be full of people celebrating the Ritual of Release. Can't you think of some way to disguise him before morning?

OKO *(Recovering, she looks at CHŌGORŌ hopefully)*: That's a good thought. The forelock will draw attention. I'll shave it off to change your appearance. Daughter-in-law, bring the razor.

OHAYA: Yes, mother.

(OHAYA exits through the curtained doorway and returns with a razor and water pot.)

CHŌGORŌ: Mother, it would cause me great shame if people thought I feared death enough to disguise myself and avoid capture. I was ready to accept the consequences when I killed the samurai, but I had to remain alive to fulfill a certain duty. *(He begins to cry.)* Living day to day, I thought of nothing but you, and I came to say goodbye so I could see your face one more time. Instead, I have only upset you. Please hand me over to Yohei.

(OKO cannot hold back her sobs.)

OKO: So you are ready to turn yourself in no matter what I say?

CHŌGORŌ: Yes.

(Throwing down her hand towel in exasperation, OKO turns away.)

OKO: Then do as you please.

TAKEMOTO:

"I will go first."

(OKO takes the razor and brings it to her wrist. CHŌGORŌ stops her with his left hand.)

CHŌGORŌ: What are you doing?

OHAYA: Chōgorō, it is just as your mother says. If you will not shave off your forelock, I will die as well.

(OHAYA tries to unsheathe CHŌGORŌ's sword, and he stops her with his right hand. The three form a tableau, with CHŌGORŌ at center holding the sword in OHAYA's grasp at his right and the razor gripped by his mother at his left. The

following lines are delivered in kuriage *style, at an accelerating pace, culminating in a climax.)*

CHŌGORŌ: Don't be rash.

OKO: Shall I die first?

CHŌGORŌ: Wait! What are you saying?

OKO: Or will you try to escape?

CHŌGORŌ: But . . .

OHAYA: Will you shave off your forelock?

CHŌGORŌ: But . . .

OKO *(Desperately)*: Will you escape?

(The three pose silently. CHŌGORŌ *looks deeply into his mother's eyes and then into* OHAYA*'s.)*

CHŌGORŌ *(To* OKO*)*: I will escape. *(To* OHAYA.*)* I will shave off my forelock. I will, I will, I will. I'm sorry. *(Bursting into a powerful expression of apology.)* Mother, please forgive me.

OKO: So you will try to escape?

CHŌGORŌ: Yes, I will.

OKO: Then you truly are my son.

OHAYA: You have made the right decision.

OKO: Let's begin shaving.

(As the mood relaxes, CHŌGORŌ *holds a hand towel to his eyes to dry his tears.* OKO *uses her hand towel to tie back her right sleeve, and* OHAYA *brings a mirror, which she sets on a stand, as* OKO *sharpens the razor on a whetstone.)*

TAKEMOTO:

Her sleeves become soaked with tears / as she thinks of how she must remove the forelock / that should have been shaved long ago.

*(*OHAYA *places the mirror before* CHŌGORŌ. *Holding back her tears,* OKO *stands behind* CHŌGORŌ. *Placing a towel over his shoulders, she wets his hair and begins to shave off his forelock, placing the shaved hair—part of a trick wig—on a tray held by the kneeling* OHAYA.*)*

What is usually a joyous occasion / is marked with their tears, / which she uses to wet his hair before shaving it. / Yet it is difficult to keep her old hand steady, / and the razor quivers in her hand and slips.

(A sharp note of the shamisen *indicates the slippage of the razor.* CHŌGORŌ *brings his hand to his forehead to stop the bleeding.)*

OHAYA: You've cut him.

OKO: How careless of me. At least we have something to stop the bleeding.

TAKEMOTO:

Saying thus, she takes an ink stick. / She gazes at her son's face as she applies the ink.

The forelock of Nuregami Chōgorō (Nakamura Tomijūrō V) is shaved by his adoptive mother, Oko (Kamimura Kichiya V), to hide Chōgorō's identity. Chōgorō's sister-in-law, Ohaya (Nakamura Tokizō V), holds a tray holding shaving accessories. (Umemura Yutaka, Engeki Shuppansha)

*(*OHAYA *brings over an ink set from near the upstage wall, and* OKO, *kneeling at* CHŌGORŌ*'s side, brushes a small amount of ink on the cut.)*

OKO: It seems to have worked. He looks much different now. Ah, but there is still the mole on his cheek.

TAKEMOTO:

She brings the razor down to scrape off the mole.

*(*OKO *stands and brings the razor to his face but cannot bring herself to cut off the mole. She tries a second time.)*

OKO *(Through her tears)*: His father had a mole in the same place. I can't bring myself to remove it. Daughter-in-law, please do it for me. *(Crosses to* CHŌGORŌ*'s left and sits.)*

OHAYA: Please don't ask this of me. How could I remove it?

OKO: Why has it become necessary to remove this reminder of his father? Even though I'm doing it to save him . . . *(Removes the towel from his shoulders and embraces him.)*

TAKEMOTO:

"It is too much to bear," / she says as she clings to him and drowns in her tears. / Suddenly out in front . . .

*(*YOHEI *approaches the house and raises the blind from the window.)*

YOHEI: I've caught you Nuregami.

TAKEMOTO:

Saying thus, he throws his silver dagger, / which grazes Chōgorō's cheek.

(He throws a dagger, perfectly aimed to cut off CHŌGORŌ*'s mole, which is actually removed by sleight of hand.)*

OHAYA: Chōgorō, the mole has been removed.

CHŌGORŌ *(Surprised)*: What? *(Bringing the mirror to his face, he looks closely.)*

OKO *(Sobbing)*: Is this also a sign of his compassion? Thank you so much.

*(*OKO *bows toward the window.)*

TAKEMOTO:

His mother turns to the outside to say these words, / but Chōgorō, who has already made up his mind to be captured, / sits quietly.

*(*CHŌGORŌ *slowly rearranges himself. Putting the hand towel in his kimono, he passes the mirror to the black-garbed* STAGE ASSISTANT [kurogo] *behind him.)*

CHŌGORŌ *(Seriously)*: Mother, it's time for you to tie me up and hand me over to Yohei.

OKO: What are you saying?

OHAYA *(Incredulously)*: Chōgorō, have you lost your mind? My husband showed his true feelings by using his dagger to take off your mole. *(Moving close to him.)* He also left this money for you as cash for the road. Do you still doubt his intentions? *(She places the money on the ground before him.)*

CHŌGORŌ *(Emotionally, to* TAKEMOTO *shamisen accompaniment)*: Yohei gave up the portrait and removed the mole. His kindness touches me down to the bone. Though I've caused my mother to grieve and scold me, I don't feel as though I'm being unfilial. The more children need help, the more responsibility and religious rules become irrelevant. It has nothing to do with loyalty or Buddhist law. My mother wanted nothing more than to help me, and I humored her, even allowing her to shave my forelock, but I'm guilty of killing not one, not two, but four men. There's no way to save me. *(Slowly to his mother, making his point.)* Instead of being caught by some nobody, I'd rather be tied up by my mother and have her hand me over to Yohei as a memorial to her. If I don't do this, you won't be able to face your husband in the next world. *(He poses silently in determination.)*

OKO: Well said, Chōgorō. *(Bowing.)* I now realize how I've forgotten my responsibilities. Forsaking my true son for the success of my stepson is the true way a human should act. Hiding Chōgorō has shown that I'm no better than a beast, a cat that protects its kitten by carrying it by the neck. You can't escape the net of heaven, and ropes will bind the relationship between parent and child that lasts only one lifetime. Daughter-in-law, bring the rope.

OHAYA *(Desperately)*: But that would be going against the intentions of my husband. Even if Chōgorō were to travel to China or India, as long as he's in this world, there's still a chance you may meet again. You must allow him to escape.

OKO *(Disagreeing)*: I showed my love by hiding him, I must now show my responsibility to my stepson by tying him up and handing him over. I protected him in the daytime and will hand him over at night. Day and night also separate my true son from my stepson. I can be both merciful and dutiful, and satisfy the memory of my late husband. *(To* CHŌGORŌ*.)* Are you ready?

CHŌGORŌ *(Determined)*: I've been waiting for this.

TAKEMOTO:

As he brings his hands together, / his mother spies the rope for the skylight. / Taking it, she binds his hands. / Having pulled the rope tight, / the skylight closes, / filling both the room and their hearts with darkness. / Oko raises her voice loud.

*(*CHŌGORŌ *slowly puts his hands behind his back and closes his eyes, waiting to be bound.* OKO *tries to make* OHAYA *get the rope, but she refuses. When* OKO *tries herself,* OHAYA *attempts to stop her. To the rhythm of the* TAKEMOTO, OKO *takes the skylight rope and throws off* OHAYA, *who crosses to the right and falls to the ground. She ties the rope around* CHŌGORŌ *with the help of the* STAGE ASSISTANT *as* YOHEI *watches from outside.* OKO *stands to* CHŌGORŌ*'s right, holding the rope.)*

OKO *(Crying out loudly)*: I have caught Nuregami Chōgorō. Where is Jūjibei? Come take him into custody and receive credit for a job well done.

TAKEMOTO:

She calls out. / Hearing her voice, Yohei returns inside.

*(*YOHEI *enters and crosses to* CHŌGORŌ*'s left as* OKO *sinks to the ground at left.)*

YOHEI: Good work. It had to be done. This villain could not hope to escape. I will drag him before my lord. Wife, what time is it?

OHAYA *(Confused)*: It is still the middle of the night.

YOHEI: How foolish. I just heard the dawn bell, and if I hesitate much longer, it will be daylight and the time allotted for my duty will be over. This rope used to open the skylight does not conform to regulations. It is tradition to make it only three feet long.

TAKEMOTO:

Taking his sword out, he cuts the rope. / The skylight slams open / and moonlight shines in.

*(*YOHEI *slices the rope behind* CHŌGORŌ*'s back and turns left, looking at the sky through the skylight.)*

YOHEI: Oh my, the night is over. I am only supposed to work at night. It is dawn of the day of the Ritual of Release. Those released on this day need feel no responsibility toward their liberator. Go as you please.

(The sound of the temple bell marking the time is heard in the distance. CHŌGORŌ *listens to the sound intently.)*

CHŌGORŌ: But that was the three-o'clock bell.

YOHEI: No, it was the bell marking the dawn.

CHŌGORŌ: The extra three hours . . .

YOHEI: Will be a gift for our mother.

CHŌGORŌ: I owe you so much.

YOHEI *(Desperately)*: No more words! Just go!

*(*YOHEI *and* CHŌGORŌ *take each other's hands and look into each other's eyes for the first and last time as brothers.* YOHEI *places the money in* CHŌGORŌ*'s hands.)*

TAKEMOTO:

They say their farewells, / and then part, / as difficult as it is.

*(*CHŌGORŌ *quickly takes his sword and straw mat and runs outside. At* shichisan, *he kneels and, at the clack of the* ki, *clasps his hands in gratitude to* YOHEI, *who stands watching from the doorway. As* YOHEI *begins to cry, he slams the door shut, leaning against the door frame for support.* OKO *and* OHAYA *pose on their knees.* CHŌGORŌ, *wrapping the straw mat around himself, exits running down the* hanamichi. *The curtain closes to shamisen, large drum, and loud* ki *pattern.)*

Three-panel woodblock print by Utagawa Toyokuni III (1786–1864). Kawarasaki-za, Edo, eleventh month 1850. The old Heike warrior, center, identified here as "Seno o Jūrō Kaneyasu," his true historical name, is stabbed by "Koman's child, Tarōkichi." Pulling up their sleeves in preparation to enter the fray, left, are Tarōkichi's grandfather, "Kurōsuke, a farmer from Ōmi" (Seki Sanjūrō II); and Kurōsuke's nephew, "Yahashi no Nisōta" (Asao Okuyama III). Heike general "Saitō Bettō Sanemori" (Kawarasaki Chōjūrō I, later Ichikawa Danjūrō IX), right, watches from inside the room while the boy's dying mother, "Koman the daughter of Kurosuke" (Ichikawa Dannosuke), crawls toward him on the ground. (Tsubouchi Memorial Theatre Museum of Waseda University)

The Sanemori Story

Sanemori Monogatari

Namiki Senryū and Miyoshi Shōraku

TRANSLATED BY KATHERINE SALTZMAN-LI

1749 TAKEMOTO-ZA, OSAKA

The Sanemori Story

INTRODUCTION

Saitō Sanemori was a warrior who fought and died bravely for the Heike clan during the Genpei wars of the late twelfth century. As narrated in the medieval chronicle *Tale of the Heike* (Heike Monogatari), he changed his allegiance from the Genji (or Minamoto) side to the Heike (or Taira), for whom he served as an important leader. He died on the battlefield at the village of Shinohara, Kaga province, at seventy-two. The battle was led by Minamoto no Kiso Yoshinaka, leader of the northern anti-Heike forces and first cousin to Yoritomo, who was the first Genji shogun after the Heike had been completely defeated.

Sanemori's deeds have been told and performed innumerable times. An important stage in the metamorphosis of his story is offered by *The Sanemori Story,* translated here and originally written for the puppet theatre and then adapted by kabuki. Also known as the "Kurōsuke's House" scene (Kurōsuke Sumika no Ba), *Sanemori* is performed independently of the full five-act history play *(jidaimono), The Genji and Heike at Nunobiki Waterfall* (Genpei Nunobiki no Taki), from which it is taken. The play was created for the puppet theatre by Namiki Senryū (Sōsuke) (1695–1751) and Miyoshi Shōraku (1696–1772) and, perhaps, a Takeda Geki, whose name appeared on the program *(banzuke).* It premiered at Osaka's Takemoto-za in the eleventh month of 1749. Along with *The Stone-Cutting Feat of Kajiwara* and *The Secret Art of Rowing,* the play is one of three in this volume dealing with the world *(sekai)* of the Heike-Genji conflict.

Sanemori presents an exemplary case of the kinds of transformations wrought on *Tale of the Heike* and other borrowed source material in Tokugawa-period plays. There are significant differences between the puppet play and both *Tale of the Heike* and the first dramatization of Sanemori, the *nō* play *Sanemori.* Among other differences, the Sanemori of these earlier versions is an old man meeting his death *(Tale of the Heike)* or having met his death (in the *nō*), and he is presented in both as a vain man who dyes his hair in old age so as to appear young. Also, the *nō* play places more emphasis on Sanemori's vanity, thus propelling his need for enlightenment and promoting one of the thematic raisons d'être of the *nō.*

These and other elements are either changed in the puppet play or placed in a distinctly different context. Plot changes are founded on an altered temporal perspective. In the puppet play, Sanemori is a young man and the play is centered on the birth of Yoshinaka. New characters (Senō, Kurōsuke, Koman) are created who offer a fresh network of typical Edo Tokugawa-period obligations and loyalties to explain the motivations for the actions that give Sanemori his place in *Tale of the Heike*. Truth to one's word takes the place of vanity as the motivating factor for Sanemori's dyed hair in his final battle; love, honor, and revenge take the place first of chance—for the choice of Tezuka (Tarōkichi) as Sanemori's slayer—and then of physical exhaustion—as the main cause of Sanemori's future death.

While the puppet play seems to have been an adaptation of a 1733 kabuki play of the same name, the kabuki version used today—first staged at Osaka's Kado no Shibai in 1757—is an adaptation of Senryū and Shōraku's puppet play. Soon after the kabuki version premiered in Osaka, it was staged in Kyoto at the Kameya-za. It was not seen in Edo until 1793, when it was put on at the Nakamura-za. The kabuki play betrays its puppet origins in many ways. The *takemoto* chanter and accompanying shamisen player perform throughout, sometimes taking over characters' lines and sometimes providing narration, as they would in the puppet play. Before and after Koman is revived, she lies on the stage like an inactive puppet. She is literally brought back from the dead, coming to life again as though a manipulator had picked up his puppet. Impossible physical occurrences, such as the re-attachment of Koman's arm, are also common in the puppet theatre.

Like many kabuki plays, *Sanemori* remains a museum piece that replicates the acting of previous generations. Sanemori, considered one of the most challenging parts for an actor of male roles *(tachiyaku)*, can be performed in one of two main Edo styles *(kata)*. The first derives from Ichikawa Danzō VII (1836–1911) and the second from Onoe Kikugorō V (1844–1903), who altered what he inherited from Bandō Mitsugorō III (1775–1831) and Bandō Hikosaburō V (1832–1877). For example, in the highlight scene of Sanemori's narration *(monogatari)*, the tradition associated with Danzō is restrained and stresses the irony of the situation, while the Kikugorō line tends to play the scene in grand and showy style. Productions today are likely to mix *kata* from the two traditions.

Sanemori is of the "patient man of judgment" *(sabakiyaku)* role type. Like Yuranosuke in the same playwrights' *The Treasury of Loyal Retainers* (Kanadehon Chūshingura, 1748; trans. Keene 1971, Brandon 1992), these characters are required to tread very slippery paths in order to achieve their goals. They are often drawn in two directions. As Senō says, "While you sustain yourself off the Heike, you protect a Genji descendant." In *Tale of the Heike,* Sanemori's sympathies are clearly with the Heike; in *Sanemori* they are with the Genji, even though we know he will continue to fight for the Heike. The wisdom of such characters and their eye-on-the-prize determination allows them to navigate difficult and changeable courses.

Senō is also complicated. He is one of the kabuki characters who "return" *(modori)* to good motives after displaying an evil nature. The play does not include a villain, other than the ineffective and disposable Nisōda, as foil for a hero. The purity of Tarōkichi's budding heroism stands in strong contrast to the compromises inevitably required of samurai in their pursuit of loyalty. Because of the dramatic qualities he represents, Tarōkichi is one of kabuki's most significant child roles *(koyaku)*. Such roles are very important for the early training of child actors.

This translation is based on both the printed version in Toita Yasuji et al., eds., *Meisaku Kabuki Zenshū,* Vol. 4, and a 1980 video of a production starring Bandō Hikosaburō VIII (b. 1943).

CHARACTERS

SAITŌ SANEMORI, *a Heike samurai, originally on the Genji side*
SENŌ NO JŪRŌ KANEUJI, *a Heike samurai*
AOI GOZEN, *widow of Kiso Yoshikata*
KURŌSUKE, *a farmer, sympathetic to the Genji*
YABASE NO NISŌDA, *nephew of* KURŌSUKE
KOYOSHI, *wife of* KURŌSUKE
KOMAN, *daughter of* KURŌSUKE *and* KOYOSHI
TARŌKICHI, *son of* KOMAN
TARŌBEI, *the village headman*
FOUR FISHERMEN
RETAINERS, *samurai (number varies) in service to* SANEMORI
STAGE ASSISTANTS, *black-garbed* kurogo
TAKEMOTO, *musical ensemble of shamisen player and chanter who accompany the action*

(The stage shows a roofed house of two rooms, one in view of the audience and one at left closed off by sliding paper doors. A split curtain hangs from a doorway leading from the visible room to the back of the house. The house is raised one step off the ground. A gate on the right end of the house marks the entrance. Behind the house, right, is a wave-filled lake backed by hills, right of the gate. A brush thicket sits on the shore in front of the lake, and a well is just to the side of the house. TAKEMOTO *musicians perform from a platform at stage left, where they are seen throughout the*

scene. KOYOSHI *sits in the house ginning cotton as the scene opens.* NISŌDA *enters the gate to her house.)*

TAKEMOTO:

This old woman lives in the village of Onohara. / Her husband is Kurōsuke, her daughter, Koman. / And here comes the nephew of the house, Yabase no Nisōda.

NISŌDA *(To* KOYOSHI*)*: What hard work. Has the cotton this year been left unharmed?

KOYOSHI: Oh, nephew! I didn't realize you had come. With Kurōsuke gone, did you come to help out with the planting?

NISŌDA: No, I hadn't known that Uncle was away. Actually, I'm trying to improve my lot lately and I'm hoping that you'll help me out with a little something. It seems that recently someone may have helped an illustrious woman from the capital by accompanying her here with the promise of protection. She is Lady Aoi, the widow of Lord Kiso Yoshikata.

KOYOSHI: There is a woman who arrived recently from somewhere, but she's an unhealthy-looking kitchen maid with coarse hands. Your uncle probably got her pregnant and then brought her here with him.

NISŌDA: Hm, doesn't sound too likely. You can't fool me with some cock-and-bull story. Anyhow, today Uncle went to Ishiyama.

KOYOSHI: Not so, your uncle went carp fishing at Kusatsu River. The Ishiyama story is completely wrong.

NISŌDA: The story about the woman being Uncle's mistress is what's wrong. With all these lies, the truth is hard to find. But the fact is that Yoshikata's wife, Aoi Gozen, is a wanted woman and there is a reward for finding her. Wouldn't you like to share it with me?

KOYOSHI: I see. Well, why don't we wait for your uncle to return and discuss it with him?

NISŌDA: No, I can't wait.

KOYOSHI: Well, so long as you're here, wouldn't you like me to prepare some fish salad?

NISŌDA: With the carp?

KOYOSHI: No, with a different fish I already have.

NISŌDA: Oh, Uncle used to eat your fish salad with me sometimes. I remember how good it tasted. You make it even when he's not here?

KOYOSHI: Yes, I'll make my best.

NISŌDA: That's too much trouble to take for a penniless simpleton like me. I need to go. I look forward to your hospitality at another time. *(He shouts as he leaves.)* Until later. *(Exits right.)*

TAKEMOTO:

Nisōda quickly leaves. / As is the way of this world, / with its impermanent dwellings and sad thoughts, / Yoshikata's wife, Aoi Gozen, finds herself pregnant / and secreted away in an inner room of Kurōsuke's house. / Downcast, on this moonlit night, / she enters.

*(*AOI GOZEN*, dressed elegantly, comes out from the room at left and stands in the main room.)*

AOI GOZEN: Oh, madam. The cry of the crow seems ominous. Oh, where could Koman be? Is there no word, no tidings at all? Haven't Kurōsuke and Tarōkichi returned?

KOYOSHI: There's no reason to worry. You say that the cry of the crow is ominous, but that is actually the joyful bird of easy birthing. My husband has gone to Ōmi to fish for the famous Gengorō carp to offer you in the hope of a safe delivery. As the wind is held in the meshes of a fishing net, may the life in you and your baby remain with us for years to come.

TAKEMOTO:

The fugitive whose fortune has so changed from before, / her pitiable lot. / What can give her hope? / But here comes Kurōsuke, the master of the house, pulling the weight of his net behind.

TARŌKICHI: Look what I've caught! Look what I've caught!

(Offstage shamisen music. KURŌSUKE *enters along the* hanamichi. *In straw sandals and simple dress, he pulls along a net. He leads a simply clad* TARŌKICHI *by the hand. The boy immediately enters the house.)*

TARŌKICHI: Look, Grandma! I've got something big here. And I caught it, I caught it!

TAKEMOTO:

He dances with joy and delight.

KOYOSHI: Good job, good for you. Tell us all about it. Father, show us this big catch, your fortune of the carp-fishing day.

KURŌSUKE: I'll show you, but this thing we caught today will shock you. It neither flies nor leaps: it is indeed the strangest Gongorō carp ever. Be prepared!

TAKEMOTO:

Out of the net, a woman's arm. / Not knowing it is the arm of his daughter . . .

(The arm falls out of KURŌSUKE*'s net. Its hand grasps a white banner.* AOI GOZEN *and* KOYOSHI *look shocked.)*

KURŌSUKE: Do you see this? It must have been snatched from the body by one of the ghosts who haunt the Rashomon Gate. Brace yourself, Mother, when you look at this.

TAKEMOTO:

She mumbles incoherently, unable to approach. / Tarōkichi can only wonder.

KOYOSHI: This makes me terribly uneasy. Father, this arm, where did you find this arm?

KURŌSUKE: I let my net out where the Kusatsu River flows into Lake Biwa, thinking to catch the carp that collect there. The arm flowed into the net and your grandson saw it. He insisted on taking it out, and although I had a bad feeling about it, I pulled it out of the net. I tried to loosen the white banner that the hand is gripping so firmly, but I couldn't. What kind of person could this hand belong to? We must mourn it, but first we must try to loosen the fingers and release the banner. Lady Aoi, help us by firmly taking the wrist, and let us use all our strength to open the hand.

(They all take hold of the arm.)

TAKEMOTO:

Nervously setting to work, they try forcing the hand open. / They cannot manage.

KURŌSUKE: This isn't working. We'll have to cut it open at the palm.

TAKEMOTO:

But Tarōkichi bursts in.

TARŌKICHI: Grandpa, first let me try to open up the hand.

KURŌSUKE: No, no, forget it. This isn't like taking dolls apart, you know. You could crush the bones.

TARŌKICHI: I won't, I won't! If I release the fingers one by one, I can do it!

TAKEMOTO:

Little imp that he is, / he goes right ahead and loosens the fingers / one at a time. / The white banner passes into the child's hands, / the arm's remaining desire now accomplished. / Amazingly, the silk of the banner unfurls. / Full of increasingly sad thoughts, / Lady Aoi hears the boy cry out.

TARŌKICHI: I got it! I got it!

*(*TARŌKICHI *takes the banner and hands it to* KURŌSUKE, *who in turn gives it to* AOI GOZEN.*)*

AOI GOZEN: Oh my, this is the white banner of the Genji, the treasure of the clan.

KURŌSUKE: Well, if this is their banner, then, well, what about the arm?

TAKEMOTO:

His query brings the same thought to all three, / Kurōsuke, Lady Aoi, and Koyoshi. / They cannot express their realization that it must be the arm of Koman. / They look at each other, drawing in a deep breath. / Just then, the village headman runs in.

(The three look at each other with a stunned expression. The village headman, TARŌBEI, *runs in, down the* hanamichi *looking all flustered. He is dressed in* haori *and* hakama.*)*

TARŌBEI: Is Kurōsuke home? Heike samurai are on their way here right now. They're conducting some investigation. You'd better clean up whatever mess you've got here, all right?

TAKEMOTO:

He leaves his warning and turns back.

(As TARŌBEI *leaves,* KURŌSUKE*'s expression shows the state of his emotions.)*

KURŌSUKE *(Whispering)*: Wife, I've heard from one of the Heike that they plan to put an end to all Genji descendants. Quickly, hide Lady Aoi! What times these are!

TAKEMOTO:

He whispers to her. / She accompanies Lady Aoi / into the inner room.

*(*KOYOSHI *takes* AOI GOZEN *and* TARŌKICHI *with her into the inner room.)*

Then in come two Heike samurai, / Saitō Sanemori / and Senō no Jūrō./ With Nisōda as informant, / they come in search of Aoi Gozen. / The village headman leads them in.

(Simultaneously with the chanting, TARŌBEI *runs ahead, opens the gate to* KURŌSUKE*'s house, bows down, and waits.* SANEMORI *enters along the* hanamichi. *His face is white. He is dressed in formal attire* [kamishimo] *and padded sandals and wears his two swords. He stops at* shichisan, *looks out at the audience, and waits as* SENŌ *enters, also grandly attired and with white hair, beard, eyebrows, and a tuft of hair standing on top of his head. He stops around the middle of the* hanamichi. *Both face the audience and are turned slightly toward each other.)*

TARŌBEI: This is the house of Kurōsuke. *(Bows deeply.)*

SENŌ: Sanemori!

SANEMORI: Senō!

BOTH MEN: Well, well!

(They look at each other. SANEMORI *turns so that his back faces the audience and he is positioned further back on the* hanamichi. *This allows* SENŌ *to walk past him and move onto the stage first.* SANEMORI *follows as the* TAKEMOTO *chants.)*

TAKEMOTO:

The gate is opened and both men . . .

*(*SENŌ *boldly enters first.* SANEMORI *pauses at the gate, turns around to look at the prostrate* TARŌBEI, *then turns back to enter.* SENŌ *nearly walks into* KURŌSUKE, *who has come back out from the inner room. In reaction, he turns to the audience and strikes a* mie *as* KURŌSUKE *bows to him.* SENŌ *then walks past* KURŌSUKE. KURŌSUKE *and* SANEMORI *walk toward each other.* KURŌSUKE *is shocked to see* SANEMORI *and, trembling, bows as* SANEMORI *continues to look at him.* SANEMORI *walks over to* SENŌ, *both men at left, with* KURŌSUKE *right.* SANEMORI *and* SENŌ *face upstage. Two black-garbed* STAGE ASSISTANTS [kurogo] *enter with tall, black, wooden stools* [aibiki] *for* SENŌ *and* SANEMORI.*)*

. . . soon enter. / Senō no Jūrō, the most despised, and Sanemori / seat themselves.

SENŌ *(In measured tones)*: Well, if it isn't Kurōsuke, the farmer of Katada Bay in Nishigo province. We've learned that you're sheltering the pregnant widow of Master Kiso Yoshikata, Lady Aoi. Drag her out here at once.

TAKEMOTO:

Kurōsuke keeps himself from faltering.

*(*KURŌSUKE *bows low, nervously.)*

KURŌSUKE: It's completely unthinkable. Such a person, here!

SENŌ: Enough! It's your own nephew, Yabase no Nisōda, who has informed me more than once. Come, confess now. You can't avoid it.

KURŌSUKE: No matter what my nephew says, he's absolutely wrong about our concealing any such person here. Why, such a person—

SANEMORI *(Interrupting)*: Kurōsuke, Kurōsuke, I'm not sure you understand. *(Short pause. He looks at the audience and subtly moves his eyebrows up and down.)* The Heike are using all of their power to search out every remaining Genji descendant. They will search even to the womb, and thus it is a serious matter if you are hiding the pregnant Aoi Gozen, as your nephew claims. *(Short pause, same as before.)* Listen carefully, if a girl descendant is found, we can do something about saving her, thanks to the compassion of Lord Kiyomori's eldest son. But if we encounter any resistance now, your house will be raided and a search will be conducted. *(*KURŌSUKE *starts up in consternation, then lowers his head again.)* This will lead to trouble for you, so tell us the truth, now.

*(*KURŌSUKE *and* SANEMORI *exchange glances.)*

TAKEMOTO:

Finding he must respond clearly, / Kurōsuke endeavors to formulate an answer despite his shock. / *(*KURŌSUKE *is at a loss.)* He tries what he can, paying no heed to right and wrong.

KURŌSUKE *(Bowing again)*: Yes, all right. Indeed, under particular circumstances, we took Aoi Gozen into our home. Because she will give birth this month and because we do not yet know if the child will be a boy or a girl, please leave her in my care until she is safely delivered of the child.

SENŌ: What a resolute old man you are. You'd have us just idly wait around until the day of birth, be it today or tomorrow. Our orders are to search the womb and to open the belly itself. It is my job to cut open the belly and it is for Sanemori to make the inspection. So bring out Aoi Gozen. After we've cut her open, if the child's a girl, we'll save it.

KURŌSUKE: Who has commanded you to cut open her pregnant belly?

SENŌ *(Loudly)*: Lord Kiyomori!

KURŌSUKE *(Shocked)*: Good lord!

TAKEMOTO *(Rapidly)*:

He is shocked at what he hears.

KURŌSUKE *(This and the following are spoken in quick and excited succession as he grows increasingly agitated)*: This is too cruel. You will take not one life but two. Please have mercy, just for the remainder of this month.

SENŌ: Absolutely not!

KURŌSUKE: At least give us until the twentieth of the month!

SENŌ: No!

KURŌSUKE: How about the tenth?

SENŌ *(Slowing down again)*: What a tedious old man! I'm going in there and dragging her out. We'll eradicate the Genji!

*(*KURŌSUKE *rushes over. Kneeling, he holds onto* SENŌ *'s leg to hold him back.* SENŌ *struggles to get free.* SANEMORI *sits motionless.)*

TAKEMOTO:

He would go, / but Kurōsuke prevents his entry.

KURŌSUKE *(Crying out his plea)*: Please be so kind as to wait. Have compassion!

TAKEMOTO:

Suddenly, in the midst of his cries, / a commotion is heard from within./ His wife's voice is heard.

KOYOSHI *(From the inner room)*: Kurōsuke! Kurōsuke! It's Lady Aoi, come help, please!

(All three men stop and listen.)

TAKEMOTO:

In shock, he starts to go. / Senō quickly pulls him back.

*(*SENŌ *prevents* KURŌSUKE *from leaving by grabbing him by the hair and holding him down.* SANEMORI *barely seems to notice.)*

SENŌ: And where do you think you're going? You who found belly-cutting so distressing, now you'll try to say that the baby's been born. Let's get the brat so we can see whether or not that's really true, shall we?

KURŌSUKE: Well . . .

SENŌ: Shall we go then?

BOTH: Well, well, well.

SENŌ: So old man, what do you say?

*(*KURŌSUKE *frees himself and runs away from* SENŌ, *who ends his question by taking a pose, turning to go to the inner room, and striking a* mie. KURŌSUKE, *on the other side of the room, also strikes a pose, then resumes his former position.)*

TAKEMOTO:

To avoid this inevitable outrage, / Koyoshi comes out of the inner room. / She carries something wrapped in brocade.

*(*KOYOSHI *comes out from the inner room holding* KOMAN *'s arm wrapped in a brocade cloth. She holds it as though holding a swaddled infant.)*

KOYOSHI *(Looking at the bundle)*: Oh, the ill luck of the Genji!

(She makes her way down from the room and sits near KURŌSUKE.*)*

TAKEMOTO:

With fate hanging in the balance, / she comes out in tears. / Kurōsuke sobs convulsively.

(KURŌSUKE *looks over at his wife, his hands shaking in agitation.)*

KURŌSUKE: Wife, if it's a boy, its life is over. Is it a girl? A girl? *(Imploring.)* Is it a girl?

TAKEMOTO:

He asks but receives no answer, sinking lower in despair. / Without knowledge, Senō jumps in.

SENŌ: So, she has nothing to say. It must be a boy. Bring the brat here!

SANEMORI: Please, Senō, be patient. The job of inspection is mine, and when I'm done, I will let you know the result. Bring the infant he-e-e-re!

(KOYOSHI *brings the bundle to* SANEMORI, *who stands and moves toward her.)*

TAKEMOTO:

Having ordered that the child be brought to him, Sanemori takes the bundle in his arms. / To try and pretend that a boy is a girl / under Senō's close scrutiny / would require the most careful and contrived of efforts. / Only under such desperate circumstances does Sanemori now unwrap the cloth. / But what does he see? / A woman's arm dyed in red! / It is too astonishing, / and Senō is even more shocked.

(He takes the bundle and cradles it. SENŌ *gets up and tries to look at the bundle.* SANEMORI *turns away and then both turn two or three times in parallel motion,* SENŌ *trying to pry,* SANEMORI *trying to conceal. Finally,* SANEMORI *quickly opens up the cloth wrapper. In shock, he lays the arm down on the ground on its wrapper. Both men react strongly through coordinated expressions and* mie.*)*

SENŌ: This is what Aoi Gozen gave birth to? My god!

(He pokes the arm two or three times with his fan. A final mie *is struck by both men.)*

TAKEMOTO:

He is thoroughly disgusted. / Kurōsuke, however, acts quickly, / tugging at his wife.

(SENŌ *and* SANEMORI *resume sitting.)*

KURŌSUKE *(Scolding* KOYOSHI*)*: This is awful! If it is known that the widow of Master Kiso Yoshikata gave birth to an arm, it will stain his reputation. Why didn't you hide it to protect him?

TAKEMOTO:

Gravely, he scolds her, and gravely she responds.

KOYOSHI: I worried about just that, but the severity of this interrogation made me feel that I had no choice.

(They look at each other. KURŌSUKE *glances over at* SENŌ. KURŌSUKE *and* KOYOSHI *resume their bowing positions.)*

TAKEMOTO:

The daughter's loyalty once more displayed. / But Senō no Jūrō only laughs.

SENŌ *(In measured tones)*: How terribly clever! Here in Japan we have an occurrence never before known in China or India: a woman giving birth to an arm. It must have been some swindling priest!

SANEMORI *(Similarly composed)*: No, Senō, it's not as you say. There is an example just like this.

SENŌ: Is that what you've heard? Tell me, Sanemori, in which country did it occur?

SANEMORI: Well, it's not well known, but an empress of the northern countries above China always suffered in hot weather and would hold onto an iron pillar during the heat. Its essence entered into her body and she gave birth to a metal ball. According to a fortune-teller's divination, it was forged into a sword. It was the sword Kanshobakuya. *(Short pause accompanied by plucks on the shamisen.)* It must be that Aoi Gozen, who has suffered so much from the misery of her situation, came under some influence from those physically caring for her and was thus unable to carry out a natural pregnancy. There is indeed no disputing the workings of this universe. Because of this strange birth, we should henceforth call this place Tebarami Village, the Village-Where-a-Hand-Was-Conceived.

TAKEMOTO:

Accepting the possibility of the explanation, / the name will be passed down. / Even Senō will speak it.

SENŌ: In all my days, this is the first time I've heard anything like this. There is virtue to be gained here. I will go and proclaim it to Lord Kiyomori. *(He rises and crosses in front of* SANEMORI *toward the gate, then turns and looks down at the arm.)* I entrust the arm to you. But what if Kiyomori gets angry?

SANEMORI: Should that occur, I will be the one to offer him apologies. My heart will guide me.

SENŌ *(With some sarcasm)*: Well, all right. If a belly can carry an arm *(he points to the arm with his fan)*, then your heart should be able to harbor a plan. *(He points the fan to his chest, then walks out the gate.* KOYOSHI *and* KURŌSUKE *turn and bow toward him.)* I'll see you later, Sanemori.

*(*SENŌ *closes the gate and looks out at the audience, evidently with much on his mind.)*

TAKEMOTO:

He looks out, no doubt thinking out his plan.

(Drums. SENŌ *walks to the beginning of the* hanamichi *and waves his opened fan toward the back. He checks to see that no one is watching, then turns to face* NISŌDA, *who is coming down the* hanamichi.*)*

NISŌDA *(Stopping near* SENŌ*)*: Senō, sir.

(Both turn, looking furtively this way and that. SENŌ *whispers to* NISŌDA, *who then sneaks off down the* hanamichi. SENŌ *carefully tiptoes back onstage,*

holding up his pants to emphasize his quiet steps, turns, poses, turns again, then enters the thicket to hide. All the while, offstage drums have softly marked the time.)

TAKEMOTO:

They move with quick steps to conceal themselves. / When all is quiet, Aoi Gozen leads Tarōkichi from the room.

(They come out of the inner room, AOI GOZEN *holding* TARŌKICHI*'s hand.* TARŌKICHI *walks down to sit with his grandparents.* AOI GOZEN *sits in the open room of the house just outside the inner room. Facing her is a kneeling, bowing* SANEMORI. *He raises his head as she finishes taking her seat. A* STAGE ASSISTANT *enters and leaves a small stand behind* SANEMORI.*)*

AOI GOZEN: I have heard of you, Sanemori, but this is the first time I've met you. I will never forget the compassion you showed today. I am so grateful. *(She lowers her head slightly.)*

TAKEMOTO:

She speaks, and Sanemori bows.

SANEMORI *(His manner more familiar than before)*: It is an honor to meet you. I originally served the Genji, but for certain reasons, I came to follow the Heike. Yes, the Heike. But though I receive a stipend from Kiyomori, I cannot forget my old attachments. I requested the task I came to perform today in order to save you from danger. But the arm, it is all so strange. When I was aboard Nisōda's boat, I slashed at someone. If this arm held a white banner, then it belonged to that person.

TAKEMOTO:

He asks and hears the response.

AOI GOZEN: Yes, indeed, it was holding a banner. *(Turning to* SANEMORI.*)* What was the approximate age of the person you killed?

SANEMORI: About twenty-three or -four. She was a light-complexioned woman of some height whose name was Koman.

TAKEMOTO:

Kurōsuke and his wife are shocked at what they hear.

*(*KURŌSUKE *and* KOYOSHI *rise up on their knees and gesture wildly with their arms, turning this way and that.* TARŌKICHI *remains seated and apparently impassive.)*

KURŌSUKE: My god, it must have been our daughter, Koman.

TAKEMOTO:

A great lament arises; / Lady Aoi, too, feels consternation and dismay penetrating to her bones. / (TARŌKICHI *lowers his head.)* A totally distraught Tarōkichi bitterly sobs. / In old age, emotion and tears well up in Kurōsuke. *(He stands as if to go after* SANEMORI, *then sits again, crying.)*

KURŌSUKE *(Completely agitated and almost babbling)*: Sanemori, what offense caused you to cut off my daughter's arm? How tragic! This girl has a father of almost sixty and a child soon to turn seven. She could never have committed theft or fraud. What was her mistake? How did she transgress? Please tell us.

TAKEMOTO:

His wife is concerned with more concrete matters.

KOYOSHI *(Both wipe their tears)*: Yes, husband, but also ask him where he disposed of the body.

KURŌSUKE *(Through his tears)*: Did she live on or die immediately, providing food for scrounging dogs? Oh, Sanemori, please feel for us and tell all. State the truth, leave nothing out. *(Continues to wail and wipe his tears.)*

TAKEMOTO:

He asks for sympathy. / The parents burst into tears, / and Sanemori feels their plight.

*(*AOI GOZEN *lowers her head and delicately wipes her tears.)*

SANEMORI *(Checking his emotions)*: So it was your daughter. *(Declaiming slowly.)* How I pity you. *(He moves to center, closer to* AOI GOZEN*.)* My cruelty was inadvertent, but I will give you a summary of what happened. Listen! Lady Aoi, please listen also.

TAKEMOTO:

They listen for his story. / The torchlight shines like stars, / the scene resembling a night battle formation.

(Here begins SANEMORI*'s narration* [monogatari]*. It is acted out from his seated position. As he gestures, he uses a fan, sometimes closed, sometimes opened, as a prop. The others react appropriately throughout.)*

SANEMORI: Master Munemori's boat set out from the capital in the direction of Setakarasaki to visit the shrine on Chikubu Island. In the midst of banqueting, a woman in her early twenties was spotted in the water swimming from the direction of Yabase. She held some white silk object between her teeth, and the hand that would be cut was seen struggling up and down in the water. She was quickly approaching. As soon as I saw her, I called for someone—a boatman or some swimmer—to jump in and save her, but none would. I alone was willing to help. "Don't kill her!" I cried, and I hurried over to the side of the boat.

*(*SANEMORI *continues to mime the story. His fan is open. Offstage drums.)*

TAKEMOTO:

At that moment, gales blew down from the mountain. / The brushwood boat offered no support for a drowning woman. / Out of pity for her, he untied some netting / and, fastening it to an oar, he flung it out to her.

SANEMORI: "Hey, woman! Don't let go of the oar; hold onto it tightly!"

TAKEMOTO:

He carefully helped her onto the boat.

SANEMORI: First, I lifted her safely aboard and then tended to her. I asked her to explain fully how she ended up in the water, where she came from, and what her name was. "Koman," she said.

TAKEMOTO:

As he was questioning her, / pursuing voices from the shore called out.

SANEMORI: "She's on the Genji side! She's concealing their white banner! Get it from her!"

TAKEMOTO:

"Get it from her!"

SANEMORI: Voices everywhere . . .

TAKEMOTO:

Hearing the shouting voices, / Hida no Saemon, present among those on the boat, / pounced on Koman. / He could not get the banner from her.

SANEMORI: Her single-minded heroism. Knowing that if the white banner were to pass to the Heike, it would be the end of the Genji, she would not save her own life only to see them pass into obscurity. And so that arm, which held so fast to the white banner, splashed into the lake.

TAKEMOTO:

He cut off her arm. / As it sank to the lake floor, the boat was rowed to shore.

SANEMORI: I placed the body on the beach. And eventually the white banner also returned to shore. Could it be that thinking of her parents and longing for her child, her arm drifted back?

TAKEMOTO:

How tragic! / A tearful tale, / each word drenching the couple in tears.

*(*SANEMORI *finishes telling the story, ending with a final powerful* mie *with his opened fan held overhead. He moves back to his old seat.* KURŌSUKE *and* KOYOSHI *wipe their tears.* KOYOSHI *faces her.)*

KURŌSUKE: Now, indeed, I see why only the little one could release the banner: his insistent request to remove it came from some premonition based in the parent-child bond. The three of us were unable: the mother's will allowed her child the success of the feat. The strength of her affection, remaining even in death, and the devotion shown by her clutched hand, do they not speak eloquently?

(More weeping, as KURŌSUKE *and* KOYOSHI *lean over* TARŌKICHI.*)*

TAKEMOTO:

Together with Lady Aoi, they are all lost in tears. / But Tarōkichi restrains his tears and runs to stand below Sanemori.

TARŌKICHI *(Facing the audience)*: Mr. Samurai, you killed my mommy!
(He strikes a pose as if confronting SANEMORI.*)*

TAKEMOTO:
In spite of the eyes glaring at him with hatred, / Sanemori, as is his way, gathers his courage to respond.

SANEMORI: Your heroic mother . . .

TAKEMOTO:
Well begun!

SANEMORI: Go look in the wrapper!

TAKEMOTO:
Tarōkichi immediately runs over to take up his mother's arm in his own.
(He runs to the arm, sits down, and hugs it.)

TARŌKICHI: Mommy! *(Facing his grandparents.)* How I wish this arm could reattach to her body. I want her! *(He runs back and forth, calling out for his mother.)* Mommy! Mommy!

TAKEMOTO:
He runs in one direction and another. / Flinging himself down, he breaks down and cries.
*(*KOYOSHI *comforts him while* KURŌSUKE *takes the arm and wraps it up again. He puts the wrapped arm in front of* SANEMORI*, then returns, weeping, to sit with* KOYOSHI *and* TARŌKICHI.*)*
In the midst of these lamentations, / local men come carrying the corpse.
(Wave pattern [nami no oto] *on the drums. Offstage shamisen music accompanies the* hanamichi *entrance of four fishermen. They are dressed in waist-length straw raincoats. They carry* KOMAN*'s body on a shutter. Rushing down the* hanamichi*, they arrive at* KURŌSUKE*'s gate. Behind them,* NISŌDA *has crept down the* hanamichi*, and, as the fishermen enter the gate, he secrets himself in the same thicket where* SENŌ *went to hide. The fishermen carry the shutter into the house and slip* KOMAN*'s body onto the floor. They then carry the shutter out the gate and pause.)*

FIRST FISHERMAN: Listen here! The daughter of this house has been killed. We fishermen come bearing her body.

SECOND FISHERMAN: Kurōsuke, missus, don't be shocked: we've brought her corpse, but one of her precious arms has been lost.

THIRD FISHERMAN: We divided up and inquired all around, but dogs probably ate it. There's no trace of it anywhere.

FOURTH FISHERMAN: At least you can now have a memorial service.

FIRST FISHERMAN: In any case, you have the body. Oh, oh, how sad!

ALL FOUR FISHERMEN *(Saying the Buddhist prayer for the departed)*: Praise be to Buddha, praise be to Buddha. Let us go now.

TAKEMOTO:

They finish the prayer and depart.

(They close the gate and leave via the hanamichi.*)*

KURŌSUKE *(Hurries with* KOYOSHI *and* TARŌKICHI *over to the body)*: Tarōkichi, give a farewell look at your mother's face. Take a good look to remember her.

TAKEMOTO:

He rushes right over to embrace her.

TARŌKICHI *(Putting his hands on* KOMAN*)*: Mommy! I'll never say anything bad again. I'll listen to whatever you say; please speak! Grandpa, help me!

TAKEMOTO:

He weeps and yearns for her.

(The old couple weep loudly.)

KURŌSUKE: What can I do? You have expressed more than I could and to such loving effect.

TAKEMOTO:

His wife also speaks, her eyes filled with tears of remorse.

KOYOSHI: There are things we might have wanted to speak of to each other at your dying hour . . . Tarōkichi, ladle some water and make a parting offering. Anise flowers will do.

*(*TARŌKICHI *removes his hands from* KOMAN. *He makes a big show of wiping his eyes and banging his feet on the floor.)*

TARŌKICHI: Am I so awful? Why don't you speak? I don't hear you! I don't hear you!

KURŌSUKE: No, no, it's not you at all.

TAKEMOTO:

This could not be more touching. / A thoughtful Sanemori sits, / arms folded. He addresses Tarōkichi.

SANEMORI: Your mother was steadfast in her bravery. After her arm was cut off, she did not stop breathing. When finally her vital organs had no spirit left in them, she still would not relinquish the white banner, clutching it with the greatest devotion. *(He rises and then kneels again at the bundle in front of him. He unwraps it, holds it, and expresses surprise.)* But how strange: there is warmth in this arm again. My god, what is happening? What would happen if we were to bring it together with Koman's body and the banner?

*(*SANEMORI *looks at* KURŌSUKE, *who gets up and goes to the arm. After rewrapping it,* KURŌSUKE *carries it back to* KOMAN*'s body. Meanwhile,* AOI GOZEN *takes the white banner out of her obi and gives it to* SANEMORI.*)*

TAKEMOTO:

Sanemori carries the white banner to the severed arm.

(He stands over KOMAN, *his back to the audience.* KURŌSUKE *and* KOYOSHI *gather around.* SANEMORI *turns and walks back to where he was sitting before. At*

SANEMORI *'s prompting,* KURŌSUKE *rushes out the gate to the well. He leans over and calls into it for the return of* KOMAN *'s soul.* KOYOSHI *rubs* KOMAN *'s back, calling "Daughter," and* TARŌKICHI *touches her with both hands, calling out "Mommy! Mommy!" Drums and eerie flute music* [netori] *are heard.)*

TAKEMOTO:

Amazingly, the arm, now holding the banner again, rejoins with the body. / Could it be due to the virtue of the banner? / Koman's soul, yearning for her child, returns to her body. / She breathes again, her eyes open.

(As KOMAN *revives,* KOYOSHI *gestures* KURŌSUKE *back from the well.* KOMAN *sits up, holding the banner. She is supported by her parents.)*

TARŌKICHI: Mommy, mommy, it's you!

KOMAN *(Her voice very weak, her gaze straight ahead)*: Daddy, Mommy, Tarōkichi, Lady Aoi.

AOI GOZEN: I'm right here.

KOMAN: Did you get the white banner?

AOI GOZEN: Yes, it made its way right here.

KOMAN: Oh, how happy that makes me . . . Father?

KURŌSUKE *(Leaning over her)*: Yes, yes.

KOMAN: Mother?

KOYOSHI: Yes, I'm right here.

KOMAN: I have something I want to tell Tarōkichi.

(Both parents nod.)

KURŌSUKE: He's right here.

(She cannot see TARŌKICHI. KURŌSUKE *tries to help her make contact with* TARŌKICHI, *but after getting up on her knees, she collapses.)*

TAKEMOTO:

Just then, her condition becomes hopeless. / She hovers between life and death. / The old couple wail aloud.

*(*KOMAN *dies.* SANEMORI *and* AOI GOZEN *pray.)*

KURŌSUKE: How miserable! That last request, I know what she wanted to say. I will tell her story. *(He takes* TARŌKICHI *back to the other side of the room and sits down with him.* KOYOSHI *fusses over the body. She retrieves the banner, goes to get the stand behind* SANEMORI, *and places the banner on it in front of* AOI GOZEN. KURŌSUKE *turns to* SANEMORI *and* AOI GOZEN.*)* Sanemori, excuse me, but she was going to tell what has been a secret, that she wasn't really our daughter. We found her as an infant, abandoned at Katada Bay. Carefully placed with her was an inscribed dagger, indicating that she was the child of a Heike. *(He places the dagger in front of* SANEMORI *and returns to his place.)* We kept thinking that her parents would come looking for her, wanting to take her back, but that never happened, and now she is dead. How cruel to think that she revived only to end like this; I cannot bear to part with her.

*(*KURŌSUKE *and* KOYOSHI *weep over the body.)*

TAKEMOTO:

He wails and wails. / *(*AOI GOZEN *also cries, holding a hand towel* [tenugui] *to her face.)* Aoi Gozen shares his grief, / but now her time is upon her. / Her body is wracked with the pain of labor, / *(suddenly, stabbed by pain, she bites on a folded paper to control her reaction)* and Sanemori is alarmed.

SANEMORI *(To* KURŌSUKE *and* KOYOSHI*)*: Stop your wailing, you two. Lady Aoi is in the throes of childbirth, help her!

*(*AOI GOZEN*'s face shows her pain.)*

TAKEMOTO:

Kurōsuke and Koyoshi escort her immediately into the inner room./ *(They help her into the inner room.)* They take all appropriate measures, / drawing the folding screen around her and supporting her belly. / While the old couple are thus occupied with the birth, / resourceful Sanemori erects the white banner.

*(*SANEMORI *paces, holds up the banner, and strikes a pose. He turns and hangs the banner at the split curtain, then kneels, praying, in front of it. With stylized gestures,* TARŌKICHI *creeps up to the inner room and peeks inside.* SANEMORI *scolds him.)*

SANEMORI *(Walking him back)*: You shouldn't do that. Be good now and sit here.

*(*SANEMORI *gently returns him to his place and then resumes praying at the banner.* TARŌKICHI *repeats his actions, although this time he only gets half-way when* SANEMORI *spots him and bangs on the floor, immediately sending* TARŌKICHI *back again.)*

TAKEMOTO:

His life the hope of the Genji, / the birth of the young lord goes smoothly. / His first cry sounds loudly.

(Offstage sound of an infant crying. KURŌSUKE*, one of his sleeves tied back with a cord, comes out from the inner room. He runs to the gate and looks around.* SANEMORI *comes down from where he has been sitting and also checks for eaves-droppers.* KURŌSUKE *comes over to him, bows, and speaks.)*

KURŌSUKE: Sanemori, the birth has taken place.

SANEMORI: And is the child a boy or a girl?

KURŌSUKE *(Elatedly)*: Joyfully, it is a jewellike boy.

SANEMORI *(Shouting)*: A boy! *(He catches himself and slaps his hands over his mouth.* KURŌSUKE *looks around, worried. Now more quietly.)* A blessed good omen for the future of the Genji! We must immediately choose our lord's infant name. Starting right now, we will call him Komaōmaru.

(He holds his hands in a grateful gesture and then returns to sit in front of the banner.)

TAKEMOTO:

This young lord, / the future general, Kiso Yoshinaka.

*(*KURŌSUKE *goes over to sit with* TARŌKICHI *and puts the dagger in* TARŌKICHI*'s belt.)*

KURŌSUKE: Sanemori, at this joyous moment, sir, would you please appoint Tarōkichi as retainer to the newly born child?

SANEMORI *(Facing the audience)*: Just think of the dead woman's loyalty: even if we were to cremate her body, the arm, with its single-minded devotion, probably would not burn. I will have a mound piled up immediately as a shrine-tomb for this arm, and from today, I give Tarōkichi the new name of Tezuka no Tarō Mitsumori, Tarō Mitsumori of the Arm Tomb. He will serve the young lord, Master Kiso, as his most trusted "right-hand" retainer. *(He points to his arm, underscoring the pun with a chuckle.)*

TAKEMOTO:

He is introduced as the "right-hand" man. / Just then, Koyoshi comes out from the inner room.

*(*KOYOSHI *enters, sits near the inner room, and addresses* SANEMORI*.)*

KOYOSHI: From the inner room, Lady Aoi could hear Kurōsuke's story regarding Tarōkichi, that although his father was a Genji, his mother was the daughter of a Heike. The network of Heike families is extensive, but she may even have been an illegitimate child of Kiyomori himself. Lady Aoi therefore wishes that Tarōkichi first prove his loyalty as an adult before he is accepted as a retainer for the young lord.

SANEMORI: That is eminently reasonable. It would be a disaster should the news of the young master's birth leak to the Heike. The child must be taken to his father's domain, Suwa in Shinshū, and entrusted to the care of Yoshikata's retainer, Gonnokami Kaneto. After Tarōkichi grows up, he can join Lord Kiso's loyal followers. Kurōsuke, missus, please get everything ready! *(He returns to pray at the banner.)*

TAKEMOTO:

He leaves the preparations to them. / Just then Senō no Jūrō / appears from behind the bushes.

*(*SENŌ *comes out of hiding. Drums accompany his movement to the gate, which he opens. He walks into the house immediately.)*

SENŌ: You're not going anywhere, nowhere at all! I thought something like this might happen, so I waited behind to watch and listen. I wasn't about to let a son of Yoshikata get away. Now hand him over. Let me have him!

SANEMORI *(Standing and speaking angrily)*: Senō, can you not let him live? He's yet an infant who knows nothing of this world, neither its seas nor its mountains. Letting him go indicates the compassion of the warrior.

SENŌ: So you say, duplicitous Sanemori! *(Slight pause.)* But your disloyalty undermines your words: while you sustain yourself off the Heike, you protect a Genji descendant. *(He puts one foot on the step leading into the house and poses, looking at* SANEMORI*, who returns his glare. He then walks over to* KOMAN*'s body.)* Ever since this woman somehow got hold of the white banner, the Heike have been unable to sleep at night. *(Looking down at* KOMAN.*)* Reflect on the seriousness of your offense!

TAKEMOTO:

He kicks Koman's body, sending it away.

(As SENŌ *kicks, the actor playing* KOMAN *unobtrusively makes his exit.)*

SENŌ: Give me the newborn brat. If there is any protest, I'll kill you all.

TAKEMOTO:

Tarōkichi, seeing his mother's body being treated in this way, / unsheathes the dagger she left him. / In spite of his inexperience, / he plunges it immediately into Senō's side. / All look on in shock.

*(*TARŌKICHI *has run over to* SENŌ *and stabbed him twice. Beats of the* tsuke *mark the stabbings.* TARŌKICHI *strikes a pose with* SENŌ.*)*

TARŌKICHI: Hey, samurai, you shouldn't tread on my mother! You shouldn't kick my mother!

*(*SENŌ *pulls off his outer costume to the waist. He falls onto a small stool provided by a* STAGE ASSISTANT.*)*

TAKEMOTO:

Senō though he is, he has been gouged through at a vital spot. / Seriously wounded, he topples over.

SENŌ *(Sitting now with* TARŌKICHI*)*: Lady Aoi, hasn't Tarōkichi now proven himself a loyal retainer to Komaō?

(Flute and shamisen music.)

SANEMORI: Yes, most assuredly.

SENŌ *(Slowly)*: He has brought down a hereditary Heike samurai, Senō no Jūrō Kaneuji. It's a great feat and benefit to you. Although he is not yet of age, please retain him. In truth, long ago when I was still a dependent, there was a serving woman who became pregnant. The child she bore was taken unknowingly to Katada Bay and abandoned by its Heike father, who was, in fact, me. *(*KURŌSUKE *looks shocked.) As* proof of its origins, I placed this sword with the infant, and now these many years later, my own grandson has stabbed me in the side with it.

TAKEMOTO:

How moving!

SENŌ *(Looking at his grandson)*: When I first became a retainer, I hated being tied to the Heike. When you first become a retainer, hatred of your Heike bonds could cloud your future and harm your chances. Serve well for seven years and you will be able to join Lord Kiso's inner circle. *(Turning with effort.)* Sanemori, please help him achieve a matchless level of service. *(Speaks with increasing difficulty.)* Now, for my head. *(To* TARŌKICHI.*)* Help me by performing another early service for your master.

*(*SENŌ *pulls the dagger out of his side, then grasps his long sword. He leans on it to raise himself up, but falls down again.)*

TAKEMOTO:

This warrior, so rooted in the ways of cruelty, / easily unsheathes his sword.

(He raises himself again and leans over to TARŌKICHI*, looking at him and leaning down in a gesture of love. Then he unsheathes his sword and looks at* TARŌKICHI*, who grabs hold of it with him. In a special piece of business designed to suggest his self-decapitation, he and* TARŌKICHI *lift the sword over his head to rest on the back of his neck. He makes ferocious facial expressions as they move the sword back and forth across his neck. Then—in what some actors perform as a partial somersault—he tumbles forward, his head hidden. As he does this, the* STAGE ASSISTANT *behind him tosses forth a property head and* TARŌKICHI *strikes a pose holding the sword to his side.)*

TAKEMOTO *(Chanted as the above actions unfold)*:

Together with his deeply agitated grandson, / he clutches it firmly with both hands. / With grunts and groans, he slices off his own head. / As is true of all Heike, / Senō has been notorious for his evil, / but his resolve in this final act is indeed praiseworthy.

*(*KURŌSUKE *comes over to the boy.* TARŌKICHI *looks down at the head. A black cloth conceals* SENŌ*'s body as it is removed.* KURŌSUKE *and* TARŌKICHI *turn around and show the head to* AOI GOZEN*, who is revealed with* KOYOSHI *as the sliding* shōji *screens of the inner room open.)*

TAKEMOTO:

To present the head, Kurōsuke escorts the boy to Lady Aoi.

*(*AOI GOZEN *looks down on him from the inner room. Seated, her outer garment is pulled down to the waist, revealing a white undergarment. She cradles her swaddled infant.)*

AOI GOZEN: You unhesitatingly killed a great Heike samurai. This meritorious feat indicates that your fate is intertwined with the young lord in lifetimes of service.

The old Heike warrior Senō (Ichikawa Danzō IX) attempts suicide by self-decapitation. Sanemori (Ichikawa Danjūrō XII) watches from behind as his son, Tarōkichi (Ichikawa Shinnosuke VII), assists. (Umemura Yutaka, Engeki Shuppansha)

TAKEMOTO:

Hearing this, Tarōkichi stands erect.

(TARŌKICHI *stands near the seated* SANEMORI.)

TARŌKICHI: So, I am to be a samurai. Now I can kill my mother's enemy, Sanemori.

TAKEMOTO:

Saying this, he moves toward Sanemori.

(TARŌKICHI *strikes a pose.*)

SANEMORI: Very commendable. I agree with your motive, but if you kill Saitō Bettō Sanemori while you are still so young, you will not gain sympathy for your deed. Go with your young master to Suwa in Shinshū and join his faithful troops when you become an adult. Those years hence, I will return to my old home, dressed in my finest, and then you can have your revenge. Until then, farewell.

(*He bows.* KURŌSUKE *takes the boy.*)

TAKEMOTO:

At the moment of his "farewell," / Yabase no Nisōda, having overheard all, / leaps out of hiding.

*(*NISŌDA *emerges from hiding in the bushes and stands outside the gate.)*

NISŌDA *(Quickly)*: I heard everything! Everything: your plan to help Komaōmaru and to go north. I'm going to inform the authorities of exactly what you're doing, just you wait!

TAKEMOTO:

He spews out these words and starts to run off. / *(He runs to the* hanamichi.*)* Without a moment's hesitation, / Sanemori throws his short sword forcefully, / striking Nisōda.

(A trick technique makes it seem that NISŌDA *is struck in the neck just as he reaches* shichisan. *He runs back onstage, struggles to pull out the dagger, and falls down dead behind the bushes at right.)*

SANEMORI *(Facing the audience)*: Retainers, hurry! Bring my horse!

(A train of RETAINERS *begins to enter on the* hanamichi.*)*

RETAINERS: Yes!

TAKEMOTO:

They respond. / Having fit the horse with its saddle, / they lead it in for service.

*(*SIX RETAINERS, *dressed in* kamishimo, *their* hakama *pulled up to the waist, are followed down the* hanamichi *by a footman leading the horse, represented by two actors in a horse prop* [nuigurumi]. *As the* RETAINERS *align themselves and kneel onstage, the "horse" is backed off to the side.)*

RETAINERS: The horse is ready.

(Drums are heard. ONE RETAINER *helps* SANEMORI *on with his sandals.)*

TAKEMOTO:

Tezuka no Tarō / takes his mother's dagger / and hangs it from his waist. / He swings onto a cotton-ginning horse.

*(*TARŌKICHI*'s outer garment is stripped to the waist where the dagger hangs. He mounts the "horse," a toy made out of his grandmother's cotton-ginning equipment.* KURŌSUKE *helps him manipulate it.)*

TARŌKICHI: Sanemori, are you going to flee after having killed my mother? *(Pretends to ride the "horse.")* I am now called Tezuka no Tarō, the Mitsumori of this dagger. Let's have it out here and now.

(He pretends to ride the "horse" again and poses with his leg out to the side.)

TAKEMOTO:

So he exclaims.

*(*KURŌSUKE *and* KOYOSHI *are seated to* TARŌKICHI*'s left.* SANEMORI *is on his right.)*

SANEMORI: We will have it out, but not now. *(He walks over to* TARŌKICHI, *pulls out some paper, wipes the boy's nose, then turns away.)* You must learn to contain your ferocity. Save the battle cries you so naturally proclaim for the day in your adulthood when you will take your revenge on me. Look at my face and remember it well, so that one day you might settle scores with me. *(Strokes* TARŌKICHI*'s head.)*

KURŌSUKE *(Kneeling)*: Yes, but Sanemori, when my grandson has grown up, your face will be wrinkled and your hair will have grayed.

SANEMORI: Yes, how true. Then I will dye my sidelocks black. If you should succeed in killing me and anyone claims that you have captured the head of another, wash it in pond water to find the true color of its hair. *(He uses his fan to mimic washing.)* We will meet again in the north, on a battlefield at Kaga in Shinohara.

*(*SANEMORI *walks back to* TARŌKICHI *and poses with one hand on the boy's shoulder and one holding his opened fan high.)*

TAKEMOTO:

They will meet, they will meet again.

*(*SANEMORI *moves away from* TARŌKICHI*.)*

AOI GOZEN *(To* SANEMORI*)*: My son *(looks down at the infant, then up again)* will remember your loyalty and prevent this revenge.

KURŌSUKE: If I live, I will be there to carry the banner.

KOYOSHI: And I will cook for the troops.

TARŌKICHI: But the slayer shall be me, Tezuka.

SANEMORI: We will grapple with each other on horseback until one of us falls between the horses.

*(*SANEMORI *does a little dance to show the struggle. The dance continues throughout the following chanting.)*

TAKEMOTO:

The pathos of the aged warrior becomes clear / when he is silenced in battle. / Like an old tree shriveled by the wind, / his will shall be broken.

SANEMORI: Until then, Tezuka.

TARŌKICHI: Yes, until then.

SANEMORI: And when you finally succeed in toppling my head, I will return to the earth of Shinohara. Farewell.

TAKEMOTO:

His name will be celebrated in the northern region.

(The "horse" is brought back onstage and into the house. With the help of his RETAINERS, SANEMORI *mounts it.* TARŌKICHI *runs over and stands at the "horse's" side. A* RETAINER *comes around and lifts him on, in front of* SANEMORI. *They take one turn together around the stage, then* TARŌKICHI *dismounts.)*

Reins in hand, he sets off, his spirits high. / With the moon-filled house behind, he hastens his horse.

Sanemori (Ichikawa Danjūrō XI) rides a kabuki horse (two men in a horse costume) down the *hanamichi.* (Tsubouchi Memorial Theatre Museum of Waseda University)

*(*SANEMORI *rides off down the* hanamichi, *with the* RETAINERS *aligned and ready to follow. The "horse" bolts at* shichisan *and moves back, raising its head up and down. Drums and* tsuke *punctuate the action.* SANEMORI *strikes a final* mie, *open fan overhead. The onstage* RETAINERS *also strike a tableau* [hippari mie], *suggesting a send-off. The curtain is drawn for an "outside-the-curtain exit"* [maku soto no hikkomi] *of the* RETAINERS, *now lined up along the stage proper, and the mounted* SANEMORI. *The latter urges the "horse" on, but it stands motionless. He strikes it with his fan and it bolts, the* tsuke *marking these movements.* SANEMORI *holds his fan between his teeth, strikes a final pose, and exits down the* hanamichi, *followed by the* RETAINERS *as exit music plays.)*

Three-panel woodblock print by Utagawa Ōsai (dates unknown). Nakamura-za, Edo, eighth month 1862. "Cherry Blossom Princess Yuki" ("Sawamura Tanosuke" III), center, watches "Matsunaga Daizen" ("Bandō Hikosaburō" V), left, summon dragons from the waterfall with his unsheathed magical sword, while "Konoshita/Hisayoshi" ("Kataoka Nizaemon" VIII), right, poses in a *mie*, holding a *go* board in his left hand. (Tsubouchi Memorial Theatre Museum of Waseda University)

The Golden Pavilion

Kinkakuji

Nakamura Akei, Asada Itchō, Toyotake Ōritsu, Mitsu Nomiko, and Kokuzō Su

TRANSLATED BY ALAN CUMMINGS

1757 TOYOTAKE-ZA, OSAKA

The Golden Pavilion

INTRODUCTION

The Gion Festival Chronicle of Faith (Gion Sairei Shinkōki), the long play in which *The Golden Pavilion* originally appeared, was written for the puppet theatre by Nakamura Akei, Asada Itchō, Toyotake Ōritsu, Mitsu Nomiko, and Kokuzō Su (all dates unknown) and first performed at the Toyotake-za in Osaka in the twelfth lunar month of 1757. Its kabuki version premiered at Kyoto's Minami no Shibai (temporarily known as the Sawamura Somematsu-za) the following year. The play is set in the second half of the sixteenth century, a time of civil war in Japan, when numerous provincial lords vied to seize control of the country.

The warlord Oda Nobunaga, although he does not appear in the scene translated here, casts his shadow over the entire play, as he did over Japanese history of the period. Nobunaga began as a minor provincial lord, but through shrewd alliances and his mastery of the latest military technology—muskets and gunpowder—succeeded in rising to a position of de facto power. In 1582, he was assassinated by one of his disaffected vassals, Akechi Mitsuhide. Mitsuhide himself was soon defeated and killed by another Nobunaga vassal, Toyotomi Hideyoshi, who went on to seize national power. The trio of Nobunaga, Mitsuhide, and Hideyoshi was an endless source of fascination to Tokugawa-period audiences and provided the source material for many plays, such as *The Picture Book of The Taikō* (Ehon Taikōki), translated in Volume II of this series. Plays dealing with this world *(sekai)* usually followed contemporary prejudices in painting Nobunaga as a despot and Mitsuhide as a tragic, if justified, revenger who was punished for his hubris. Hideyoshi, on the other hand, was idolized as a man who had risen from the lowliest peasant beginnings to glory and magnificence, a man who had brought peace to a country long wracked by civil war. Hideyoshi's legend was especially honored in his seat of power, the Kamigata region of Osaka and Kyoto. This is the world that *The Gion Festival Chronicle of Faith* presents, and Nobunaga, Hideyoshi, and Mitsuhide all appear in it.

It is recorded that the puppet play first opened under the title of *Gion Sairei Shinchōki.* But inasmuch as *"shinchō"* is an alternate reading of the characters for Nobunaga's name, the overt political reference was clearly too much for the censors and the word was changed to *"shinkō"* for virtually all subsequent productions. Kabuki historian Ihara Seiseien (also known as Ihara Toshirō) speculates that the Gion Festival in Kyoto was especially popular at the time, hence the reference to it in the title.[1] Whatever the reason, the innovative and spectacular use of the stage lift *(seri)* to raise and lower the entire set in *Golden Pavilion* was such a sensation and the thirst of Osaka audiences for plays about Hideyoshi was so great that the play ran for some fifteen months. When competing kabuki versions by the Sawamura Somematsu and Nakamura Kumetarō troupes opened in Kyoto during the first month of 1758 and the first Edo production took place in the fifth month of the same year, the play's lasting popularity was sealed. *Golden Pavilion* has remained an enduring staple of the kabuki stage throughout the Tokugawa period and up until the present day.

Structurally, the original is a typical puppet history play *(jidaimono)* in five acts. *Golden Pavilion* was originally part of Act IV and is the only section still regularly performed. This scene is primarily concerned with the treachery of an evil aristocrat called Matsunaga Daizen, who earlier in the play tricked the mistress of Shogun Ashikaga Yoshiteru into murdering her beloved. Other highlights of earlier acts include the love affair of Yuki and Naonobu and Yamaguchi Kurōjirō's (meant to represent Akechi Mitsuhide) attack on Oda Harunaga (the usual kabuki alias for Oda Nobunaga). The final act shows Daizen's defeat and decapitation by the forces of Ashikaga Yoshiaki and Harunaga. Daizen is clearly based on the historical character of Matsunaga Hisahide, who was indeed involved in the actual assassination of Yoshiteru but whom, like Richard III, popular tradition has painted much blacker than he probably was. Apart from the historical elements, various earlier puppet plays were cannibalized in the writing of *Golden Pavilion*. The story of Princess Yuki and her magical, dragon-summoning sword had previously appeared in Uji Kaganojō's (1635–1711) *The Female Artist Kanō no Yukihime* (Onna Eshi Kanō no Yukihime) and Chikamatsu Monzaemon's (1653–1725) *Matahei the Stutterer* (Domo Mata), translated in this volume. The full-length version of the latter, *The Courtesan of the Hangon Incense* (Keisei Hangonkō), contains an episode in which a painting comes to life to save its artist. Other plays are thought to have been influential as well.

History plays by their very nature tended to deal with the big themes, presented in bold brush strokes: good versus evil, proper government versus illegitimate tyranny, spirit and intelligence versus brute power. In *Golden Pavilion*, too, we are far from the ambiguous moral greys of everyday life of kabuki and puppet domestic plays *(sewamono)*. This tendency is reinforced by some of the unique presentational aspects of the play. First, the characters are all neatly identifiable as major kabuki role types. Daizen, with his almost supernatural sense of wicked-

1. Ihara Seiseien, *Sajiki kara Shosai e* (From the Theatre Boxes to the Study), p. 55.

ness, is an archetypal aristocratic "nation-destroyer" *(kuni kuzushi)*. His adversary, Tōkichi /Hisayoshi, is a typically patient, problem-solving hero *(sabakiyaku)*. Princess Yuki is a "red princess" *(akahime)*, a reference to the color of kimono most typically worn, though most current female-role specialists *(onnagata)* wear pink. Her husband, Kanō Naonobu, is the epitome of the gentle and ineffectual *wagoto* lover. Gunpei / Satō Masakiyo is often played with bravura *aragoto* elements, and finally the "red-face" *(akattsura)* Kitōda is a typical comic villain. Each of the characters is given a scene in which the actor can demonstrate his abilities: Tōkichi has the well scene; Yuki, the "toe and mice" *(tsumesaki nezumi)* sequence, where she draws mice in the blossoms with her foot; Gunpei, his final vigorous appearance as Satō Masakiyo.

Second, as the kabuki scholar Watanabe Tamotsu has suggested, the very scale of the characters involved lifts the play out of the realm of reality and into that of myth.[2] The portrayal of the evil Daizen is obviously larger than life, not only in the tradition of kabuki villains but also in the impersonal vilification that had already attached itself to the historical Matsunaga Hisahide. Yuki's family history as the granddaughter of the famous painter Sesshū and the daughter of the equally revered Sesson has the potential to transform her into an embodiment of art, and thus her triumph is not just of good over evil, or of the spirit over material existence, but also of art over despotism. Tōkichi, too, with his hidden identity as the local hero, Hideyoshi, must have resonated deeply with contemporary Osaka audiences. Incidentally, the revelation of Tōkichi's true identity would not have been such a surprise to contemporary audiences: it is well flagged through the disguised use of Hideyoshi's previous name of Kinoshita Tokichirō (here, Konoshita Tōkichi) and the reference to his famously short stature.

The acting style, too, has many elements that raise the actors above the everyday plane. Ihara has commented that the play is even more effective when the actors play their roles as puppets, giving form to the words of the *takemoto* chanter. For example, in one performance tradition, in the section where Yuki is freed by the mice, the *onnagata* playing her mimics the stiff actions of a manipulated puppet using the unique "puppet-movement" *(ningyō buri)* technique. Certainly the pervasive environment of unreality, and the more fantastic and supernatural elements in the play, such as the magical sword and the mice coming to life, suited puppet performance. Following Watanabe's perspective, kabuki actors were able to carry off these scenes because their acting was not bound to realistic techniques. That said, however, these techniques do not necessarily emotionally distance audiences from the action of the play. Daizen is not a character for whom we are made

2. Quoted in Watanabe Tamotsu, *Kabuki Techō* (Kabuki Guidebook), p. 130.

to feel much sympathy, but he is given an engagingly human side with his obsession for the game of *go* and his undisguised lust for Princess Yuki. The scene in which Yuki parts from her husband and laments her fate in a pink snowstorm of cherry blossoms can be unbearably moving, an effect that, perhaps paradoxically, is enhanced by its aesthetically formal beauty.

Yuki is at the emotional center of the play, the character on which the audience inevitably focuses. With some justification, her part is ranked as one of the important and challenging "three princesses" *(san hime)* roles: the others are Princess Yaegaki in *Japan's Twenty-Four Paragons of Filial Piety* (Honchō Nijūshikō), translated in this volume, and Princess Toki in *The Kamakura Trilogy* (Kamakura Sandaiki). Nakamura Utaemon V (1865–1940) has explained the particular difficulties of the part: "Princess Yuki hasn't received a samurai education. Nevertheless, besides her courage she must retain a most graceful refinement. And since she is a woman well aware of the situation in which she finds herself, she must also display sufficient eroticism."[3] This clearly elucidates what audiences find so appealing about Yuki: in spite of her beauty and obvious refinement, she is not one of those typical weeping princesses seemingly enervated by her own social position. Rather, she is prepared to sacrifice herself for her husband and to physically take on Daizen and his minions. The play is undeniably spectacular, full of magnificent sets and grandiose posturing, but Yuki is the drama's living heart, that which gives it life and has ensured its popularity over three centuries.

For this translation, the main text consulted was that in Toita Yasuji et al., eds., *Meisaku Kabuki Zenshū,* Vol. 4, as well as the puppet theatre text in Yamada et al., eds., *Toyotake-za Jōruri-shū III,* a volume in *Sōsho Edo Bunkō 37.* The scene can open with several maidservants summarizing the previous action: the kidnapping of Keijuin, Naonobu, and Yuki, and Daizen's dissipation and villainous intentions toward the princess. Stage directions are based on a videotape of the November 1997 production at the Kokuritsu Gekijō (National Theatre of Japan), which starred Ichimura Uzaemon XVII (b. 1916) as Daizen, Nakamura Ganjirō III (b. 1931) as Tōkichi, and Nakamura Jakuemon IV (b. 1920) as Princess Yuki, and on the June 1998 production at the Kabuki-za.

CHARACTERS

MATSUNAGA DAIZEN HISAHIDE, *a villain plotting to seize power*

KONOSHITA TŌKICHI, *a master strategist in the employ of Oda Harunaga, in reality, the general* MASHIBA HISAYOSHI *in disguise*

3. Ibid.

SOGŌ GUNPEI, *a retainer of* DAIZEN, *in reality,* SATŌ TORANOSUKE MASAKIYO, *retainer to* HISAYOSHI

KANO NO SUKE NAONOBU, *an artist imprisoned by* DAIZEN, *husband of* YUKI

PRINCESS YUKI, *wife of* NAONOBU, *daughter of the artist Sesson*

MATSUNAGA KITŌDA, *younger brother of* DAIZEN

KEIJUIN, *the shogun's mother, imprisoned by* DAIZEN

SOLDIERS

MAIDSERVANTS

TAKEMOTO, *narrator and shamisen player who accompany the action*

(A plaintive melody and singing offstage, during which the traditional striped curtain opens to the sound of accelerating ki *clacks. The scene revealed is of the Temple of the Golden Pavilion in the Kitayama district of Kyoto, now the lair of the evil* MATSUNAGA DAIZEN. *The pavilion itself dominates the center of the stage: it is a gorgeous three-story structure with black-lacquered pillars, gold fittings, and painted golden screens. The effect is of the utmost luxury. The main room is concealed by a bamboo blind. To left is a smaller room, its interior again concealed by bamboo blinds; it is connected to the main pavilion by a raised walkway. Two large cherry trees in bloom are situated on either side of the pavilion. To the right is a painted waterfall, vertical bands of blue and white between rocky outcrops. In front of the waterfall is a well, surrounded by a low parapet. The* TAKEMOTO *narrator and shamisen player are seated on a platform at left. The music dies away, and a loud, single* ki *clack signals the* TAKEMOTO *musicians to begin.)*

TAKEMOTO *(Slowly and with dignified grandeur)*:

What then is the Golden Pavilion? / It is the mountain retreat of / Chamberlain Lord Yoshimitsu, who built the Rokuon Temple. / A lofty three-tiered palace / with willows and cherries planted around, / truly it is the brocade of Kyoto!

(The bamboo blinds roll upward to reveal the inner room. Gold panels with huge painted tigers flank a striped curtain of green, yellow, and purple, which conceals another inner room. MATSUNAGA DAIZEN *and his brother,* KITŌDA, *face each other across a* go *board, intent on their game.* DAIZEN, *left, is dressed in a white kimono over which he wears a heavy brocade jacket tied in front with a huge bow. His "prince"* [ōji] *wig, appropriate to a superhuman villain, is worn long and loose, cascading down his back and chest. His makeup is a blue-tinged white, suggesting a refined and supernatural evil. He leans on a brocade armrest with a tobacco tray in front of him.* KITŌDA, *right, wears the comical wig of a minor villain, his face colored a deep red and accented with black lines around his mouth and eyes. His*

formal attire [kamishimo] *is patterned in red and gold with white at the shoulders and hem.)*

Kitōda encircled by his opponent. / Winning two games in a strand, / Daizen gloats with pleasure.

*(*DAIZEN *laughs.)*

DAIZEN *(Magisterially)*: Kitōda, you've lost this time as well.

KITŌDA: I fancy myself as a skilled player of *go*, but I can never match your skill, brother, you who wield dominion over the land. We must switch sides.

TAKEMOTO:

Proudly he clears away the black and white stones.

*(*KITŌDA *begins to separate the* go *stones into two bowls, while* DAIZEN *turns to face front and grasps a large silver pipe in his right hand.)*

DAIZEN: It is Asakura Yoshikage whom I feel sorry for. After Harunaga's scheming exposed him, I thought soon to take revenge, but as I could find no capable general, regretfully I have had to hide myself away here at this Golden Pavilion. Just when I had been searching for a doughty warrior, it seems that a certain Konoshita Tōkichi has taken leave from Harunaga and desires to enter my service. Though I am suspicious, Gunpei has suggested that if it is one of Harunaga's plots, we should pretend ignorance and employ this man. Thus, I have sent Gunpei to bring him here. Is there still no sign of them?

KITŌDA: Gunpei is doubtless taking every precaution. But brother, you seem to be downcast today. Why not have some sake while we wait?

DAIZEN: Until Princess Yuki gives me her answer, I can find no pleasure in drinking. *(Calls out.)* Maids, open the screens!

MAIDS *(From offstage)*: At once, master.

TAKEMOTO:

Almost before their words are spoken / the dividing screens are pushed open. / The pitiful Princess Yuki, / like Wang Chou-chün in the barbarian land, / a blossom losing its scent and color. / Daizen softens his words.

(A blind rises within the smaller pavilion at left. Through the translucent sliding screens, PRINCESS YUKI *is dimly visible, flanked by two* MAIDSERVANTS. *They push open the screens and* YUKI *is finally revealed. She wears a kimono and over-robe* [uchikake] *of pink, gorgeously embroidered with red and gold flower motifs. Her wig is the elaborate "blown circle"* [fukiwa], *with the large topknot constructed around a silver drum. Her delicacy and vulnerability are emphasized by the rows of silver hair ornaments rising in a halo above her face. With every slight movement, they shake and catch the light. The two* MAIDSERVANTS *are dressed in typical fashion, one in light blue, the other in purple. The gold screen behind shows a large cherry tree over a pond.* YUKI *is obviously melancholic. Her movements are slow, and her manner is downcast.)*

DAIZEN: Princess Yuki, your husband, that wretch Naonobu, endures agonies in my smallest dungeon because he will not paint a dragon as Keijuin wishes. Will you paint the dragon in his place, or will you submit to my desires? Come now, what is your answer?

TAKEMOTO:

Pressed, at last the princess raises her head.

(Raising her head, she dabs at her eyes with the hem of her sleeve.)

YUKI *(Weakly, but with grace)*: Your request is both unexpected and unreasonable. The secrets of painting have been handed down in our family from my grandfather, and so I have no grounds to decline.

TAKEMOTO:

Instead of landscapes, birds, or flowers, / her family's métier is ink-painted dragons.

YUKI: A secret scroll was passed down from Sesshū to my father, Sesson, but he was killed by some unknown assailant and the scroll was lost. Without it, what can I use as a model to paint from?

TAKEMOTO:

"And so I beg for your forgiveness."

(She bows deeply, with both hands before her.)

YUKI: Further, it was thanks to the Lady Keijuin that Naonobu and I were united as man and wife. A woman's modesty could never allow me to betray that bond. That you have imprisoned not just me but my husband as well is truly too cruel. Do not force me to endure such misery. I would rather that you kill me.

TAKEMOTO:

She slumps to the ground, / weeping.

(Weeping loudly, YUKI *buries her face in her sleeves.)*

DAIZEN: Did you hear that, Kitōda? I ask her to paint a dragon and she tells me that she has lost some secret scroll; I ask her to submit to my desires and she tells me that she must be faithful to that wretch Naonobu. Either way, Naonobu is the fly in the ointment. When Gunpei returns, I will have him drown Naonobu in the well; then my plans will go smoothly. Until you give me a favorable answer, I will torture you with pleasure in my bed. Princess Yuki, raise your voice and sing for me. Sing!

(As his speech builds to a climax, DAIZEN *raises his voice and bangs his pipe on the floor in emphasis, leering lecherously at* YUKI.*)*

TAKEMOTO:

To his demands, / the Princess can make no reply. / All she can do is weep.

(Trembling, YUKI *again bursts into tears, slumping against her padded armrest as the* MAIDSERVANTS *move to close the screens.)*

TAKEMOTO:

Just then Sogō Gunpei appears, / leading Konoshita Tōkichi, / a naked blade held to his neck.

*(*GUNPEI *enters along the* hanamichi, *leading* TŌKICHI. *Two* SOLDIERS *bring up the rear.* GUNPEI *is a typical henchman: his face is red, and he wears red and gold formal attire* [kamishimo] *over a black kimono. Both are tucked up into his waist to reveal his red legs and yellow* tabi. *He holds a long, unsheathed sword in his right hand. The white-faced* TŌKICHI, *too, wears formal attire, his with a pattern of silver gourds on a black background, worn over a pale blue kimono. He walks humbly but with some assurance, in spite of the fact that he is unarmed. One of the guards carries his swords. The whole party stops at* shichisan, *where* TŌKICHI *and the guards kneel.* GUNPEI *remains standing with his sword held over the prisoner.)*

KITŌDA *(Calling out)*: Is that you, Gunpei? My brother has been awaiting you.

TAKEMOTO:

Daizen speaks.

DAIZEN: Gunpei, who is that you have in custody?

GUNPEI: This is none other than Konoshita Tōkichi, who desires to enter your service and has come of his own accord. Just in case he has some trick up his sleeve, I have taken every precaution, as you can see.

DAIZEN *(Laughs)*: Ha, ha. Since Tōkichi desires to serve me, no such precautions will be necessary. Release him. Release him.

GUNPEI: Yes, sir.

TAKEMOTO:

As he sheaths his sword, / Gunpei, too, kneels down.

DAIZEN: So you are the Konoshita Tōkichi of whom I have heard much. Stand not on formality. Come closer. Come closer.

*(*TŌKICHI *bows deeply.)*

TAKEMOTO:

Obeying his words, / he approaches. / Daizen speaks.

(Led by GUNPEI, *the party approaches the main stage.* GUNPEI *and* TŌKICHI *kneel below* DAIZEN, *to his right, while the* SOLDIERS *line up farther right.)*

DAIZEN: That you have forsaken Harunaga and wish to enter our service is a most auspicious omen for our campaign against him. But it is unseemly that you should be unarmed. Return his swords. Come closer, come closer.

TAKEMOTO:

Taking back his swords / entrusted to a soldier, / Tōkichi is restored to dignity. / He bows deeply, hands before him.

(A SOLDIER *brings* TŌKICHI *a sword. Gravely, he tucks the short one into his obi, lays the other by his side, and bows to* DAIZEN. *The* SOLDIERS *exit right.)*

TŌKICHI *(Modestly, but with spirit)*: As you may see, I am less than four feet in height. Compared to the legendary general Yamamoto Kansuke of Kōshū, I am a remarkably small man. But if your lordship could find some use for me as a groom or in holding his horse's bridle, I would be eternally grateful.

TAKEMOTO:

Humbly, he prostrates himself.

(The musicians draw out the phrase. TŌKICHI *moves his sword from his left to his right, thus indicating his peaceful intent, and then performs an elaborate, deep bow in time with the shamisen.)*

DAIZEN: In the past, there was a man called Sei no Anshi, who, although he stood only three feet high, surpassed all the barons and governed the country. A warrior's soul is what matters, and one should judge a man on whether he is good or evil, or so they say. But every man has his vices, and one of mine is the game of *go*. Here is the board. What say you to a game, Tōkichi?

TŌKICHI *(Politely)*: As you command, my lord, but I am a poor and unpracticed player and thus not a worthy adversary, I fear.

KITŌDA: I won't take "no" for an answer. Come to the board. *(Powerfully.)* Come.

TŌKICHI: Then, as you command.

TAKEMOTO:

To the fray, Tōkichi / enters the pavilion.

(Taking his sword, TŌKICHI *approaches the pavilion as* GUNPEI *makes way for him. Removing his sandals, he steps up into the pavilion and sits, bowing to* DAIZEN. KITŌDA *places the* go *board before his brother.)*

DAIZEN: This should be interesting. Approach the board.

TŌKICHI: As you command.

TAKEMOTO:

Tōkichi faces the board. / Who shall make the first move?

*(*GUNPEI *crosses to left.)*

GUNPEI: There isn't a more pleasant way to pass the time. I shall observe from here.

TAKEMOTO:

He sits himself down to observe.

*(*GUNPEI *sits on the veranda and, holding his sleeves out, strikes a comical* mie *as he faces the competitors. The game progresses.)*

TAKEMOTO *(Slowly and delicately)*:

The separating screens slide softly open. / Princess Yuki suffering within, / in her heart, a plan.

(The inner blind rolls and the screens of the neighboring pavilion slide open to reveal YUKI. *Hand to her breast, she kneels.)*

YUKI *(To herself)*: Luckily, they have imprisoned me in this pavilion. Now is my chance to rescue the Lady Keijuin, to whom I owe so much. And I must save my husband's life.

(Using different cadences, the narration moves back and forth between YUKI, DAIZEN, TŌKICHI, *and* GUNPEI. *The characters mime the lyrics.)*

TAKEMOTO:

Ah . . . eyes downcast, / she wonders how, / brains racked for the opening gambit, / Daizen lays his first stone. / As on the ivy-covered paths of Utsu, / Tōkichi launches his attack and / takes Daizen's piece. / Calm on the sidelines, Gunpei's words of advice, / heeded not by Daizen, / she fixes on a plan and nods.

YUKI: Should I sacrifice myself and give him the answer he desires?

TAKEMOTO:

"If I consent / he will surely free my darling Naonobu / from his prison cell."

*(*YUKI *bows deeply, miming making her request to* DAIZEN.*)*

YUKI: If I say no, it will mean my husband's life.

DAIZEN: That was a dangerous move. My pieces are already in position.

TŌKICHI: I'm afraid not. It's this white piece that I will take.

DAIZEN: Looks like you're a slippery fish.

TŌKICHI: With eyes only for the white ones.

DAIZEN: White fish?

TŌKICHI: Or white flesh?

(The two men are deeply absorbed in their game, taking pieces from small bowls on the floor beside them and placing them on the go *board.)*

TAKEMOTO:

Listening to their predictions, / she tries to calm her beating heart.

YUKI: Indeed, in the past, there was the example of Lady Tokiwa, who gave herself to her husband's enemy, Kiyomori. That was for the sake of her children, but I must do the same for my beloved husband's sake. I must, I must.

TAKEMOTO *(Slowly)*:

So saying she stands / and, on trembling legs, / timidly she approaches Daizen from behind.

*(*YUKI *slides open the door at the side of her room and crosses over to the main pavilion. Peeping in at* DAIZEN, *eventually she plucks up the courage to enter. She kneels behind him.)*

YUKI *(Trying to catch his attention)*: Excuse me, Lord Daizen. My reply from earlier is . . . Excuse me . . .

TAKEMOTO:

Although she bows, / intent on the game, / he doesn't even raise his head.

DAIZEN: Who's that?

Konoshita Tōkichi, in reality Mashiba Hisayoshi (Nakamura Baigyoku IV), left, plays the game of *go* with his enemy Matsunaga Daizen Hisahide (Ichimura Uzaemon XVII), watched by Daizen's brother, Matsunaga Kitōda (Kataoka Gatō V), center. Daizen's daughter, Princess Yuki (Nakamura Fukusuke IX), motions retainer Sogō Gunpei (Nakamura Kichiemon II), right, to be patient. (Umemura Yutaka, Engeki Shuppansha)

YUKI: It's me.

DAIZEN: Me who?

YUKI: My reply from earlier . . .

DAIZEN: Princess Yuki, face white like my *go* stones. And your reply is that you will sleep with me?

YUKI *(Distraught)*: Ye . . . es . . .

DAIZEN *(Triumphant)*: That "yes" is like a caress. Ha, ha, ha. And here with Tōkichi looking on . . . love makes fools of us all. Forgive me. Forgive me.

TŌKICHI: Your apologies are unnecessary. Although we may be master and retainer, when it comes to *go,* one need not hold back. Isn't that right, Gunpei?

(The following dialogue is dotted with punning references to go *moves.)*

GUNPEI: True indeed. Now because of a woman, Lord Daizen has his back to the wall.

DAIZEN: Tonight I will ravage your queen, pinning her down like this.

TŌKICHI: And I will break your pin, thus.

DAIZEN *(Musing)*: Fascinating. But if I kill Harunaga and Naonobu, that will leave no more obstacles.

GUNPEI: That's the truth.

DAIZEN *(A sudden flash of inspiration)*: Gunpei, kill him! Cut off his head!

GUNPEI: Yessir!

TAKEMOTO:

Sogō Gunpei hurries off. / The princess is shocked.

*(*GUNPEI *stands, bows to* DAIZEN, *and stomps off vigorously to left.* YUKI *runs to the edge of the veranda.)*

YUKI: Wait, please. Who are you going to kill?

GUNPEI: That's obvious. Naonobu.

*(*GUNPEI *strikes a brief* mie *with both hands on his sword.)*

YUKI *(Holding up her hand)*: Wait, I beg you. I came here to tell my lord Daizen that I would submit to his desires in order to save my husband's life. But as he was so intent on his game, I spoke once and then kept silent. Please wait, I beg you.

TAKEMOTO:

As she weeps imploringly, / Daizen says . . .

DAIZEN: So, Yuki, you will submit to me then?

YUKI *(Anguished)*: Ye . . . es.

DAIZEN: This is so sudden, I know not what to think. Gunpei, wait.

GUNPEI: Just because she's given in to you, there's no reason to kill him?

DAIZEN: I was so absorbed in the game that I spoke without thinking. That was nearly the end of Naonobu. Tōkichi, a certain text tells the story of a great king of the country of Harano in India who, like me, was so intent on his game that he killed a priest by mistake. That was truly an act of fate. If you agreed to submit to me, then I would not kill that wretch Naonobu; that was our agreement. So I shall consent to spare him.

TAKEMOTO:

His words calm her slightly. / Daizen gazes intently at the board.

*(*YUKI *bows deeply to* DAIZEN, *her head shaking.)*

DAIZEN: It would seem that the game is mine. I shall deliver the final blow.

TŌKICHI: Then let us proceed.

TAKEMOTO:

The enemy Tōkichi faces / is Oda Harunaga.

*(*DAIZEN *and* TŌKICHI *speak rhythmically, "riding"* [nori] *on the strings of the* TAKEMOTO *shamisen accompaniment.* GUNPEI *resumes his place on the veranda, and* YUKI *crosses upstage left, sitting with her back to the audience as the players alternate in placing their* go *pieces on the board.)*

DAIZEN: Having strengthened my rear guard, now for the offensive . . .

TŌKICHI: Maybe it comes, maybe it doesn't. Tread not on the plain of bamboo grass.

DAIZEN: What matter if I do? I'll take what I please.

TŌKICHI: Taking comes not easy—taking power, that is.

DAIZEN: I'll take the country. Greatness and grated yams, all will be mine.

TŌKICHI: To go from eating peasant yams to the delicacy of eels . . .

DAIZEN: A more rapid rise there's never been.

(TŌKICHI *lays his final stone.)*

KITŌDA *(Shrieking with surprise)*: Good gracious, heavens above, brother, you've lost!

TAKEMOTO:

Not pausing to gather the stones, / the short-tempered Daizen / seizes and overturns the board. / Tōkichi laughs in triumph.

(DAIZEN *looks up in shock and flips the board over, scattering the stones in every direction.* TŌKICHI *takes a step back.)*

TŌKICHI *(Laughing, then rapidly)*: Ha, ha. One should never play solely to win; the greatest secret is to play not to lose. My vice is to hate losing, not just at the *go* board but in debate and on the battlefield, too. If you want to play again, I'm ready any time. Tōkichi will play you as many times as you like.

TAKEMOTO:

Even when playing with a handicap / Tōkichi knows all the ruses.

(Still kneeling, TŌKICHI *moves closer to* DAIZEN, *finally striking a defiant* mie *to the sound of two* tsuke *beats.)*

DAIZEN: A most interesting metaphor. Your spirit is stronger than your appearance would suggest. Now, how should I test your wits? . . . Hmm.

TAKEMOTO:

Deep in thought / he takes hold of the nearby *go* bowl, / his target the well beneath the rocks / and with a splash he hurls it in.

(DAIZEN *gazes around him, finally catching sight of the* go *bowls. He seizes one of them and, with a shout, throws it into the well to right.)*

DAIZEN: Now, Tōkichi. *(Strikes a* mie.*)* That *go* bowl I threw into the well, is there any way to retrieve it without getting your hands wet? What say you?

TŌKICHI *(Looking toward the well for a moment, then bowing deeply)*: My lord.

TAKEMOTO *(With water pattern* [mizu no oto] *drumbeat accompaniment)*:

Without delay, / he steps down into the garden. / And with the metal drainpipe, / he directs the waterfall's / cascading flow into the well. / This sleight of hand devised in an instant.

(TŌKICHI *steps into the garden, slips on his wooden sandals, and approaches the waterfall but, holding his sleeve up to his face, is driven back by the force of the water. He strikes a strong* mie *in front of the well, gazing at the drainpipe.)*

Water flows over the well curb. / He takes the floating bowl / and upturns the waiting board.

(He rips a long drainpipe from the side of the pavilion and, standing upstage of the well with his right foot resting on the well curb, uses the pipe to raise the level of water in the well. The bowl floats to the surface. TŌKICHI *takes the* go *board, upturns it, and, inserting his closed fan into the bowl, places the bowl on the board. He tosses the fan away and strikes a* mie, *still holding the upturned board.)*

TŌKICHI: This *go* bowl within these four legs is the head of your enemy Harunaga readied for your inspection. A most auspicious beginning.

TAKEMOTO *(Alluding to the legend of a famous Chinese general)*:

Holding the board in one hand, / Chang Liang on the bridge of Kahi, / offering up the boot of Huang Shih Kung, / must have looked as valiant as this.

(In an impressive display of balance, TŌKICHI *strikes a famous* mie, *facing center with his legs apart and the* go *board supported on his left hand.)*

GUNPEI: Bravo! Bravo! My lord, we must celebrate with a banquet in his honor.

DAIZEN: A splendid display of quick thinking! *(*TŌKICHI *passes the* go *board to* DAIZEN *and kneels* below DAIZEN.*)* My congratulations. Now we can toast you as my strategist. Kitōda, Gunpei, lead the way.

KITŌDA: As you command. Come, Master Tōkichi.

TŌKICHI: Then, my lord, I trust we will meet later. *(Bows.)*

TAKEMOTO:

The schemes they both harbor / are deep as Daizen's chest. / Asking for a position, / Tōkichi departs to an inner room, / leaving his thoughts with the princess. / Daizen gazes after him.

*(*KITŌDA *exits through curtain to rear,* GUNPEI *exits left.* TŌKICHI *moves toward left, pauses in front of cherry tree, and looks back for an instant before leaving.* YUKI *moves to sit beside standing* DAIZEN.*)*

DAIZEN: Now it is your turn, Princess Yuki. Come.

TAKEMOTO:

He takes her hand, but . . .

DAIZEN: Wait. First, I will have you paint that picture of a dragon. What do you say? Eh?

TAKEMOTO:

He sidles up to her.

YUKI: Since I have agreed to submit, I cannot refuse this request. But without my family's secret scroll on dragon painting as a model, I will be unable to paint your dragon.

DAIZEN: Mmm. A reasonable excuse.

TAKEMOTO:

He nods, but then / his eyes stray to the nearby sword.

*(*DAIZEN *see the sword, upstage, and is suddenly struck by an idea.)*

DAIZEN: But, if I were to show you a model, then you could no longer refuse. Agreed?

YUKI: If I had a sample drawn by Sesshū, then I could paint it for you immediately. You possess such a sample?

DAIZEN: I do . . . I do.

TAKEMOTO:

Daizen accompanies / the princess into the garden, / unsheathing his sword. / When he shines its light upon the waterfall, / ah, how can it be? / Within the falling water, the shape of a dragon! / Filled with suspicion, Princess Yuki / is unable to look away. / As the sword reflects once more in the water, / the rainmaking Kurikara Dragon appears as though alive. / When hidden, the dragon vanishes. / The magical sword / held in Daizen's hand / makes even him shiver with fear.

(During the narration, DAIZEN *takes the sword, still encased in a brocade sheath, and enters the garden with* YUKI. YUKI *crosses to and kneels in front of the well, facing front. His back to her,* DAIZEN *unsheathes the sword. A supernatural drum pattern* [usudorodoro] *is beaten and builds to a violent water pattern as* DAIZEN *turns and approaches the waterfall, sword held high. A silver dragon—a prop suspended by a string—repeatedly appears within the waterfall, only to vanish when* DAIZEN *hides the sword. Turning,* YUKI *seems astonished at the sight. Finally,* DAIZEN *turns, still with the sword held high, and he and* YUKI *strike a* mie.*)*

Without a moment's hesitation / the princess readies herself. / Daizen tries to protect himself, but / she seizes the sword and gazes upon it.

(As DAIZEN *returns to the pavilion,* YUKI *rushes after him, seizes his sword arm, and examines the sword.)*

YUKI: There can be no doubt. This is the sword Kurikaramaru for which I have been searching. Daizen, you murdered my father. Your crime will not go unavenged! *(She seizes the sword and goes to attack* DAIZEN, *but, as the* tsuke *beat, he pushes her back and she kneels, back to the audience, at right.)*

DAIZEN: What is your proof that I murdered your father?

TAKEMOTO:

She doesn't let him finish.

YUKI *(Rising and speaking excitedly as she kneels again, facing front)*: This sword is my proof. It is a family heirloom, called Kurikaramaru, which my grandfather, Sesshū, brought back with him from China. When reflected in the morning sun, an image of the god Fudō appears, when turned toward the evening sun, the form of a dragon. It possesses the mystic power of both Kurikara and Fudō; hence, its name. The sword was handed down to my father, Sesson, but he was murdered beneath Kanchogataki Waterfall on Mount Jigaji in Kawachi, and the sword was lost. *(Weeps.)* I hid the existence of the sword and spread a rumor that I was searching for our secret scrolls, but my only aim was to find this sword. Just now you have shown me the power of this sword, so there can be no doubt that you are my father's murderer. Now we shall have a true reckoning.

TAKEMOTO:

She lunges at him, / but he seizes back the sword.

*(*YUKI *rises and, as the* tsuke *beat, attacks* DAIZEN *with the sword, but he quickly disarms her and throws her to the ground, holding her down with his foot.)*

DAIZEN: Stop waving that thing around! In my desire for power, I sought out three magical instruments. On my quest, I happened to go to the Kanchogataki Waterfall, and there I saw an old man conjuring up the shape of a dragon in the water with this masterpiece of a sword. I demanded that he give it to me, but the old codger refused. As we were all alone, I killed him. That old man was your father, Sesson. I laugh at how you've suffered all these years not knowing who the murderer was. Now I, Daizen, hunger not for power alone but for love, too. How dare you call me your enemy, you little trollop.

(During his speech, the gloating DAIZEN *tramples* YUKI *underfoot.)*

TAKEMOTO:

As he tramples and kicks her, / Kitōda rushes out, / and as he is binding her, / there appears Konoshita Tōkichi.

(Enter KITŌDA *rapidly from the upstage curtain, carrying a rope. As the* tsuke *beat, he subdues* YUKI *and is about to tie her up when* TŌKICHI *enters from left.)*

TŌKICHI: What's this? Release her.

TAKEMOTO:

As his hand goes to draw his sword, / Daizen says . . .

DAIZEN: Wait, Tōkichi. I have my reasons. Do not interfere. *(Calling out.)* Gunpei, come.

GUNPEI *(From offstage)*: My lord.

TAKEMOTO:

He replies and then enters.

GUNPEI *(Enters from left and kneels)*: What is your command?

DAIZEN: Take that wretch Naonobu, whom I placed in your care, and lead him to Mount Funaoka. When the bell strikes five, cut him to ribbons!

GUNPEI: Got it, boss. But I should take Princess Yuki with me, too.

DAIZEN: You will not.

GUNPEI: But why?

DAIZEN: An ignorant lout like you could never understand. Look at her, all tied up. She'll be like a peach blossom bedraggled by the rain. Tie her to that cherry tree. Her punishment shall come after I have enjoyed watching her suffer.

GUNPEI: Understood, boss.

TAKEMOTO:

He hurries away. / Daizen does not look up; / a hawk intent on its kill. *(GUNPEI exits to left. DAIZEN and KITŌDA return to the main pavilion, where KITŌDA kneels at right of DAIZEN, who remains standing.)*

DAIZEN: Kitōda, I entrust this sword to you. Keep it safe. And ensure that Keijuin is securely guarded.

KITŌDA *(Taking sword)*: As you command, brother.

DAIZEN: Tōkichi, from now onward, you are my retainer. If Oda paid you one thousand pieces of silver, I will pay you two thousand, or ten thousand. Now, bind that honey trap, Princess Yuki. Make her suffer.

TŌKICHI: Yes, my lord. *(Bows.)*

TAKEMOTO:

Saying "Yes, my lord," / he drags her to her feet / and binds her to the cherry trunk. / Master and retainer retreat together.

(TŌKICHI binds the distraught YUKI to the trunk of the cherry tree, left, leaving her enough rope to move several paces. She approaches him, but he pushes her away. DAIZEN and KITŌDA exit to rear. Looking around to check that he is unobserved, TŌKICHI gazes upward toward the second story of the pavilion, then at YUKI, and finally exits left. The TAKEMOTO platform revolves to reveal a new narrator and shamisen player. The large bell tolls once. The new narrator speaks, slowly and emotionally.)

Retreating inside, / the vespers bell, too, / shrouded in mist, / helpless and alone. / Kano Nosuke Naonobu, / his end due at the toll of five, / is driven ahead by Gunpei, / his steps those of the sheep to slaughter, / unwillingly lingering. / She is face to face with her husband.

(YUKI weeps, her whole body trembling. The bell tolls several times. Finally she rises and moves as far right as her rope will allow. NAONOBU enters weakly from left, hands tied behind him, driven on by GUNPEI and two SOLDIERS, one of whom holds a rope tied around NAONOBU's shoulders. NAONOBU is the archetypal young lover, sensitive and refined, in a simple, black kimono, his face painted white. He looks drawn from his long confinement. At last, YUKI turns and the two are face to face.)

YUKI: Ah! My husband.

NAONOBU: Yuki . . .

TAKEMOTO:

They try to embrace, / but the soldier pulls him back, / the rope held tight. / All they can do is gaze, / voices choked with tears.

NAONOBU *(Tearfully)*: I never imagined that we would come to this. All I wished to do was to rescue my mistress and find my father-in-law's murderer. How it pains me that I must die having achieved neither. I beg you to look after our lady with whatever remains of your life.

YUKI *(Weeping)*: It is I who should be begging you. Though you are innocent, they will put you to the sword. What shall I do without you? All I want is to go with you, to die with you.

TAKEMOTO:

"All I want to do is to go with you, / to die with you." / As she cries out, / Gunpei sneers.

(She struggles several steps nearer to NAONOBU *but again collapses in floods of tears.)*

GUNPEI: You would do better to stop this useless sniveling and obey Lord Daizen's commands. Guards, take him away!

SOLDIERS: Prisoner, move it out.

NAONOBU *(Gazing emotionally at her)*: Yuki, farewell . . .

TAKEMOTO:

Farewell, farewell, / his words of goodbye.

(The two lovers strain at their bonds, gazing into each others' eyes.)

This their final parting in this world, / in their hearts, evening falls / as he is hurriedly dragged away.

(The lovers pause, gazing at each other. NAONOBU *is dragged right by the* SOLDIERS, GUNPEI *bringing up the rear.* YUKI *stands and tries to catch a final glimpse of her beloved, but* GUNPEI *jabs her with his elbow and she falls.)*

SOLDIERS: Move it along!

*(*NAONOBU, SOLDIERS, *and* GUNPEI *exit along the* hanamichi *to the slow and mournful beating of the large drum. With* YUKI *still lying center, the drumbeats increase to a climax. A second shamisen player joins the* TAKEMOTO *musicians. Cherry blossom petals slowly begin falling along the width of the stage. The narration becomes slow and heavily ornamented.)*

TAKEMOTO:

Pitiful Princess Yuki lies helpless / within the falling petals.

(Distraught, YUKI *slowly rises to her knees, trembling. Gradually the petals begin to swirl down more thickly.)*

Bound, unable to even gaze after him, / unable to move, she stretches her body / for one final glimpse. / The beckoning wind brings with it / the tolling of a bell from a country temple, / echoing within the falling cherry blossoms.

(She tries to run after NAONOBU *but is pulled back. Desperate for one last glimpse, she climbs the steps of the pavilion. The petals are now falling so thickly*

Princess Yuki (Nakamura Jakuemon IV) draws images of mice in the fallen cherry blossom petals. By magic, two white mice appear. Manipulated by stage assistants in black, they gnaw through the ropes binding Princess Yuki and free her. (Umemura Yutaka, Engeki Shuppansha)

that she almost vanishes in a blizzard of pink. She tries and fails to loosen the rope, as the bell tolls again.)

Like the branches, her body droops / as ceaselessly flow her tears. / But at last, she opens her eyes.

(Center, YUKI *sinks to her knees amid the fallen petals, weeping in desperation and grief. Gradually the petals cease to fall.)*

YUKI *(The bell tolls)*: Is that evening, or is it still the bell for dusk? There were so many things I wanted to say to you, my husband, while you still lived. *(The bell tolls.)* Naonobu, my father's murderer was Daizen. I so wanted you to know that. *(Another toll of the bell.)* Ah, if only I could undo this rope.

TAKEMOTO:

Trying to undo it, / the more she struggles, the tighter it binds, / bringing pain upon herself / like those trying to rid themselves of passions.

YUKI: Daizen, you demon, you serpent.

TAKEMOTO:

"Does justice exist? / No matter what he does to me . . ."

(She enters the pavilion and glares at the inner curtain.)

YUKI: You shall not go unpunished!

TAKEMOTO:

Tears of frustration stream down, / stream down, / like the dew strewing jewels.

YUKI *(Kneeling at center, before the pavilion)*: Ah, I remember. Grandfather Sesshū, when once a monk at Hōfuku Temple neglected his studies, absorbed in painting, like this his teacher tied him to a pillar in the main hall as punishment. From morning till night, he suffered, shedding tears. So he drew a mouse on the floor with his foot until it chewed through his ropes and set him free.

TAKEMOTO:

"His blood flows in my veins, too. / Though I have not his talent, / I lack nothing in determination." / With her feet, she gathers blossoms, / gathers them, rakes them together. / Lacking a brush, the tips of her toes will serve, / for ink, the pale petals of her tears. / Drawing freely with her foot, / her ardor enters the picture.

(With new energy, YUKI *stands and rakes the petals into piles with her feet and the hem of her robes. Intently, she draws the image of a mouse in the petals with the tips of her toes. Finished, she kneels again in despair as a* dorodoro *pattern sounds softly, signifying the supernatural.)*

Is that rustling movement just the wind? / Amongst the petals, two white-haired mice / suddenly appear. / At the hempen rope, / the magical mice gnaw, bite, / and chew, and, at last, / the rope snaps.

(Manipulated by two black-clad STAGE ASSISTANTS [kurogo] *using long poles* [sashigane], *two white mice appear amid the petals. They gnaw at* YUKI*'s bonds. The rope snaps and she falls forward in surprise. Rubbing her bruised hands, she notices the mice.)*

YUKI *(Standing)*: How happy I am! The ropes have broken. The mice that I drew with my foot must have chewed through them.

TAKEMOTO:

She searches the fallen blossoms for the mice. / A sudden gust, and with the petals, they scatter and vanish. / The princess wakes from her dream.

(She searches with her sleeves draped over her palms. As a drum signals the wind, the STAGE ASSISTANTS *raise their poles and the bodies of the mice split in half, showering* YUKI *with more cherry blossoms. On her knees in joy, she strikes a gorgeous* mie *surrounded by the slowly spiraling petals.)*

She calms her beating heart, / so overjoyed is she that / her feet touch not the ground. / Just then, from behind, comes running / Matsunaga Kitōda.

*(*KITŌDA *appears from behind the rear curtains, still carrying the magical sword. He stands to the right, arms outstretched, blocking* YUKI*'s path.)*

KITŌDA: Where do you think you're going, you stubborn slut? Just try and get past me.

TAKEMOTO:

He grabs her by the scruff of the neck, / pulling her back. / "Let go of me!" / But as they struggle fiercely, / a swiftly thrown dagger. / And Kitōda's life is at an end.

(A brief choreographed fight scene [tachimawari] *ensues. Just as* KITŌDA *manages to subdue* YUKI, *there is a shout from offstage and a dagger strikes him in the throat. He collapses in front of the well.)*

She is startled, / and as she looks about . . .

TŌKICHI *(From offstage)*: Princess Yuki. Wait.

TAKEMOTO:

A voice calls out. / Mashiba Hisayoshi, Lord of Chikuzen, / enters with dignity.

(The rear curtains are pulled open to reveal TŌKICHI, *now in his true identity as* MASHIBA HISAYOSHI. *He wears armor and is flanked by two* SOLDIERS.*)*

YUKI: Tōkichi, why are you dressed like that?

HISAYOSHI *(Sitting on a camp stool)*: I will reveal all. This is the sword Kurikaramaru for which you have been searching, the sword that your grandfather Sesshū received in China from the Ming emperor.

TAKEMOTO:

Taking the sword from the corpse, / he passes it to her for examination.

*(*HISAYOSHI *signals one of his soldiers, who retrieves the sword. Exit* SOLDIERS. STAGE ASSISTANTS *hold up a small black curtain to disguise* KITŌDA*'s exit.)*

YUKI: This is indeed Kurikaramaru. Now I have the sword. Next is my father's murderer, Matsunaga Daizen.

TAKEMOTO:

As she rises, / Hisayoshi says . . .

HISAYOSHI: Wait, Princess Yuki. I well understand your haste, but Daizen is not just your father's murderer, he is an enemy of the state. I have given orders to Gunpei, so you need not worry about the safety of your husband, Naonobu. Hurry now to Mount Funaoka to tell him of what has occurred here. Leave the rescue of Lady Keijuin to me.

YUKI: I will. I leave my mistress in your keeping.

TAKEMOTO:

The sword at her waist, / she lifts up her hems and, / her skirts swirling up a wave of petals, / rushes off toward Mount Funaoka.

(She pauses at shichisan. *Rediscovering her femininity,* YUKI *pulls the sword slightly from its sheath and uses it as a mirror to retouch her hairstyle. She wraps the sword in its brocade cover and moves daintily off to drum,* tsuke, *and shamisen accompaniment.)*

The evening moon already on the wane, / as are the fortunes of Daizen. / A drunken slumber, the perfect chance. / Hisayoshi hesitates, / and just at that moment . . . "Now I've got you" . . . comes the attack. / He breaks free of the hold / and with a blow sends the man tumbling. / Another throw leaves a man / standing on his head.

*(*HISAYOSHI *is attacked by six of* DAIZEN*'s* SOLDIERS. *In stylized combat, he makes short work of them, without having to draw his sword.* HISAYOSHI *strikes a* mie *on the* hanamichi *with his foot on a* SOLDIER*'s back. He crosses to left, moving unconcernedly past his attackers, and strikes another* mie. *Having disposed of the attackers, who exit left, he strikes one more* mie, *then crosses to the cherry tree right of the pavilion, ties on his sword so that it is at his back, and climbs the cherry tree rear of the pavilion to reach the second-story balcony of the pavilion. In a breathtaking piece of stagecraft, the entire pavilion is lowered on the stage lift* [seri] *to show the upper room, still hidden by a striped curtain matching the one below.)*

HISAYOSHI: Lady Keijuin, Lady Keijuin.

(He kneels and lifts the curtain. KEIJUIN, *within, is dressed as a nun in a purple robe and white hood. She prays in front of burning incense, a rosary clasped in her hands.)*

TAKEMOTO:

Keijuin is engaged in contemplation. / She sits still, not looking up. / In her presence, Hisayoshi bows his head.

HISAYOSHI *(A bell tolls)*: I am Mashiba Hisayoshi, a retainer of Oda Harunaga. I have come to rescue you. Do not be alarmed.

TAKEMOTO:

At his words, she ceases her chanting.

KEIJUIN: So Harunaga has sent for me. You have done well to come this far, and I am well pleased. However, the sutras teach us not to begrudge our lives. I have already resigned myself to death, so I beg you to leave me here that I may gain virtue in the next world.

TAKEMOTO:

She closes her eyes, clasps her hands, / and bows her head once more.

HISAYOSHI: Your words are unexpected. My soldiers have surrounded this pavilion, and I must summon them. I will signal that you are safe.

TAKEMOTO:

He lights the signal flare hanging at his waist. / Drums echo in reply.

HISAYOSHI: So, Lady Keijuin, farewell.

KEIJUIN: Farewell, Hisayoshi.

HISAYOSHI: We will meet again.

(He kneels beside KEIJUIN, *and the curtain closes on them. Drums, flute, and bell. The entire pavilion again rises on the lift, carrying* HISAYOSHI *and* KEIJUIN *out of sight. Drumbeats increase in force; shouts and sounds of battle. On the main stage, ten* SOLDIERS *dressed in colorful, flower-patterned fighting costumes* [hana

yoten] *and carrying spears enter from the lower curtain and run to the* hanamichi *pursued by* DAIZEN, *now dressed in a white kimono and carrying a halberd. Short combat during which* DAIZEN *forces the* SOLDIERS *to flee down the* hanamichi. *At* shichisan, *he strikes a vigorous* mie *holding his halberd high.)*

HISAYOSHI *(From offstage)*: Matsunaga Daizen, hold. Mashiba Hisayoshi, Lord of Chikuzen . . .

GUNPEI *(His voice echoes from behind the* hanamichi *curtain)*: And Satō Toranosuke Masakiyo . . .

HISAYOSHI: Now reveal . . .

BOTH: Themselves to you.

DAIZEN *(Vigorously)*: How dare you!

(To rapid offstage drum and flute accompaniment [hayabue], GUNPEI, *now revealed to be* HISAYOSHI*'s retainer* SATŌ TORANOSUKE MASAKIYO, *rushes in from the rear of the* hanamichi. *His transformation into* MASAKIYO *is indicated by a costume change: his hair now hangs loose, he wears a fringed gold apron over a gold kimono with a bullseye pattern, and he carries a spear. He forces* DAIZEN *to return to center.* HISAYOSHI *appears from the rear curtain of the pavilion, accompanied by four* SOLDIERS.*)*

DAIZEN: Tōkichi, wait.

HISAYOSHI: Daizen, you fool. *(Sits on camp stool.)* You killed Lord Yoshiteru, and, what's more, you even took Lady Keijuin hostage. I knew that you had hidden yourself here at the Golden Pavilion and were biding your time, so my plans were plots within counterplots.

MASAKIYO *(Sitting)*: I, Satō Toranosuke Masakiyo, became your retainer and infiltrated the pavilion. We have rescued Lady Keijuin and have you surrounded in every direction.

HISAYOSHI: There is nothing you can do, Daizen. Show some dignity and prepare to die.

DAIZEN: Your plan was cunning. I suspected something was amiss but had no idea of Gunpei's identity until this moment. Since Lady Keijuin is rescued, it would seem that my plans are ruined. But I will leave a mountain of corpses before I am taken.

MASAKIYO: No matter how well you fight, we have you surrounded so completely that there is no chance of you getting away, Daizen. I'll have your head now. *(Strikes a* mie.*)*

HISAYOSHI: Masakiyo, hold. *(To* DAIZEN.*)* It would be an easy matter to take your life here. But since we have rescued Lady Keijuin, we shall let Lord Yoshiaki take to the field and attack you at your castle in Shigi.

DAIZEN: A valiant proposal. I will persuade the priests of Mount Hie to take my side, and we shall give you a battle worthy of the name.

Matsunaga Daizen Hisahide (Jitsukawa Enjaku III), center, standing on a three-step platform and holding a halberd aloft, poses in a powerful scene-ending tableau *(hippari mie)* with Sogō Gunpei (Matsumoto Kōshirō VIII, later Matsumoto Hakuō), left, threatening him with a lance, and Mashiba Hisayoshi (Nakamura Kanzaburō XVII), right, standing defiantly. (Umemura Yutaka, Engeki Shuppansha)

HISAYOSHI: We shall meet again on the battlefield.
DAIZEN: Until then . . .
HISAYOSHI: Matsunaga Daizen . . .
DAIZEN: Mashiba Hisayoshi . . .
ALL: Farewell.

(DAIZEN *mounts a three-step red dais that* STAGE ASSISTANTS *have placed center. He solemnly traces the Chinese characters for "full house"* [ōiri] *with his halberd in the air, as a symbol of the play's success. With* DAIZEN *holding his halberd horizontally over his head,* MASAKIYO *on one knee, to the right and* HISAYOSHI, *standing, at the left, they strike a tableau* [hippari mie] *as the curtain is run closed to music and accelerating* ki *clacks.)*

One-panel woodblock print by Utagawa Kunimasa III (1848–1920). Shintomi-za, Tokyo, May 1886. "Ichikawa Danjūrō" IX is identified as the actor of two roles, the goddess "Benten" and the "Heron Maiden" (shown here). Danjūrō also played a third role, the Maiden's lover, Yasuna. The inscription reads: "Three sections, moon, snow, and flower, with *nagauta, takemoto, kiyomoto,* and *tokiwazu* onstage musical ensembles" (upper right). (Tsubouchi Memorial Theatre Museum of Waseda University)

The Heron Maiden

Sagi Musume

Anonymous (text); Kineya Tadajirō (music)

TRANSLATED BY CODY M. POULTON

1762 ICHIMURA-ZA, EDO

The Heron Maiden

INTRODUCTION

The Heron Maiden was first performed by Segawa Kikunojō II (1741–1773), one of the leading actors of female roles *(onnagata)* of his time, as part of a dance finale called *The Chirping of Tiny Birds in the Willows* (Yanagi ni Hina Shochō no Saezuri); it featured the first use of the revolving stage *(mawari butai)* for a dance play. The piece quickly became a classic of the dance play *(shosagoto)* repertoire, one that continues to challenge every important *onnagata.* In recent years, the dance has become a showpiece for the talents of Bandō Tamasaburō V (b. 1950) and is an excellent vehicle for the display of this talented *onnagata*'s eerie eroticism. Music is provided by a full onstage *nagauta* ensemble consisting of eight to ten singers, an equal number of shamisen players, four or five drum players, and a flutist.

This play is the earliest extant example of a "transformation piece" *(henge-mono),* a spectacular type of dance that originated during the Genroku period (1688–1704). Its chief aim is to demonstrate, through a series of quick changes *(hayagawari),* a striking variety of costumes and identities. Until the end of the eighteenth century, transformation pieces were exclusively performed by *onnagata* to the accompaniment of a ballad in *nagauta* style. With the introduction of special effects *(keren)* and virtuoso acting in the early nineteenth century, actors of leading male roles *(tachiyaku)* also began performing transformation pieces. These later dances featured a wide variety of personalities, both male and female, young and old. Early pieces generally presented no more than four or five changes, but later on, as many as twelve were performed. Two types of classical changes are used: *hikinuki* and *bukkaeri.* Each involves the removal by a stage assistant of basting threads holding the costume together. At the proper moment, the assistant suddenly whisks off the outer costume to reveal another one underneath, all of this being done before the audience's eyes as the actor performs. In *hikinuki* ("pulling out"), the entire outer kimono is removed, while in *bukkaeri* ("sudden change"), only the upper portion drops to cover the lower part of the original costume. A stage assistant may hold the disassembled fabric up around the actor as he strikes a pose framed by the new colors revealed. New dance pieces were often composed for styles of kabuki music, such as *tokiwazu,* created around 1739, and *kiyomoto,* founded in 1814.

Although the chief purpose of a transformation piece may be to show off the lead dancer's skill through the dazzling display of sudden costume changes, an early piece such as *Heron Maiden* also reveals that—as in many *nō* plays—the spectacle of transformation expresses an underlying theme of metamorphosis. *The Heron Maiden* portrays the resentful spirit *(onryō)* of a heron, who, having assumed the form of a young woman, falls in unrequited love with a man. Five costume changes take place as, before our eyes, we see the heron first take the form of an innocent young girl and then an older and more experienced woman. In the end, she is wounded, and, having resumed the form of a heron, dances out her death throes. In short, this play depicts different facets of a woman's psyche, as well as a kind of montage of both human and avian identity.

The composition of the dance sequences in *Heron Maiden* closely follows the six-part structure of *nagauta* music, which provides a considerable variety of musical and emotive effects. It begins with a quiet "prelude" *(oki)* and proceeds to the entrance of the dancer, during which the full chorus sings a "travel scene" *(michiyuki)*. Both dance and music become more lyrical in the "lament" *(kudoki)*, which is typically a vocal solo accompanied by one shamisen. The music grows swifter and brighter in the fourth section, called a "drum chorus" *(taikoji)* or sometimes a "dance section" *(odoriji)*. The music continues to increase its pace and complexity in the "scattering" *(chirashi)* section, in which the music seems to compete with the dancer, culminating in a feverish climax. The pace and tone return to a solemn lyricism in the "finale" *(dangiri)*.

Performance variations exist for most sequences in the work. For example, depending on the leading actor's preference, the musical prelude to the dance can be performed while the curtains are still closed, in the dark, or with the lights up. Frequently, the dancer is already onstage, but in past productions an elevator trap would likely have raised him into view on a dais. The interlude during the lament is an opportunity for the *nagauta* orchestra to display its skill; the quick change during this section is frequently performed onstage (as in this translation), but sometimes the actor will exit and execute the change offstage. The dance during the drum chorus is usually performed with a single umbrella, but Nakamura Ganjirō III (b. 1931) has revived an older version in which he dances with two umbrellas. In the intermediate sections of the dance, costume changes will reveal kimono that vary in color and pattern from actor to actor. However, the lead actor always wears a white kimono at the beginning and the end to signify the heron's identity. The major innovation in performance business *(kata)* for this dance occurs in its ending. In early *kata,* the dancer struck a defiant pose, then either disappeared via a trap or remained standing while the curtain was run closed. Some performers today prefer this conclusion, but under the influence of Russian ballerina Anna Pavlova's performance earlier this century of "The Dying Swan," which strongly influenced Onoe Kikugorō VI (1885–1949), a more pathetic depiction of the heron's death became popular. The stage notes here, based on Tamasaburō's performance, reflect this modern interpretation.

The play's meaning is clear enough even without an understanding of the *nagauta* ballad, but the lyrics are beautiful. Typical of much classical Japanese verse, the lyrics are highly elliptical and rife with phonetic effects and associations; a translation into English can only hope to give an approximate sense of these poetic effects. Like the linked verse *(renga)* of *nō* drama, a slim narrative is told almost exclusively in a telescopic flow of images, most of which have to do with water or some other form of moisture: clouds, snow, dewdrops, marshes, and, inevitably, tears. These are linked to cherry blossoms as well as to the maiden's umbrella, the latter also serving to symbolize the wheel of karma, driving the dancer into the jaws of hell in retribution for her wrongful attachment to a man. One can only pity this spirit and feel that her fate was excessively cruel. Perhaps for this reason, the lyrics for the "torture segment" *(seme no dan),* depicting the heron-maiden's torture in hell, are usually greatly abbreviated in performance. Throughout the play, its anonymous author has skillfully strung images together, creating an atmosphere that is intensely visual, almost even palpable, accentuating not only the erotic qualities of moisture, the airiness, and the evanescence of snow and blossoms but also the burden of snow and sorrow. This work succeeds in achieving the same integrity of word, sound, and image that we see in the best *kuse* sequences in *nō* plays. Indeed the music, with its eerie flute, drums, and calls *(kakegoe),* pays tribute to *nō*. For this translation, I have used the 1892 text of the production starring Ichikawa Danjūrō IX (1838–1903) at the Kabuki-za in Tokyo, published in Toita Yasuji et al., eds. *Kabuki Kessakushū,* Vol. 19.

CHARACTERS

HERON MAIDEN, *spirit of a heron who assumes the form of a woman*

STAGE ASSISTANT, *a formally dressed* kōken

NAGAUTA, *chorus of singers accompanied by an orchestra of shamisen, drums, and flute*

(Before the curtain opens, the beat of a stick drum and the eerie sound of a flute [netoribue] *are heard from offstage* [geza], *signifying the presence of a spirit or*

The spirit of the Heron Maiden (Nakamura Jakuemon IV) appears in human form carrying an umbrella over her shoulder, her head modestly covered. (Umemura Yutaka, Engeki Shuppansha)

apparition. The beat of a hand drum [kotsuzumi] *joins the prelude* [oki] *of the formal musical composition that is sung and played from behind the curtain: "Lost in you, my love is a night's moon / drowned in clouds of delusion." The curtain opens to reveal the* NAGAUTA *singers and instrumentalists seated on a dais at right. To right and left stand "wave boards"* [namiita], *screens painted with a marsh scene, and stakes to indicate the water's edge. A willow tree is planted at right. The* HERON MAIDEN *stands at center with her back to the audience, wearing a plain, white, long-sleeved kimono* [furisode] *with a black satin obi. Her hair, dressed in a style popular among young women, is covered in a white hood of glossy silk. She wears black lacquered clogs and holds an umbrella covered with flakes of snow. The chorus begins the travel scene* [michiyuki] *section of the music and of the play.)*

NAGAUTA:

Though the gales of love blow seeds of dissent / and burden my umbrella with snow, / this growing passion's but the slightest of flakes / vanishing on this vain journey!

(Slowly, the MAIDEN *turns around to face the audience, then closes her umbrella. A soloist sings.)*

The darkness of my heart, deep in thoughts of you, / so wretched this evening. / A heron drenched in drifting snow, / so lovely in her solitude!

(The MAIDEN *swirls, spreads her arms, lays down the umbrella, and kneels. She stands and raises one leg at a time, miming birdlike steps. Presently, to a quiet interlude of hand drum and drummer's calls, she removes her hood. Eerie flute music joins the shamisen to support the solo singer.)*

The thin course of this vagrant heart / is a single, trickling stream of droplets. / The white heron knows naught but bitterness: / at home in water, her dripping steps / only vanish like the dew.

(The MAIDEN *mimes with her sleeves the flapping of wings. She removes her hairpin, letting her hair fall, then mimes the delicate footsteps of the heron walking through the marsh. Her gestures simultaneously mime the actions of a bird and express a woman's regrets. Flute, hand drum, and shamisen accompany her first quick change of costume* [hikinuki], *which reveals underneath a beautiful kimono of red silk crepe with a collar of black satin. The dancer has now assumed the identity of a young townswoman, and the pace of the music becomes more sprightly.)*

When even tears have dried, / sleeves stay damp in moonlight, / that talk we had the night we met forgotten.

(The MAIDEN *kneels, clasps her hands in prayer, stands, then kneels again. The music's pace slows, becoming more reflective. A soloist sings the young girl's lament* [kudoki] *for a lost lover.)*

After a quick change of kimono *(hayagawari)*, the spirit of the Heron Maiden (Ichikawa Monnosuke VII) dances sensuously in human form. (Tsubouchi Memorial Theatre Museum of Waseda University)

Oh, god who joins two lovers, / you have stolen away a happiness / that shames me with so many hues and scents.

(Holding a scarlet hand towel [tenugui], *she mimes tying—that is, joining—lovers. The singing stops and instrumental music continues as she moves behind the umbrella to prepare for a rapid onstage costume change* [bukkaeri]*: the outer kimono top is peeled off to reveal an inner blue kimono with a pattern of flakes of snow and flowing water. She drapes the scarlet hand towel across her shoulders. The full chorus sings.)*

Harder than drawing salt on Suma beach / is catching my lord's heart. / Believe me when I tell the truth!

(The MAIDEN *mimes the actions of drawing saltwater. A soloist now sings, accompanied by a bamboo flute.)*

Harder than plaiting folds in satin *hakama* / is soothing my master's breast. / Believe me, I would truly tell the truth.

(The MAIDEN *dances using gathering, untying, and sweeping movements. She takes one end of the towel in her teeth, expressing her jealousy and frustration. The key of the music changes, becoming more solemn and melancholy.)*

The white heron's wings scattering snow, / though like a scene of swirling blossoms, / alas, they would blow away these flurried thoughts! / They will blow away the snow! / A heart worn down by love, / laden with a blizzard of blossoms, / but this umbrella, these sleeves, are loath to brush them away.

(The MAIDEN *opens the umbrella. Then, kneeling behind it, she undergoes her fourth quick onstage change, this one using the thread-pulling* [hikinuki] *method, revealing a pink kimono with a pattern of cherry blossoms. Once again, she takes up the umbrella and holds it aloft, proceeding to dance a catalogue of umbrellas* [kasa zukushi]. *So begins the drum song* [taikoji]. *The music becomes faster and brighter. And the full chorus sings.)*

Oh umbrella, / if I must open you, / give me shade against the blazing sun! That's the way! / If I really must take shelter under you, / let's go to Yoshino and see the cherries, / a parasol for fragrant flowers. Yes, that's the way! / This parasol's a turning, turning wheel / of karma, moon, and sun. / That's the way, yes, that's the way!

(The MAIDEN *tosses her umbrella in the air, catches it, and poses* [kimari].*)*

That's the way romance begins: / I'd be with him, but I cannot, / and the keen blades of jealous talk, / they drive me from this world / to the very Mount of Swords.

(The MAIDEN *dances to a sprightly rhythm, marking the beginning of the next dance section, the scattering* [chirashi]. *The tempo becomes swifter, introducing the torture sequence portraying the heron maiden's sufferings in hell. She takes the corner of the scarlet towel in her teeth, expressing frustration and jealousy. With the*

Stage assistants drop the costume top of the Heron Maiden (Ichikawa Monnosuke VII) to reveal a white and pink kimono with feather designs beneath it, transforming the figure into its real bird form. (Tsubouchi Memorial Theatre Museum of Waseda University)

aid of a formally dressed STAGE ASSISTANT [kōken], *the dancer performs a* hikinuki *costume change, instantly revealing a scarlet underkimono beneath the removed layer. Then, this layer, too, is removed in a flash, through* hikinuki, *to reveal a white kimono decorated with a feather pattern. A red slash across the shoulder signifies that the* HERON MAIDEN *has suffered a mortal wound. She loosens her long hair and poses on her knees, facing away from the audience. She arches her torso backward in a "prawn-shaped pose"* [ebizori no mie]. *To the swift accompaniment of stick and hand drums and shamisen, the chorus continues to sing.)*

Under a sheltering tree, I am afraid! / My eyes are filled with scenes of hell: / the judge of sins, King Enma, / verily I see his iron stave.

(The thin, trailing branches of the willow tree are likened to the iron staves of Enma and his demons. The MAIDEN*'s movements become more violent and painful. The snow falls heavily. She swoons, then collapses. When she rises, her movements are once again birdlike. The chorus continues to the accompaniment of flute and hand and stick drums.)*

A hell for those who've taken life, / or a multitude of cries and screams; / the incessant beating of titans' drums. / Hell's minions swarm on me from every side, / wielding staves and gnashing teeth.

(The MAIDEN *mimes her suffering and physical torture, culminating in a final quick costume change* [bukkaeri] *in which the kimono top is suddenly dropped, revealing a pattern of red and orange flames on its underside.)*

Again and again, / all day and night, / 'round and 'round they pursue me now, / my body squeezed and crushed beneath. / Have mercy on this wretched flesh.

(As she mimes her sufferings in hell, the MAIDEN *gradually loses strength and swoons. She falls prostrate. A temple bell tolls, followed by a ghostly flute melody* [netori]. *Shamisen quietly play "snow melody"* [yuki aikata], *marking the musical finale of the piece* [dangiri]. *The* MAIDEN *dies. The curtain is run closed to* ki *clacks as the bird-woman lies alone on stage.)*

Two-panel woodblock print by Utagawa Toyokuni III (1786–1864). Nakamura-za, Edo, third month 1850. "Princess Yaegaki" (Ichikawa Kodanji IV) flies in the air carrying the magic helmet. Ichikawa Danjūrō VIII is pictured in his two contrasting roles: Yaegaki's handsome betrothed, "Takeda Katsuyori," hand on sword, and "Shirasuga Rokurō," wearing bold red makeup *(kumadori)*, a warrior in the service of villain Nagao Kenshin. (Tsubouchi Memorial Theatre Museum of Waseda University)

Japan's Twenty-Four Paragons of Filial Piety

Honchō Nijūshikō

Chikamatsu Hanji, Miyoshi Shōraku, Takeda Inaba,
Takemoto Saburōbei, and Takeda Hanbei

TRANSLATED BY PAUL M. GRIFFITH

THE TEN TYPES OF INCENSE

Jusshukō no Ba

FOX FIRES IN THE INNER GARDEN

Okuniwa, Kitsunebi no Ba

1766 TAKEMOTO-ZA, OSAKA

Japan's Twenty-Four Paragons of Filial Piety

INTRODUCTION

Japan's Twenty-Four Paragons of Filial Piety was first performed as kabuki in the fifth month of 1766 at the Naka no Shibai in Osaka. It was based on the puppet play written by Chikamatsu Hanji (1725–1783) and others that was staged a few months before at Osaka's Takemoto-za. Since then, it has had numerous revivals on both puppet and kabuki stages. The work is regarded as a classic of the history play genre *(jidaimono)* not only for its strong narrative structure but also, in a plot filled with intrigue and suspense, for its pure theatricality. The two scenes from Act IV translated here are the ones most often performed in kabuki today.

Set in the sixteenth century in an age of turbulent warfare, the play takes as its theme the fierce rivalry between the Takeda and Uesugi clans, led by the great warlords Takeda Shingen and Uesugi Kenshin (here called Nagao Kenshin). As the play opens, the Takeda and Uesugi clans are feuding over possession of the Suwa Hosshō helmet, a great treasure bestowed on the Takeda clan by the god of Suwa himself. The Japanese term *"hosshō"* refers to the unchanging essence of all universal matter, the Buddha's absolute reality. This helmet was lent to the Uesugi clan and they now refuse to give it back. In order to make peace, it is suggested that the two families be united by marriage. Thus Shingen's son, Katsuyori, is betrothed to Kenshin's daughter, Princess Yaegaki.

At this point, the shogun, Ashikaga Yoshiharu, is assassinated. As both Shingen and Kenshin were supposed to be attending the shogun but were absent, blame falls upon them for neglect of duty, and in order to allay suspicions, they promise to find the culprit. If, after three years they fail to do so, they will present the heads of their only sons in apology. Three years pass and no culprit is found. Katsuyori's head is now forfeit, but, instead of sacrificing him, Shingen substitutes the head of another young man who looks very much like his son. Shingen then orders that Katsuyori disguise himself as a humble servant called Minosaku and that he go to Kenshin's mansion to steal back the sacred Suwa Hosshō helmet. He is to go with a lady-in-waiting named Nureginu. She, in fact, was the lover of the deceased young man substituted for Katsuyori and, though her loyalty to the Takeda clan is beyond question, her genuine grief at the loss of her lover, and her mixed emotions in having to accompany one whom her lover so resembles, make her the most poignant character in the play. Her suffering is made all the worse because her own father, whom she has now rejected, is, in fact, the shogun's assassin and is therefore the original reason for her lover's substitution and death.

When the "Incense" scene opens, Minosaku and Nureginu have successfully entered Kenshin's mansion, he as a gardener and she as lady-in-waiting to Princess Yaegaki. However, unknown to them, Kenshin has seen through their disguise and, surprisingly, has decided to promote Minosaku to the rank of samurai in order to send him with a letter to his military barracks in Shiojiri. Waiting at the barracks is the official envoy who had previously come to Kenshin's mansion demanding the head of his son, which, like that of Shingen's son, is forfeit for the failure to find the shogun's assassin. Furthermore, though they do not actually appear in the following two scenes, also staying at Kenshin's mansion are the late shogun's consort and her son, who is to become the next shogun. They are being protected by Kenshin, and this is the "young lord" to whom Minosaku refers in his opening speech.

The two scenes take place against this background of breathtaking intrigue, plot, and counterplot. The character of Yaegaki stands out against this dramaturgic complexity: in the midst of all the political scheming, she is the one character who refuses to take part, remaining constant and true even to the death. Her motivation is simple: she is led by an ideal of love for the man she is to marry and there is nothing that can sway her from her chosen path. Such unbending idealism is very close to the heart of the "red princess" *(akahime)* role type. Yaegaki is classified as one of the three great princess roles *(san hime)* in the kabuki repertoire not only because her actions are so laudable but also because the role requires an actor to express and maintain exceptional emotional intensity. Princess Yuki of *The Golden Pavilion,* translated in this volume, is another. It is often said that the portrayal of elegance and refinement is paramount for princess roles, but Yaegaki seems to go far beyond this. Indeed, much of the scene's effect relies on her shocking forwardness toward Minosaku, which goes against every rule of etiquette with which she was raised. It is debatable exactly when in the play Yaegaki becomes convinced of Minosaku's true identity, but the only real explanation for her behavior is her absolute certainty that this is the man to whom she is betrothed and to whom, therefore, she owes her love and allegiance.

In the "Incense" scene, Yaegaki's "entreaty" *(kudoki)* highlights her single-minded devotion. Speaking to Minosaku, she insists that they are fated to be together, and when she speaks of birds with wings the same color, she refers to a mythical pair of lovebirds whose bodies were joined, sharing the same pair of wings *(hiyoku no tori).* It is interesting that this particular section, which is an emotional climax, has given rise to different acting traditions *(kata),* all of which seek to give a concrete illustration of the lyric. The standard *kata* today stems from Nakamura Utaemon V (1865–1940) and is used for this translation. Here, Yaegaki calls Minosaku's attention to the one-panel screen with its painting of a pair of birds. In other acting traditions, such as that created by Onoe Kikugorō IV (1808–1860), Yaegaki brings out a fan on which a pair of mandarin ducks (symbols of marriage and devotion) are painted, while Kikugorō VI (1885–1949) is known to have used model mandarin ducks floating in a pond. In all cases, we see how physical props are invested with significant meaning beyond their normal function and are used to externalize a character's psychology.

Some critics have claimed that Yaegaki is considered one of the three great princess roles for the "Fox Fires" dance, rather than for the "Incense" scene. This is because of the extreme technical skill in the manipulation of props and costumes that the dance requires over and above the portrayal of character. The actor's handling of the kimono's long sleeves is considered especially important in princess roles, and this can easily be appreciated in such sections as Yaegaki's entreaty, in which the actor's skill imparts an air of gentle refinement that is central to the role type. The dance is even more difficult in this respect because the multilayered quick-change *(hikinuki)* costume is heavier than usual.

In the "Fox Fires" scene, the technique of "puppet gestures" *(ningyō buri)* may also be performed. The technique was first developed in the Kamigata region during the Tenpō era (1830–1843), and was made popular in Edo by Ichikawa Kodanji IV (1812–1866). He first introduced *ningyō buri* in the "Fox Fires" scene at the Nakamura-za in the third month of 1850, and the technique is still seen occasionally. The "Fox Fires" scene is one of relatively few currently performed kabuki dances—along with *The Butterflies' Travel Dance* (Chō no Michiyuki) and *Oshichi in the Tower* (Yagura Oshichi)—that have *takemoto* accompaniment. Furthermore, most dances originating in the puppet theater are "travel scenes" *(michiyuki)* designed to lighten the mood between long and often static scenes of dialogue. The "Fox Fires" scene is again an exception. Though known for its stunning visual beauty and special stage effects *(keren),* the dance is nevertheless a logical extension of the drama of the previous scene, the strong emotions of which are intensified by the fact that we now find the character alone for most of the time.

The sources for this translation were the unpublished scripts *(daihon)* used for the Kabuki-za productions of February 1994, April 1998, and April 1999, with additional reference made to the text in Toita Yasuji et al., eds., *Meisaku Kabuki Zenshū,* Vol. 5.

CHARACTERS

YAEGAKI, *teenage princess, daughter of* KENSHIN *and betrothed to* KATSUYORI

NUREGINU, *lady-in-waiting to* KENSHIN, *in reality a spy working for the Takeda house and known to* MINOSAKU

MINOSAKU, *in reality* KATSUYORI, *son and heir of* TAKEDA SHINGEN, *who has infiltrated* KENSHIN*'s mansion disguised as a gardener*

NAGAO KENSHIN, *general, enemy of* SHINGEN *and* MINOSAKU

SHIRASUGA ROKURŌ, *samurai in* KENSHIN*'s service*

HARA KOBUNJI, *samurai in* KENSHIN*'s service*

TWO SAMURAI, *retainers of* KENSHIN

STAGE ASSISTANTS, *black-garbed* kurogo

TAKEMOTO, *chanters and shamisen players who narrate the action*

The Ten Types of Incense

(The curtain opens to accelerating ki *clacks and offstage music* [kagen] *played by the large drum, flute, and shamisen, creating an imposing and grand atmosphere. A large room in* KENSHIN's *mansion is revealed. Center are the panels of a sliding door on which is painted a stream meandering through a garden of chrysanthemums. A one-panel standing screen, left, is decorated with a picture of two birds on a bare branch in the snow. On either side of this central section are two small rooms with sliding doors now closed. The* TAKEMOTO *chanter and shamisen player are seated on a raised platform at left.)*

TAKEMOTO *(Singing slowly and solemnly)*:

Like flowing water / are our lives in constant flux, / and now transformed in / formal robes, Minosaku / studies his refection, / as calmly, with composure, / he makes his way into the room.

(The central sliding doors draw apart and MINOSAKU*—in reality,* KATSUYORI *—enters. He is a handsome, white-faced youth, with forelock still unshaven. He wears formal garb* [kamishimo], *consisting of a purple vest* [kataginu] *and trailing trousers* [nagabakama] *over a red kimono, and bears the two swords of a samurai. Holding his long sword in his left hand, he steps forward, then pauses.)*

MINOSAKU: It is fortunate that I was brought up among common folk, for people do not know my face. Disguised as a gardener, I have penetrated this estate and I can now protect our young lord should any attempt be made upon his life. Yet, my intentions have been discovered, and I have been made a samurai. What am I to do now?

(He makes his way to the edge of the stairs and seats himself with the aid of a black-robed STAGE ASSISTANT [kurogo].*)*

TAKEMOTO:

Puzzled by this turn of events, / pensively he hangs his head, / his mind shut in with worry, / while, shut in her room, / is the daughter of the house, / Princess Yaegaki. / He who was her dear betrothed, / Lord Katsuyori, / gave his life through suicide, / since which dreary day, / within this single room, has / she confined herself, / contemplating the picture / hung in the alcove / and chanting sutras with the / sound of a prayer bell.

(In the small room, right, white silk blinds are rolled up behind the sliding doors. Through the translucent doors themselves can now be seen YAEGAKI*, dressed in the typical red kimono and silver tiara of a youthful "red princess"* [akahime]. YAEGAKI *has been told that* KATSUYORI *is dead, and as yet she has no idea that the man who committed suicide was a substitute who looked exactly like him. Seated with her back to the audience, she prays to a hanging scroll that is a portrait of her betrothed. A single prayer bell rings out poignantly.)*

TAKEMOTO:

From the other side as well / comes a cricket's chirp, / crying tears that wet her sleeve / as Nureginu / mourns the departed on this / death anniversary, / now facing his name tablet / with hands in prayer.

(In the small room right, white blinds behind the translucent doors are rolled up to reveal NUREGINU, *seated facing front and praying as she strikes a small bell. She wears a simple black kimono as befits a serving lady. Finally, the sliding door is pulled back to show her in full view. She puts down the bell hammer and, holding her Buddhist rosary, puts her hands together to pray for her deceased love.)*

NUREGINU *(Sadly)*: In all the wide world, who else is there to mourn for you, even today, on the anniversary of your death? How heartless! It is pitiable to think that you passed away quite unaware of father's evil. Surely, you must be lost in the next world. I, your wife, Nureginu, can only offer this meager service, but think of it as though a thousand . . . ten thousand sutras have been recited, and please attain salvation from this world! Hail to Amida Buddha. Hail to Amida Buddha.

TAKEMOTO *(Passionately)*:

Hail to Amida Buddha!

*(*MINOSAKU *has overheard* NUREGINU*'s words and is moved at the memory of the man who died in his place and who was called by his name.)*

MINOSAKU: Indeed, today is the twentieth of the eleventh month, the very day on which my substitute died. It is the anniversary of the other "Katsuyori's" death.

TAKEMOTO:

Days and months passed slowly by . . . / It has been over one year. / May the spirits of the dead / attain enlightenment / and reach speedy salvation!

*(*MINOSAKU *points into the distance and then gestures "one" to represent one year. He brings his hand to his chest in prayer. The doors to* YAEGAKI *'s room slide open. Though he cannot see her,* MINOSAKU *overhears* YAEGAKI *'s words.)*

YAEGAKI *(Speaking sadly to the portrait)*: My dear Katsuyori, hearing that our engagement had been arranged between our parents, I could hardly wait for the day I would become your bride, so I ordered that your likeness be painted. The more I look at it now, the more beautiful you are . . . And to think of lying beside such a husband!

(The smoke from the incense YAEGAKI *burns at the altar table slowly wafts upward toward the painting, almost as if it represented* YAEGAKI *'s own deep yearnings.)*

TAKEMOTO:

"It was my luck to be born / a pampered princess, / enjoying the beauty of / both moon and flowers. / By the side of your portrait, / is this incense smoke / of the ten fragrances, now / tribute to the dead?"

*(*YAEGAKI *bows before the scroll and then turns to face the audience with her Buddhist rosary in hand.)*

"It was not for the purpose of / prayers for the deceased / that I had your form painted / as a picture scroll. / Now, may your soul come back in / the smoke of 'Returning Soul Incense'!"

*(*YAEGAKI *is aware of the ancient belief that the spirit of a deceased lover could reappear in the smoke of this incense, and she now prays for her own betrothed to come before her.)*

"If a famous work of art / truly has power, / then I long to hear your voice . . . / I long to hear you / speak but a single word in / calling me your love." / So saying, by the picture, / she prostrates herself / and dissolves in bitter tears.

(She rises, turns toward the painting, and falls to her knees, weeping.)

MINOSAKU *(Sympathizing)*: That tearful voice must be Princess Yaegaki's. She calls my name, thinking of me as her true husband. Here, the mourning princess . . . There, the mourning Nureginu.

TAKEMOTO:

Indeed, how wretched! / Beyond all words to express / is the sadness that lingers / in these women's hearts. / Thinking thus, despite himself, / he is moved to tears.

MINOSAKU *(Lifting a hand to wipe his eyes)*: Without realizing, I wept.

TAKEMOTO:

Adjusting his collar, he / rises to his feet, / while from behind, with heavy heart, / Nureginu sees . . .

(MINOSAKU walks to the back of the room, turns front, and seats himself on a tall stool [aibiki] *placed by a STAGE ASSISTANT. NUREGINU is attracted by the sound and goes to look through a gap in her sliding doors. Recognizing MINOSAKU, with whom she is in league, she is baffled by his changed appearance. She slides the door open, walks out, and kneels just outside her room.)*

NUREGINU: Minosaku, what's become of your appearance? Why do you dress in those robes?

MINOSAKU: Yes, you are right to be suspicious. Though not part of my plan, Kenshin has taken me into service, and now I wear the attire of a warrior and these two swords.

NUREGINU: Indeed, though foolish to think that just because you now wear the crested robes of a samurai, you could look the same as my husband, nevertheless, in that apparel . . . *(Tearfully.)* "This keepsake itself, is now the cause of my grief, for without it here . . . "

(The TAKEMOTO chanter continues for her with a slightly altered quotation from the famous poetry collection Kokinshū.*)*

TAKEMOTO:

" 'Then perchance I could forget / my memories of you.' / So go the lines of the old verse, / a sad song of parting."

(NUREGINU is shocked at the close resemblance between her late husband and MINOSAKU now that he is similarly dressed. She takes a square of white silk cloth from her kimono breast, a memento of her lover stained with his blood. She slowly unfolds it and holds it out for MINOSAKU to see.)

"Yet, regardless of my keepsake, / your appearance now / differs not one particle / from my dear husband's, / and seeing you here like this, / I cannot forget."

(She clutches the keepsake to her breast.)

NUREGINU: It seems that I am lost on the path of transmigration.

(She caresses the keepsake to her cheek and dabs her tears. Just as she is about to cry out, she checks herself, rushes back into her room, and there begins weeping as she recalls her deceased husband.)

TAKEMOTO:

Now begging his forgiveness, / she sinks to the ground / as her weeping voice is heard / in the next room, where, / standing suspiciously, is / Princess Yaegaki. / Through a gap in the sliding door, / stealthily she peeks / and, making no mistake, she / recognizes him.

(YAEGAKI, until now lost in a reverie, is aroused by the sound of someone crying outside. She stands and goes to her sliding door. Seeing him, she, too, is shocked at MINOSAKU's resemblance to KATSUYORI's portrait.)

YAEGAKI: Can it be Katsuyori?

TAKEMOTO:

She strains to calm herself as / her heart leaps in her breast. / The thought that he resembles / the one who's passed away / is only the result of / a mind's delusion.

(She begins to rush out of her room but holds herself back after one step. She retreats, closes the door, and poses against the pillar. Thinking she is deluding herself, she shakes her head, glances back at the picture, and hides her face with her sleeve in embarrassment.)

"Before this painted portrait, / how ashamed I feel," / as back she now returns, / hands clasped together, / chanting the sutras again / with her prayer bell.

(She returns to kneel and pray before the picture. The sound of her bell rings out.)

Meanwhile, Lord Katsuyori, / guessing the feelings / in Nureginu's heart, speaks / with a cheerless voice.

*(*NUREGINU *comes out of her room and assumes a kneeling position near the door.)*

MINOSAKU: A woman's heart is fragile, and your grief, understandable, . . . but you had best resign yourself to the ways of this uncertain world.

*(*MINOSAKU *sympathizes with* NUREGINU *'s loss, for he, the real* KATSUYORI, *was spared through her lover's death. He meditates sadly on the quirk of fate that brought about these circumstances.)*

TAKEMOTO:

With these words, he counsels her, / while on the other side / is one grasping at pure air, / imagining now / that her betrothed were alive / rather than deceased. / How she would long for him and / yearn to be at his side. / So, again, she takes a peek, / and when his features / with the portrait she compares, / rather than a likeness, / he seems the living image! / Is this not the real . . . / the genuine Katsuyori / who sits before her? / Without another thought, / she bursts from her room.

(Looking through a gap in the door, YAEGAKI *is shocked again at* MINOSAKU*'s likeness to* KATSUYORI*. After glancing back at the picture, she rushes out of the room, pauses, throws down her Buddhist rosary, and tidies her hair before going to sit at* MINOSAKU *'s side, where she shyly places her right hand on his lap.)*

YAEGAKI *(Passionately)*: Katsuyori! How I have longed for you!

TAKEMOTO:

But when she clings to him, and / begins to shed tears, / he reacts with a start. / Then, feigning ignorance . . .

MINOSAKU: Your words are most unexpected. I am a gardener named Minosaku who was only recently taken into military service, for which reason I have changed

Princess Yaegaki (Nakamura Utaemon VI), center, flirts with Katsuyori (Ichikawa Ebizō IX, later Ichikawa Danjūrō XI), urged on by Lady Nureginu (Onoe Baikō VII). (Tsubouchi Memorial Theatre Museum of Waseda University)

into these robes and donned these swords. I have no memory of this Katsuyori of whom you speak.

TAKEMOTO:

He pushes her aside.

(He gently pushes her away, and she crosses several feet to his left. Though YAEGAKI *is correct in assuming that he is* KATSUYORI, *he still refuses to admit his true identity because she is* KENSHIN*'s daughter and may, therefore, be untrustworthy.)*

YAEGAKI: What's that? You are a samurai newly taken into service by my father, and before that you were the gardener Minosaku? *(Embarrassed, and beginning to doubt herself.)* I, of all people, should have known! Yet, as your features resemble his so closely I thought that perhaps . . . *(Slowly, deeply mortified.)* This results from my heart's passion. Here, before you both . . .

TAKEMOTO:

"How ashamed I feel."

*(*YAEGAKI *glances back at* MINOSAKU, *then, behaving as though he were indeed a total stranger to whom she suddenly felt attracted, she looks bashfully away again.)*

YAEGAKI: Nureginu, come here.

NUREGINU: Yes, madam.

(Offstage musicians begin a sweet, romantic melody played by shamisen and Chinese fiddle [kokyū]. NUREGINU *bows and follows her lady into her room, left, where both seat themselves,* NUREGINU *at right.)*

YAEGAKI: Nureginu, that man who calls himself Minosaku, or whatever . . . Have you been close to him for long?

NUREGINU *(Enthusiastically at first, then after realizing what she's saying, more seriously)*: Yes . . . No, not at all! *(She shakes her head strongly.)*

YAEGAKI: Do not dispute it. He is surely someone known to you.

NUREGINU: Why, for my lady, of all people, to say such things! I only set eyes on him a moment ago. How could I possibly . . .

YAEGAKI: Do not conceal it! Judging from your manner with him just now, are you not having a secret affair? . . .

TAKEMOTO:

"For so very intimate / do you both appear?" / But at such unexpected words, / there is horror and surprise.

*(*YAEGAKI *coyly revolves a finger at her lady-in-waiting as though teasing her, and then shields her face in embarrassment.* NUREGINU *is alarmed and worried about giving away her own and* MINOSAKU*'s plans.)*

NUREGINU: Why, as for what my lady says, how unbecoming to take an interest in such a man.

YAEGAKI: If you say it is unbecoming, then he must certainly be known to you.

NUREGINU *(Hesitantly)*: No, that was not my meaning . . . What I meant to say was, how unbecoming it would be of me to deceive my precious lord, your father, by taking a secret lover.

YAEGAKI: In that case, if he is neither your acquaintance nor your lover . . . then, from now, I myself would like to receive his love.

*(*NUREGINU *is shocked by this open confession.)*

TAKEMOTO:

Pressing her fervently, she begs / that Nureginu / perform the task of go-between, / as, in the blinding light / of the setting sun, she lifts / a sleeve to her face. / How charming and endearing / is her appearance.

(Imploring, YAEGAKI *gestures in* MINOSAKU*'s direction, and when* NUREGINU *hesitates, she pushes her gently from behind. At last,* NUREGINU *consents, and* YAEGAKI *begins to check her appearance. They stand, and* NUREGINU *leads her lady out of the room. As they approach,* YAEGAKI *pulls back bashfully, but* NUREGINU *forces her on until she is sitting beside* MINOSAKU*, hiding her face.)*

NUREGINU *(Sitting at the left and speaking to* YAEGAKI*)*: Being one of your position, I still thought of my lady as a child and hardly expected such boldness with that Minosaku.

YAEGAKI *(To one side)*: My love began the moment I saw him, but let us speak no more of this. Here, at once . . .

NUREGINU: You mean that I should mediate?

YAEGAKI *(Bashfully)*: That is so.

NUREGINU: But my, my . . . How true that even a great lord's daughter may fall into the path of love if she is careless. But, if that is how things stand, I will be the go-between.

MINOSAKU *(Shocked that* NUREGINU *seems about to give their secret away)*: Wait, Nureginu! Do not be reckless in what you say.

NUREGINU: I understand everything. I . . . understand. *(She looks meaningfully at him and taps her right hand on her breast to reassure him that she knows what she is doing.* NUREGINU *has been struck by the lengths to which her young mistress will go for the sake of love and now believes she can turn this to her own advantage. She speaks to* YAEGAKI.*)* It isn't that I refuse to be the go-between, but do you truly love Minosaku from the bottom of your heart?

TAKEMOTO:

Asked this question, all the more, / her face blushes red.

*(*YAEGAKI *slowly steals a glance at* MINOSAKU, *then, breaking into a smile, she covers her face with both sleeves.)*

"With conduct ill becoming / a high-born princess, / would I say I loved him if / it were no more than . . ."

YAEGAKI: A lie?

TAKEMOTO:

"For what possible reason / would I be so false?"

*(*YAEGAKI *coyly opens her fan, staring through its ribs at* MINOSAKU. *In a reverie, she looks out over it, drops the fan absently, and hides her face in embarrassment.)*

NUREGINU: If you are certain in your heart, then you need only show me some definite evidence of your pledge, and, upon seeing that, I will act as go-between.

YAEGAKI: Indeed, that is an easy request. Perhaps if I wrote it down . . .

NUREGINU: In this case, I have a special wish. The pledge that I desire is . . . *(she looks around to check that they are not being overheard, then, with conviction)* that you steal the Suwa Hosshō helmet!

YAEGAKI *(Shocked)*: What do you ask? Did you say steal the Suwa Hosshō helmet? *(She turns toward* MINOSAKU. *Now realizing that he must indeed be the real* KATSUYORI, *she speaks rapidly.)* So, you are Katsuyori after all!

TAKEMOTO:

At such words, he quickly covers her mouth.

(He lifts his fan to YAEGAKI *'s face to silence her, horrified that someone else may be listening.)*

MINOSAKU: Why, how absurd to call me Katsuyori! I am Minosaku and have no idea at all to whom you refer. Do not talk so rashly.

TAKEMOTO:

Thus he speaks, and, into his face / deeply she gazes.

(Slowly, she looks up at him. YAEGAKI *is now certain that he is the real* KATSUYORI, *and she makes a fervent entreaty* [kudoki] *that he confide in her.)*

"No more than betrothed, we had yet / a single pillow to share, / and though natural / for you to conceal feelings / of conjugal love, / yet are we like a pair of birds / with wings the same hue. / Though mankind little suspects / the ties that bind them, / still is it the custom for / all living creatures / to call with affection to / their parent or spouse."

*(*NUREGINU *helps* YAEGAKI *to take off her outer robe* [uchikake], *which she places behind the standing screen. Bowing to* MINOSAKU, YAEGAKI *calls his attention to the two birds painted on the screen, then she rises to pose by its side. Overwhelmed by emotion, she steps back, colliding with a pillar. Somewhat embarrassed, she poses* [kimari] *with her arms wrapped around the pillar.)*

"However hard for others / to distinguish your face, / how could I mistake the / appearance of one / for whom I have so longed, my / dear Katsuyori?"

(She looks sadly at MINOSAKU *and returns to her room to look up lovingly at the painting. Coming out again, she sits beside him.)*

"While from the world and from men / you remain hidden, / and your person is kept / carefully disguised, / what need is there for such reserve / with I who am your wife? / I beg you reveal clearly / your identity / and reassure my heart . . ."

(She lets out a sob.)

MINOSAKU: Take care!

(Startled by her loud cry and alarmed that others may overhear, MINOSAKU *picks up his sword and stands to go, but, kneeling at his side, she holds on to the sheath and prevents him from leaving. They pose. He kneels again.)*

TAKEMOTO:

"I beg only this! / If now, my earnest desire / cannot be granted, / then I beseech you to kill me. / Kill me, I implore!" *(She taps ground to emphasize her feelings.)* Thus, clinging to his person, / bitterly she weeps. / *(She cries.)* Katsuyori, purposely, / speaks in an angry tone.

MINOSAKU: Your words are ludicrous nonsense! No matter how much you insist to the contrary, I am a menial servant and have no recollection of whom you speak. You should be more circumspect lest others see you. Move aside at once!

TAKEMOTO:

He pushes her away . . .

YAEGAKI *(Shocked by his strong denial)*: Then, no matter how much I implore, you are not Katsuyori? *(Shamed and frustrated, she begins sobbing.)*

TAKEMOTO:

With a start, Minosaku / is taken aback / as, by the hilt of his sword, / she takes up the blade. / Seeing such impulsiveness, / Nureginu stops her quickly.

*(*NUREGINU *rushes to* YAEGAKI*'s side and holds on to the sword.)*

NUREGINU: My lady! Wait!

YAEGAKI: No, no. Let me go at once. Let me die. If this man is not Katsuyori . . .

TAKEMOTO:

"Of my foolish ravings, / I am now ashamed, / and before my love's image, / I cannot excuse my heart's defilement. / No longer can I go on / living in this world." / Again they wrestle together, / and once more she is restrained.

(As they struggle with the sword, YAEGAKI *glances at* MINOSAKU *and shakes her head remorsefully. Briefly she covers her breast with her sleeve and looks over toward the portrait. At last,* NUREGINU *manages to win the sword over and goes to return it by* MINOSAKU *'s side. Seeing that she is beaten,* YAEGAKI *bursts into tears.* NUREGINU *returns to kneel at* YAEGAKI *'s left.)*

NUREGINU: My lady, wait. *(In a comforting tone.)* I expected no less from the child of a warrior's family. Your determination is splendid and, having witnessed your sincerity, I will let you meet Katsuyori after all. *(In a more cheerful voice.)* You guessed correctly, for Minosaku over there is indeed the real Katsuyori. Go to meet him at once.

TAKEMOTO:

Now as she's pushed toward him, / as one would expect, / her former bitterness shrinks / to a mere one-hundredth.

*(*NUREGINU *points toward* MINOSAKU, *and* YAEGAKI *becomes bashful, trying to escape back into her room. However,* NUREGINU *pushes her in his direction.)*

YAEGAKI *(Coyly)*: My, but just look!

TAKEMOTO:

Though with all her heart she protests / at her cruel treatment, / after all is said, they both / draw close together / and, just as their passion grows, / Nureginu's heart / begins to beat more quickly.

(After some resistance, YAEGAKI *goes to sit beside* MINOSAKU *and places one sleeve on his lap. Both are happy and, at this show of intimacy,* NUREGINU, *left, takes out her fan and begins to cool herself excitedly.)*

Just at that moment, / her father Kenshin's / voice is clearly heard . . .

KENSHIN *(Offstage)*: Where is Minosaku? The hour grows late, and my reply must be delivered to Shiojiri.

(Surprised, MINOSAKU *gestures for the women to retreat quickly into* YAEGAKI*'s room while he himself descends to the bottom of the stairs and sits right.* NUREGINU *leads* YAEGAKI *off left and closes the sliding door.)*

TAKEMOTO:

At which, he enters the room.

(The painted doors at the back open to reveal KENSHIN *with a black lacquered letterbox in his left hand. Inside the box, supposedly, is his reply to the shogunate envoy, who is now waiting at his military barracks in Shiojiri. Having taken holy orders,* KENSHIN*'s head is shaved, he has a short mustache, and he wears the typical high-collared, stiff brocade outer robe* [omigoromo] *of a high-ranking aristocrat. With his entrance, the atmosphere changes completely, for, in his aspect and speech, he exudes the authority of a powerful warlord.)*

TAKEMOTO:

Minosaku is surprised / and starts to one side.

MINOSAKU: If all is prepared, I will leave at once.

KENSHIN *(Severely)*: The particulars are contained inside this letterbox. Do not hesitate, but go this instant.

MINOSAKU: Yes, my lord.

TAKEMOTO:

He acknowledges receipt, / and with letterbox in hand, / now toward Shiojiri / he goes with all speed.

*(*MINOSAKU *carefully replaces his long sword in his obi, goes to take the letterbox in his right hand, bows slightly, and immediately makes his way to the* hanamichi, *where he pauses at* shichisan. KENSHIN, *aided by a* STAGE ASSISTANT, *sits on a stool on the platform center.* MINOSAKU *still does not know* KENSHIN*'s real intentions, but he suspects that* KENSHIN *has seen through his disguise. For this reason,* MINOSAKU *now transfers the letterbox to his left hand, keeping his right hand free to draw his sword in case of attack. He departs warily. Offstage stick drum, shamisen, and flute play until he disappears. The raised dais on which the* TAKEMOTO *musicians sit revolves to reveal a new chanter and shamisen player.)*

TAKEMOTO:

Kenshin, with eyes fixed, / watches till he's gone.

(Satisfied that MINOSAKU *has really left,* KENSHIN *nods to himself with a sinister air.)*

KENSHIN: Shirasuga Rokurō! Come here at once!

ROKURŌ: Yes, my lord!

(Offstage musicians indicate the sounds of battle [tōyose]. ROKURŌ, *carrying a naked sword, runs in from left to rapid* tsuke *beats. He wears a wide-sleeved brocade garment with hems split at the sides* [yoten], *and his hair is tied up with a headband. He moves right and bows, placing his sword on the ground.)*

TAKEMOTO:

With immediate reply, / Shirasuga Rokurō / advances before his lord. / Kenshin, forcefully . . .

KENSHIN *(Rhythmically, in time with the* TAKEMOTO *shamisen* [nori]*)*: Here in Suwa are the waters of the lake completely frozen over and impassable by boat. *(Faster, no longer in rhythm.)* The journey to Shiojiri must be made over land through a difficult mountain pass . . . Take care that you do not fail! *(*KENSHIN*'s implicit meaning is that they should overtake, ambush, and kill* MINOSAKU.*)*

ROKURŌ: Yes, my lord!

TAKEMOTO:

"Your command will be obeyed!"

*(*ROKURŌ, *anxious to impress his lord, poses in a powerful* mie.*)*

ROKURŌ *(Rhythmically, to* TAKEMOTO *shamisen* [nori]*)*: Even if Katsuyori should prove fearless, I, in turn, will display my mastery of the secret arts.

TAKEMOTO:

"Cliffs of sheer rock rise sharply / at Shiojiri, / where, over peaks and through valleys, / through high mountain passes, I'll persevere. / Though I must soar above heaven and earth, / still will I slash and cut and slash again / in pursuit of the foe."

(With the sounds of battle in the background, ROKURŌ *poses, looking up at the mountain peaks and then down into the valleys. Taking up his sword, he mimes fighting, ending in a stone-throwing* [ishinage] mie *to two* tsuke *beats.)*

ROKURŌ: Presently, I will have good news to report!

KENSHIN: That is well spoken. Now, go at once!

ROKURŌ: Yes, my lord.

(He bows and runs to the hanamichi, *where he poses in a* mie. *Then, beginning with slow and powerful steps, he gradually quickens his pace until he is running energetically to intercept* MINOSAKU.*)*

TAKEMOTO:

Both heart and limbs are filled with / the hot blood of youth / as the young warrior departs, / following swiftly.

KENSHIN: And now, Hara Kobunji! Come at once!

KOBUNJI: Yes, my lord!

TAKEMOTO:

Springing to attention is / Hara Kobunji, / making his way with all speed / into his lord's sight.

(To the sounds of battle and rapid tsuke *beats,* KOBUNJI *dashes in from left holding a spear. Like* ROKURŌ, *he wears the brocade garment with split hem of a warrior in combat. His face is red and his hair falls loosely about his ears. He halts left and bows, placing the spear on the ground.)*

KENSHIN: I have just dispatched Rokurō, but I am still dubious of the outcome if he is alone. Go now to assist him.

KOBUNJI: I humbly receive my lord's command and will go to join Rokurō at once.

TAKEMOTO:

"Like the leaves scattering in / the trees of autumn, . . . / one blade of pampas, / two blades of pampas . . . / with one thrust here and another there, / I will follow on."

(He mimes the leaves tumbling down and, balancing on one leg while leaning on his spear, he performs a stone-throwing mie.*)*

KOBUNJI: Once defeated, Katsuyori's head . . .

TAKEMOTO:

"Will be struck clean off / in the blink of an eye."

(He mimes cutting off the head.)

KOBUNJI: Of that my lord can rest assured.

TAKEMOTO:

Truly, with such energy, / such courage and strength, / he well deserves a lasting name / for loyalty in the house / of Uesugi.

(He bows low.)

KENSHIN *(Impatiently)*: Quickly, go!

KOBUNJI: Yes, my lord!

TAKEMOTO:

And now, with renewed vigor, / he dashes away.

(Again, to the sounds of battle, he makes his way to the hanamichi, *where he poses heroically in a* mie *and exits.)*

In his wake, a suspicious / Princess Yaegaki . . .

*(*YAEGAKI *and* NUREGINU *reappear and look on with expressions of concern. They approach* KENSHIN *and seat themselves on either side of him,* YAEGAKI *to his left.)*

YAEGAKI: Father, what was all the commotion?

KENSHIN: That young man was none other than Takeda Katsuyori. I have sent the other two to dispose of him.

YAEGAKI *(Horrified)*: What? You mean to kill Katsuyori?

The villainous Nagao Kenshin (Bandō Mitsugorō VIII) prevents Princess Yaegaki (Nakamura Utaemon VI), right, and Lady Nureginu (Nakamura Shikan VII), center, from interfering with his order to have Katsuyori killed. (Umemura Yutaka, Engeki Shuppansha)

TAKEMOTO:

So stunned is she at the news, / she falls to the ground.

*(*YAEGAKI *lets out a cry and exchanges a desperate look with* NUREGINU. *Slowly she leans back in dismay.* NUREGINU *is also alarmed but is helpless to do anything in front of* KENSHIN.*)*

"On this day, whatever else / may have come to pass, / to meet again my husband, / who just now departed, / was like the rare blossoming / of the most precious flower. / But from him in whom I rejoiced / must I now be parted / yet another time?"

(She stares longingly after MINOSAKU *and briefly crosses her sleeves to represent their union, then stands, overcome with tears.)*

Calling upon her father / to be merciful, / to spare her dear lover's life, / she humbly implores. / Yet, though she clings to him weeping, / he pays no regard.

(Kneeling at his side, she tries to move him, but he brushes her away.)

KENSHIN *(To* NUREGINU, *with loathing and hostility)*: As for you who are Takeda's spy, there are detailed questions I must put to you! Disappear within!

TAKEMOTO:

Begrudging in compassion, / the rough-mannered general / retires deep within his / private bedchamber.

*(*NUREGINU *is shocked that* KENSHIN *knows she is a spy in league with* MINOSAKU. *Resolving to hurry after and warn* MINOSAKU *of his danger, she stands and straightens her kimono with a decisive air. Just as she reaches the top of the stairs,* KENSHIN *pins her to the ground with his fan and holds* YAEGAKI *back with his left hand, a fierce and unforgiving expression on his face. They pose in a final tableau* [emen no mie], *with* KENSHIN *center,* YAEGAKI *left, and* NUREGINU *below. A single loud* ki *is the signal for offstage stick drum and flute to play excitedly* [hayabue], *expressing the conflicting tensions as the curtain is closed to an accelerating* ki *pattern.)*

Fox Fires in the Inner Garden

(The curtain opens to offstage beats of the large drum, representing flowing water [mizu no oto], *and accelerating* ki *to reveal the garden inside* KENSHIN*'s mansion. A brushwood fence with covered gate, right, leads to the mansion itself, while across a stone bridge over the pond, a small shrine, left, contains the treasured Suwa Hosshō helmet. A large stone lantern, lit, stands at center. A landscape of mountains is visible against the night sky. One stroke of the temple bell* [hontsurigane] *suggests the late hour and the loneliness of the scene. We should imagine the strains of a sad song filtering out from the mansion. A large ensemble of* TAKEMOTO *musicians sits on a raised platform left. A brief introduction by solo shamisen is followed by offstage koto music.)*

TAKEMOTO *(Slowly)*:

"By my thoughts of you / am I consumed, burning like / fox fires in the open plains, / deep into the night."

(A soft drumroll offstage [dorodoro] *signals the entrance of a white fox on the* hanamichi *stage lift* [suppon]. *Played by a child in a costume* [nuigurumi], *the fox makes its way to the main stage and onto the stone bridge to look down at its reflection in the pond.)*

"Burning like fox fires, / fox fires of the open plains . . . / the fields ablaze with fox fires, / deep into the night."

(Offstage dorodoro *is heard as the fox causes blinds around the shrine to lift of their own accord. The fox hops up into the shrine, poses at each pillar, and magically disappears into the main altar. The drum pattern for flowing water sounds as* YAEGAKI *enters warily through the gate, on her way to warn* KATSUYORI *of his danger. Holding a lantern in one hand, she lifts up the hem of her kimono with the other. She wears a pale mauve long-sleeved kimono, a silver tiara on her head, and thick garden clogs of black lacquer on her feet. The bell tolls intermittently to suggest that she is quite alone as she walks about checking with her lantern. Koto music continues, as if coming from the mansion.)*

YAEGAKI *(Noticing the music)*: From an inner room, I hear the blind musician . . .

TAKEMOTO:

"How well it describes me, the song / that he is singing."

(She turns to look back toward the mansion and sadly glances down at her own person.)

"Yet the one to be pitied / is Lord Katsuyori. / Though his life is now threatened / by an evil scheme, / of this, his present danger, / he is unaware."

(At the mention of her betrothed, YAEGAKI *looks into the distance, worried. She turns to the back and a* STAGE ASSISTANT *helps her out of her clogs and takes her lamp.)*

"The cause of our parting, too, / was my pitiless father, / for though I begged and protested, / his cruel heart remained unmoved / by my pleading words."

*(*YAEGAKI *kneels and looks toward the mansion, thinking of her father,* KENSHIN. *She bows dutifully and shakes her head at the thought of his merciless nature. She taps the ground to show the depth of her feelings but shakes her head once more as she recalls the words she spoke to him. She rises, begins to move about, and then sinks again to her knees.)*

"If you could feel compassion / at your daughter's grief, / then spare the life of my betrothed / and let us marry, I beg." / Thus, lamenting bitterly, / she falls to the ground.

YAEGAKI *(She begins to cry but stops herself)*: No, no. This is no time for tears. I must reach Katsuyori ahead of his pursuers and warn him of his danger. The shorter path is . . .

TAKEMOTO:

"Across the lake of Suwa! / Now must I hurry / and ask the boatman to take me / lest I be too late." / With courage and devotion, / she draws up her hems / and hastens toward the lake.

(She gestures in the lake's direction, stands, and mimes pulling up her kimono. The water drum pattern offstage creates a sense of urgency as YAEGAKI, *holding both ends of her obi, hurries to* shichisan. *Looking ahead, she takes two tentative steps but then turns back.)*

YAEGAKI: No, no, no. *(Dropping her obi, she pauses briefly to think.)* The lake is now frozen over, and a boat will be unable to cross. I must go on foot, yet, with only a woman's strength, how am I to overtake Katsuyori's pursuers?

(Glances down at her legs, then looks in the pursuers' direction.)

TAKEMOTO:

"What cruel fate determines that / I should stand helpless / as before my very eyes / my husband should die?"

(She looks back desperately across the frozen lake, hits her arms in frustration, and falls to the ground in tears.)

YAEGAKI *(In despair)*: If only I had wings . . . How I long for wings that I might fly to his side to warn him!

(Rising to her feet, she gently moves her long sleeves like wings. She stamps lightly to emphasize her emotions.)

TAKEMOTO *(Passionately)*:

"I yearn to meet . . . I yearn to see . . ." / For her spouse she longs, / and now with countless gloomy thoughts / is her mind confused. / For a hundred, a thousand years, / she'd weep through the nights, / but though she would cry her life away / and drown in bitter tears, / how little it would profit / her dearest husband.

(Desperate to reach her betrothed but helpless, she gazes and gestures across the lake. Grasping her sleeves, she sinks to the ground and holds one sleeve over another to represent her eternal bond with him. She shakes her head and wipes away a tear. Standing to think, she slowly turns toward the shrine, and it suddenly occurs to her to pray for assistance.)

Her only recourse . . . to beg the / gods and Buddha for help. / And so, now to the alcove / wherein is enshrined / the helmet of supreme truth / before which she prays.

(As she makes her way to the building, left, the offstage drum pattern for water indicates the pond she must cross, while a single shamisen plays with increasing speed to

suggest her nervousness. Stepping up into the holy shrine, she sits, blesses herself, and bows low.)

YAEGAKI: If this helmet is the sacred treasure bestowed upon the Takeda House by the god of Suwa, then it must be invested with no less than the deity's spirit itself. *(Bows in awe.)* Now, at Lord Katsuyori's time of crisis, I beg for assistance.

TAKEMOTO:

Imploring that he be saved, / she goes to take the helmet, / raising it to her head, / lifting it in reverence. / Fearful that others / would now suspect her actions / if they saw her face, / warily she steps down to / tread the stepping stones with care.

*(*YAEGAKI *lifts up her arms in supplication to the gods and turns to bow before the helmet. A hidden* STAGE ASSISTANT *takes the helmet from the altar and hands it to her. She looks around furtively to check that no one is watching and, in her anxiety, trips over the edge of the shrine. Supporting herself with one foot on the stair, she poses clutching the helmet to her breast. Offstage, a large drum plays the water pattern. A large full moon appears in the sky as she makes her way to the stone bridge.)*

TAKEMOTO:

Reflecting on the surface / of the garden pond, / now by the light of the moon, / she beholds a doubtful form! / With shock and astonishment, / she leaps to one side.

(Holding the helmet overhead, she sees an image in the water. Startled, YAEGAKI *dashes off the bridge and falls to the ground, right, frozen with fear. The helmet is placed on the ground by her side.)*

YAEGAKI: Without doubt, what I saw just now . . . *(pauses, terrified)* was a fox's shape! Why, reflected on the surface of the garden pond . . .

TAKEMOTO:

"What an uncanny sight!" / The pounding in her chest / she tries to stroke down . . . she tries to stroke down. / Though nervous and trembling, / now by slow degrees, / she goes back to look once more / upon the water, / yet all she sees reflected / is her own image.

(By placing her hand in the breast of her kimono, she soothes her nerves. Standing, she inches slowly back onto the bridge. She shields her face with her sleeve until she has enough courage to look down.)

YAEGAKI: Just now, the shape of a fox was reflected in this water. Yet, to look again, there is only my own reflection. Was it some phantom spirit I saw, or did my nervous state lead me to imagine it?

(She slips a hand into her kimono breast and stands deep in thought. Suddenly, two loud strokes of the TAKEMOTO *shamisen break the tension.)*

TAKEMOTO *(Strongly)*:

"How mysterious this is!" / Jittery and tense, / to the helmet she returns, / lifting it in respect. / Now, again, she goes to peek, / and in dawn's moonlight clear, / clearly, clearly on the water, / a white fox's shape! / Like the pond's muddy verges / is her breast all choked, / as there by the water's edge / bolt upright she stands / gazing down in wonder at / the marvelous sight.

*(*YAEGAKI *crosses right to retrieve the helmet. Lifting it to her forehead reverently, she goes back to the bridge. The water drum pattern offstage suggests her pounding heart, shifting to a loud* dorodoro *when she looks down. She is shocked to see the fox's reflection again. Turning away in fear, she shields herself with the helmet as a* STAGE ASSISTANT *begins to pull out the threads holding the top layer of her kimono in place. Facing front, she crouches, trembling behind the helmet. The strokes of the shamisen quicken, she stands upright, and the* STAGE ASSISTANT *pulls off the outer layer of kimono* [hikinuki], *revealing a white kimono beneath. With the helmet held above her left shoulder, she poses* [kimari] *to loud* dorodoro, *two* tsuke *beats, and one toll of the bell.* Dorodoro *softens and flute and drums play the magical fox pattern* [raijo]. *The* STAGE ASSISTANT *attaches the helmet to the end of a long pole* [sashigane] *and gently lifts it out of* YAEGAKI*'s hand, taking it right. Startled to find that the helmet is no longer at her side, she sees it hovering in midair. Hoping to catch it with her sleeves, she runs toward it, but it eludes her and floats away left. Chasing after it, she manages to bring it to the ground, emphasized by a single* tsuke *beat.* Dorodoro *swells, then silence. The* STAGE ASSISTANT *takes the helmet off the pole and runs off.)*

YAEGAKI *(Kneeling above the helmet)*: It is true . . . I have heard that the god of Suwa has the fox as his emissary, and if this helmet represents his divine person, then there will be countless fox spirits in attendance. How miraculous, for without doubt they are protecting it!

*(*YAEGAKI *lifts up the helmet and stands. The offstage water pattern is played as she approaches the lake, but she is stopped by a pair of samurai who suddenly appear from behind the fence. They wear yellow* tabi *and small knee patches.* Hakama *over their brocade upper kimono are tucked up, leaving their legs bare and free for combat. One samurai wrests the helmet from* YAEGAKI, *but, mysteriously, she is able to hold him back. The three pose to a shrill note from the flute and two* tsuke *beats. Indicating her possession by the fox spirits,* YAEGAKI*'s right hand is curled under like a fox paw. Aided by the foxes' strength,* YAEGAKI *continues the dance battle* [shosadate] *with the samurai, retrieving the helmet and causing the men to somersault onto their backs. Momentarily they lie defeated.)*

YAEGAKI: Yes, now I remember! If the lake is frozen over, one need only find where a fox has already crossed. Following its footprints, even men and horses may

Princess Yaegaki (Bandō Tamasaburō V) holds the magical helmet overhead and gazes into the pond, where she sees the reflection of a fox spirit. (Umemura Yutaka, Engeki Shuppansha)

pass without worry. Yet, to cross before a fox would mean drowning beneath the water. All men know this of Suwa Lake!

TAKEMOTO *(Boldly, courageously)*:

Even if across the ice / no fox has yet passed, / the thought of her dear husband / gives her strength of will. / Added to that, the helmet / with its power divine / that now must be returned to / Lord Katsuyori. / This is the sacred wish of / the god of Suwa.

(Seated, YAEGAKI *hits the ground with her knees to emphasize her resolute spirit. She bows to her beloved and then turns toward the shrine, lifting her hand and lowering her head in gratitude.)*

YAEGAKI: I will obey!

(She puts her hands together and rubs them in heartfelt prayer.)

TAKEMOTO:

"I will obey . . . I will obey! / How thankful . . . grateful I am!" / Thus, taking up the helmet / to place upon her head, / instantly, the dancing shapes / of fox fires ablaze, / flickering all about her, / burning here and there.

*(*YAEGAKI *stands and the two samurai reappear to challenge her. She holds the helmet above her head and the samurai pose on either side of her to loud* dorodoro, *flute, and* tsuke *beats. Balls of flame representing fox fires float through the air, suspended on poles held by* STAGE ASSISTANTS. YAEGAKI, *left, holds the helmet aloft as the men attempt to pull her from behind.)*

Flames roaring in confusion, / how wondrous the sight! / Here protecting the helmet / of the Buddha's supreme truth!

(The fight continues to offstage dorodoro *and* tsuke *beats. The men cannot defeat the power of the fox spirits.* YAEGAKI *disappears behind the fence, right, as the men pose, holding the helmet between them. The helmet held by the* STAGE ASSISTANT *flies left, causing the men to revolve dizzily. It leads them across the bridge into the shrine. Using the shrine's sacred straw rope, they try but fail to catch the helmet, which flies back toward* YAEGAKI. *Controlled by the fox spirits, the men take out short silver truncheons* [jitte] *and begin to fight each other to loud offstage* dorodoro.*)*

At last, to Suwa Lake she goes, / starting now to cross / . . . as though taking to the air.

(Now in a pink kimono, YAEGAKI *reappears through the fence with helmet in hand. With the offstage water pattern creating suspense, she stands motionless, invisible to the two samurai. Once again they approach the helmet and challenge, only to be confronted by* YAEGAKI, *who defeats them again and again. She forces them back into the shrine building, where they hold the sacred rope over their shoulders.* YAEGAKI *hurries to* shichisan *to fast beats of the* tsuke, *trips, and falls to her knees. Turning to the men inside the shrine, she rises and, with a single wave of the*

helmet, causes both to somersault and lie unconscious. She poses triumphantly to two tsuke *beats. The blinds come down to close off the shrine. The helmet now seems alive in her hand.* YAEGAKI *briefly stumbles back, overwhelmed by its power. The large drum sounds forcefully offstage* [ōdoro] *together with the stick drum and flute playing a fast fox pattern* [haya raijo] *as* YAEGAKI *starts down the* hanamichi, *at times struggling in fear against the helmet but pulled forward toward the frozen lake.* Tsuke *beats echo her footsteps and the curtain closes to accelerating* ki.*)*

GLOSSARY

This glossary is restricted to terms used in Volume 1. Glossary terms in other volumes will differ somewhat, as may the definitions themselves. Long vowels are given only for italicized words and not for terms likely to be found in a standard English dictionary. Cross-referenced words are in bold italic type. A literal translation is given only for selected terms.

adauchi (revenge), the subject of vengeance, which fills so many plays. Also ***katakiuchi.***

aibiki, a black stool, either high or low, placed under an actor by a ***kōken*** or ***kurogo*** to ease the strain of sitting or standing over a long period. Often it helps to give the actor additional stature.

ai guma (blue shadow), stylized ***kumadori*** makeup of bold blue-grey lines on a white background, suggesting an evil nature.

aikata, melodic excerpt played during dialogue or action by offstage shamisen to suggest mood or emotional context.

akahime (red princess), young, upper-class, female role type of extreme refinement and fragility, so-named because the character usually wears a bright red, long-sleeved ***(furisode)*** kimono.

akattsura (red face), role of a red-faced minor villain in a ***jidaimono.***

aragoto (rough business), bravura acting style, a specialty of the Ichikawa Danjūrō acting family, particularly in ***Kabuki Jūhachiban*** plays.

arahitogami, a powerful character who may be considered a kind of demigod.

asagimaku (light blue curtain), large curtain of light-blue cotton rigged downstage in order to cover the full width of the stage. When dropped, a new scene is suddenly revealed.

banzuke, program or poster advertising a play and its cast.

batabata. See ***tsuke.***

Bon. See ***Obon.***

boshi, hat or purple cloth worn on the crown of a woman's wig.

bukkaeri (sudden change), a quick, onstage costume change technique by which stage assistants remove basting threads so that, at the proper moment, the top half of the costume falls about the actor's waist with the inside lining covering the lower half of the kimono. This lining matches the newly revealed upper half, the effect being as if the entire costume has been changed. The actor strikes a ***mie*** and the assistants hold up the rear portion of the dropped fabric to increase the actor's size. See also ***hayagawari, hikinuki.***

bunraku, popular term for a commercial puppet theatre form based in Osaka. The term derives from the name of late eighteenth–early nineteenth-century producer Uemura Bunrakuen (or Bunrakuken). See ***ningyō jōruri.***

buyō (dance), specifically dance in kabuki, which may also be called ***nihon buyō*** (Japanese dance).

chikaragami (power paper), stiff, winglike paper forms projecting upward from a ***gohon kuruma bin*** wig to add volume to an ***aragoto*** hero's head.

chirashi (scattering), a segment of musical composition, usually rapid, played just before the finale ***(dangiri).***

chobo, team of one ***takemoto*** chanter ***(tayū)*** and one shamisen player in kabuki.

chūnori (riding in the air), stage trick ***(keren)*** of an actor flying, via ropes and pulleys, over the stage or audience.

daigashira, genre of sung storytelling and sometimes dance beginning in the Muromachi period (1568–1600) and taken into early kabuki; related to the ***kōwakamai*** performance genre.

daihon (stage book), handwritten script written by the playwright and his assistants for a specific production and used by actors and producers in rehearsal. Also called ***gikyoku.***

daikon (radish), or *daikon yakusha* (radish actor), a slur at an actor, shouted out in the theatre for a poor performance.

daishō iri, offstage musical accompaniment using shamisen, large drum ***(ōdaiko),*** and small drum ***(kotsuzumi)*** and heard during ***tachimawari*** scenes.

dan, division of a play, most commonly an act within a dialogue play. Also, a section or sequence of a dance play, such as "waving sleeves and stamping section" (*momi no dan*) and "bell section" (*suzu no dan*).

dangiri, also *dangire,* two offstage drumbeats chiefly used at the closing of the curtain in a ***jidaimono.*** Also, the final musical section of a dance play.

danjiri, an Osaka-style festival percussion rhythm.

degatari (onstage narrative), the convention of musical narrative groups (***takemoto, kiyomoto, tokiwazu,*** etc.) performing onstage, where they sit on special platforms and wear formal costumes, as in *Lady Kuzunoha.*

dokugin (solitary recital), solo offstage singing accompaniment in ***meriyasu*** style designed to heighten the plaintive atmosphere of certain scenes.

doma, the "pitlike" seating area in the middle of a theatre.

dorodoro, onomatopoeic word for an intermittent, rolling pattern of the offstage large drum ***(ōdaiko)*** that denotes tension, mystery, or the supernatural.

ebizori (no mie) (prawn-shaped pose), type of ***mie,*** performed by female characters, in which the kneeling actor, overcome by an opponent's power, bends his body backward in a posture resembling the shape of a prawn. Also called *ebigaeri no mie.* One of the rare *mie* associated with female characters.

eboshi, tall, black, lacquered hat worn, as a rule, by nobility.

Edo *sanza,* the three large, officially licensed theatres of Edo: the Nakamura-za, Morita-za, and Ichimura-za. Also called *sanza.*

eiri kyōgen bon, Tokugawa-period illustrated scenarios. Principal form in which plays were published before the Meiji era.

emen no mie (picture pose), picturelike tableau that concludes an act, usually of a ***jidaimono.*** Each character poses in a ***mie*** appropriate to his or her nature.

fukiwa (blown circle), elaborate wig worn by high-ranking female character in a ***jidaimono.*** The topknot is constructed around a large drum of silver or gold.

fumidashi. See ***mie.***

furisode (hanging sleeve), kimono style worn by young women, so-called because of its very long sleeves.

gagaku (elegant performance), ceremonial music of the imperial court.

gassaku (joint writing), coauthorship, a common practice in kabuki and puppet theatre. Also a coauthored play.

genroku mie, a powerful ***aragoto***-style ***mie*** in which left and right arms and legs point in opposite directions, the actor raises one hand in a fist, and the body faces on the diagonal, creating a tense pose.

geta, wooden clogs worn outdoors.

geza (lower seat), offstage musicians' room, located stage right (the "lower" side of a kabuki stage). Also, the shamisen, drum, gong, flute players, and singers who perform here, watching the unfolding stage action through slits in the scenery. Also, the background music and songs performed throughout a play by these offstage musicians.

gidayū, one style of narrative theatre music. Created ca.1685 by chanter Takemoto Gidayū for the puppet theatre and now standard music for puppet plays. Also called ***takemoto*** when performed in kabuki.

gikyoku. See ***daihon.***

giri (obligation), sense of duty to someone else, usually one's lord or a superior; a major motive of characters in kabuki plays, often set in opposition to human feelings ***(ninjō).***

go, board game in which a player, using either black or white stones, attempts to surround and eliminate the stones placed by his opponent.

gohon kuruma bin (five-spoked wheel wig), wig with five heavily lacquered, projecting "spokes" of bound hair radiating from each side of the head, forming a kind of halo.

hachimaki, small cloth, rolled or folded and tied around the head as a headband.

hakama, wide, ankle-length, pleated culottes worn over kimono by commoners or together with a vest ***(kataginu)*** by samurai. ***Nagabakama*** (long *hakama*), worn by samurai on the most formal occasions, trail behind the wearer six or eight feet.

hanamichi (flower path), rampway running from the rear of the auditorium, through the audience, and connecting at a right angle to the main stage at stage right; used for major entrances and entrances.

hanare kyōgen, the simple one-act plays of early kabuki prior to the development of multiact dramas ***(tsuzuki kyōgen).***

hana yakko. See ***yakko.***

hana yoten. See ***yoten.***

hanten, laborer's short, open work jacket, usually made of indigo-dyed cotton.

haori, thigh-length, open, outer robe worn by men over kimono as an informal garment by samurai and a formal garment by commoners.

haradashi (belly-thruster), evil, red-faced, bare-bellied minor samurai, as in *Just a Minute!*

haragei (gut acting), truthful, intuitive acting that goes beyond the conventions; begun by Ichikawa Danjūrō IX in the late nineteenth century.

haru kyōgen (spring play), plays produced during the New Year season (first lunar month, usually mid-February), the beginning of spring on the lunar calendar. This was the second major production of the theatre year. Called *ni no kawari* (second change) in Kamigata. *Haru kyogen* titles in Edo customarily contained the word "Soga," or in Kamigata, the word ***"keisei."*** Also called *hatsuharu kyōgen* ("early spring play"), and *hatsu shibai* (first play).

hashigakari, the runway used for important entrances in ***nō*** theatres.

hayabue (fast flute), lively offstage musical pattern played by drum and flute to suggest tension or conflict in ***jidaimono,*** as in *The Golden Pavilion.*

hayagawari (quick change), any one of a variety of quick-change costume techniques, such as ***hikinuki*** or ***bukkaeri.***

haya kagura (fast court music), offstage music played by flute, stick drum ***(taiko),*** and large drum ***(ōdaiko)*** that suggests ***gagaku*** music of the imperial court; played for the opening scene of the ***kaomise*** program.

haya raijo (fast lightning), rapid offstage musical pattern played by ***nō*** flute, stick drum ***(taiko),*** and large drum ***(ōdaiko)*** to signify the fast exit of a fox character. See also ***raijo.***

haya sagariha, stately offstage music played by the flute and three drums of the ***nō*** ensemble to indicate a palace scene.

hengemono (transformation dance), a kind of dance that evolved during the nineteenth century in which a single actor played up to twelve roles in sequential dance scenes. Only some of the individual scenes from these longer dance works still survive, except for *The Six Poet Immortals*, which is sometimes still produced with all five of its original scenes. Also called *henge buyō.*

hikimaku, kabuki's standard draw curtain, pulled open and closed by stage assistants.

hikinuki (pulling out), onstage quick costume change in which basting threads are pulled out of an outer kimono so it can be removed instantly to reveal an inner kimono of a different color.

hinadan (doll platform), long, two-step platform covered with a red cloth on which sit the fifteen to twenty instrumentalists and singers of a ***nagauta*** musical ensemble.

hinin (nonhuman), outcast; the status of kabuki actors was beneath and outside the four defined social classes: samurai, farmer, artisan, and merchant.

hippari mie (pulling tableau), group ***mie*** showing tension of unresolved conflict between hero and opponent, or among additional characters, at a play's final curtain.

hiyoku no tori (joined birds), a mythical Chinese pair of birds physically joined and sharing one pair of wings and eyes, symbolizing abiding marital love.

hontsurigane (main bell), large offstage bronze bell and its sound. Struck with a mallet, its long reverberation tolls the time and creates a pensive or expectant mood.

hyōshigi. See ***ki.***

ie no gei (family art), a group of plays or a style of acting associated with a particular acting family. The *ie no gei* of the Ichikawa Danjūrō line is both its ***Kabuki Jūhachiban*** play collection and its ***aragoto*** acting style.

ishinage no mie (stone-throwing pose), a ***mie*** executed, usually by a heroic male figure, with one hand held above the head, fingers open, as if the character has just thrown a stone.

ito ni nori. See ***nori.***

jidai (period), a scene played in history play style. See ***jidaimono.***

jidaimono (period piece), one of the major dramatic genres, a history play concerning rulers, gods, imperial nobility, or samurai. Usually, but not necessarily, set in the distant, pre-Tokugawa-period past.

jidai-sewamono (period-domestic piece), long, all-day play in which the first part (often *ichibanme*, "first part") is a ***jidaimono*** and the concluding part (often *nibanme*, "second part") is a ***sewamono.***

jiri-jiri, onomatopoeic word for a heel-toe sliding foot movement that edges the actor sideways; used in situations of tension or conflict.

jitte, short metal truncheon held in one hand by police or fighting chorus ***(yoten)*** that serves as both weapon and symbol of authority.

jōruri, generic term for narrative theatre music, sung-chanted and accompanied by shamisen; performed in several styles, including ***takemoto, ōzatsuma, tokiwazu,*** and ***kiyomoto*** in kabuki and ***gidayū*** (another name for ***takemoto***) in the puppet theatre. Often used to refer to the puppet theatre as a whole.

junsui (pure), plays composed directly for kabuki production rather than being adapted from the puppet theatre, ***nō,*** or ***kyōgen.***

Kabuki Jūhachiban (Eighteen Famous Kabuki Plays), a group of plays performed mainly in ***aragoto*** acting style; created by several generations of actors in the Ichikawa Danjūrō family line. Finalized by Danjūrō VII in 1840, the collection includes *The Medicine Seller* and *Just a Minute!*

kabuki odori (kabuki dance), the name given to the performances originated by Okuni in the early seventeenth century.

kabuku, the old verb meaning "to incline," from which the word kabuki was derived.

kagen, offstage musical pattern played by ***nō*** flute, large drum ***(ōdaiko),*** and often shamisen, mimicking ancient imperial ***gagaku*** music *(kangen);* used to suggest impressive grandeur of a court scene in a ***jidaimono.***

kagura (god dance), dances associated with the Shinto religion; performed at shrines, the imperial court, or in villages on auspicious occasions.

kakegoe, well-timed shouts directed at the actors by spectators to encourage a performance or, sometimes, to criticize it.

kakinuki (excerpted writing or "sides"), dialogue booklets containing one actor's lines and used in rehearsal.

kami (deity, spirit), transcendent presence in Shinto religion, usually in form of a deity, spirit of natural phenomena, or deified human.

kamishimo (top-bottom), formal samurai male outer garments worn over basic kimono and consisting of stiffened vest ***(kataginu)*** and wide, ankle-length, pleated culottes ***(hakama).***

kane no oto (bell sound), the single or multiple tolling of the large temple bell ***(hontsurigane)*** to indicate time or atmosphere.

kanzen chōaku (reward good, punish evil), Confucian formulation of the proper didactic aim of literature.

kaomise kyōgen (face-showing play), the first play of the annual theatre season, in the eleventh lunar month (usually mid- or late December), constructed to showcase a troupe's new lineup of stars.

karami (grappler), minor soldiers or policemen who are easily defeated foils of a principal character in battles **(tachimawari).**

kari hanamichi (temporary *hanamichi*), the secondary runway sometimes set up on the audience right side of the auditorium. In the past, this was a permanent part of theatre architecture, but in modern productions, it is set up only if needed. Formerly *higashi no ayumi.*

kasa zukushi (umbrella catalogue), section of *The Heron Maiden* in which a dancer performs a lyrical sequence to a description of umbrellas. Kabuki often has scenes in which a common item or concept is enumerated.

kata (form, pattern), conventional forms of acting, makeup, scenery, music, or costumes handed down over generations but nonetheless changeable according to each actor's taste.

kataginu, formal, stiff, vestlike garment worn with **hakama** over kimono by samurai. See **kamishimo.**

katakiuchi. See **adauchi.**

kaze no oto (wind sound), or **kazaoto,** a pattern of the offstage large drum **(ōdaiko)** that suggests a strong wind.

keisei (castle toppler), courtesan, a common character in kabuki plays. Of various ranks, the highest is **tayū.**

keren, spectacular stage trick or special effect, including quick costume changes, character transformations, acrobatics, flying in the air, and stunts using real water.

ki, or **hyōshigi,** two tapered hardwood clappers, struck together in the air to produce a clear musical sound that signals a technical change in a scene. A continuous pattern (*kizami, hon maku,* or *hyōshi maku*) accompanies the opening or closing of the draw curtain. A single clack signals the start of a scene (*ki o naosu*) or the end of a performance (*tomegi*); a curtain to fall or the stage to revolve (*itchōgi*); or sets up the final moments of a scene (*kigashira* or *ki no kashira*).

kigashira. See **ki.**

kimari (pose), brief pose to emphasize emotion, intention, or reaction. Softer and shorter in duration than a **mie,** it is often performed by a female character.

kinuta (fulling block), offstage music suggesting the beating of cloth on a fulling block.

kiri (cutting or end), in a puppet play script, the final scene of a multiscene act.

kitsune no bi (fox fires), the blue-green lights believed to hover where magical foxes congregate. Represented in kabuki by phosphorescent flames attached to ***sashidashi*** and manipulated by stage assistants.

kitsune kotoba (fox words), section of *Lady Kuzunoha* in which the character's speech suggests her fox nature.

kiyomoto, major musical style for dance plays, which originated in the nineteenth century. The musicians appear on stage when they perform.

kizami. See ***ki.***

kōjō (announcement), formal announcement from the stage by an actor or stage manager ***(tōdori)*** to the audience, such as a comment about the play or performance or a proclamation of an actor's name change, often in a special name-taking ceremony.

ko jōruri (old *jōruri*), puppet plays from before the time of Chikamatsu Monzaemon and Takemoto Gidayū, who revolutionized the nature of puppet performance and dramaturgy.

kōken (see from behind), acting assistant who, crouching unobtrusively behind an actor, helps him with properties, costumes, or makeup. In spectacular pieces, such as *Just a Minute!*, *The Medicine Seller,* and *The Heron Maiden*, the *kōken* wears a formal costume ***(kamishimo)*** and wig; in less formal plays, the *kōken* wears black garments (hence the nickname ***kurogo***). Some plays employ both types of assistant.

kokyū, small, offstage stringed instrument played with a bow, originally introduced from China; used to create a mood of romantic melancholy.

koshibai, small theatres, in contrast to the major theatres ***(ōshibai).*** They operated during the Tokugawa period under various restrictions. See also ***miya shibai.***

kotsuzumi, small drum, struck by the hand.

kōwakamai, all-male medieval performing art that presented dances based on war chronicles.

kowakare (child separation), scene of pathos in which a parent and child must part from one another.

koyaku (child role), roles for child actors.

kuchidate, the old art of ad-libbing, which kabuki actors used in the creation of their earliest plays.

kudoki (entreaty or lamentation), plea of a female character to her lover or expression of pathos or deep sorrow, usually through mime, to sung lyrics in a dance play or to chanted narrative from the puppet theatre.

kumadori (following the shadow), highly stylized makeup consisting of a solid base on which are applied strong red or blue lines that follow and emphasize bone contours. Primarily used for heroic or supernatural figures in ***aragoto***-style plays.

kuni kuzushi (nation destroyer), aristocratic arch-villain in a ***jidaimono,*** such as Matsunaga Daizen Hisahide in *The Golden Pavilion.*

kuriage, during a confrontation between two characters, an exchange of a repeated word or phrase that rises to a crescendo and ends in a unison line.

kurisage (scooped and dropped), wig in which hair rises in bunches around a shaved pate. Worn by minor comic villains (*hagataki*) in ***jidaimono.***

kurogo (black clothes), nickname for black-robed and hooded stage assistants. Also *kuronbo* (black boy). See ***kōken.***

kuruwa, legally licensed prostitution quarters (pleasure quarters or gay quarters), such as Yoshiwara in Edo, Shinmachi in Osaka, and Shimabara in Kyoto.

kuse, a musical section of ***nō*** plays, sung largely by the chorus and performed while the ***shite*** is either sitting or dancing.

kyōgen (farcical words), genre of short comic plays performed alternately with ***nō*** plays on a theatre program. In kabuki, a generic term for a play, such as ***natsu kyōgen*** (summer play).

kyōgen kata (play person), backstage functionary and apprentice playwright.

maku soto no hikkomi (outside-the-curtain exit), lead actor's exit down the ***hanamichi*** after the main curtain has been closed behind him; used to conclude an act or play and/or to focus audience attention on the ***hanamichi.***

manaita obi. See ***obi.***

mawari butai (revolving stage), originally a manually turned disk placed atop the stage proper; later, built into the stage and, eventually, operated by electricity.

meriyasu, brief, offstage segment of ***nagauta*** music, usually sung by a solo singer to shamisen accompaniment during scenes without dialogue to accentuate the emotional feeling of the action. It is heard mainly in scenes with a melancholic or romantic flavor.

michiyuki (travel scene), scene in which two characters—usually lovers—travel to their destination; performed as an independent dance or a dance scene within a longer play. Often associated with a double suicide.

mie (pose), powerful acting technique in which the actor makes several rhythmic movements that culminate in a freeze of several seconds. Often, one foot may be planted strongly (*fumidashi*), arms are thrust outward, head is rotated (*senuki*), and, at the final moment, one eye is crossed in a glaring look (*nirami*) that expresses intense feelings. ***Tsuke*** beats accompany the foot planting and the two-part head rotation. Usually performed by powerful male characters and far less frequently by females. Numerous types of ***mie*** exist, many being known by technical names, such as ***ishinage no mie.*** See also ***kimari.***

migawari (substitution), plot convention whereby one character is substituted for another to protect the life of a superior.

mimasu (three measuring boxes), the Ichikawa Danjūrō family's distinctive crest of three nested rice-measuring boxes.

minarai (look-and-learn), apprentice playwright.

miokagura, offstage percussion music indicating precincts of a shrine in ***jidaimono.***

miya shibai (temple/shrine ground theatre), or *miya shibai,* temporary theatre set up under special licensing arrangements on the grounds of a temple and shrine. They competed with the ***ōshibai.*** See also ***koshibai.***

miya kagura (shrine music), offstage shamisen and percussion pattern, featuring ***ōdaiko, taiko,*** bamboo flute, and small bronze cymbals, indicating the precincts of a shrine.

mizu no oto (water sound), drumbeat pattern of the offstage large drum ***(ōdaiko)*** suggesting flowing water.

mizu nuno (water cloth), ground cloth simulating water; used in scenes taking place near lakes, ponds, or streams.

modori (return), playwriting technique in which a seemingly evil character returns to good behavior.

monogatari (narration), solo narrative of an important event from the past by a male character; a major dramatic sequence in kabuki plays derived from the puppet theatre.

mudra, symbolic hand position, usually of a Buddhist figure.

nagabakama. See ***hakama.***

nagauta (long song), music of shamisen and singers with the flute and three drums of the ***nō*** ensemble that became the basic form of kabuki music. A lyric style, as opposed to a narrative style. Played onstage for dance plays or offstage ***(geza)*** as background music during dialogue plays.

namazu guma (catfish makeup), humorous makeup style suggesting the face of a catfish.

namiita (wave boards), scenic convention of waves painted on a two-dimensional groundrow for scenes set near water.

nami no oto (wave sound), drumbeat pattern of the offstage large drum ***(ōdaiko)*** that suggests continuous swelling and falling of waves.

narabi daimyō (lined-up lords), group of high-ranking lords aligned at the back or side of the stage to increase a scene's visual effect.

netori (roosting bird), eerie rising and falling of an offstage flute melody suggesting the supernatural. Also *netoribue* (roosting bird flute).

nichō, shamisen melody in lively tempo used to highlight movement sequences or in pauses between formal speeches.

nihon buyō (Japanese dance), recital dance drawn from the kabuki repertory.

nimaime sakusha, the second-ranking playwright in a kabuki company. See **gassaku.**

ningyō buri (puppet gestures), acting that imitates the movement of puppets, including the presence of black-robed puppet manipulators to make the illusion even more puppetlike.

ningyō jōruri (musical-narrative puppet theatre), the major form of commercial puppet theatre, centered in Osaka; popularly called **bunraku.**

ninjō (human feelings), unmediated human impulses, desires, or feelings. In kabuki drama, these feelings are often in conflict with one's social obligations ***(giri).***

nō, austere, classical genre of theatre, predating kabuki. During the Tokugawa period **nō** was made the official theatre of the samurai class, while kabuki catered to commoners.

nō-kyōgen, the composite art of serious, chanted, masked **nō** and humorous, spoken **kyōgen.** A standard program consists of several plays of each genre offered in alternation.

nori (riding), vocal technique in which an actor recites dialogue in time to **takemoto** shamisen rhythm, a technique borrowed from the puppet theatre. Also *ito ni nori* ("riding the strings" of the shamisen).

nuigurumi (sewed-on wrapping), costume worn by an actor portraying an animal.

Obon (also Bon), late-summer Buddhist festival for the spirits of the dead; the occasion for plays (*bon kyōgen*) about characters who have died tragically.

ōdaiko (large drum), large offstage drum played with a pair of either thick or light sticks to provide a wide range of atmospheric rhythmic patterns.

ōdaimono (great age plays), a group of **jidaimono** set in the Nara (696–794) and Heian (794–1185) periods, prior to the wars between the Genji and Heike clans. Also called *ōchō mono.*

odoriji (dance section), lively concluding section of a dance or dance play using rhythmic and often abstract movements.

ōdoro (large *dorodoro*), drumbeat pattern of the offstage large drum ***(ōdaiko)*** that is an exaggerated form of **dorodoro,** indicating a ghostly apparition or other impending supernatural event.

oiemono (feudal house piece), ***jidaimono*** based on feudal clan controversies; also *oiesōdō* (internal clan turmoil). A play involving a struggle for succession to clan leadership, frequently involving a missing heirloom that sets the plot in motion. Generally set in the pre–Tokugawa past to avoid censorship.

ōiri, full or sold-out house. During a performance, an actor may write in the air the simple three-stroke character for "large" (*ō*) and the two-stroke character for "enter" (*iri*) as a symbol of good fortune.

ōji (prince), wig on which hair hangs loose from a shaved pate to below the shoulders. Worn by aristocratic villains (*kugeaku*) in ***jidaimono.***

oki, prelude section of many dance plays.

omigoromo, elegant floor-length brocade outer coat with stiffened collar, worn indoors by high-ranking male nobility.

ōmukō, the gallery at the rear of the theatre, facing the stage. Its low-cost seats were usually occupied by aficionados.

onnadate, a female character who is strong willed, gallant, and fearless. Equivalent to the male **otokodate.**

onnagata (female form), male actor of female roles.

onryō, angry ghost who may come back to seek revenge.

ōshibai, large theatres during the Tokugawa period, in contrast to small theatres ***(koshibai*** and ***miya shibai).***

ōtachi (large sword), exaggeratedly long sword carried by ***aragoto*** heroes.

otokodate, virtuous Tokugawa-period commoners or "street knights" who acted as protectors of the townsmen against samurai abuse.

Ōtsu-e, folk painting from the area of Ōtsu, near Kyoto.

ōzatsuma, early type of narrative music used in Edo for ***aragoto***-style plays. Usually performed by onstage musicians.

raijo (lightning), offstage musical pattern played by ***nō*** flute, stick drum ***(taiko),*** and large drum ***(ōdaiko)*** to indicate the entry of a fox character. See also ***haya raijo.***

renga, classical "linked-verse" style of poetry.

roppō (six directions), stylized, bravura masculine walk usually performed on the ***hanamichi*** as an exaggerated way of exiting. One type is the *tobi roppō* (flying in six directions), a leaping, bounding exit.

sabakiyaku (sagacious role), judicious, problem-solving hero, usually in a ***jidaimono*** (for example, Sanemori in *The Sanemori Story*).

sakaro, secret technique of rowing against the wind and tide; valuable in naval maneuvering.

sakusha, playwright on the staff of a theatre company and part of a writer's hierarchy. See also ***tate sakusha.***

sanbo kagura, a lively tune heard in *The Felicitous Soga Encounter.*

san hime (three princesses), the three most important and difficult princess roles in kabuki, including Princess Yaegaki in *Japan's Twenty-Four Paragons of Filial Piety* and Princess Yuki in *The Golden Pavilion.*

sanmaime sakusha, the third-ranking playwright in a kabuki company. See ***gassaku.***

san nyōbo (three wives), the three most challenging wife roles in kabuki, including Otoku in *Matahei the Stutterer.*

saru guma, a monkeylike makeup worn by Asahina in *The Felicitous Soga Encounter.*

sashidashi (thrust forth), long, thin pole with a candle at one end, used by ***kurogo*** or ***kōken*** to light an actor's face. Still used in certain plays to recapture the feeling of old-time kabuki.

sashigane (thrust metal), long, thin pole used by ***kurogo*** or ***kōken*** to bring to magical life a butterfly, bird, mouse, or other object attached by a wire to its tip.

sekai (world), well-known cluster of characters and situations from the past for which a playwright fabricates a plot ***(shukō)*** to create a new play.

seme no dan (torture segment), brief portion of *The Heron Maiden* in which the title figure suffers the tortures of hell, but in a very highly stylized, even abstract, way. Other plays feature realistic torture scenes (*semeba*).

seri, stage elevator used to raise or lower scenery and/or actors. See also ***suppon.***

sewaba (domestic scene), a scene of poverty in a ***sewamono*** or of family tragedy, such as separation of parent and child ***(kowakare),*** in a ***jidaimono.***

sewamono (domestic piece), a play concerning commoners of any period, although usually set during the Tokugawa period.

shagiri, ceremonial drum ***(taiko*** and ***ōdaiko)*** and flute music played at the end of an act.

shibai jaya, teahouse attached to and serving a theatre.

shichigochō (seven-five meter), verse written for puppet performance or dialogue written for kabuki composed in alternating phrases of seven and five syllables. Usually sung in puppet-derived plays, and spoken in rhythmic style in pure kabuki plays.

shichisan (seven-three), an actor's strongest position on the ***hanamichi,*** located in the midst of the audience seven units from stage and three from back of auditorium. An actor entering or exiting the ***hanamichi*** stops at this position in order to shift focus toward or away from the scene onstage. In the twentieth century, with the advent of projecting balconies, *shichisan* was moved forward to a position three units away from the stage and seven units from the back of the auditorium so an actor in this position may be seen by all audience members.

shiokumi (dipping brine), offstage song suggesting melancholy.

shiro nuri (painted white), a white-faced character, indicating refinement, in both kabuki and the puppet theatre.

shite (doer), main character in a ***nō*** play; often masked.

***shōji*,** sliding doors of latticed framework covered with white paper used to divide rooms or serve as entrance and exit doors to a residence.

shosa (posture or gesture), dance or mime.

shosabutai (dance stage), polished cypress platforms placed over the main stage and ***hanamichi*** for dance or ***aragoto***-style plays. The platforms facilitate smooth sliding steps and reverberate when stamped on.

shosadate*,** fighting techniques ***(tate) performed as dance.

***shosagoto*,** a dance play.

shukō (plot or arrangement), the manipulation of events and characters to create a newly constructed plot; considered the "horizontal" aspect of playwriting, vis à vis the "vertical" aspect of known worlds ***(sekai)*** of subject matter. Kabuki plays are famous for intricately elaborated and complex plots.

***shūme*,** the formal name-taking ceremony performed when an actor publicly changes his name.

suji guma (muscle shadow), strong type of ***kumadori*** makeup using bold red lines on a white background.

***suō*,** voluminous outer robe worn by samurai in a ***jidaimono*.**

suppon (snapping turtle), small stage elevator ***(seri)*** located at ***shichisan*** on the ***hanamichi*;** used for the appearance or disappearance of a single character, usually a ghost or other supernatural figure.

sutezerifu (thrown away dialogue), dialogue not written in a script but ad-libbed or extemporized by actor.

tabi*,** bifurcated socks for men or women of all stations, worn indoors, or outdoors with sandals ***(zōri) or clogs ***(geta)*.**

tachimawari (standing and turning), stylized fight scene consisting of choreographed movement sequences ***(kata)*** that culminate in ***mie*.** It may involve two or three major characters or may pit a hero against a mass of opponents, in which case it may also be called ***tate*.**

tachiyaku (standing role), originally a term that distinguished actors, who stood and moved, from seated musicians. It now means a leading male role of a wide range of types.

tada uta (solo song), arresting, melancholy song sung offstage to shamisen accompaniment, usually for the exit of a female character.

taiko, stick drum.

taikoji (drum chorus), a musical segment, such as in *The Heron Maiden.*

taimen (encounter), ritualized confrontation between hero and villain.

taimen sanju, offstage shamisen music used for the entrance of Gorō and Jūrō in *The Felicitous Soga Encounter.*

takageta, tall wooden clogs, worn mainly by courtesans but also worn by a few male characters, such as Gongorō in *Just a Minute!,* in order to greatly increase their height.

takemoto, emotional, highly dramatic style of narrative music ***(jōruri)*** adapted to kabuki from the puppet theatre where it is called ***gidayū.*** Performed by a team of one chanter-singer ***(tayū)*** and one shamisen player for dialogue plays and by a large ensemble for dance plays.

tanka (short poem), a type of poetry consisting of five lines of 5–7–5–7–7 syllables.

tatami, straw-covered mats used for residential flooring.

tate, the codified sequences of fight choreography used in ***tachimawari.***

tate sakusha, chief playwright of a theatre company and supervisor of second-ranking playwright ***(nimaime sakusha),*** third-ranking playwright ***(sanmaime sakusha),*** and writing and rehearsal assistants (***kyōgen kata*** or *kyōgen sakusha*) attached to the company.

tayū (chief performer), chanter of ***takemoto*** music. Also a top-ranking courtesan ***(keisei).***

tengu, demon or goblin often depicted with hawk's beak and wings or red face and long nose.

tenugui, hand towel ubiquitously carried by commoners, second only to the fan in its variety of uses.

tobi roppō. See ***roppō.***

tōdori, a backstage functionary of considerable importance. Something like an assistant manager, he made stage announcements as well.

tokiwazu, important style of kabuki narrative music created in the eighteenth century and used in dance plays.

Tokugawa period (1603–1868), period of feudal rule through fifteen shoguns of the Tokugawa samurai clan. Noted as a time of peace, seclusion from outside contact, and mercantile and urban growth. Because shoguns resided in Edo, also called Edo period.

tōmi (distant view), flat or drop painted with a distant view. Also, placing actors or small scenic models upstage to suggest that they are far in the distance.

tomimoto, early style of highly emotional narrative music created in kabuki to accompany dances. Now largely defunct.

tonbo (dragonfly), short for *tonbogaeri,* a flip or somersault performed by a combat specialist during ***tachimawari.***

torii, simple wood or stone gateway consisting of two posts topped by one or two beams that marks the entry to a Shinto shrine.

tōshi kyōgen (full play), performance of an entire, or nearly entire, play text. Most programs are composed of selected scenes from several plays; these are called *midori.*

tōyose, offstage musical pattern of conch shell blasts and large drum ***(ōdaiko)*** signifying a call to battle and battle sounds.

tsuke, two wood blocks beat alternately on a wooden board placed on the floor near the stage left proscenium. *Tsuke* beats (*tsuke uchi*) accompany and emphasize stage action: a single beat (*hiro te*) for a small action; a double beat (*batan*) for a strong action or a ***mie;*** a continuous pattern (*batabata*) to accompany running; and a rising and falling pattern (*uchiage*) to highlight a climactic ***mie.*** A three-beat pattern (*battari*) may also be used to emphasize ***mie.***

tsunagi (tie together), quiet music or ***ki*** beats played during brief interval in which a set is changed, usually with house lights dimmed.

tsurane (in succession), bravura monologue delivered by a hero in ***jidaimono*** to boast of his virtues and power. Formerly composed by the actor, playwrights have developed elaborate speeches written in ***shichigochō*** with puns, word play, insults, lists of related words, and other entertaining verbal devices. May also refer to less flamboyant but nevertheless dramatic speeches of self-introduction in ***sewamono.***

tsurieda (hanging branches), decorative border of cherry or plum blossoms, maple leaves, lightning flashes, or other features of nature that frames an outdoor setting.

tsuzuki kyōgen, multiact plays first introduced into kabuki in 1664.

tsuzumi, drum, in two sizes, struck by the fingers and palm of one hand. The “large drum” (*ōtsuzumi*) is held on the player’s hip and produces a hard, metallic sound. The “small drum” ***(kotsuzumi)*** is held on the player’s shoulder and produces a smaller, softer tone.

uchikake, woman’s elegantly trailing outer robe worn over kimono on formal occasions; usualy padded, heavily embroidered, and left open at the front.

usudorodoro, a light drumbeat pattern to create an ominous mood. See ***dorodoro, ōdoro.***

wagoto (soft business), gentle, comic-erotic acting style developed primarily by actors in the Kamigata region.

wajitsu (gentle truth), role type combining the gentleness of a ***wagoto*** role with the upright behavior found in roles of conscientious, mature, and intelligent men *(jitsugoto).*

wakashu (young man), role of an adolescent. Also, adolescent actors who were important in early kabuki.

waki (beside), secondary character in **nō** who is the unmasked questioner of the main character ***(shite).***

warizerifu (divided dialogue), also *kakeai zerifu,* dialogue antiphonally spoken, usually by two characters and usually composed in phrases of seven and five syllables ***(shichigochō)*** with the final phrase spoken in unison.

wataribyōshi (passing rhythm), lively offstage percussion music often employing shamisen and song and used to accompany a courtesan procession or crowd entrance.

watarizerifu (passed-along dialogue), a long speech divided among a group of characters who speak in sequence then join together to deliver the last phrase or line in unison.

yagō (house name), the name of an actor's house, family, shop, or "guild," which audience members shout to show appreciation (see **kakegoe**). Used as a kind of nickname for a kabuki actor.

yagura, the drum tower located above a theatre entrance as a mark of official approval to produce plays.

yakko (footman), attendant who, in spite of his lowly position, is dynamic and independent. Often featured in dance scenes that call for vigorous movement. *Hana yakko* (flower attendant) carry blossoming branches or flower-decorated poles.

yakugara (role type), categorization of role types, including basic role types of **tachiyaku, onnagata,** comic, villain, and elderly characters.

yamadai (mountain platform), single-level platform covered with a red cloth and placed onstage to seat a **takemoto, kiyomoto, tokiwazu,** or **ōzatsuma** narrative musical ensemble in a dance play.

yamagata (mountain shape), two-part fighting movement with sword, pole, or other weapon, first striking down from the center to the left and then from the center to the right, forming the shape of a mountain.

yarō, the adult male actors to whom kabuki was restricted after **wakashu** actors were banned in 1652. They ushered in the age of *yarō* kabuki, during which the theatre's artistic qualities greatly increased.

yoshino, the onstage seating area in Tokugawa-period theatres located upstage right and facing the audience. Named for the view it afforded of the decorative cherry blossoms framing the stage, which were reminiscent of the blossoms on Mount Yoshino.

yoten, wide-sleeved garment with hems split at the sides worn by minor samurai or by groups of policemen or constables in fight scenes. Also, the characters who wear these costumes. *Hana yoten* (flower yoten) wear colorful costumes of this type and wield branches of cherry blossoms as weapons. See also ***karami.***

yuka (floor), a location downstage left where a team of ***takemoto*** chanter and shamisen player ***(chobo)*** sits, either in view of the audience on a small revolving dais placed on the stage or behind a blind above the stage left entrance.

yuki aikata (snow melody), shamisen accompaniment during a quiet scene of falling snow.

zagashira (troupe head), actor-manager of a troupe. Called ***zamoto*** in Kamigata.

zamoto (troupe/theatre foundation), in Edo, the person licensed by the government to produce kabuki plays at a theatre. In Kamigata, the actor-manager of a troupe.

zankoku no bi (aesthetic of cruelty), quality of beauty arising in scenes of torture or death that are performed in stylized, musical fashion.

zōri, straw sandals with thongs.

SELECTED BIBLIOGRAPHY

Apart from a small number of standard English-language works about kabuki, the bibliography is limited to sources used in the preparation of this volume's introductions and translations. Sources related to specific plays are given with an abbreviation for the play following their listing. Works without abbreviations apply to more than one play.

FSE The Felicitous Soga Encounter

GP The Golden Pavilion

HM The Heron Maiden

JAM Just a Minute!

JTP Japan's Twenty-Four Paragons of Filial Piety

LK Lady Kuzunoha

MP The Medicine Peddler

MS Matahei the Stutterer

SA The Secret Art of Rowing

SCF The Stone-Cutting Feat of Kajiwara

SF Summer Festival: Mirror of Osaka

SK The Skylight

SS The Sanemori Story

Atsumi Seitarō. *Kabuki Buyō* (Kabuki Dance). Tokyo: Sōgensha, 1956. HM

Bakhtin, Mikhail. *Problems of Dostoevsky's Poetics.* Caryl Emerson, trans. and ed. Minneapolis: University of Minnesota Press, 1950. MP

Bowers, Faubion. *Japanese Theatre.* New York: Hermitage House, 1952. Reprint, Rutland, Vt.: Tuttle, 1974.

Brandon, James, ed. *Chūshingura: Studies in Kabuki and the Puppet Theater.* Honolulu, University of Hawai'i Press, 1982.

———, trans. *Kabuki: Five Classic Plays.* Cambridge: Harvard University Press, 1975. Paperback ed., Honolulu: University of Hawai'i Press, 1992.

Brandon, James R., William P. Malm, and Donald Shively. *Studies in Kabuki: Its Acting, Music, and Historical Context.* Honolulu: University of Hawai'i Press, 1978.

Cavaye, Ronald. *Kabuki: A Pocket Guide.* Rutland, Vt.: Tuttle, 1993.

Chikamatso Hanjietal. "Honchō Nijūshikō" (Japan's Twenty-Four Paragons of Filial Piety). Unpublished Kabuki-za production script *(daihon)*, February 1994. JTP

———. "Honchō Nijūshikō" (Japan's Twenty-Four Paragons of Filial Piety). Unpublished Kabuki-za production script *(daihon),* March 1998. JTP

———. "Honchō Nijūshikō" (Japan's Twenty-Four Paragons of Filial Piety). Unpublished Kabuki-za production script *(daihon),* April 1999. JTP

Chikamatsu Monzaemon. "Keisei Hangonkō" (The Courtesan of the Hangon Incense). Unpublished Kokuritsu Gekijō production script *(daihon),* July 1998. MS

Engekikai Bessatsu: Buyō Meisaku Jiten (Dictionary of Famous Dances). Tokyo: Engeki Shuppansha, 1986. HM

Ernst, Earle. *The Kabuki Theatre.* New York: Grove Press, 1956. Rev. ed., Honolulu: University of Hawai'i Press, 1974.

———, ed. *The House of Sugawara.* In *Three Japanese Plays from the Traditional Theatre.* New York: Grove Press, 1959.

Gunji, Masakatsu. *Kabuki,* 2d ed. John Bester, trans. Tokyo and New York: Kodansha, 1985.

Halford, Aubrey S., and Giovanna M. *The Kabuki Handbook.* Tokyo and Rutland, Vt.: Charles E. Tuttle, 1956.

Hasegawa Senshi and Matsuda Bunkōdō. "Kajiwara Heizō Homare no Ishikiri" (The Stone-Cutting Feat of Kajiwara). Unpublished Kabuki-za production script *(daihon),* January 1999. SCF

Hattori Yukio, ed. *Kanjinchō* (The Subscription List), *Kenuki* (The Tweezers), *Shibaraku* (Just a Minute!), *Narukami* (The Thunder God), *Ya no Ne* (The Arrow Sharpener). *Kabuki On-Sutēji* (Kabuki On-Stage), Vol. 10. Tokyo: Hakusuisha, 1985. JAM

Huizinga, Johan. *Homo Ludens: A Study of the Play Element in Culture.* Boston: Beacon Press, 1950.

Ichikawa Danjūrō I. *Kichirei Soga no Taimen* (The Felicitous Soga Encounter). In Toita Yasuji et al., eds., *Meisaku Kabuki Zenshū* (Collection of Kabuki Masterpieces), Vol. 13. Tokyo: Tōkyō Sōgensha, 1969. FSE

———. "Kotobuki Soga no Taimen" (The Felicitous Soga Encounter). Unpublished Meiji-za production script *(daihon),* March 1993. FSE

Ichikawa Danjūrō II. "Uirō Uri" (The Medicine Peddler). Unpublished Kabuki-za production script *(daihon),* May 1993. MP

Ihara Seiseien (Toshirō), ed. *Kabuki Nenpyō* (Kabuki Chronology), Vol. 2. Tokyo: Iwanami Shoten, 1957. SF

———. *Sajiki kara Shosai e* (From the Theatre Boxes to the Study). Tokyo: Genbunsha, 1925. Included in *Kokuritsu Gekijō Jōen Shiryōshū 388* (National Theatre Production Sources, No. 388). Tokyo: Nihon Geijutsu Bunka Shinkō Kai, 1997. GP

Iizuka Yoichirō. *Kabuki Saiken* (A Close Look at Kabuki). Tokyo: Daiichi Shobō, 1926. GP

Ishibashi Ken'ichirō. *Kabuki Midokoro Kikidokoro* (What to See and Hear in Kabuki). Kyoto: Tankōsha, 1993.

Jones, Stanleigh H., Jr., trans. and ed. *Sugawara and the Secrets of Calligraphy*. New York: Columbia University Press, 1985.

———. *Yoshitsune and the Thousand Cherry Trees*. New York: Columbia University Press, 1993.

Kawataki Mokuami. *Kotobuki Soga no Taimen* (The Felicitous Soga Encounter). In Kawatake Shigetoshi, ed., *Mokuami Zenshū* (The Works of Mokuami). Tōkyō: Shunyodō, 1925. FSE

Kawatake Shigetoshi. *Kabuki: Japanese Drama*. Tokyo: Foreign Affairs Association of Japan, 1958.

Kawatake Toshio. *Japan on Stage: Japanese Concepts of Beauty as Shown in the Traditional Theatre*. P. G. O'Neill, trans. Tokyo: 3A Corporation, 1990.

Keene, Donald, trans. Chūshingura: *The Treasury of Loyal Retainers*. New York: Columbia University Press, 1971.

Kincaid, Zoe. *Kabuki: The Popular Stage of Japan*. London: Macmillan, 1925.

Koike Shōtarō, ed. *Ichinotani Futaba Gunki* (Chronicle of the Battle of Ichinotani), *Ōmi Genji Senjin Yakata* (The Castle of the Genji Advance Guard at Ōmi), *Ehon Taikōki* (The Picture Book of the Taikō), *Kajiwara Heizō Homare no Ishikiri* (The Stone-Cutting Feat of Kajiwara). *Kabuki On-Sutēji* (Kabuki On-Stage), Vol. 4. Tokyo: Hakusuisha, 1985. SCF

Koike Shōtarō, ed., "*Kuzunoha* Saiken." (A close look at *Kuzunoha*), *Kabuki* no. 33, 1976. LK

Kokuritsu Gekijō Chōsa Yoseibu Geinō Chōsa Shitsu, ed. *Kokuritsu Gekijō Jōen Shiryoshū 352: Futatsu Chōchō Kuruwa Nikki* (National Theatre Production Sources No. 352: Chōgorō and Chōkichi: A Diary of Two Butterflies in the Pleasure Quarters). Tokyo: Kokuritsu Gekijō, 1994. SK

Kokuritsu Gekijō Chōsa Yoseibu Geinō Chōsa Shitsu, ed. *Kokuritsu Gekijō Jōen Shiryoshū 388: Gion Sairei Shinkōki* (National Theatre Production Sources No. 388: The Gion Festival Chronicle of Faith). Tokyo: Kokuritsu Gekijō, 1997. GP

Kokuritsu Gekijō Chōsa Yoseibu Geinō Chōsa Shitsu, ed. *Kokuritsu Gekijō Jōen Shiryoshū 394: Hiragana Seisuiki: "Sakaro"* (National Theatre Production Sources No. 394: A Beginner's Version of the Rise and Fall of the Heike and Genji Clans: "The Secret Art of Rowing"). Tokyo: Kokuritsu Gekijō, 1998. SA

Kominz, Laurence. *Avatars of Vengeance: Japanese Drama and the Soga Literary Tradition*. Ann Arbor: Center for Japanese Studies, University of Michigan, 1995. FSE, MP

———. *The Stars Who Created Kabuki: Their Lives, Loves and Legacy*. Tokyo: Kodansha, 1997.

Leiter, Samuel L., trans. and commentator. *The Art of Kabuki: Five Famous Plays.* 2d ed. rev. Mineola, N.Y.; Dover, 2000. Originally published as *The Art of Kabuki: Famous Plays in Performance.* Berkeley: University of California Press, 1979.

———. *New Kabuki Encyclopedia: A Revised Adaptation of* Kabuki Jiten. Westport, Conn.: Greenwood, 1997.

Malm, William P. *Nagauta: The Heart of Kabuki Music.* Tokyo and Rutland, Vt.: Tuttle, 1963.

Matsuda, Bunkodō et al. "Sakaro" (The Secret Art of Rowing). Unpublished Kabuki-za production script *(daihon),* March 1998. SA

Matsuzaki Hitoshi, ed. *Natsu Matsuri Naniwa Kagami* (Summer Festival: Mirror of Osaka), *Ise Ondo Koi no Netaba* (The Ise Dances and Love's Dull Blade). *Kabuki On-Sutēji* (Kabuki On-Stage), Vol. 3. Tokyo: Hakusuisha, 1987. SF

Mizuhara Hajime, ed. *Shintei Genpei Jōsuiki* (The Rise and Fall of the Genji and Heike Clans). Tokyo: Shinjinbutsu Ōraisha, 1989. SA

Mochizuki Tainosuke. *Kabuki no Geza Ongaku* (Kabuki Offstage Music). Tokyo: Engeki Shuppansha, 1997.

Murayama Shūichi, "Abe Seimei no Onmyōdō" (Abe Seimei and Yin-yang Divination), Kokuritsu Bunraku Geikijō, ed., *Dairokujūnikai Bunraku Kōen* (Bunraku Production No. 62). Osaka: April 1996. (Bunraku Program.) LK

Namiki Senryū (Sōsuke), Miyoshi Shōraku, and Takeda Koizumo. "Natsu Matsuri Naniwa Kagami" (Summer Festival: Mirror of Osaka). Unpublished Kabuki-za production script *(daihon),* July 1987. SF

———. "Natsu Matsuri Naniwa Kagami" (Summer Festival: Mirror of Osaka). Unpublished Misono-za, Nagoya, production script *(daihon),* February 1990. SF

———. "Natsu Matsuri Naniwa Kagami" (Summer Festival: Mirror of Osaka). Unpublished Kabuki-za production script *(daihon),* July 1997. SF

———. "Natsu Matsuri Naniwa Kagami" (Summer Festival: Mirror of Osaka). Unpublished Kabuki-za production script *(daihon),* June 1999. SF

Nojima Jusaburō. *Kabuki Jinmei Jiten* (Dictionary of Kabuki Names). Tokyo: Nichigai Associates, 1988.

Ogita Kiyoshi, Kawari Masumi, Tsuchida Mamore, eds. *Kinsei Bungaku Sen Geinō Hen* (A Selection of Edo-Period Literary Works: Performance Volume). Osaka: Ishumi Shoin, 1994. MP

Ortolani, Benito. *The Japanese Theatre: From Shamanistic Ritual to Contemporary Pluralism.* Rev. ed. Princeton, N.J.: Princeton University Press, 1995.

Raz, Jacob. *Audience and Actors: A Study of Their Interaction in Japanese Traditional Theatre.* Leiden: Brill, 1983.

Scott, A. C. *The Kabuki Theatre of Japan.* London: George Allen and Unwin, 1955. Reprint, Mineola, N.Y.: Dover, 1999.

Shaver, Ruth. *Kabuki Costume*. Rutland, Vt.: Tuttle, 1966.

Taguchi Shōko. "Kamigata Kabuki no Engi: Edo to Kamigata" (Kamigata Kabuki Performance Style: Comparing Edo and Kamigata). *Kabuki: Kenkyū to Hihyō* (Kabuki Research and Criticism) 15 (1995): 35–54. SF

Takeda Izumo II et al. "Hikimado" (The Skylight). Unpublished Kabuki-za production script *(daihon)*, September 1994. SK

———. "Kuzunoha" (Lady Kuzunoha). Unpublished Kokuritsu Gekijō production script *(daihon)*, June 1998. LK

Thornbury, Barbara E. *Sukeroku's Double Identity: The Dramatic Structure of Edo Kabuki*. Ann Arbor: Center for Japanese Studies, University of Michigan, 1982.

Toita Yasuji et al., eds., *Meisaku Kabuki Zenshū* (Complete Collection of Kabuki Masterpieces), 25 vol., Tokyo: Tōkyō Sōgensha, 1969–1971.

Torigoe Bunzō, ed. *Keisei Hangonkō* (The Courtesan of the Hangon Incense). *Kabuki On-Sutēji* (Kabuki On-Stage), Vol. 12. Tokyo: Hakusuisha, 1989. MS

Tsubouchi Shōyō and Yamamoto Jirō. *History and Characteristics of Kabuki, the Japanese Classical Drama*. Ryōzō Matsumoto, trans. Yokohama: Heiji Yamagata, 1960.

Tsunoda Ichirō and Uchiyama Michiko, eds. *Takeda Izumo, Namiki Sōsuke Jōruri-shū* (Collection of Puppet Plays by Takeda Izumo and Namiki Sōsuke). In *Shin Nihon Koten Bungaku Taikei* (New Compendium of Japanese Classical Literature), Vol. 93. Tokyo: Iwanami Shoten, 1991.

Watanabe Tamotsu. *Kabuki Techō* (Kabuki Guidebook). Tokyo: Shinshindō, 1982. GP

Yamada Masando et al., eds. *Toyotake-za Jōruri-shū III* (Toyotake Theatre Puppet Play Collection III), a volume in *Sōsho Edo Bunko 37* (Collection of Edo Literature, Vol. 37). Tokyo: Kokusho Kankōkai, 1995.

Yoshida Yukiko et al., eds. *Nihon Buyō Zenshū* (Collection of Japanese Dances), Vol. 4. Tokyo: Nihon Buyōsha, 1980. JTP

CONTRIBUTORS

EDITORS

James R. Brandon

Professor Emeritus and former Chair of the Department of Theatre and Dance at the University of Hawai'i at Manoa, Honolulu. Ph.D. in Theatre and Television, University of Wisconsin-Madison. Translator-director of eleven English-language kabuki productions in the United States and Europe, including *Sukeroku: Flower of Edo, Narukami the Thundergod, The Subscription List,* and *The Scarlet Princess of Edo.* Founding editor, *Asian Theatre Journal* (1984–1971) and author/editor/translator of sixteen books, including *Kabuki: Five Classic Plays* (1975; 2d ed. 1992); *Chūshingura: Studies in Kabuki and the Puppet Theater* (1982); *Two Kabuki Plays:* The Subscription List *and* The Zen Substitute (with T. Niwa, 1966); *Kabuki Dancer* (trans. of Ariyoshi Sawako's *Izumo no Okuni,* 1994); *Studies in Kabuki, Its Acting, Music and Historical Context* (with W. Malm and D. Shively, 1978); *Nō and Kyōgen in the Modern World* (1997); *Cambridge Guide to Asian Theatre* (1993); and the forthcoming *The Death of Kabuki and Other Myths: Kabuki under American Occupation.* Among honors are the Order of the Rising Sun–Gold Rays with Rosette from the Japanese government; the Uchimura Prize of the International Theatre Institute; the John D. Rockefeller III Award in Asian Arts; and Outstanding Theatre Teacher of the Year of the Association for Theatre in Higher Education.

Samuel L. Leiter

Head, Graduate Program, Department of Theatre, Brooklyn College, City University of New York, and faculty member, Ph.D. Program, City University of New York. Ph.D., Dramatic Art, New York University. Author/editor/translator of seventeen books on American theatre, international stage directors, and Japanese theatre, including *The Art of Kabuki: Famous Plays in Performance* (1979; rev. ed. 2000); *Kabuki Encyclopedia: An English-language Adaptation of* Kabuki Jiten (1979); *New Kabuki Encyclopedia: A Revised Adaptation of* Kabuki Jiten (1997); *Japanese Theatre in the World* (1997); *Zeami and the Nō Theatre in the World* (with Benito Ortolani, 1998); *Japanese Theatre and the International Stage* (with Stanca Scholz-Cionca, 2000); *The Man who Saved Kabuki: Faubion Bowers and Theatre Censorship in Occupied Japan* (trans./adapt. of Okamoto Shiro's *Kabuki o Sukutta Otoko,* 2001); *A Kabuki Reader: History, Performance* (2001); *Frozen Moments: Writings on Kabuki, 1966–2001* (2001); etc. Founding editor, *Asian Theatre Bulletin;* editor, *Asian Theatre Journal* (1992 to present); and editorial board member, *Theatre Symposium.* Honors include East-West Center Fellowship (1962–1964), Fulbright Fellowship to Japan (1974–1975), Claire and Leonard Tow Professorship (1997–1998), Wolfe Fellowship in the Humanities (1999–2000), Broeklundian Professorship (2001–2006), Brooklyn College Award for Creative Achievement (2001), seven CUNY Research Foundation grants, and Visiting Scholar at Waseda University (1994, 1995).

TRANSLATORS

Holly Blumner

M.A., Asian Theatre, University of Hawai'i. Ph.D. candidate, University of Hawai'i; dissertation topic: "The *Wagoto* Style of Kabuki Acting." Studied kabuki for four years in Kyoto and at Waseda University; continues to practice *nihon buyō* and *nagauta* singing. Commentator/translator for English "Earphone Guide," Kabuki-za and Kokuritsu Gekijō, Tokyo. Coeditor of *101 Years of Kabuki in Hawai'i* (with J. A. Iezzi), and coauthor of "Sukeroku: A History" (with N. Maeshiba, 1995).

Alan Cummings

M.A., Waseda University. Specialist in kabuki of late Tokugawa and Meiji periods. Ph.D. candidate, University of London; dissertation topic: "Mokuami and Meiji Kabuki." Commentator/translator for English "Earphone Guide," Kabuki-za and Kokuritsu Gekijō, Tokyo.

Paul M. Griffith

Associate Professor, Education Faculty, Saitama University. D.Phil. candidate, St. Anthony's College, Oxford University, with focus on Tokugawa-period art history. Worked in Far Eastern Department, Victoria and Albert Museum (London), on their kabuki woodblock print collection. Recipient of Japanese Ministry of Education Fellowship (1981–1983) and Japan Foundation Scholarship (1985–1987) for study in Japan. Translator for the NHK (Nippon Hōsō Ryōkai) Television bilingual program *Traditional Japanese Performing Arts.* Producer and translator/commentator for the English "Earphone Guide," Kabuki-za and Kokuritsu Gekijō, Tokyo. Studies *nihon buyō* under Fujima Hideka.

Julie A. Iezzi

Assistant Professor, Department of Theatre and Dance, University of Hawai'i. Ph.D., Asian Theatre, University of Hawai'i. Student of *nagauta, gidayū,* and *tokiwazu.* Translator/commentator for English "Earphone Guide," kabuki performances, Tokyo. Coeditor of *101 Years of Kabuki in Hawai'i* (with H. Blumner), and author of "Sounding Out Kabuki: Music Behind the Scenes" (1995).

Matthew Johnson

B.A., University of California, Los Angeles. Producer and translator/commentator for English "Earphone Guide," kabuki and *bunraku* performances, Tokyo. For ten years, a resident of Japan. Active as *nihon buyō* dancer (stage name Fujima Mitsugi) and as shamisen player. Collaborator with actor Ichimura Manjirō on creation of Internet web site, "Kabuki for Everyone."

Laurence R. Kominz

Professor of Japanese and Director, Institute for Asian Studies, Portland State University, Oregon. Ph.D., Japanese Literature, Columbia University. Author of *The Stars Who Created Kabuki: Their Lives, Loves and Legacy* (1997) and *Avatars of Vengeance: Japanese Drama and the Soga Literary Tradition* (1996), and many articles on kabuki. Student of *nihon buyō* and *kyōgen.* Translator/commentator for English "Earphone Guide," kabuki performances, Tokyo.

William Lee

Assistant Professor, Asian Studies Centre, University of Manitoba. Ph.D., Japanese Theatre and Literature, McGill University, Montreal. Specialist in kabuki, augmented by study and performance of *kagura.* Articles include "Chikamatsu and Dramatic Literature in the Meiji Period"

(1999) and "Japanese Folk Performing Arts Today: The Politics of Promotion and Preservation" (2000).

Mark Oshima

Instructor, Sophia University, Tokyo. A.B., East Asian Studies, Harvard University. Ph.D. candidate, East Asian Languages and Civilizations, Harvard University. Professional singer of *kiyomoto* (stage name Kiyomoto Shimatayū) and student of *nihon buyō* (stage name Fujima Toyaki). Translator/commentator for English "Earphone Guide," kabuki and *bunraku* performances, Tokyo; writer of English-language programs for the Kabuki-za; and performance translator for NHK Television. Translator of Nakamura Matazō's *Kabuki Backstage, Onstage: An Actor's Life* (1990) and kabuki plays *Yotsuya Ghost Stories* and *A Maiden at Dōjōji* (1998). Author of *Konnichiwa Kabuki Dance: Heaven and Earth, the World of Contradictions* (1992).

Cody M. Poulton

Associate Professor, Pacific and Asian Studies, University of Victoria, Canada. Teaches Japanese literature and theatre. Ph.D., Japanese Studies, University of Toronto. Studied at the International Research Institute for Japanese Studies in Kyoto. Translator of plays by Kara Jūrō, Hirata Oriza, Okamoto Kanoko, Shiga Naoya, and Ibuse Masuji. Author of *Spirits of Another Sort: Major Plays of Izumi Kyōka* (2001).

Katherine Saltzman-Li

Assistant Professor, East Asian Languages and Cultural Studies, University of California, Santa Barbara. Teaches premodern Japanese theatre. Ph.D., Japanese Literature, Stanford University. Author of *Creating Kabuki Plays: "Context for Valuable Notes on Playwriting"* and the article "The *Tsurane* of *Shibaraku*: Communicating the Power of Identity" (both forthcoming). Studied kabuki and other oral arts for three years at Waseda University Memorial Theatre Museum under sponsorship of the Japan Foundation and Japanese Department of Education.

INDEX

The index includes terms, plays, and actors found in the editors' and translators' introductions.

KABUKI PLAYS ON STAGE

VOLUME 1, BRILLIANCE AND BRAVADO, 1697–1766

1697 The Felicitous Soga Encounter (Kotobuki Soga no Taimen)

1697 Just a Minute! (Shibaraku)

1708 Matahei the Stutterer (Domo Mata), from *Keisei Hangonkō* (The Courtesan of the Hangon Incense)

1718 The Medicine Peddler (Uirō Uri)

1730 The Stone-Cutting Feat of Kajiwara (Kajiwara Heizō Homare no Ishikiri), from *Miura no Ōsuke Kōbai Tazuna* (The Plum-Blossom Reins of Miura no Ōsuke)

1734 Lady Kuzunoha (Kuzunoha), from *Ashiya Dōman Ōuchi Kagami* (A Courtly Mirror of Ashiya Dōman)

1739 The Secret Art of Rowing (Sakaro), from *Hiragana Seisuiki* (A Beginner's Version of the Rise and Fall of the Heike and the Genji Clans)

1745 Summer Festival: Mirror of Osaka (Natsu Matsuri Naniwa Kagami)

1749 The Skylight (Hikimado), from *Futatsu Chōchō Kuruwa Nikki* (Chōgorō and Chōkichi: A Diary of Two Butterflies in the Pleasure Quarters)

1749 The Sanemori Story (Sanemori Monogatari), from *Genpei Nunobiki no Taki* (The Genji and Heike at Nunobiki Waterfall)

1757 The Golden Pavilion (Kinkakuji), from *Gion Sairei Shinkōki* (The Gion Festival Chronicle of Faith)

1762 The Heron Maiden (Sagi Musume)

1766 Japan's Twenty-Four Paragons of Filial Piety (Honchō Nijūshikō)

VOLUME 2, VILLAINY AND VENGEANCE, 1773–1799

1773 Great Favorite Subscription List (Gohiiki Kanjinchō)

1777 The Precious Incense and Autumn Flowers of Sendai (Meiboku Sendai Hagi)

1778 The Temple Gate and the Paulownia Crest (Sanmon Gosan no Kiri)

1780 The Tale of Shiroishi and the Taihei Chronicles (Go Taiheiki Shiroishi Banashi)

1780 Nozaki Village (Nozakimura), from *Shinpan Utazaimon* (The Balladeer's New Tale)

1781 The Revenge at Tengajaya (Katakiuchi Tengajayamura)

1782 Mirror Mountain: A Women's Treasury of Loyalty (Kagamiyama Kokyō no Nishiki-e)

1784 The Barrier Gate (Seki no To)

1794 Five Great Powers that Secure Love (Godairiki Koi no Fūjime)

1796 A Message of Love from Yamato (Koi no Tayori Yamato Ōrai)

1796 The Ise Dances and Love's Dull Blade (Ise Ondo Koi no Netaba)

1799 The Picture Book of the Taikō (Ehon Taikōki)

VOLUME 3, DARKNESS AND DESIRE, 1804–1864

1804 The Tale of Tokubei from India (Tenjiku Tokubei)

1812 Sanbasō with His Tongue Stuck Out (Shitadashi Sanbasō)

1813 The Scandalous Love of Osome and Hisamatsu (Osome Hisamatsu Ukina no Yomiuri)

1818 Yasuna

1823 The Execution Ground at Suzugamori (Suzugamori), from *Ukiyozuka Hiyoku no Inazuma* (The Floating World's Pattern and Matching Lightning Bolts)

1823 Kasane, from *Kesa Kakematsu Narita no Riken* (A Surplice-Hanging Pine and the Sharp Sword of Narita)

1825 The Ghost Stories at Yotsuya on the Tōkaidō (Tōkaidō Yotsuya Kaidan)

1826 The Wisteria Maiden (Fuji Musume), from *Kaesu Gaesu Nagori no Ōtsu* (Ōtsu of the Ever-Returning Farewells)

1831 The Six Poet Immortals (Rokkasen)

1836 Masakado, from *Yo ni Utō Sōma no Furugosho* (Filial Love at the Abandoned Sōma Palace)

1851 The Tale of the Martyr of Sakura (Sakura Giminden)

1860 The Three Kichisas and the New Year's First Visit to the Pleasure Quarters (Sannin Kichisa Kuruwa no Hatsugai)

1864 Gorozō the Gallant (Gosho no Gorozō), from *Soga Moyō Tateshi No Goshozome* (The Soga Design and the Gallant's Dyed Kimono)

1864 Scarface Otomi (Kirare Otomi), from *Musume Gonomi Ukina no Yokogushi* (A Female Version of the Boxwood Comb Lover's Scandal)

VOLUME 4, RESTORATION AND REFORM, 1872–1905

1872 Two Lions (Renjishi)

1873 Sakai's Drum (Sakai no Taikō)

1873 Shinza the Barber (Kamiyui Shinza)

1877 The Woman Student (Onna Shōsei Shigeru)

1881 The Renowned Banzui Chōbei (Kiwametsuki Banzui Chōbei)

1883 The Demon Ibaraki (Ibaraki)

1883 The Fishmonger Sogorō (Sakanaya Sogorō)

1885 Benkei Aboard Ship (Funa Benkei)

1887 Viewing the Autumn Foliage (Momijigari)

1892 The Dropped Robe (Suō Otoshi)

1893 The Mirror Lion, A Spring Diversion (Shunkyō Kagami Jishi)

1905 A Sinking Moon Over the Lonely Castle Where the Cuckoo Cries (Kojō Rakugetsu Hototogisu)